LIGHT THE LAMP

Papers on World Trade and Investment
in Memory of Bijit Bora

World Scientific Studies in International Economics

(ISSN: 1793-3641)

---

*Published**

Vol. 5 Institutions and Gender Empowerment in the Global Economy
edited by Kartik Roy (University of Queensland, Australia), Hans Blomqvist (Swedish School of Economics and Business Administration, Finland) & Cal Clark (Auburn University, USA)

Vol. 6 Globalization and Systemic Risk
edited by Douglas D. Evanoff (Federal Reserve Bank of Chicago, USA), David S. Hoelscher (International Monetary Fund, USA) & George G. Kaufman (Loyola University Chicago, USA)

Vol. 7 Fostering Monetary and Financial Cooperation in East Asia
edited by Duck-Koo Chung (North East Asia Research Foundation, South Korea) & Barry Eichengreen (University of California, Berkeley, USA)

Vol. 8 Challenges of Economic Development in the Middle East and North Africa Region
by Julia C Devlin (University of Virginia, USA)

Vol. 9 Globalization and International Trade Policies
by Robert M Stern (University of Michigan, USA)

Vol. 10 The First Credit Market Turnoil of the 21st Century: Implications for Public Policy
edited by Doughlas D Evanoff (Federal Reserve Bank of Chicago, USA, Philipp Hartmann (European Central Bank, Germany) & George G Kaufman (Loyola University, USA)

Vol. 11 Free Trade Agreements in the Asia Pacific
edited by Christopher Findlay (University of Adelaide, Australia) & Shujiro Urata (Waseda University, Japan)

Vol. 12 The Japanese Economy in Retrospect, Volume I and Volume II
Selected Papers by Gary R. Saxonhouse
by Robert M Stern (University of Michigan, USA), Gavin Wright (Stanford University, USA) & Hugh Patrick (Columbia University, USA)

Vol. 13 Light the Lamp
Papers on World Trade and Investment in Memory of Bijit Bora
edited by Christopher Findlay (University of Adelaide, Australia), David Parsons (KADIN Indonesia) & Mari Pangestu (Trade Minister of Indonesia)

*The complete list of the published volumes in the series, can also be found at
http://www.worldscibooks.com/series/wssie_series.shtml

13 World Scientific Studies in International Economics

LIGHT THE LAMP

Papers on World Trade and Investment in Memory of Bijit Bora

edited by

Christopher Findlay
University of Adelaide, Australia

Mari Pangestu
Trade Minister of Indonesia

David Parsons
KADIN Indonesia

World Scientific

NEW JERSEY • LONDON • SINGAPORE • BEIJING • SHANGHAI • HONG KONG • TAIPEI • CHENNAI

Published by

World Scientific Publishing Co. Pte. Ltd.
5 Toh Tuck Link, Singapore 596224
USA office: 27 Warren Street, Suite 401-402, Hackensack, NJ 07601
UK office: 57 Shelton Street, Covent Garden, London WC2H 9HE

British Library Cataloguing-in-Publication Data
A catalogue record for this book is available from the British Library.

World Scientific Studies in International Economics — Vol. 13
LIGHT THE LAMP
Papers on World Trade and Investment in Memory of Bijit Bora

ISBN-13 978-981-4299-39-8
ISBN-10 981-4299-39-1

Typeset by Stallion Press
Email: enquiries@stallionpress.com

Printed in Singapore by B & Jo Enterprise Pte Ltd

Contents

Author Affiliations

Kym Anderson, School of Economics, University of Adelaide

Chunlai Chen, Crawford School of Economics and Government, Australian National University

Christopher Findlay, School of Economics, University of Adelaide

Michael Francis, Bank of Canada

Noel Gaston, School of Business, Bond University

Uwe Kaufmann, School of Economics, University of Adelaide

Xuepeng Liu, Coles College of Business, Kennesaw State University

Mari Pangestu, Trade Minister of Indonesia

David Parsons, KADIN Indonesia (Indonesian Chamber of Commerce and Industry)

Richard Pomfret, School of Economics, University of Adelaide

Hussain G. Rammal, Business School, University of Adelaide

David K. Round, Centre for Regulation and Market Analysis, University of South Australia

Shujiro Urata, Graduate School of Asia–Pacific Studies, Waseda University

Corinne Luu, Bank of Canada

Preface

Bijit Bora (pictured), a highly regarded economist, academic and international public servant, died suddenly in Adelaide in October 2006, aged 45.

We dedicate this volume to his memory.

Its contributors include friends and colleagues from around the world. We have also included a couple of papers that Bijit was drafting at the time of his death.

Listed below is a summary of Bijit's published work. His interests ranged across trade policy, sectoral studies and empirical work, but investment remained a major theme.

A milestone in that respect was the release of Bijit's edited collection, published by Routledge, on research issues in foreign direct investment. A reviewer of the volume said that it was "essential reading for anyone with a serious interest in theoretical, methodological or government policy issues associated with foreign direct investment."[1]

[1]Thomas L Brewer (2004). *Transnational Corporations*, 13(3), 141–145.

We thank especially Patrick Low and Bijit's colleagues in the World Trade Organization (WTO) for their help in identifying the set of papers associated with his name.

Many of Bijit's friends have already dedicated collections of papers or reports to him, for example, the Kiel Institute/CEPR Trade Policy Monitoring Paper 1 on "Monitoring Trade Policy: A New Agenda for Reviving the Doha Round," reports of work on second-hand clothing markets in Africa in which Bijit was involved,[2] the WTO's World Trade Report of 2007 and the book *Trade and Health: Seeking Common Ground*, which included Bijit's paper on tariffs on malaria nets.

We add our collection to this list. We think he would like this compilation, one which reflects his own diverse interests, his work on data and his interest in policy.

Bijit's life and work truly spanned the globe. At the time of his death he was living and working in Switzerland as a researcher at the WTO Secretariat.

His work covered trade and development issues across Africa, Asia, the Indian subcontinent and Latin America.

He was born in India but grew up in Canada, spending most of his life there before moving to Adelaide in 1991 to take up a position in the Economics Department at Flinders University.

This role, and his joint research and teaching with colleagues at the University of Adelaide, put him in touch with many of the city's students of economics in the 1990s. They still ask us about him.

For Bijit and his family, Adelaide became their nominated home, and it stayed their home even after more than eight years of living in Geneva.

While in Adelaide he and his Canadian-born wife, Laura, became Australian citizens and their family grew to include two daughters and a son.

From his base at Flinders University he contributed to international economics and economic development. This took him on a path to the Asia–Pacific region and eventually to the United Nations Conference of Trade and Development (UNCTAD) and the WTO.

---

[2] See http://sds.ukzn.ac.za/files/RR71%20Velia.pdf.

Working through the Pacific Economic Cooperation Council, a network of regional scholars, business people and officials from 23 Asia–Pacific economies, Bijit helped to bring new ideas to the region, particularly on investment. These ideas contributed directly to initiatives adopted by APEC ministers. Mari Pangestu in her chapter in this collection recalls her work with Bijit in these settings.

This work took Bijit on secondment to UNCTAD in 1998 to contribute to the World Investment Report. He stayed until 2001, when he took a permanent appointment in the Economic Research and Statistics Division of the WTO Secretariat.

Bijit was a young and popular figure in these international networks. He brought a special enthusiasm and openness to his relationships that reflected his honesty. Added to that was a sometimes innocent optimism about work and life. These values drove his work and his engagement with others, but could lead to disappointments as he struggled with systems or bureaucracies that seemed to him to be driven by other forces.

Yet he maintained his enthusiasm for his work. He moved between ministers, ambassadors to the WTO and struggling trade officials in the least-developed countries of the world with the same "can do" attitude and sense of respect.

Sport was important to him and he was ready to try most things. For a short time in earlier years he played on the professional tennis circuit. He had a passion for triathlons, which he developed at the Meteors Triathlon Club in Adelaide, and a few months before his death he competed in the Monaco Ironman competition.

He enjoyed life, seeking out new experiences and chances to engage with new people. Travelling with him was a delight. He was always ready to talk — on the flight, in the airport, and over dinner and afterwards.

He became a lively and engaging presenter at conferences and workshops. He was sought after for panels with senior colleagues, and, like a good teacher, his enthusiasm and knowledge of the material brought people along with him.

We have tried to capture some of these dimensions of Bora's life in the title of this book.

Lighting the lamp refers to scoring a goal in the popular Canadian sport of ice hockey — so a commentator might scream that the scorer "squeezed the stick, pulled the trigger and lit the lamp!" And that's what he did in his work and life with us.

Bijit had returned home to Adelaide one last time in 2006 to bring his knowledge and experience to two weeks of teaching at the School of Economics at the University of Adelaide.

He is survived by his wife Laura, herself an international public servant, daughters Kendall and Katie, and son Zac.

Christopher Findlay, Mari Pangestu and David Parsons

Selected Publications of Bijit K Bora

Books

Marginalisation of LDCs and Small Vulnerable States in World Trade, edited with R Grynberg and MA Razzaque. Commonwealth Secretariat, 2005.

Foreign Direct Investment: Research Issues, editor. London: Routledge, 2002.

Priority Issues in Trade and Investment Liberalisation: Implications for the Asia Pacific Region, edited with M Pangestu. Singapore: Pacific Economic Cooperation Council, 1996.

Regional Integration and the Asia Pacific, edited with C Findlay. Melbourne: Oxford University Press, 1996.

Journal Articles

Industrial policy and the WTO, *World Economy*, 23(4), 543–559, 2000 (with P Lloyd and M Pangestu).

Workplace characteristics and their effects on wages: Australian evidence, *Australian Economic Papers*, 38(3), 276–289, 1999 (with M Wooden).

Investment policy making APEC style, *Asia Pacific Investment Review*, 3(2), 37–48, 1997.

The Australian financial system: Evolution, regulation and globalization, *Law and Policy in International Business*, 28(3), 787–812, 1997 (with M Lewis).

Chapters in books

Rolling back malaria and the WTO development agenda. In *Trade and Health: Seeking Common Ground*, C Blouin, J Heymann and N Drager (eds), ch. 5. Montreal and Ontario: McGill–Queens University Press, 2007.

Market access barriers and poverty in developing East Asia. In *East Asia Integrates: A Trade Policy Agenda for Shared Growth*, K Krumm and H Kharas (eds), Washington DC: World Bank and Oxford University Press, 2004.

New regional trading developments in the Asia–Pacific region. In *Global Change and East Asian Policy Initiatives*, S Yusef, M Anjum Altaf and K Nabeshima (eds). Washington DC: World Bank and Oxford University Press, 2004 (with J Gilbert and R Scollay).

Locational determinants of international production. In *Research Issues and Foreign Direct Investment*, B Bora (ed). London: Routledge, 2002.

Environment. In *Research Issues and Foreign Direct Investment*, B Bora (ed). London: Routledge, 2002.

Trade related investment measures. In *Development, Trade, and the WTO: A Handbook*, B Hoekman, A Mattoo and P English (eds). Washington DC: World Bank, 2002.

Industrial policy and the WTO. In *Millennium Round and Developing Countries*, W Martin and B Hoekman (eds). London: Blackwell, 2001 (with P Lloyd and M Pangestu).

Foreign direct investment and the East Asian financial crisis. In *East Asia: Recovery and Beyond*, R Newfarmer and C Wood (eds). Washington DC: World Bank, 2000.

East Asia and options for negotiations on investment. In *Options for Global Trade Reform: A View from the Asia–Pacific*, W Martin and M Pangestu (eds), Cambridge: Cambridge University Press, 1999 (with SY Chia, N Freeman and S Urata).

Can APEC deliver on investment? In *Whither APEC? The Progress to Date and Agenda for the Future*, F Bergsten (ed). Washington DC: Institute for International Economics, 1997 (with EM Graham).

The internationalisation of China. In *China the Emerging Giant*, East Asian Analytical Unit. Canberra: Australian Department of Foreign Affairs and International Trade, 1997 (with C Chen).

The role of multinational corporations in globalisation. In *The Handbook of Globalisation*, A Levy (ed). Cheltenham, UK: Edward Elgar Publishing, 1997.

The policy implications of Canada's trade and investment linkages with East Asia. In *Canada Among Nations 1997*, M Molot, F Hampson and M Rudner (eds). Ottawa: Carleton University Press, 1997.

Trade and investment developments in APEC. In *International Trade and Migration in the APEC Region*, P Lloyd and L Williams (eds). Melbourne: Oxford University Press, 1996.

Foreign direct investment. In *Regional Integration and the Asia Pacific*, B Bora and C Findlay (eds). Melbourne: Oxford University Press, 1996.

International air transport. In *Regional Integration and the Asia Pacific*, B Bora and C Findlay (eds). Melbourne: Oxford University Press, 1996 (with C Findlay and P Forsyth).

North American Free Trade Agreement. In *Regional Integration and the Asia Pacific*, B Bora and C Findlay (eds). Melbourne: Oxford University Press, 1996.

The role of regional trading arrangements in regulatory reform: the international air transport industry. In *Regional Integration and the Asia Pacific*, B Bora and C Findlay (eds). Melbourne: Oxford University Press, March 1996.

APEC's Non-Binding Investment Principles: one step forward? In *Investment Issues in the Asia Pacific*, C Green and T Brewer (eds). Dobbs Ferry, NY: Oceania Press, 1995.

Implications of globalisation for Australian foreign investment policies. In *Globalisation: Issues for Australia*. Canberra: Australian Government Publishing Service, 1995.

Manufacturing sector. In *Australia's Trade Policies*, R Pomfret (ed). Melbourne: Oxford University Press, 1995 (with R Pomfret).

APEC's Non-Binding Investment Principles. Centre for Asia Pacific Affairs Report No. 19, San Francisco: Asia Pacific Foundation, 1995. Also published in B Bora and M Pangestu, *Priorities in Trade and Investment Liberalisation: Implications for the Asia Pacific*. Singapore: Pacific Economic Cooperation Council, 1995 (with EM Graham).

International factor flows. In *Australia's Trade Policies*, R Pomfret (ed). Melbourne: Oxford University Press, 1995.

Internationalisation, trade and foreign direct investment: comment. In *International Integration of the Australian Economy*, J Dwyer and P Lowe (eds). Sydney: Reserve Bank of Australia, 1994.

Open regionalism: concept and application in the Asia Pacific. In *Pacific Economic Development Report*, M Borthwick (ed). Singapore: Pacific Economic Cooperation Council, 1994 (with C Findlay and J Crowley).

Towards a regional investment agreement. In *Pacific Economic Development Report*, M Borthwick (ed). Singapore: Pacific Economic Cooperation Council, 1994.

Foreign direct investment cooperation in the Asia Pacific region: the PECC Investment Code. In *New Directions in Regional Trade Liberalisation and Cooperation*, G Yen (ed). Taiwan: Taiwan Institute of Economic Research, 1994.

Alternative investment arrangements: conceptualising the issues. In *Pacific Initiatives for Regional Trade Liberalisation*, M Pangestu (ed). Jakarta: Centre for Strategic and International Studies, 1993.

Australia's response to NAFTA. In *NAFTA, Australia and New Zealand*, J Higley, R Cushing and M Sutton (eds). Austin: University of Texas at Austin Press, 1993 (with C Findlay).

Hard landings and soft rights: forces for change in the Pacific air transport markets. In *Pacific Initiatives for Regional Trade Liberalisation*, M Pangestu with C Findlay (eds). Jakarta: Centre for Strategic and International Studies, 1993.

Overview

Christopher Findlay, Mari Pangestu and David Parsons

Our book begins with a discussion of the question of the future of world trade policy. Pangestu's response to this question is that while there are new complexities, mainly related to the global financial crisis of 2007 and 2008 that carries with it some new risks of protectionism, at its core the business of trade policy remains the same — to contribute to growth and development. She also identifies the application of the principles of good trade policy to new issues such as food and energy security as well as climate change. She talks about the institutions of trade policy and the rapidly rising interest in the role of the G20, but also examines the institutions of more familiar focus such as the WTO. She comments on the use of bilateral agreements and the management of the risks they involve, and spends time on the contribution of regional bodies such as APEC and ASEAN. Pangestu concludes with a commentary on how these organisations contribute to the confidence in the ability to manage change in liberalising developing countries.

Bora and Liu (Chapter 2) evaluate the impact of the WTO's Information Technology Agreement, which eliminates tariffs on an agreed list of products. The tariff cuts apply to all WTO members, whether or not they are signatories to the ITA. The authors apply a gravity model framework so that they can test the effects on trade among ITA members and WTO members. They find that the Agreement has a significant effect on the value of trade, and that WTO membership provides a significant benefit in avoiding what are otherwise significant trade-diverting effects. Bora and Liu also find that most of the progress in ITA trade liberalisation was made by developing rather than developed countries.

Bora and Kaufmann in Chapter 3 examine the role of economic analysis in WTO arbitration cases. The mandate of the arbitrators is to interpret WTO law in a legally consistent and robust way. They argue that economic analysis supports the arbitrators by assisting with the application of their mandate and by providing a method for quantifying the impact of a policy measure that is not consistent with WTO law. The authors find that the role of economic analysis is complementary to the legal analysis and not sequential. This work on the dispute settlement process highlights the amount of resources and time that is actually invested in these cases, including how many procedures have to be followed. This feature, and the lags involved in the process — for example, the time given to the offending member to continue with its "wrongdoings" while a case is considered — lead to questions about options for further reform in the process. Exploring these options is worthwhile, although the mechanism is already playing a vital role in the WTO set-up.

The extent of biases against trade and against agriculture in Australian industry assistance policy is the topic of the chapter by Anderson (Chapter 4). He asks how the evolution of the pattern of distortions in Australia compares to that in other high-income countries. Anderson makes use of an extraordinary data set that he built which includes rates of protection for manufacturing and agriculture over six decades (part of a data set covering 69 countries). He finds significant anti-trade and anti-agriculture biases in Australia's industry assistance in the decades after World War II, but that the disincentives these policies created for Australian farmers have fallen steadily to virtually zero now. He observes, however, short-term variation in this trend, as agriculture and manufacturing sector policies changed at different times. Within agriculture he comments on the trends in the variation in assistance within the sector (more recently disappearing), and notes that the structure of assistance for agriculture has not been biased against exporting industries as it has in many other countries. He notes that, like New Zealand, Australia has been able to cut its farm subsidies to zero.

The lessons that Anderson draws from this experience are that it helps agricultural reform if assistance is reformed concurrently in other sectors, not just in manufacturing but as wider microeconomic reform that adds to productivity growth. Second, the process of adjustment to cuts in assistance is easier the greater the variation in assistance within agriculture and the greater the variation in efficiency among firms within an industry. Third, transparent and well-informed policy debates as well as the quality of the public institutions that implement the reform have been invaluable.

Francis and Luu (Chapter 5) examine the implications of one of the significant changes in the world economy — India's entry into world markets. As they say, India is big (the fourth largest economy in the world in PPP terms) and has been growing rapidly. They focus on commodity markets, and on the expectation that a rapidly growing economy at India's stage of development might be expected to have significant effects in those markets. They find otherwise, and attribute this effect to the distortions in Indian policy through their effects on relative prices and on Indian supply and demand, and on the sectoral composition of growth. However, they find more significant effects since 2004, which they attribute to policy reform. Continuing reform and demographic change could be expected to shift India's demand for commodities.

Chen (Chapter 6) looks at another big economy, China, and the inflows of foreign direct investment. He evaluates China's performance in attracting inflows, discusses the effects of flows to China on the other Asian economies, and looks at various effects of the inflows. He argues that China has attracted the share of FDI that might be expected according to its size and that there is some evidence that inflows to China have been complementary to flows to other Asian economies. Exploring a rich data set, Chen finds a number of interesting features of China's FDI inflows, including its uneven regional distribution (at the same time, the continuing scope for western China to attract capital inflow) and the more recent inflows of FDI into services compared to the earlier heavier emphasis on manufacturing. Following an extensive review of the literature, he calls for further work on the spillover effects of FDI onto the productivity of local firms.

Chen's focus was on FDI in China, including its contribution to China's trade growth. Urata (Chapter 7) notes the rapid growth of both trade and FDI in the whole East Asian region and studies the relationships between them. He reports that intra-regional trade has grown faster than the region's trade with the rest of the world and that, related to this, trade in components accounts for a rising share of regional trade. He finds that the importance in trade of machinery products (especially electronic and electrical products) has increased and that intra-industry trade has grown faster than inter-industry trade. His assessment is, therefore, that these features reflect the rising degree of the division of labour within East Asia.

Urata studies the trade patterns of Japanese multinational corporations. He notes their relatively strong export orientation, particularly in the machinery sector. He finds that trends in multinational trade match those in overall East Asian trade and identifies the extent to which trade by multinationals is intra-firm. He concludes that multinational strategy in East Asia has been an important driver of the observed patterns of trade and offers this relationship as evidence of the extent to which the notable features of East Asian trade have been driven by market forces. However, he also explains how the liberalisation of trade and FDI policies facilitated this process. Finally, Urata comments on the growing interest in regional preferential trade agreements and asks whether market-driven regionalisation is giving way to an institution-driven process. He notes some of the positive effects of preferential agreements but also reports the concerns about preferential reform. He argues the case for more work on how to move from preferential agreements to global liberalisation.

Urata identified the growing importance of the electronics sector in regional trade and, in Chapter 8, Parsons and Rammal examine that sector in more detail. They are interested in the factors that impede integration in this sector, especially non-tariff barriers and supply chain impediments. Their focus is ASEAN and they find a relatively low level of NTMs compared to other sectors. Within electronics, NTMs are rare in the component trade but are more likely to be seen in the consumer product trade. Interviews reveal that more important are impediments in the supply chain that raise trade costs. Many of these are related to poor administration, processing and policing in areas where government responsibilities affect the supply chain, such as customs procedures. Interview respondents also reported their concerns about areas where the problem was the lack of government action, such as in matters related to transport infrastructure, rather than problems of intervention or matters of commission. The authors review the scope for regional cooperation to support national efforts to solve these problems and discuss items that might be included in the ASEAN "Roadmap for the Integration of the Electronics Sector."

Urata noted the growth of intra-regional trade and its links to the development of supply chains within the region. Pomfret (Chapter 9) observes that the policy counterpart of this development has been to work to reduce the costs of crossing borders. The case study by Parsons and Rammal also highlights the significance of these costs in ASEAN. Pomfret reviews a number of trade facilitation measures in ASEAN and uses data on trade costs to infer their impact. He finds a significant reduction in the costs of trade (by his measure, trade costs in *ad valorem* terms fell from 10 percent to less than 4 percent from 1990 to 2007). Pomfret also suggests that the contribution to trade facilitation is an important element of the regional free trade agreement, AFTA, and asks whether the emergence of the regional supply chains led to both pressure on governments to reduce trade costs and to do so not only by unilateral measures but also through bilateral and plurilateral agreements.

In Chapter 10, Gaston returns to the FDI theme, but with a focus on labour markets. He observes that home countries worry about the loss of jobs associated with outbound FDI. Host country concerns include the extent to which FDI firms invest on worker training compared to local firms, the extent of the race-to-the-bottom in social policy, the implications of the presence of FDI firms for labour union bargaining power and the contribution of FDI firms to earnings inequality. He reviews the theoretical work and empirical studies of the effects of FDI in labour markets. He finds that a theme of the theoretical work is that

FDI flows are associated with rising levels of inequality, a result that is borne out in much of the empirical work.

Most chapters in the book refer to trade in goods, and in the final chapter, Round and Findlay review trans-border issues related to air transport. Their observation is that while airline strategy is global, the regulation of the sector is national. Airline strategy is often constrained by the rules of the systems providing access to markets, and which often limit foreign ownership, but airlines seek other routes to cooperation. This strategy still triggers interest from competition policy regulators. The authors observe that, in this setting, independent decision-making by regulators may not lead to the "right answer" on the proposal for cooperation from a global perspective but argue that over time the gaps between the positions of the various regulators may close. Another response, however, is to seek to build a global regulatory agency. Its implementation involves many challenges but consideration of that model does provide guidance for a program of work on these issues. Round and Findlay stress the value of a clear statement of, and focus on, national welfare in decision-making and argue that transparency in decision-making is an important contributor to that result. They highlight a role for one country, or a group of countries — for example, a regional arrangement such as APEC — to take the lead in promoting common policy directions and the associated capacity building.

Chapter 1

The Future of World Trade Policy[1]

Mari Pangestu

Dedication

I dedicate this talk today to all my PECC colleagues, and in particular to the late Bijit Bora, who was a very, very good friend, and a very good sparring partner! Bijit and I had many, many occasions to share ideas, including during PECC meetings as well as in APEC, and later in the WTO.

My recollections of work with Bijit and then being at this meeting today also remind me of the critical role that research can play in policy making. Institutionalising the access of researchers to policy-making processes is extremely valuable, as Bijit and I often discussed. The role of academics and policy institutions working alongside and within the policy-making process will remain important, and in fact can make the process more effective, to ensure a more cohesive, comprehensive and coherent trade policy in the future. Meeting these goals is a challenge but also an opportunity for PECC, which should continue to provide this type of effective input to policy makers on a continuing basis.

[1] This chapter is based on a speech to the 18th General Meeting of the Pacific Economic Cooperation Council in Washington, 13 May 2009.

I have been a regular contributor to and participant in PECC meetings and projects. I would like to think I am a better trade minister because of my experience with PECC, which exposed me to so many dimensions of trade policy. It gave me a better bag of tools so that now, when confronted with a trade policy situation, I can often say, "Well, we've thought about this before, haven't we?" This is one of my themes today: to what extent are we now looking at old issues in a new light and what will be new in trade policy?

What is the future of trade policy? Will it be different from what we have been used to? Yes and no! Yes, because we have to re-think the way we look at trade policy because of the changing contexts and challenges — the financial crisis of 2007 and 2008 has brought on a new dimension. No, because the future role of trade policy will be more or less the same. Trade remains critical to growth. Its role has been rehearsed in all the summits (G-20, ASEAN, World Bank and the IMF), and individual countries agree. So, while the role of trade policy will remain similar, there will also be subtle differences, complexities and dimensions.

The new complexities are mostly related to the financial crisis of 2007 and 2008. Trade was not its cause, but is a casualty. There is decline in demand, so a decline in trade flows occurs. There has also been, as a consequence, discussion of rebalancing growth, which was mentioned in the International Monetary Fund's (IMF) report on the *Regional Economic Outlook* (*REO*) *for Asia and Pacific* (6 May 2009) regarding prospects for the Asia–Pacific region. That report talks about the need to look more at domestic consumption as the source of growth. This discussion is being replayed in Germany, with a debate between Chancellor Merkel and the Governor of the Bundesbank. The amplification of the crisis through trade has been bad for many countries, especially those that are part of the production and supply chain. There remains a general anxiety about globalisation as well.

Another dimension of the crisis that needs to be understood is what Baldwin calls "murky protectionism." As Baldwin and Evenett say,

> Most examples of murky protectionism ... are not direct violations of WTO obligations; they are abuses of legitimate discretion which are used to discriminate against foreign goods,

> companies, workers and investors. Examples include abuses of health and safety regulations, and clauses in stimulus packages that confine spending to domestic producers (p. 14).

The fear of increased protectionist measures emerged in 2008 with concern that trade wars might be replayed, as occurred in the 1930s. Surveys of new protectionist measures find that some measures in trade, and fiscal, policy have had discriminatory elements with regard to favouring domestic goods vs foreign goods, domestic workers vs foreign workers, domestic banks vs foreign banks, etc. These evaluations by the multilateral agencies find increased dumping, safeguards, increased tariffs up to the bound level, and non-tariff measures, etc, which are of concern. The World Bank has concluded that developed countries rely more on subsidies than on measures such as tariff and non-tariff measures.[2] There has also been an increase in policies in the name of green policy, or green growth, which is another dimension that will benefit from critical analysis in the design of future trade policy. Developing countries face serious risks in the incorrect application of measures on environmental grounds.

On the other hand, a crisis is an opportunity — in Asia this certainly has been a very important theme. Lessons from earlier crises are that to continue, and not to reverse, reforms are important. Acceleration of reforms, including those in the trade and investment areas, is also a way forward. The role of trade policy, however, is linked with energy and food security, as well as with issues of climate change, all of which should be objectives in the medium term.

So, given these changes in circumstance, has the objective of trade policy changed? After all, trade policy is not an end in itself; it is a means to an end. So what is the goal that we are all looking for? The answer is that the goal remains the same — growth and development. How does trade policy give us growth and development, and, in the context of the crisis, how do we minimise loss of growth during this very crucial time of the downturn? All the summits and leaders say,

---

[2] See Elisa Gamberoni and Richard Newfarmer, 'Trade protection: Incipient but worrisome trends', 4 March 2009. See http://www.voxeu.org/index.php?q=node/3183.

and development concerns must be continued in the way the DDA is approached.

Aid for trade and trade financing are the complementary measures that are valuable, especially for developing countries. New measures for trade financing should be an outcome of the G-20 work program, then followed up at the Asian Development Bank (ADB), and then followed up again at the spring meetings of the World Bank.

The WTO adopts a single undertaking approach in which "(v)irtually every item of the negotiation is part of a whole and indivisible package and cannot be agreed separately. 'Nothing is agreed until everything is agreed.' "[4]

Should this be abandoned to move to sector-by-sector and issue-by-issue agreements? This is a hard question. There were a few suggestions of what might be extracted from the current model — trade facilitation, for example. This might sound easy, and rather like an "early harvest." But in practice, it is difficult to make it work. When negotiators return to their country they can say, "OK, we're going to have to give up on this, but we're going to get this benefit," and that becomes a very important part of being able to convince people to sign on to the agreement. An "early harvest" is valuable, but in order to be effective it should eventually be linked to all the other parts.

How should regional commitments play a role in future trade policy discussions? It is important that the ASEAN Economic Community (AEC) remains on track. There is scepticism as to whether the "score card and blue print," which is the new instrument to ensure that countries are on track, will be effective in ensuring the achievement of the AEC. Therefore, for the AEC to be achieved, policy makers are aware that monitoring the implementation through the score card needs to work and there is now a lot of discussion as to how to make the score card more transparent (including member-specific information), accessible to peer review and useful for policy makers for the purposes of coordination and keeping to timelines.

---

[4]See http://www.wto.org/english/tratop_e/dda_e/work_organi_e.htm.

It is true that regionals and bilaterals are "messy," as many commentators have observed, including the incorporation of the downside effects of using up scarce negotiating resources of developing countries and the risks of increasing the costs of doing business because of the famous "spaghetti bowl" effect. But from a national point of view, it is important to be involved to avoid the costs of losing out to others who are moving faster.

Yet this game is risky, and it is also important to manage those risks. There has been a great deal of learning-by-doing, and in an effort to have model free trade agreements, some efforts to standardise rules of origin and the scheduling of tariffs have been undertaken in the ASEAN and ASEAN plus dialogue partner agreements. The ASEAN–New Zealand–Australian agreement is the most comprehensive agreement signed with a dialogue partner and includes comprehensive scheduling of tariff cuts, investment and services and also, for the first time, includes measures related to labour movement and the environment. Even though the labour and environment sections are referred to as cooperation and comprise bilateral memorandums of understanding, inclusion is already a sign of progress. Using existing agreements as benchmarks has also been practiced. For instance, when there were problems in reaching an agreement with Korea on the investment component of the ASEAN–Korea FTA, the ASEAN–New Zealand–Australian agreement was used as the benchmark.

At the same time, countries should continue the unilateral reform agenda in a concerted way. International commitments, whether they are regional or multilateral, help national governments frame the reform agenda and also limit reversal of reforms. The current global financial crisis has prompted big questions such as: Can we continue reforms? Should reforms, in fact, be accelerated? These are politically difficult to answer and thus support for finding answers is important. This is where APEC can play a role through its agenda for domestic reforms and capacity building.

Another immediate challenge is how to address increased protectionism that is WTO-consistent, but still has restrictive effects on trade and investment. This is the "murky protection" already noted.

Greater transparency, the role of surveillance mechanisms, and peer pressure are being looked at as options. The spirit of APEC, that is the spirit of cooperation in the Pacific region, has been about confidence-building measures to carry out reforms together, and peer pressure has developed as part of this overall process. A great deal has been learned from that process, which has been and can be fed into WTO discussions. The advantage of APEC is that it is not a negotiating forum and enables policy makers to interact and conduct dialogue in a more open way.

The G-20 countries also pledged to refrain "from increasing new barriers to trade in goods and services, imposing new export restrictions, and implementing WTO-inconsistent measures to stimulate exports." There is another sentence in that statement: "We will also minimise the negative impact on trade and investment of their domestic policies and actions, including fiscal policy and actions in supporting the financial sector."[5]

Therefore, the issues are not just the usual trade policy concerns, but also refer to fiscal measures that can have a trade impact. How can we make sure that the G-20 countries refrain from new fiscal measures and refrain from protectionism? It has been agreed that the WTO Trade Policy Review Board will manage the mechanism and a report listing measures taken by countries is published every three months, with the first report coming out in December 2008.[6] No judgement will be made on whether the measures are protectionist or non-protectionist, but the reports add to transparency. The reports will also state whether reforms or liberalisation have been undertaken, so if something positive has been achieved, it is also reported. The processes involved with the report provide incentives for self-notification and also encourage countries to clarify the policies that are listed by the WTO. Furthermore, the report mentions principles for undertaking any increased measures

[5]See http://www.g20.org/Documents/final-communique.pdf.

[6]The WTO Director General produces a report for the Board such as WTO documents JOB(09)/2 (26 January 2009), WT/TPR/OV/W/1 (20 April 2009) and WT/TPR/OV/W/2 (15 July 2009). See http://www.wto.org/english/news_e/news09_e/tpr_13jul09_e.htm.

that can impact trade, such as making the policy temporary and subject to review.

ASEAN also plans to adopt a similar approach, and an initiative called "Open ASEAN" will soon be implemented. Before taking on new policies, the review board will need to be notified to enable partners to review the policies. An agreement has already been reached to have a notification process, a review process, and a transparency process. Specific contact points will be identified within each government as to who to contact for a certain policy. And peer review with a private sector as well as other stakeholders has also been implemented.

What APEC and PECC can do is to examine more closely the peer-review process and the transparency of policies. Talk of a similar policy notification process has also been undertaken in APEC. The advantage that APEC has of not being a negotiating forum should be optimised and it is perhaps the right place to take a more analytical look at the WTO Trade Policy Review Body reports. These policies should not be looked at from the point of view of whether they are put in the protectionist box or in the WTO-inconsistent box. They should be looked at from a development point of view. Many developing countries cannot afford subsidies, and the only measures they use are trade policy measures. That discussion is to occur at further WTO Trade Policy Review Body meetings, where the importance of the sunset clause, the review clause, transparency, and the idea that subsidies for consumption are better than production, will be topics. A key concern is also that policies adopted in the name of climate change do not end up being trade-distortionary.

As noted, some of the methodology that APEC developed may now become part of the ASEAN Economic Community methodology. But at the same time, there is a sense that reusing previous ideas has lost its appeal, and there is some loss of momentum (within APEC for the Individual Action Plan process) and confidence in APEC's ability to really affect reform. People are asking whether there is a need to think differently about APEC and to give it a different, broader mission.

This discussion is continuing but APEC's role does include that of a cheerleader for reform, and encouraging its members through various initiatives that are difficult to take to the WTO. In that respect, it is noteworthy that Singapore, the Chair in 2009, has proposed a multi-year program of work. This program includes:

- accelerating trade and liberalisation at the border (this could include the Free Trade Area of the Asia–Pacific [FTAAP] in the long term, or other building blocks) and dealing with issues of trade facilitation;
- building the notification process (which was a worthwhile exercise because, by reporting to the WTO and now ASEAN, it enabled consistency among other ministries within a country);
- improving the business environment through regulatory reform behind the border to speed up business transactions; and
- instituting better physical connectivity (strengthening regional transportation and logistics networks across borders).

It is also important to have an Asia–Pacific caucus within the G-20 for the financial architecture issues, as it is also important in the WTO. There has always been a problem with APEC finance ministers who follow a meeting schedule that is not integrated with the leaders' summit. If APEC is going to be relevant, APEC finance ministers must be made more a part of the APEC process.[7]

In conclusion, while some old ideas are being reused or looked at again in a new way, the goal remains the same: greater openness. There are more challenges and complexities, and not just about trade liberalisation but also related to fiscal measures, and maintaining and strengthening the disciplines that are already in the current framework is of great value. Negotiations remain critical, but developing countries have to add to their capacity to negotiate. Confidence building, peer pressure, capacity building, and having ongoing confidence to continue reforms are part of the package, all helping to keep reforms on track, and even accelerating reforms. At one level, the political push from the

[7] It is heartening to note that after this speech was delivered, in the lead-up to the APEC Trade Ministers Meeting in July, the SOM of the APEC Trade and Foreign Ministers process met back-to-back with the SOM from the APEC Finance Ministers process, with one overlapping session on Trade Finance. This is an important start.

G-20 is critical, but in developing capacity and building confidence, PECC and APEC can play a very important role.

Reference

Baldwin R and Evenett SJ (2009). Introduction and recommendations for the G20. In *The Collapse of Global Trade, Murky Protectionism, and the Crisis: Recommendations for the G20*, R Baldwin and S Evenett (eds), pp. 1–12, Vox.eu publication, http://www.voxeu.org/index.php?q=node/3199.

Chapter 2

Evaluating the Impact of the WTO Information Technology Agreement

Bijit Bora and Xuepeng Liu*

This paper provides an empirical assessment of the Information Technology Agreement (ITA) under a gravity model framework. Our results show that, all other things being equal, an ITA member would import at least 7 percent more in ITA products if the exporter is a WTO member compared to a baseline case of neither being a member of the WTO (trade creation effect of the ITA). If the importer is a member of the WTO but does not participate in the ITA, then it would import at least 6 percent less in ITA products than the baseline case (trade diversion effect of the ITA within the WTO). If only one country in a pair is a WTO member, they would trade at least 17 percent less in ITA products than the baseline case (trade diversion effect of the WTO). We also find that most of the progress in ITA trade liberalisation has been made by developing rather than developed countries. Taken together, these

*The views expressed in this paper are of a personal nature and should not in any way be associated with the WTO Secretariat, or Members of the WTO.

results indicate that participation in the ITA will increase the value of bilateral trade and that being a WTO member can avoid a large trade diversion effect.

> "As we embark into the last lap of the Doha Development Agenda, it is important to keep in mind the contribution that an ambitious initiative to cut barriers to trade, such as the ITA, can make to development."
>
> WTO Director-General Pascal Lamy, in opening the WTO Information Technology Symposium on 28 March 2007.

2.1. Introduction

Since the 1990s, the information technology (IT) industry has been increasingly characterised by intense competition, price sensitivity, falling prices and declining profit margins around the world. Trade barriers increase IT product suppliers' relative costs in global markets and play an important role in determining international competitiveness. Tariffs on many electronic products, such as finished computers, have been significantly reduced or eliminated among major IT-producing countries, but the tariffs on other electronics such as semiconductors and software remain high. Market access negotiations during the Uruguay Round negotiations yielded a number of tariff reduction approaches. Among the various formulas and other modalities that were proposed, the United States, as the largest trader in IT products, proposed to extend its offer to eliminate all agricultural tariffs to a number of non-agricultural products, including some electronic equipment (Croome, 1999, p. 159). The United States considered free trade in all electronic products one of the major objectives in the Uruguay Round negotiations of the GATT. Differences in views about the value of concluding a zero-for-zero approach in electronic equipment led to its exclusion from the final Uruguay Round package. However, the interest in concluding zero-for-zero negotiations in electronic products did not abate. At the WTO Singapore Ministerial Conference in December 1996, the Ministerial Declaration on Trade in Information Technology Products (ITA) was concluded by

29 countries.[1] In the ensuing months, a number of other countries accepted the ITA. By April 1997, the total value of trade accounted for by all the ITA participants finally surpassed the minimum 90 percent requirement.

The Agreement has as its objective the bound elimination of duties as specified in its annex. Product coverage includes computers, telecommunications, semiconductors, semiconductor manufacturing equipment, software, instruments and apparatus. Participants cannot choose from the product list and have to implement the tariff elimination objective. The only area for negotiation is the implementation period for the reduction and final elimination of tariffs. The Agreement specified that this had to be done no later than 1 January 2000, although flexibility was provided for longer staging on a product-by-product basis. Extended staging, however, is available only for developing countries and must be approved by other participants. A number of participants, including Costa Rica, India, Indonesia, the Republic of Korea and Chinese Taipei, took advantage of the possibility of extensions, with the requirement that the final date for elimination not be beyond 2005. The commitments undertaken under the ITA in the WTO are on a most-favoured-nation (MFN) basis, and, therefore, benefits accrue to all other WTO members.[2]

Membership of the ITA has been expanding steadily and, by 2007, it had 70 member states or separate customs territories and represented about 97 percent of world trade in IT products. As shown by Bora (2004), the average of simple average tariffs over all ITA products at six-digit HS92 level is 3.6 percent and 11.2 percent for ITA members and non-members, respectively.[3] Most ITA members have lower tariffs on

---

[1]These include Australia, Canada, Chinese Taipei, the EU (15 members, not including the EU expansion after 2004), Hong Kong SAR, Iceland, Indonesia, Japan, Korea, Norway, Singapore, Switzerland (including Liechtenstein), Turkey and the United States.

[2]The ITA is solely a tariff-cutting mechanism. While the Declaration provides for the review of non-tariff barriers (NTBs), there are no binding commitments concerning these.

[3]However, these average figures are from different years for different countries, ranging from 1999–2004. See Bora (2004) for more details of tariffs on ITA products.

ITA products than non-members. The key non-ITA member countries are Brazil, Mexico and South Africa.

The ITA, as a sectoral agreement on an MFN basis, holds a unique place amongst the different multilateral trade agreements. The purpose of this paper is to conduct an empirical evaluation of the ITA. A gravity model approach is taken as our empirical framework. Given that this sectoral agreement is embedded in the WTO framework, we need to design our variables specifically to test this plurilateral agreement by using bilateral ITA trade data.

This study contains important policy implications. If the ITA is effective, then it will justify this sectoral agreement on an MFN basis as an alternative to the general WTO agreement. If WTO negotiations become deadlocked, sectoral agreements may be a good avenue to follow. Such agreements are better than regional trade agreements (RTAs) in the fact that they are on an MFN basis and do not suffer from the problems of rules of origin, overlapping or many other implementation issues. Besides the traditional argument for free trade, trade in IT products, in particular, is expected to have additional benefits to trade in general. As we know, IT products are highly value added in terms of technology. Trade in IT products can reasonably increase the technology diffusion across countries. In sum, it is important to know if the ITA is effective in promoting trade in IT products.

The rest of this paper is organised as follows: Section 2 describes some facts on ITA trade, Section 3 discusses the gravity model approach and the dataset, Section 4 shows the regression results and Section 5 concludes.

2.2. Some Facts on ITA Trade

As shown in Figure 2.1, the value of ITA imports grew consistently from 1988 to 2000, when they peaked. The growth was so strong that ITA trade accounted for as much as 16.5 percent of world trade in 2000. After 2001, the IT industry experienced a recession, but started to recover after 2003.

In 2002, Asia was the largest trading region for ITA exports, accounting for 60 percent of world exports and 47 percent of world

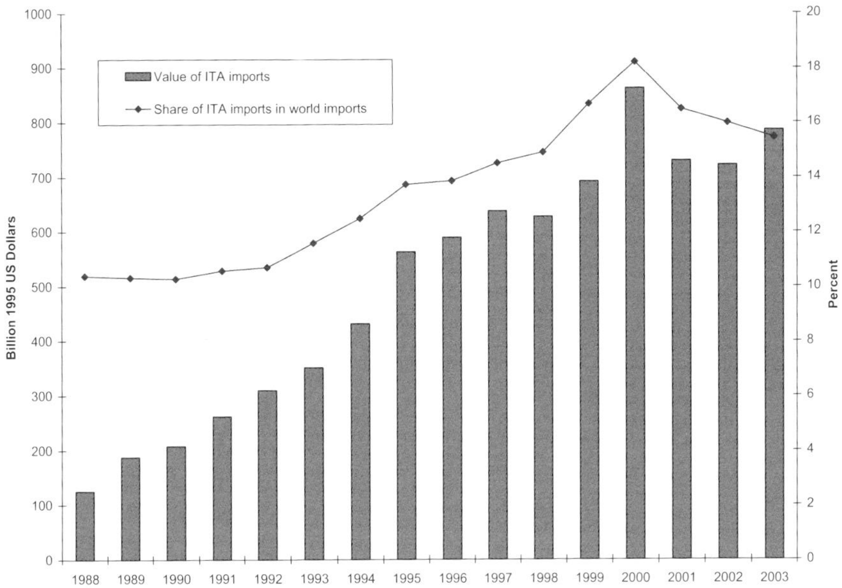

Fig. 2.1. Total real ITA imports and the share of ITA imports in world imports. *Source*: UNCTAD COMTRADE.

imports (Fig. 2.2). The second and third largest regions in the same year were North America[4] and Western Europe. North America accounted for 20 percent of total world exports and 26 percent of world imports. The comparable figures for Western Europe were 13 percent and 17 percent. The ITA does not specify different types of products, but provides only a list of products. Nevertheless, it is possible to classify the various ITA products into different groups such as computers, telecommunications equipment and semiconductors. A full list of ITA products by type is provided in Appendix 2. Figure 2.3 breaks down ITA trade by type of product and shows that the most important products, in terms of trade value, are computers, semiconductors and telecommunications equipment. Together, they account for 83 percent of world ITA exports and 84 percent of world ITA imports.

[4] Defined as Canada and the United States. It does not include Mexico.

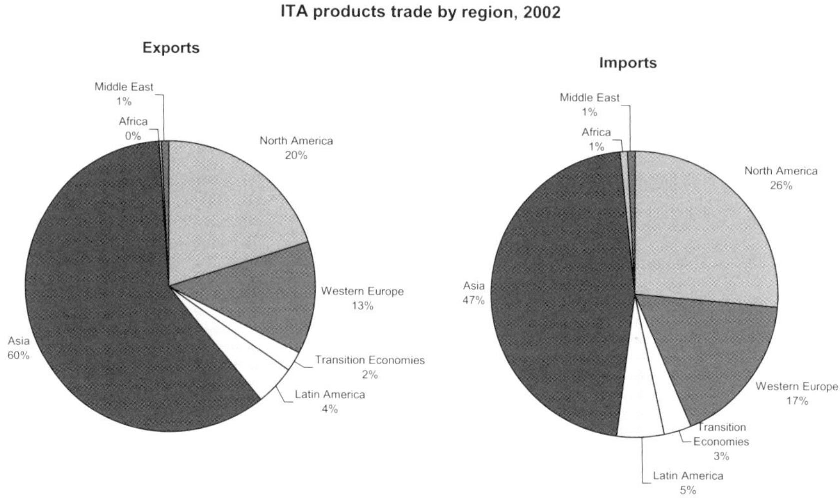

Fig. 2.2. ITA exports and imports by region, 2002.
Source: UNCTAD COMTRADE.

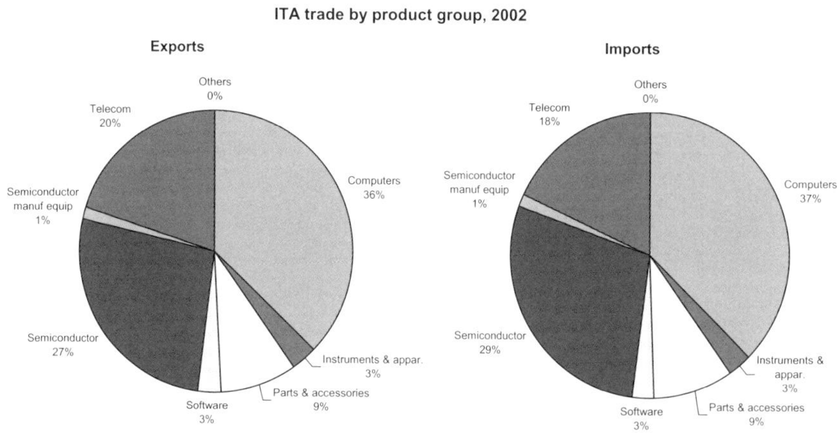

Fig. 2.3. ITA exports and imports by type of ITA product, 2002.
Source: UNCTAD COMTRADE.

Individual country data for the top 20 exporters for 1996 (the last year before the ITA came into force) and 2002 are provided in Table 2.1. This shows that the top exporters are developed countries, with the United States as the largest exporter and importer in

Table 2.1. Construction of the key ITA variables.

Importer		Exporter	Variable Names	Notes
ITA	WTO	WTO		
Yes	Yes	Yes	*ita*wto	Trade creation of the ITA
No	Yes		*_itawto*wto	Trade diversion of the ITA within WTO
No	No		*_wto*wto	Trade diversion of GATT/WTO
Yes	Yes	No	*ita*_wto	
No	Yes		*_itawto*_wto	
No	No		*_wto*_wto	Baseline: neither country in GATT/WTO

both years. The EU was the third largest exporter and second largest importer, if it is counted as one and intra-EU trade is excluded. The most notable development is the emergence and growth of China as one of the world's most important exporters. In 1996, it accounted for 2.7 percent of world export. By 2002, it had increased its share to 9.7 percent, making it the world's fourth largest exporter.

Additional observations about the data in Table 2.1 include the dominance of East Asian countries, especially the so-called newly industrialising economies (NIE) of Chinese Taipei, Republic of Korea, Hong Kong SAR and Singapore, as well as the emergence of Hungary. The trade performance of the four NIE economies is complemented by four members of the Association of Southeast Asian Nations (ASEAN) — Indonesia, Malaysia, the Philippines and Thailand.[5] Hungary was not part of the top 20 in 1996. In 2002, however, it became the 14th largest exporter and the 15th largest importer. The Czech Republic is the only other transition economy to make it onto the list.

One of the most interesting aspects of Table 2.1 is the fact that two non-ITA signatories (Brazil and Mexico) are on the list. Mexico, in particular, has been a consistently strong trader. In 1996, it was ranked

[5]It should be noted that Singapore is also a member of ASEAN, bringing the total number of ASEAN Members in the top 20 exporters to five.

as the 11th largest exporter and importer. Despite the growth in trade of China and other countries, it has managed to stay at the same level of importance in 2002 (10th largest exporter and importer). Brazil was not on the top 20 list of exporters in 1996, but was ranked 16th as an importer. In 2002, Brazil was ranked 19th in ITA exports and imports. The most important non-ITA member in terms of exports after Mexico and Brazil is South Africa (not shown in the table), which accounts for 0.1 percent of world exports and 0.4 percent of world imports. When the value of exports originating from Mexico, Brazil and South Africa are added, almost 99.9 percent of world exports in IT products would be covered by the ITA.

2.3. The Impact of the ITA: A Gravity Model Approach

We estimate the effect of the ITA on bilateral trade flows in a gravity model framework. The basic gravity model explains (the logs of) bilateral trade with (the logs of) the distance between the countries and their joint GDP.[6] In practice, this model is often augmented with many other covariates that can potentially affect bilateral trade, such as geography, culture, history and political or military relations.

Previous papers on the GATT/WTO such as Rose (2004) usually use two variables to capture the effect of the GATT/WTO on trade: "Bothin" and "Onein." "Bothin" is a binary variable that is unity if both countries in a pair are GATT/WTO members; and "Onein" is a binary variable that is unity if only one country in the pair is a GATT/WTO member. The first variable is used to capture the trade creation effect of the GATT/WTO, while the second is for the trade diversion effect. It is tempting to follow this tradition and create similar variables for the ITA, but this is inappropriate as the ITA is on an MFN basis. If the importer is an ITA member, then it will offer its ITA tariff rates to all WTO members, no matter if the exporter is an ITA member

---

[6]By using the joint GDP or GDP per capita, people restrict the coefficient on two countries' characteristics to be equal. In our regressions, we do not put this restriction on GDP, GDP per capita, or land area.

or not. For this reason, we create the dummy variables of interest as shown in Table 2.1.

The italic parts of the variable names are associated with importers, with the rest being for exporters. Assuming that all ITA members are also WTO members,[7] an importer falls into the following three categories: ITA member; WTO member but not ITA member; and non-WTO member. Because of the MFN nature of ITA commitments, we only distinguish exporters by their WTO memberships. As long as an exporter is a WTO member, it enjoys the tariff reductions of ITA members, no matter if the exporter is an ITA member or not. The underscore before "ita" or "wto" means that the country is not an ITA or WTO member. The first binary variable is 1 if the importer is an ITA member and the exporter is a WTO member, which measures the trade creation effect of the ITA. The second binary variable is 1 if the importer is a WTO member but not an ITA member and the exporter is a WTO member, which measures the trade diversion of the ITA within the WTO. The third to fifth variables are for the scenarios when one of the two countries is not a WTO member. We combine them into a single variable "onewto," which measures the trade diversion of the GATT/WTO.[8] The last variable is unity if neither country is a WTO member, which is taken as the baseline category in our analyses. All the variables we use in our regressions are listed in the following specification. The coefficients of interest to us are β_{18}, β_{19} and β_{20}.

$$\begin{aligned}\ln M_{ijt} = {} & \beta_0 + \beta_1 \ln(Y_i Y_j)_t + \beta_2 \ln(Y_i Y_j / Pop_i Pop_j)_t + \beta_3 \ln D_{ij} \\ & + \beta_4 Border_{ij} + \beta_5 \ln(Area_i Area_j) \\ & + \beta_6 Island_{ij} + \beta_7 Landlock_{ij} + \beta_8 ComLang_{ij} + \beta_9 EverCol_{ij} \\ & + \beta_{10} ComCol_{ij} + \beta_{11} Hostility_{ij} + \beta_{12} Remote_{ijt}\end{aligned}$$

[7] There are some exceptions. Estonia joined the ITA two years before joining the WTO (1997 vs. 1999); Lithuania (2000 vs. 2001) and Chinese Taipei (1997 vs. 2003). Among these countries/territories, only Chinese Taipei has a large number of observations in our dataset. Dropping Chinese Taipei from our analyses, however, changes very little in our results.

[8] Using separate variables has little impact on our results.

$$
\begin{aligned}
&+\beta_{13}Alliance_{ijt}+\beta_{14}GSP_{ijt}+\beta_{15}GSP_{jit}+\beta_{16}CU_{ijt}\\
&+\beta_{17}RTA_{ijt}+\beta_{18}itawto_{ijt}+\beta_{19}\_itawtowto_{ijt}+\beta_{20}onewto_{ijt}\\
&+\sum_{t=1988}^{2003}\beta_{21}^{t}a_t+\sum a_{ij}+\varepsilon_{ijt}
\end{aligned}
$$

where the subscripts i and j denote importer and exporter, respectively, and t denotes year; M_{ijt} is the c.i.f. import of i from j in year t; Υ is real GDP and *Pop* is population; $Dist_{ij}$ is the great-circle distance between i and j; $Border_{ij}$ dummy equals one if i and j share a land border; *Area* is the geographic area of a country; $Island_{ij}$ is the number of island nations in a pair (0, 1 or 2); $Landlock_{ij}$ is the number of landlocked nations in a pair (0, 1 or 2); $ComLang_{ij}$ dummy equals one if i and j have a common language; $EverCol_{ij}$ dummy equals one if i has been a colony of j; $ComCol_{ij}$ dummy equals one if i and j have been colonised by the same coloniser; $Hostility_{ij}$ is the military conflict intensity between i and j; $Remote_{ijt}$ is the distance of a country pair to the rest of the world weighted by all the other countries' GDPs in year t (see the next section for the formula); $Alliance_{ijt}$ dummy equals one if i and j were in a formal alliance in year t; GSP_{ijt} dummy equals one if i offered GSP to j in year t; GSP_{jit} dummy equals one if j offered GSP to i in year t; CU_{ijt} dummy equals one if i and j used the same currency in year t; RTA_{ijt} dummy equals one if i and j belonged to the same regional trade agreement in year t; a_t is the year dummy variable; a_{ij} is the country pair dummy; ε_{ijt} is the residual; and $\{\beta\}$ is the coefficient vector to be estimated.

The panel dataset used in this paper includes 217 countries over the years 1988–2003. These countries or territories are listed in Appendix 1. In the brackets following some country names are the years of entry into the ITA.[9] We use multiple dyadic import data, that is, each country pair appears twice a year corresponding to the import from country i to country j and the import from j to i.[10] Import

[9] See also http://www.wto.org/english/tratop_e/inftec_e/itapart_e.htm.

[10] We use import flows for trade data, rather than the sum of imports and exports for the following reasons. First, import data are usually regarded as more reliable than

data are from the UNCTAD COMTRADE dataset, aggregated over all ITA products at the six-digit HS92 level. The import of country i from country j is filled by the export of j to i when the former is missing and the latter is available. A 10 percent, c.i.f. is assumed when using the reverse flows and the US. In our log-linear gravity regressions, the dependent variable $\ln(M_{ijt})$ is substituted by $\ln(M_{ijt} + 1)$ to keep the zero trade values after taking logarithms. The measurement error created is small because trade data are converted into dollars (rather than million or billion dollars) before the one dollar is added. The data on all the other variables are from Liu (2009). Please see Table 2.2 for the descriptive statistics for the variables used in our analyses.

2.4. Regression Results

In our gravity regression results, we not only look at the impact of the ITA on trade in general, but also investigate the asymmetry of the impact between developed and developing countries. Because most European Union members are in the same customs union from the beginning of our sample in 1988,[11] it is senseless to estimate the impact of the ITA on intra-EU trade. Hence, we drop all intra-EU bilateral trade from all the regressions, although the results are not significantly different from that with intra-EU trade.

2.4.1. *ITA members vs. non-ITA members*

The regression results are reported in Table 2.3. In column (1), we run pooled OLS with only year dummies. This shows that the ITA is very effective with large trade creation and diversion effects. This result uses both within and between country pair variations. The between variations, however, often suffer from the endogeneity problem (i.e., reverse causation): the more a country trades in ITA products, the more likely

export data because customs departments are more interested in tracking imports than exports for tariff revenue reasons. Second, country or country pair's characteristics usually affect import and export differently. With directional import data, we can avoid mixing the effects on imports and exports.

[11] Austria, Sweden and Finland joined the EU in 1995.

Table 2.2. Descriptive statistics.

Variable	Obs	Mean	Std Dev	Min	Max
*ita*wto	133352	0.15	0.36	0	1
*dita*wto	133352	0.08	0.27	0	1
*uscajp*wto	133352	0.01	0.12	0	1
*aunz*wto	133352	0.01	0.09	0	1
*deuita*wto	133352	0.06	0.24	0	1
*dgita*wto	133352	0.07	0.26	0	1
_*itawto*wto	133352	0.45	0.50	0	1
onewto	133352	0.34	0.47	0	1
_*wto*_wto	133352	0.03	0.18	0	1
log(real import)	133352	4.59	3.90	−7.03	17.50
log(GDPi)	133352	10.95	2.22	1.91	16.10
log(GDPj)	133352	11.54	2.08	1.91	16.10
log(GDPPCi)	133352	1.82	1.11	−1.97	3.82
log(GDPPCj)	133352	2.09	1.01	−1.97	3.82
log(Distance)	133352	8.13	0.86	3.68	9.42
Land Adjacency	133352	0.03	0.17	0	1
log(AREAi)	133352	11.85	2.52	0.69	16.92
log(AREAj)	133352	12.03	2.48	0.69	16.92
Island	133352	0.37	0.56	0	2
Landlocked	133352	0.28	0.49	0	2
ComLang	133352	0.11	0.31	0	1
Ever Colony	133352	0.02	0.15	0	1
Com Colony	133352	0.14	0.34	0	1
Hostility	133352	0.02	0.15	0	3
Alliance	133352	0.09	0.29	0	1
Remoteness	133352	4.24	0.05	3.98	4.40
GSPij	133352	0.18	0.38	0	1
GSPji	133352	0.26	0.44	0	1
FTA	133352	0.18	0.39	0	1
CU	133352	0.02	0.14	0	1

Note: All continuous variables are in logarithm.

Table 2.3. Regression results.

	(1) Pooled OLS full sample		(2) Fixed effects full sample		(3) Random effects full sample		(4) Fixed effects large traders	
	coef.	z	coef.	z	coef.	z	coef.	z
*ita*wto	0.42***	10.50	0.07**	2.29	0.15***	5.31	0.11***	4.79
_*itawto*wto	−0.27***	−7.47	−0.06**	−2.07	−0.12***	−4.45	−0.01	−0.48
onewto	−0.37***	−10.45	−0.16***	−5.11	−0.20***	−7.03	−0.12***	−4.78
log(GDP*i*)	0.79***	115.9	−0.86***	−6.79	0.68***	46.80	−0.82***	−8.74
log(GDP*j*)	1.20***	178.6	0.20	1.51	1.00***	70.04	0.91***	7.80
log(GDPPC*i*)	0.38***	34.6	1.96***	15.54	0.29***	13.18	1.92***	20.17
log(GDPPC*j*)	0.93***	79.3	1.16***	8.35	0.73***	32.32	0.48***	3.74
log(Distance)	−0.82***	−64.1			−0.73***	−28.9		
Land Adjacency	0.97***	20.6			1.12***	9.28		
log(AREA*i*)	−0.05***	−9.45			−0.04***	−3.25		
log(AREA*j*)	−0.28***	−52.9			−0.23***	−18.7		
Island	0.23***	12.6			0.28***	6.81		
Landlocked	−0.13***	−7.99			−0.17***	−4.98		
ComLang	0.21***	6.41			0.14**	2.00		
Ever Colony	1.76***	39.3			2.18***	15.2		
Com Colony	0.52***	18.3			0.38***	6.10		
Hostility	−0.66***	−12.3			−0.45***	−3.66		
Alliance	0.14***	4.69	0.25***	3.18	0.17***	3.20	0.47***	9.79
Remoteness	1.60***	6.62	0.65	1.21	0.88**	2.33	2.66***	6.44

(*Continued*)

Table 2.3. *(Continued)*

	(1) Pooled OLS full sample		(2) Fixed effects full sample		(3) Random effects full sample		(4) Fixed effects large traders	
	coef.	z	coef.	z	coef.	z	coef.	z
GSP*ij*	−0.39***	−14.38	0.22***	3.78	−0.03	−0.84	0.34***	8.40
GSP*ji*	0.28***	12.76	0.22***	4.51	0.44***	12.1	0.07**	2.38
FTA	0.22***	10.05	0.42***	10.88	0.39***	12.7	0.30***	11.66
CU	0.64***	11.67	0.48	0.59	0.37***	2.87	0.97*	1.75
Year dummy	Yes		Yes		Yes		Yes	
R2	0.51		0.82		0.50		0.88	
# obs	133352		133352		133352		64078	

Notes:

1. Dependent variable is the logarithm of the real import of country A from country B.
2. All continuous variables are in logarithm.
3. ***, ** and * denote the significance levels at 1 percent, 5 percent and 10 percent respectively.
4. Regression (1) is OLS with year dummies and robust standard errors.
5. Regression (2) has both year dummies and country pair fixed effects.
6. Regression (3) has both year dummies and country pair random effects.
7. Regression (4) has both year dummies and country pair fixed effects (real import > $10,000).
8. The R2 for random-effect regression is the overall R2.
9. The R2 for fixed-effect regression is the adjusted R2 recovered from country pair dummy variable least square regression (DVLS), which is not comparable with the R2 in the random-effect regression.

it will join the ITA. In the following regressions, we include country pair fixed or random effects. The fixed-effects regressions use only the within variations (i.e., the demeaned data). The question we ask here is: Do two countries trade more in ITA products after one or both joins the ITA, compared with their trade before joining the agreement? The country pair's fixed effects control for the unobserved characteristics for each country pair. This partially fixes the endogeneity problem. The results from the fixed-effects model in column (2) show that a country will import 7 percent more ITA products if it is an ITA member and the exporter is a WTO member, compared with the baseline case of neither being a WTO member, ($e^{0.7} - 1 \approx 7\%$). This smaller magnitude looks more reliable than that from the pooled OLS regression, given that the ITA was implemented only a few years ago and most developed countries already had low tariffs on ITA imports before joining the ITA. The coefficient of variable "*_rtawto*wto" is negative. This means that although both importer and exporter are WTO members, if the importer is not an ITA member, it will on average import 6 percent less than the baseline case. It suggests that a non-ITA WTO member would import 14 percent more from WTO members if it joins the ITA, ($e^{(0.07+0.06)} - 1 \approx 14\%$), ceteris paribus. The trade diversion effects of the GATT/WTO are even stronger, ($e^{(0.16)} - 1 \approx 17\%$), as shown by the coefficient of the variable "onewto." This means that the imports would be 17 percent less if only one country is in the GATT/WTO, compared with the baseline case. The smaller magnitude of the coefficient of "*_rtawto*wto" (-0.06) than that of "onewto" (-0.16) implies that being a WTO member helps to avoid very large trade diversion even if the country does not sign the ITA. Regression (3) uses random effects and offers stronger trade creation effects. But the random-effects model is based on a more stringent condition, that is, the error term must be uncorrelated with country pair dummies. The Hausman test rejects this condition, so we take the fixed-effects regression as our preferred specification. Acknowledging that a small subset of the large ITA traders account for most of the world ITA trade, we drop all the bilateral trade observations with import values less than $100,000 (in 1995 real terms) in regression (4). The fixed-effects regression results are not substantially different from that in column (2). For the big traders, the trade creation effect of the ITA is even stronger, ($e^{0.11} - 1 \approx 12\%$), but the coefficient of "*_rtawto*wto" is less significant, implying a weak trade diversion effect of the ITA within the GATT/WTO.

Our results from the fixed-effects regression show that the coefficients of other covariates generally have the expected signs. GSP, RTA and Alliance significantly increase bilateral ITA trade. Currency union, however, has a significant trade creation effect only for large traders. "Remoteness" positively affects bilateral trade as expected.

2.4.2. *Developing vs. developed countries*

The ITA is expected to have asymmetric impacts on market access for different countries. The effect depends on the protection level prior to the ITA, price elasticity, etc. Because developed countries, such as the United States, Canada, Japan and the EU, were already liberalised in ITA trade before the ITA, we would expect little changes in tariffs in these countries. A larger impact is expected from the developing world. The most promising market potential comes from the East and Southeast Asian countries/territories, such as China, India, Indonesia, Thailand, Malaysia, Korea and Chinese Taipei. The high trade barriers in these countries (0–50 percent) are expected to be much lower with the implementation of the ITA. We test these hypotheses by splitting ITA membership into developed and developing countries.

Table 2.4 shows the asymmetries of the impacts in developed and developing countries.[12] We show only our preferred fixed-effect regression results. Regression (1) splits variable "*ita*wto" into two variables: "*dita*wto" (the importer is a developed ITA member) and "*dgita*wto" (the importer is a developing ITA member). As expected, the coefficient on "*dita*wto" is very small and insignificant, while the trade creation effect of "*dgita*wto" is 13 percent ($e^{(0.12)} - 1 \approx 13\%$)

[12]The developed countries include Australia, Austria, Belgium, Canada, Denmark, Finland, France, Germany, Greece, Iceland, Ireland, Italy, Japan, Luxembourg, Netherlands, New Zealand, Norway, Portugal, Spain, Sweden, Switzerland, the UK and the USA; they are now all ITA members.

Table 2.4. Fixed effects regression results, developing vs. developed countries.

	(1) Full Sample		(2) Large Traders		(3) Full Sample		(4) Large Traders	
	coef.	z	coef.	z	coef.	z	coef.	z
*dita*wto	0.01	0.29	0.01	0.57				
*uscajpita*wto					0.11*	1.81	0.06	1.44
*aunzita*wto					0.28***	3.60	0.05	0.79
*deuita*wto					−0.05	−1.36	0.00	−0.09
*dgita*wto	0.12***	3.55	0.18***	7.34	0.12***	3.55	0.18***	7.34
_*itawto*wto	−0.07**	−2.24	−0.02	−0.81	−0.06**	−2.19	−0.02	−0.78
onewto	−0.16***	−5.03	−0.11***	−4.53	−0.16***	−5.01	−0.11***	−4.52
log(GDP*i*)	−0.93***	−7.27	−0.95***	−9.93	−0.98***	−7.65	−0.96***	−10.01
log(GDP*j*)	0.23*	1.72	0.97***	8.24	0.26*	1.88	0.97***	8.29
log(GDPPC*i*)	2.02***	15.86	2.03***	21.06	2.07***	16.19	2.04***	21.11
log(GDPPC*j*)	1.12***	8.08	0.41***	3.23	1.10***	7.92	0.40***	3.17
Alliance	0.26***	3.18	0.47***	9.83	0.26***	3.24	0.47***	9.85
Remoteness	0.63	1.18	2.59***	6.28	0.71	1.33	2.61***	6.32
GSP*ij*	0.20***	3.53	0.32***	7.85	0.22***	3.89	0.32***	7.84
GSP*ji*	0.23***	4.63	0.09***	2.77	0.22***	4.60	0.09***	2.76
FTA	0.41***	10.80	0.30***	11.49	0.42***	11.05	0.30***	11.58
CU	0.48	0.60	0.98*	1.78	0.48	0.60	0.99*	1.79

(Continued)

Table 2.4. *(Continued)*

	(1) Full Sample		(2) Large Traders		(3) Full Sample		(4) Large Traders	
	coef.	z	coef.	z	coef.	z	coef.	z
Year dummy	Yes		Yes		Yes		Yes	
R2	0.82		0.88		0.82		0.88	
# obs	133352		64078		133352		64078	

Notes:
1. Dependent variable is the logarithm of the real import of country *i* from country *j*.
2. All continuous variables are in logarithm.
3. ***, ** and * denote the significance levels at 1 percent, 5 percent and 10 percent, respectively.
4. All regressions have year dummies and country pair fixed effects.
5. Regressions (1) and (3) use the full sample.
6. Regressions (2) and (4) restrict the data to only bigger traders (real import > $10,000).
7. R2 is the adjusted R2 recovered from country pair dummy variable least square regression (DVLS).
8. *dita*wto is 1 if importer is developed ITA member and exporter is in WTO, and 0 otherwise.
9. *uscajpita*wto is 1 if importer is US/Canada/Japan and exporter is in WTO, and 0 otherwise.
10. *aunzita*wto is 1 if importer is Australia/New Zealand and exporter is in WTO, and 0 otherwise.
11. *deuita*wto is 1 if importer is *developed* European ITA member and exporter is in WTO, and 0 otherwise.
12. *dgita*wto is 1 if importer is *developing* ITA member and exporter is in WTO, and 0 otherwise.

for the whole sample, which is much bigger than the overall impact (7 percent) as shown in regression (2) in Table 2.3. We find a similar pattern when restricting the sample to large traders in regression (2) in Table 2.4.

The extents of liberalisation of trade in ITA products may be different for different developed countries. We further split the variable "*dita*wto" into three variables: "*uscajpita*wto" (importers are the United States, Canada or Japan); "*aunzita*wto" (importers are Australia or New Zealand) and "*deuita*wto" (importers are developed European countries).[13] Results from regression (3) in Table 2.4 show that the trade creation effect of the ITA is the largest for Australia and New Zealand, followed by the United States. But these strong effects are not robust to restricting the analysis to only bigger traders, as shown in regression (4). The European countries did much worse (negative although insignificant trade creation effects) in both regressions (3) and (4). It is the European countries that drive the trade creation effects of developed ITA membership into insignificance in regressions (1) and (2) in Table 2.4.[14]

2.4.3. *Time-varying country fixed effects*

Recent developments in the theoretical foundation of a gravity specification suggest that time-varying country fixed effects can fully absorb the "multilateral resistance" effects in a panel data gravity regression (e.g., Baldwin and Taglioni, 2006). This method, however, is computationally cumbersome because of the very large number of interaction terms in regressions.

To reduce the number of dummies for the year and importer/exporter interactions, we take two consecutive years as one period and then use the new period dummy to interact with importers and

[13]The developed European countries include Austria, Belgium, Denmark, Finland, France, Germany, Greece, Iceland, Ireland, Italy, Luxembourg, Netherlands, Norway, Portugal, Spain, Sweden, Switzerland and the UK.

[14]Iceland is more protected than other developed European countries, but dropping Iceland from the dataset does not change our results by much.

exporters. This enables us to run the regressions with thousands of interactions, although it still requires huge memory in Stata (2GB). We expect that this new period variable should capture most of the variations over time. The corresponding results are reported in Table 2.5. All the covariates discussed in this paper are included in the left panel of this table. The coefficients of the key variables in which we are interested are even larger in absolute values than those from the pooled data regression reported in Table 2.3. The result in column (1) show that a country will import 68 percent more ITA products if it is an ITA member and the exporter is a WTO member, compared with the baseline case of neither being a WTO member ($e^{0.52} - 1 \approx 68\%$). If both importer and exporter are WTO members but the importer is not an ITA member, it will, on average, import even 20 percent less than the baseline case ($e^{0.18} - 1 \approx 20\%$). The trade diversion effects of the GATT/WTO are also stronger than those in the previous results ($e^{(0.44)} - 1 \approx 55\%$).

If we use year dummies to interact with countries, year-varying country specific variables such as GDP, and GDP per capita would be dropped. These year-varying country specific variables, however, are still kept in the regression because we group years into periods. Dropping these variables, however, does not change the results by much, as shown by the right panel in Table 2.5.

2.5. Conclusions

Overall, our results indicate that participation in the ITA increases the value of bilateral trade and being a WTO member can avoid the large trade diversion effect. The analysis yielded a number of observations about the ITA that could be useful for the future round of negotiations and trade policy in general. The same analysis can be applied to other sectoral agreements under the GATT/WTO, such as the Uruguay Round zero-for-zero agreements, chemical harmonisation and the agreements on civil aircrafts. We leave this for future research.

The gravity approach captures a variety of influences on trade, beyond specific parameters. Since the ITA requires ITA tariffs to be bound at zero, the gravity approach captures the institutional effect

Table 2.5. Regression results with time-varying country fixed effects.

	(1)		(2)	
	coef.	z	coef.	z
*ita*wto	0.52***	9.00	0.50***	9.21
_*itawto*wto	−0.18***	−3.97	−0.29***	−6.58
onewto	−0.44***	−14.72	−0.51***	−17.82
log(GDP*i*)	1.03*	1.91		
log(GDP*j*)	1.36**	2.13		
log(GDPPC*i*)	0.03	0.06		
log(GDPPC*j*)	−0.74	−1.11		
log(Distance)	−1.24***	−112.6	−1.22***	−116.8
Land Adjacency	0.62***	15.44	0.63***	16.34
log(AREA*i*)	0.01	0.00		
log(AREA*j*)	−0.91**	−2.29		
Island	4.90	0.97	−1.15	−0.64
Landlocked	−1.74	−1.30	−0.11	−0.08
ComLang	0.58***	20.20	0.53***	19.69
Ever Colony	1.31***	28.02	1.36***	30.53
Com Colony	0.33***	12.66	0.35***	14.21
Hostility	−0.54***	−12.29	−0.48***	−11.53
Alliance	0.63***	21.17	0.65***	22.56
Remoteness	0.01	0.01	1.39***	2.49
GSP*ij*	−0.15***	−4.99	−0.15***	−5.08
GSP*ji*	−0.25***	−8.66	−0.26***	−9.68
FTA	0.20***	9.78	0.19***	10.15
CU	0.28***	5.58	0.39***	8.17
Time-varying country FE	Yes		Yes	
Adj-R^2	0.69		0.69	
# Obs	133352		147319	

Note: To reduce the number of dummies for the year and importer/ exporter interactions, we take two consecutive years as one period and then use the new period dummy to interact with importers and exporters.

of being a member of the WTO and a participant in the ITA. While the results of the regression analysis send a positive signal to WTO members as they debate the overall value of a sectoral approach, it is important to recognise the specific nature of the ITA and the mechanisms by which it can affect trade. The gravity equation approach is an *ex post* analysis that seeks to explain past trade patterns and values. The actual trade values that may arise from liberalising ITA tariffs will depend on a number of parameters, such as the value of trade, the values of elasticities and other structural variables such as geography. This type of *ex ante* analysis might provide useful information, but differs from the type of analysis undertaken in this paper.

References

Baldwin, R and D Taglioni (2006). Gravity for dummies and dummies for gravity equations. NBER Working Paper No. 12516.

Bora, B (2004). The Information Technology Agreement and World Trade. Draft, WTO, Geneva, Switzerland.

Croome, J (1999). *Reshaping the World Trading System*. The Hague: Kluwer Law.

Liu, X (2009). GATT/WTO promotes trade strongly: sample selection and model specification. *Rev. of Int. Econ.*, 17(3), 428–446.

Rose, AK (2004). Do we really know that the WTO increases trade? *Am. Econ. Rev.*, 94(1), 98–114.

Appendix 1. Countries covered in the paper (Total: 217).

Afghanistan	Djibouti	Laos	St. Lucia
Albania (1999)	Dominica	Latvia (1999)	St. Pierre & Miquelon
Algeria	Dominican Rep.	Lebanon	St. Vincent & Grenadines
Andorra	East Timor	Lesotho	Samoa
Angola	Ecuador	Liberia	Sao Tome & Principe
Anguilla	Egypt (2003)	Libya	Saudi Arabia
Antigua & Barbuda	El Salvador (1997)	Lithuania (1999)	Senegal
Argentina	Equatorial Guinea	Luxembourg (1997)*	Serbia & Montenegro
Armenia	Eritrea	Macao, China (1997)	Seychelles
Aruba	Estonia (1997)	Macedonia	Sierra Leone
Australia (1997)*	Ethiopia	Madagascar	Singapore (1997)
Austria (1997)*	Falkland Islands	Malawi	Slovakia (1997)
Azerbaijan	Faroe Islands	Malaysia (1997)	Slovenia (2000)
Bahamas	Fiji	Maldives	Solomon Islands
Bahrain (2003)	Finland (1997)*	Mali	Somalia
Bangladesh	France (1997)*	Malta (2004)	South Africa
Barbados	French Guiana	Marshall Islands	Spain (1997)*
Belarus	French Polynesia	Martinique	Sri Lanka
Belgium (1997)*	Gabon	Mauritania	Sudan
Bel.-Lux.	Gambia	Mauritius (1999)	Suriname
Belize	Georgia (1999)	Mexico	Swaziland
Benin	Germany, Dem. Rep.	Micronesia	Sweden (1997)*
Bermuda	Germany (1997)*	Moldova (2001)	Switzerland (1997)*
Bhutan	Ghana	Monaco	Syria
Bolivia	Gibraltar	Mongolia	Tajikistan
Bosnia & Herzegovina	Greece (1997)*	Morocco (2003)	Tanzania
Botswana	Greenland	Mozambique	Thailand (1997)
Brazil	Grenada	Namibia	Togo
Brunei	Guadeloupe	Nauru	Tonga
Bulgaria (2001)	Guatemala	Nepal	Trinidad & Tobago

(Continued)

Appendix 1. (*Continued*)

Burkina Faso	Guinea	Netherlands (1997)*	Tunisia
Burma	Guinea-Bissau	Netherlands Antilles	Turkey (1997)
Burundi	Guyana	New Caledonia	Turkmenistan
Cambodia	Haiti	New Zealand (1997)	Tuvalu
Cameroon	Honduras	Nicaragua	USSR
Canada (1997)*	Hong Kong SAR (1997)	Niger	Uganda
Cape Verde	Hungary (2004)	Nigeria	Ukraine
Cayman Islands	Iceland (1997)*	Norway (1997)*	United Arab Emirates
Central African Rep.	India (1997)	Oman (2000)	United Kingdom (1997)*
Chad	Indonesia (1997)	Pakistan	United States (1997)*
Chile	Iran	Palau	Uruguay
China (2003)	Iraq	Panama (1998)	Uzbekistan
Chinese Taipei (1997)	Ireland (1997)*	Papua New Guinea	Vanuatu
Colombia	Israel (1997)	Paraguay	Venezuela
Comoros	Italy (1997)*	Peru	Vietnam
Congo, Dem. Rep. of	Jamaica	Philippines (1997)	Wallis & Futuna
Congo, Rep. of	Japan (1997)*	Poland (1997)	Western Sahara
Costa Rica (1997)	Jordan (1999)	Portugal (1997)*	Yemen, People's Rep. of
Cote D'Ivoire	Kazakhstan	Qatar	Yemen, Rep. of
Croatia (1999)	Kenya	Reunion	Yugoslavia
Cuba	Kiribati	Romania (1997)	Zambia
Cyprus (2000)	Korea, North	Russia	Zimbabwe
Czech Rep. (1997)	Korea, South (1997)	Rwanda	
Czechoslovakia	Kuwait	St. Helena	
Denmark (1997)*	Kyrgyzstan (1999)	St. Kitts & Nevis	

Notes: (1) Countries with years of ITA entry in brackets are ITA members by September 2004. (2) Countries with * are developed countries. (3) In regressions, countries that entered the ITA at the second half of a year are considered as ITA members from the next year.

Appendix 2. ITA product list by HS92.

GROUPING	HS	GROUPING	HS	GROUPING	HS
CO	846910	P	381800	SC	854190
CO	847010	P	850440	SC	854211
CO	847021	P	850450	SC	854219
CO	847029	P	853210	SC	854220
CO	847030	P	853221	SC	854280
CO	847040	P	853222	SC	854290
CO	847050	P	853223	SC	845690
CO	847090	P	853224	SC	854310
CO	847110	P	853225	SC	901020
CO	847120	P	853229	SC	903089
CO	847191	P	853230	SC	903140
CO	847192	P	853290	T	851710
CO	847193	P	853310	T	851720
CO	847199	P	853321	T	851730
CO	847290	P	853329	T	851740
CO	847321	P	853331	T	851781
CO	847329	P	853339	T	851782
CO	847330	P	853340	T	851790
CO	847340	P	853390	T	851810
CO	852530	P	853400	T	851822
CO	853120	P	853650	T	851829
CO	853190	P	854380	T	851830
I	900911	S	852311	T	852020
I	900912	S	852312	T	852510
I	900921	S	852313	T	852520
I	900922	S	852320	T	852790
I	900930	S	852390	T	852910
I	900990	S	852421	T	852990
I	902610	S	852422	T	854441
I	902620	S	852423	T	854449
I	902680	S	852490	T	854451
I	902690	SC	854110	T	854470
I	902720	SC	854121	T	900110
I	902730	SC	854129		
I	902750	SC	854130		

(*Continued*)

Appendix 2. (*Continued*)

GROUPING	HS	GROUPING	HS	GROUPING	HS
I	902780	SC	854140		
I	902790	SC	854150		
I	903040	SC	854160		

Notes: ITA products are grouped into the following six categories: CO — Computers; I — Instruments & Apparatus; P — Accessories; S — Software; SC — Semiconductors & Semiconductor Manufacturing Equipment; T — Telecommunication.

Chapter 3

Economic Analysis and WTO Arbitration Cases

*Bijit Bora and Uwe Kaufmann**

As the number of cases brought to the WTO's dispute settlement mechanism grows, there is an increased focus on the intellectual underpinnings of these decisions. In examining the role of economic analysis in the arbitration cases so far adjudicated, this paper shows that there is evidence of both economic concepts and empirical, or quantitative, economic analysis. While the proportion of each differs across cases, the emphasis has been on quantitative economic analysis. The paper then identifies areas where the economics profession can strengthen the confidence of users of the WTO dispute settlement in economists and thus solidify the complementary role of economic and legal analysis in the WTO's dispute settlement process.

---

*The views in this paper are those of the authors and should not, in any way, be interpreted as those of the World Trade Organization and its member states. Citations to the paper should refer to the authors and never to the WTO.

This paper has benefited greatly from comments from and discussions with Marion Jansen, Alex Keck and Robert Teh. All errors and omissions, however, are ours.

3.1. Introduction

One of the more publicised aspects of the creation of the World Trade Organization (WTO) in 1995 was the establishment of a binding dispute settlement process to enforce its legal decisions. Before 1995, when countries were signatories to the General Agreement on Tariffs and Trade (GATT), decisions by panels adjudicating trade disputes were purely academic; when a country was found in breach of an obligation, the lack of an enforcement mechanism did little to persuade it to bring its policy into conformity with GATT articles.

The key element of the enforcement process in the WTO dispute settlement mechanism is the authorisation of "retaliation" by a complaining Member when an offending Member's policies do not conform with the WTO Agreements. The mandate for the authorisation can be found in two places: Article 22 of the Understanding in Dispute Settlement and Article 4 of the Agreement on Subsidies and Countervail Measures. These provisions have been used 10 times and, given the increasing number of disputes, arbitration procedures will continue to play an important role in facilitating trade, contributing to the stability of the multilateral trading system and to enforcing the overall agreement (Brown and Ruta, 2008).

A number of the articles published on the WTO's arbitration process focus on the role and need of arbitration to ensure a viable dispute settlement process (Lawrence, 2002). In this context, the unique nature of the WTO's procedure is analysed and compared to other arbitration procedures. After analysing the economics of the WTO's arbitration process, other researchers have concluded that, although not perfect, it strengthens the multilateral trading system (Bagwell and Staiger, 2002).

Despite this growing literature, one aspect of the arbitration process not examined is the role of economics *in* the arbitration process, a question separate and distinct from the economics *of* the arbitration process. Research on the first question has been limited, although a few articles have stressed the difference between welfare analysis and trade analysis in the context of the second (Anderson, 2003; Bernstein and Skully, 2003). Simply put, there is a difference between an economic analysis of the legal text of a provision and the role of economics in interpreting that text. These two avenues of research also differ from the economic analysis of the outcome of a legal decision (Breuss, 2004). In a recent working paper, Brown and Ruta (2008) use the Bagwell and Staiger interpretation of the WTO principles of retaliation and establish a theoretical approach in examining the construction of countermeasures for each of the two major categories — WTO-inconsistent import restricting policies and WTO-inconsistent export promotion policies.

The only robust methodology, given the task at hand, is to review the existing decisions and isolate the ways in which economics has been used. This type of *ex post* analysis is necessarily limited, since the only available data are the final decisions. Not surprisingly, access to submissions and the rationale behind why possible paths of analysis are discarded by the arbitrators is, understandably, prohibited. But, as will be illustrated, interesting lessons about economics and trade law can be learned from past cases that could be useful for future cases. It should be noted that this approach does not, in any way, rejudge the cases since a what-if analysis is not employed in this paper.

The next section reviews the mandates for arbitration provided in the WTO agreements. It also notes that, while these are clear in the context of the legal process after an Appellate Body ruling, there are other instances where final judgments can be made on trade issues. These include binding arbitration under Article 25 of the DSU and non-binding good offices, conciliation and mediation under Article 5. Section 3 reviews the economic concepts behind interpreting the man date, while Section 4 examines the ways in which arbitrators have implemented the quantification aspects of their mandate. The paper closes with some observations as to how economics can be used to contribute to the WTO quasi-judicial process.

3.2. The Mandate

A starting point for isolating and examining the role of economics in a legal process is an understanding of that legal process. Accordingly, this section reviews the various mandates given to the arbitral process in the WTO. The first is found in Article 22 of the Dispute Settlement Understanding as it pertains to violations of the GATT and GATS and of other WTO Agreements, including the SCM Agreement in general. The second mandate relates specifically to cases of prohibited export subsidies. Both will be discussed below in separate sub-sections.

In addition to these two processes, the DSU foresees the possibilities of two other dispute settlement processes aside from that arising in the post-panel and Appellate Body phase. The first regards situations where the issues under dispute are "clearly defined by both parties," and bypass the panel/appellate body process. This provision is contained in Article 25 of the DSU.

The second process involves good offices, conciliation and mediation, provided in Article 5 of the DSU. No Member has taken advantage of this situation, so there is little that can be said. In September 2002, however, the European Communities, the Philippines and Thailand requested the Director-General of the WTO to act as a mediator in a trade dispute, which was *outside* the covered agreements. The third sub-section reviews this case and the only Article 25 case.

3.2.1. *Arbitration arising from violation of GATT and GATS Articles and sector(s) and agreement(s) (TRIPs Agreement)*

The arbitral process in the context of the GATT and GATS is specified in Article 22 entitled "Compensation and the Suspension of Concessions." It defines compensation and arbitration as "temporary measures available in the event that the recommendations and rulings are not implemented within a reasonable period of time." A complaining Member's first recourse to a settlement in the absence of compliance is compensation. Under Article 22.2, it has the right to negotiate an amount of compensation. However, if such an amount cannot be agreed on, it can then request authorisation from the DSB to suspend the application of concessions or other obligations to the Member concerned under the covered agreements.

If the request for suspension is not agreed to by the Member concerned, the matter is then referred to arbitration. The precise mandate for the arbitrator as stated in Article 22.6 is:

> However, if the Member concerned objects to the level of suspension proposed, or claims that the principles and procedures set forth in paragraph 3 have not been followed where a complaining party has requested authorization to suspend concessions or other obligations pursuant to paragraph 3(b) or (c), the matter shall be referred to arbitration.

The jurisdiction of the arbitrator is spelled out in Article 22.7, which states that:

> The arbitrator acting pursuant to paragraph 6 shall not examine the nature of the concessions or other obligations to be suspended but shall determine whether the level of such suspension is equivalent to the level of nullification or impairment.

It makes clear that the decision of the arbitration is binding: "The parties shall accept the arbitrator's decision as final and the parties concerned shall not seek a second arbitration."

The task of the arbitrator, therefore, is to operationalise the concept of equivalence between the requested level of suspension and the level of nullification and impairment. In doing so, two outcomes are possible: it can either agree with the requested amount, or disagree and establish another level. In either outcome, the basis for the decision needs to be explained, since the unknown is always the level of nullification and impairment. This task is precise, especially if the requested amount is in terms of a specific value.[1] If, as in the United States' Anti-Dumping Act of 1916, the request is of a qualitative nature, the task

---

[1] The arbitrators in the so-called Bananas case ("Regime for the Importation, Sale and Distribution of Bananas") highlight this difficulty when they state: "It is impossible to ensure correspondence or identity between two levels if one of the two is not clearly defined. Therefore, as a prerequisite for ensuring equivalence between the two levels at issue we have to determine the level of nullification or impairment." (paragraph 4.3).

becomes more complex. This issue will be taken up in more detail in the next section.

The mandate in relation to the sector(s) and agreement(s) in which suspension is sought is found in Article 22.3 (b) & (c),

> which sets out certain principles and procedures to be followed by a complaining party seeking to suspend concessions or other obligations, as to the sector(s) and/or covered agreement in which the suspension can be sought. Subsequent subparagraphs of Article 22.3 further elaborate on the factors that must be taken into account in applying these principles and procedures as well as the definition of "sectors" for the purposes of this provision and the procedural requirements to be followed in requesting authorization to suspend concessions or other obligations in another sector or under another covered agreement.

The *EC–Bananas III* case and the US–Remote Gambling case are the only disputes so far whose claims relate to the observance of the principles and procedures of Article 22.3 of the DSU. In the *EC–Bananas III* dispute, the arbitrators state that:

> the fact that the powers of Arbitrators under subparagraphs (b)–(c) are explicitly provided for in Article 22.6 implies *a fortiori* that the authority of Arbitrators includes the power to review whether the principles and procedures set forth in these subparagraphs have been followed by the Member seeking authorization for suspension.[2]

In the US–Remote Gambling dispute, the arbitrators'

> mandate with respect to suspend concessions or other obligations under the TRIPS Agreement is therefore to review whether the principles and procedures set forth in the various subparagraphs of Article 22.3 of the DSU have been followed by Antigua, as the Member seeking authorization for suspension in this dispute.[3]

---

[2]Decision of the Arbitrator *EC–Bananas III* (Ecuador) (Article 22.6–EC), para. 50.
[3]WT/DS285/ARB, para. 2.13.

3.2.2. *Arbitration arising from violating the agreement on subsidies and countervailing measures*

A different task faces arbitrators in prohibited subsidy cases. Their mandate is described in Article 4.10 of the Agreement on Subsidies and Countervailing Measures (SCM), which states that "the arbitrator shall determine whether the countermeasures are appropriate." Further guidance about how to define "appropriate" is provided in footnote 9 of the agreement, stating that "this expression is not meant to allow countermeasures that are disproportionate in light of the fact that the subsidies dealt with under these provisions are prohibited."

The starting point in SCM cases is the term, countermeasures, which is not defined in the agreement. The arbitrators in the FSC approach the problem of defining the word as follows:

> In the context of Article 4 of the *SCM Agreement*, the term "countermeasures" is used to define temporary measures which a prevailing Member may be authorized to take in response to a persisting violation of Article 3 of the *SCM Agreement*, pending full compliance with the DSB's recommendations. This use of the term is in line with its ordinary dictionary meaning as described above: these measures are authorized to counteract, in this context, a wrongful action in the form of an export subsidy that is prohibited *per se*, or the effects thereof.

Their approach assigns two tasks to the measures proposed by a complaining member — either to counteract a wrongful action or to counteract the effects of the wrongful action. Together, their objective is to ensure that the "Member withdraws the subsidy without delay" as dictated by Article 4.7 of the SCM Agreement.

The words "appropriate" and "disproportionate" in prohibited subsidy cases stands in stark contrast to "equivalence" in DSU cases. Equivalence imposes a degree of discipline by laying down a certain benchmark and methodology. This is not the case in prohibited subsidy disputes. This difficulty can be found in each of the three cases that have been adjudicated under Article 4.11 of the SCM Agreement, where the arbitrators seek to determine the parameters of the terms "appropriate" and "disproportionate" in the context of the agreement and also as an adjective to countermeasures.

In these cases, references are always made to the absolute standard imposed of "nullification and impairment" as stated in Article 22.4 of the DSU and its inapplicability to cases under Article 4.10 of the SCM Agreement. Reference is also made to the fact that where trade concepts are explicitly contemplated, they are defined in other parts of the agreement.[4] In particular, Article 7, paragraphs 9 and 10 of the SCM Agreement, which is the provision equivalent for actionable subsidies to Article 4, paragraphs 10 and 11 for prohibited subsidies, uses the phrase "commensurate with the degree and nature of the adverse effects determined to exist."

The lack of precision arising from the adjective "appropriate" has implications for the consistency of the standard to be used by arbitrators across subsidy cases. This point is recognised by the arbitrators in the FSC case, who state that "countermeasures should be adapted to the particular case at hand." They go further by stating that "there is an element of flexibility, in the sense that there is thereby an eschewal of any rigid *a priori* quantitative formula." Despite this flexibility, the arbitrators also recognise "an objective relationship which must be absolutely respected."

The relevant provisions are not designed to lay down a precise formula or otherwise quantified benchmark or amount of countermeasures that might be legitimately authorised in each and every instance. Rather, the notion of "appropriateness" is used to provide a degree of flexibility, at the same time recognising that there is a relationship that needs to be respected.

3.2.3. *Agreed arbitration and mediation processes*

The WTO Dispute Settlement mechanism envisages the resolution of disputes that are not based on a finding of inconsistency of a measure with a WTO agreement. The procedures for these types of disputes

[4] Brazil–Aircraft (WT/DS46/ARB), para. 3.49.

are specified in Article 5 and 25 of the DSU. These processes differ in one important respect from arbitrations that are resolved under Article 22.6 of the DSU and Article 4.9 of the SCM in that the standard for the resolution is up to the parties.

The only case brought to the Dispute Settlement Body (DSB) under Article 25 was by the European Communities and the United States. In this case, a WTO panel found that the US had a measure that was inconsistent with the Agreement on Trade-Related Aspects of Intellectual Property Rights (TRIPs). By mutual agreement the parties invoked Article 25 and established an arbitration panel to establish the level of concession to be suspended by the EC.

Despite the flexibility provided to Members under Article 25 to establish their guiding principles, the two parties agreed to follow Article 22 of the DSU. This guidance included using the concept of "nullification or impairment" as the standard for the arbitrators, which was operationalised by estimating the value of royalties realised by copyright holders.

In contrast to the US–Copyright case, on 4 September 2002 the European Communities, the Philippines and Thailand jointly requested WTO mediation after talks failed to resolve the disagreement over greater market access to European markets for canned tuna products from the two countries. The purpose of the mediation was to:

> Examine the extent to which the legitimate interests of the Philippines and Thailand are being unduly impaired as a result of the implementation by the European Communities of the preferential tariff treatment for canned tuna originating in ACP states.[5]

The request for mediation granted an additional mandate to the mediator to propose a solution:

> In the event that the mediator concludes that undue impairment has in fact, occurred, the mediator could consider means by which this situation may be addressed.[6]

[5]WT/GC/66, 16 October 2002.
[6]WT/GC/66, 16 October 2002.

The source of the dispute is the granting of a waiver to the EC for its system of non-reciprocal preferences, which it grants to a group of countries from Africa, the Caribbean and the Pacific (ACP). The preferential access provides ACP exporters with an approximate margin of preference of up to 22 percent. Interestingly, the dispute was not a "dispute" within the context of the DSU, since no WTO agreement was breached. Hence, it was not considered to be within any of the mandates of the various WTO agreements. This is clear from the use of the wording "unduly impaired" as the description of damages. In comparison, the wording for damages in the context of the GATT is nullification or impairment. Furthermore, the concept of "interests" could be interpreted as damage beyond basic trade damages. This issue will be taken up later in this paper in the context of trade effect and broader economic effects. Unfortunately, the procedure for the mediation was such that no report of the process was published, thus it is impossible to describe the methodological process used.

3.3. An Economic Interpretation of the Mandate

The starting point for the analysis of nullification or impairment is to operationalise the concept of benefits. As noted above, the arbitrators in the various dispute cases to date have been provided with broad mandates, requiring them to deliver their own interpretation as to its meaning. Despite this breadth, a common approach to interpreting "nullification or impairment" has been the level of trade that would arise if the offending measure is brought into conformity with the WTO rules. This approach, more commonly called the trade effects approach, equates nullification or impairment with the value of trade foregone and/or the revenue that would have arisen. This in itself is the use of economics, since it requires an analysis of the market for the goods and services, including the various factors that determine demand, supply, imports and exports.

For goods and services, and thus the arbitration cases on violation of GATT and GATS Articles, this basic concept is illustrated in Figure 3.1, which depicts a market for imports. For simplicity, the benchmark of a WTO-consistent measure is assumed to be the world price, which is

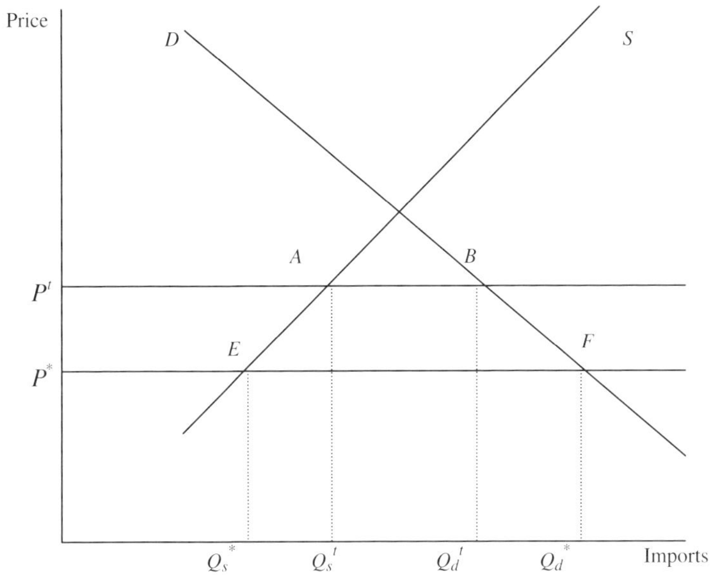

Fig. 3.1. Counterfactual trade effect analysis.

marked as P^* in the figure. The effect of a WTO-inconsistent measure, *which by definition* prejudices imports, can be modelled as an *ad valorem* increase in the import price. In Figure 3.1, this is assumed to be price P^t, making the difference between it and the world price the implicit tariff arising from the WTO-inconsistent measure.

Since the problem facing arbitrators is the counterfactual situation of compliance, the value of imports under P^* has to be compared with the value of imports under P^t. The trade effects of this decrease in the price of imports is the combined effect of reduction in domestic quantity supplied and an increase in quantity demanded. In Figure 3.1, this is depicted as the difference between *EF* and *AB*.

The calculated increase in imports depicted in Figure 3.1 is for the specific curves in that diagram. The curves depict the responsiveness of quantity demanded (curve *D*) and quantity supplied (curve *S*) to changes in price. If the *D* curve is flatter, which reflects a greater responsiveness of quantity demanded to price, a given reduction in prices arising from WTO compliance will result in a greater increase in imports. Similarly, a more responsive supply curve will also lead to the same result.

In summary, the three main factors determining the size of the trade effect, hence the level of nullification and impairment in a specific market, are the effects of the measure on the price of imports and the responsiveness of quantity demanded and quantity supplied.

Although all the GATT cases reviewed in the previous section adopted the concept of trade effects, defined as the trading opportunities arising from the implementation of a DSU ruling, the possibility that nullification or impairment could be something broader than trade has arisen a number of times.

This point was originally raised in *EC–Bananas*, when the US argued that the loss of exports of goods or services between the US and third countries arising from the WTO-inconsistent measure should also be taken into account. They further argued that the US content of lost exports, such as US fertilisers, pesticides and machinery shipped to Latin America and US capital or management services used in banana cultivation, from other complaining countries to the EC should be taken into account.

The issue of nullification or impairment being interpreted as something beyond the trade effects was also affirmatively argued in US 1916, where the ECs argued that "level" could imply either a qualitative or a quantitative equivalence. It is not clear from their argument whether or not this should be a general case, or whether it is specific to cases where quantification is impossible. In deciding on this issue, the arbitrators took the view that quantification of the trade effects was necessary to ensure that the level of suspensions does not *exceed* the level of nullification and impairment. In doing so, they made explicit the distinction between trade effects and economic effects by suggesting that to a large extent a cushion for an error in estimation could be interpreted as being "punitive" in nature.

The concept of direct versus indirect effect also arose in the context of something economists call the "chilling effect" of an anti-dumping measure. The argument here is that the mere existence of an anti-dumping measure, in this case the US 1916 Act, will deter or "chill" imports. In countering this claim, the US argued that the introduction of the chilling effect into the interpretation of nullification or impairment would reduce the level of precision in quantifying damages. In the end, the arbitrators took the view that, since the "chilling effect" could not be measured, the EC could not include it in their calculation of nullification or impairment.

Another area in the US 1916 dispute, where a broader concept than trade effect was discussed, was in the area of litigation costs associated with contesting an offending measure. The EC argued that such costs should be concluded, but the arbitrators in adhering to the concept of trade effects stated that they "are not aware of any basis in the WTO Agreements to support the view advanced by the European Communities that legal fees can be claimed as a loss of a benefit accruing to a WTO Member."[7]

The idea that economic costs could be broader than the value of trade foregone is illustrated in Figure 3.2. The diagram in this case

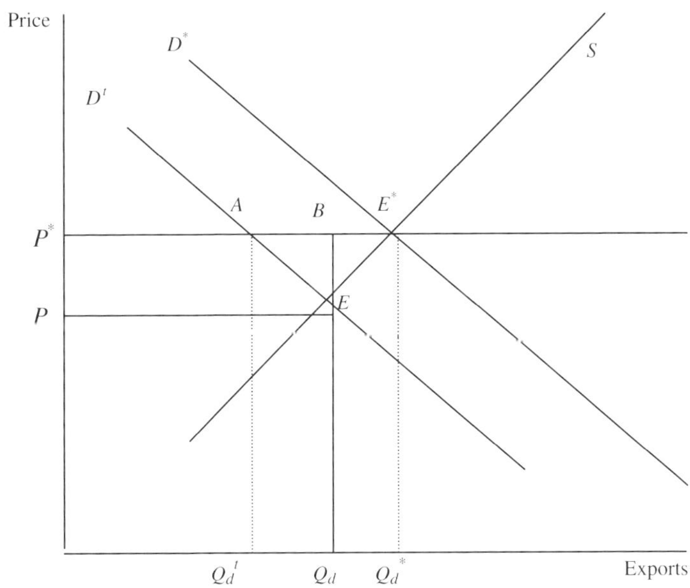

Fig. 3.2. Economic loss.

[7] Decision by the Arbitrators in US — 1916 Act (Article 22.6 — US), para. 5.73.

is drawn with the quantity of exports on the x-axis, in contrast to Figure 3.1, which uses imports. An implicit tariff, which raises the cost of exports into a market, will shift the export demand curve to the left. In Figure 3.1, this is illustrated by the demand curve D^*, which is drawn for a free trade price of P^*, and the demand curve D^t, which is drawn for the case where a member has an inconsistent measure in place. The effect of this measure, assuming a perfectly elastic supply curve, is to contract exports from Q_d^* to Q_d^t, which is the same value as $EF-AB$ in Figure 3.1.[8] The lost value of exports can also be calculated from the figure using the P^* curve, if perfect competition in the market for exportables is assumed. In this case, the lost value is given as the rectangle $Q_d^* Q_d^t AE^*$.

The area $P^* PEE^*$ also has an important economic interpretation, which is the loss in producer surplus to exporters in the case where the WTO-inconsistent measures affect the world price. In this case, the contraction of imports results in a decline in world price from P^* to P at a new equilibrium E. Since the price has fallen, the decline in imports arising from the measure is necessarily smaller than the decline when there is no price change.

An arbitral award that calculates the total amount of the lost trade value would have to sum the value of lost exports at the old price (P^*), which is equal to $Q_d^* Q_d^t AE^*$, and the lost revenue from selling exports at a lower price (P), which is equal to $PP^* BE$. In total, the area is $P^* E^* Q_d^* Q_d EP$.

It should also be noted that the area BEE^* of the lost export value is the producer surplus associated with those exports. The remaining area of the rectangle reflects the cost of producing the expanded output if the offending measure was brought into conformity.

Taken together, it would appear that the granting of the lost value of exports, with or without the price change, has an implicit economic interpretation — the opportunity cost of producing the additional exports and any associated lost producer surplus.

Disputes that have been arbitrated under the SCM Agreement have used a different standard. All three cases have used the value of the

---

[8] When the supply curve is infinitely elastic, it becomes horizontal at the prevailing price.

subsidy as meeting the mandate, but have left open the door to other standards, especially trade effects as they are used in GATT and GATS dispute cases. This point is made clear by the arbitrators in Canada Aircraft, who state that a member can propose any standard they wish as long as they are "appropriate and not disproportionate."[9]

The line of argument that trade effects should play a supporting role was first put forward by the arbitrators in US–FSC. They argued that the use of the subsidy does not preclude the possibility that trade effects can be taken into consideration. Their specific approach was whether or not a trade effects analysis would question the viability of using the value of the subsidy as a benchmark. After examining the various submissions on how to model the trade effects, they concluded that the requested amount of $4034 million was within the range of possible trade effects, which they estimated to be between $3253 and $4294 million.

In assessing Brazil's application to suspend concessions to a total of $3.36 billion, which was based on the lost orders of aircraft, the arbitrators did not disregard the concept of trade effects. However, they pointed out that the level of proposed suspensions was three to six times greater than Canada's exports to Brazil and thus decided that the requested level of suspensions was not appropriate. So, despite using the level of the subsidy to calculate the value of the arbitral reward, the arbitrators did use the trade effects test to ensure that their mandate was being properly executed.

The extent to which the value of the subsidy in itself meets the mandate of the arbitrators appears to be more to do with ease than with any specific economic analysis. Both parties to the first case, Brazil Aircraft, argued for the value of the subsidy, which made it easier for the arbitrators to use it as a benchmark. The arbitrators in the FSC case considered the value of the subsidy to be not disproportionate because of its direct relationship to the offending measure. They are careful to distinguish between proportionality of the countermeasures and the measure itself by noting that the "impact" of the measure is something completely different.

---

[9]Canada Aircraft (WT/DS222/ARB), para. 3.36.

3.4. An Economic Taxonomy of WTO Arbitration Cases

The concept of trade effects appears to have become the standard by which to judge GATT and, recently, GATS violation cases. As highlighted in the previous section, it also appears to play a supporting role in cases involving a transfer of funds by the exporting government to either exporting firms or import-competing firms. This sub-section reviews the economic concepts associated with using trade effects as a standard in these cases. The analysis is divided into two sub-sections. The first analyses policies that are either border policies and/or domestic policies acting as such and that are restricting trade in goods and services in nature. The second analyses cases involving a government transfer of funds to domestic firms. Table 3.1 lists the various arbitration cases by the type of economic analysis: trade restrictiveness or government transfer cases.

3.4.1. *Trade restrictiveness cases*

When all the relevant data are available, estimating trade effects in the context of trade restrictiveness cases is straightforward. The standard case is when exports of a member are discriminated in a market by policies that raise their cost to consumers. Another form of discrimination, as in the *EC–Bananas III* case, is when exports from one country are discriminated against by exports of another country. Of course, an extreme case of discrimination is when there is a complete ban on imports, as in the EC–Hormones case or similarly in the US–Remote Gambling case.

Figure 3.1 is theory. WTO arbitration case is practice. Converting the economic intuition in that figure into practice is not an easy task. To estimate the counterfactual trade value, product-specific elasticities, which are rarely available, are required.

(i) *European Communities — Measures Concerning Meat and Meat Products (Hormones)*

The panel and Appellate Body in this case concluded that an EC ban on imports of high-quality beef and edible beef offal was inconsistent

Table 3.1. Arbitration and mediation cases in the WTO, 1995–2004*.

Full case title and citation	Measure	Requested level	Counter level	Award
Trade restrictiveness cases				
European Communities — Regime for the Importation, Sale and Distribution of Bananas — Recourse to Arbitration by the European Communities under Article 22.6 of the DSU, WT/DS27/ARB, 9 April 1999, DSR 1999:II, 725	Article XIII of GATT 94	US$520 million		US$191.4 million
European Communities — Measures Concerning Meat and Meat Products (Hormones) — Original Complaint by Canada — Recourse to Arbitration by the European Communities under Article 22.6 of the DSU, WT/DS48/ARB, 12 July 1999, DSR1999:III,1135	SPS Agreement	C$75 million	C$3.537 million	C$11.3 million
European Communities — Measures Concerning Meat and Meat Products (Hormones) — Original Complaint by the United States — Recourse to Arbitration by the European Communities under Article 22.6 of the DSU, WT/DS26/ARB, 12 July 1999, DSR 1999:III, 1105	SPS Agreement	US$202 million	$53.301 million	US$116.8 million

(*Continued*)

Table 3.1. *(Continued)*

Full case title and citation	Measure	Requested level	Counter level	Award
European Communities — Regime for the Importation, Sale and Distribution of Bananas — Recourse to Arbitration by the European Communities under Article 22.6 of the DSU, WT/DS27/ARB/ECU, 24 March 2000, DSR 2000:V, 2243	Article XIII of GATT 94			US$201.6 million
United States — Measures Affecting the Cross-Border Supply of Gambling and Betting Services — Recourse to Arbitration by the United States under Article 22.6 of the DSU, WT/DS285/ARB, 21 December 2007.	Article XVI:1; XVI:2 (a) & (c)	US$3.443 billion	US$3.3 million	US$21 million
Governmental transfer cases				
United States — Continued Dumping Subsidy Offset Act, 2000 — Recourse to Arbitration by the United States under Article 22.6 of the DSU, WT/DS217/ARB/EEC	Art. VI.1, VI.2 GATT 1994; Art. 1, 4, 5.5 Anti-Dumping Agreement	Full value of payments	US$0.0	0.72 X value of payments
United States — Tax Treatment for "Foreign Sales Corporations" — Recourse to Arbitration by the United States under Article 22.6 of the DSU and Article 411 of the SCM Agreement, WT/DS108/ARB, 30 August 2002	Prohibited Export Subsidies; SCM	US$4.043 million	US$1.110 million	US$4.024 million

(Continued)

Table 3.1. *(Continued)*

Full case title and citation	Measure	Requested level	Counter level	Award
Brazil — Export Financing Programme for Aircraft — Recourse to Arbitration by Brazil under Article 22.6 of the DSU and Article 411 of the SCM Agreement, WT/DS46/ARB, 28 August 2000	Prohibited Export Subsidies; SCM	US$705.6 million		US$344.2 million
Canada — Export Credits and Loan Guarantees for Regional Aircraft — Recourse to Arbitration by Canada under Article 22.6 of the DSU and Article 411 of the SCM Agreement, WT/DS222/ARB, 17 February 2003	Prohibited Export Subsidies; SCM	C$3.36 billion		C$247.796 million

*This table does not include the United States Anti-Dumping Act of 1916 (Original Complaint By the European Communities) Recourse to Arbitration by the United States under Article 22.6 of the DSU, WT/DS136/ARB, 24 February 2004, where violation of Art. VI.1, VI.2, XVI.4 GATT 1994; Art. 1, 4, 5.5 Anti-Dumping Agreement were found and an amount equivalent to final judgments and settlement awards under the 1916 Act.

with the Sanitary and Phytosanitary Agreement. After the reasonable period of time had expired and the parties could not agree on a level of compensation, authorisation for Canada to suspend concessions to the European Community of up to C$75 million and a similar award of US$116.8 million to the United States was granted.

The arbitrators in this case adopted the same approach taken in the bananas case — to equate the level of suspensions to the estimated value of nullification or impairment. In this case, the counterfactual is the value of imports into the EC from Canada and the United States if the ban on imports is lifted.

In some ways, the methodology to calculate nullification or impairment is straightforward, since in the absence of the import ban exporters from both Canada and the United States would have to face a binding quota of 11,500 tons on high-quality beef. Furthermore, this quota is not unique, since it was shared between Canada and the United States. Therefore, the counterfactual in this case would be Canada's share of the 11,500-ton quota times the price of the product.

In following through on this methodology, the arbitrators estimated that Canada's share of the quota would be 8 percent at a price of C$8594 per ton, leaving the US with the remaining 92 percent at a price of US$5342 per ton. The arbitrators also noted that the quota includes hormone-treated and hormone-free products. Since there was no WTO-inconsistent measure against imports of hormone-free high-quality beef, the arbitrators deducted these exports from the Canadian and American totals. The final amount, therefore, is the product of the price, the share of the quota and the quota value, less exports of hormone-free beef, which the arbitrators estimated to be C$7,906,480. The methodology adopted by the arbitrators for both high-quality beef and edible offal is illustrated in Table 3.2 using the US case as an example.

(ii) *European Communities — Regime for the Importation, Sale and Distribution of Bananas*

A number of legal issues made this case quite complex. The core issues were the way the European Communities established a duty-free quota for imports of bananas originating from Africa, the Caribbean

Table 3.2. Counterfactual estimates for the Beef Hormones case.

			WTO (DSB)	US	EU	Average of US & EC estimate
			High Quality Beef (HQB)			
(1)	Volume of lost trade	mt	11,500	11,500		
(2)	Adjustment factor		92%	100%		
(3)	Price	$/mt	$5,342	$5,342		
(4) = (1) × (2) × (3)	Value of lost trade		$56,518,360	$61,433,000	$33,488,129	
(5)	Gross value of current imports		$31,804,779		$31,804,779	
(6)	Adjustment factor		75%		100%	
(7) = (5) × (6)	Adjusted value of current imports		$23,853,584	—	$31,804,779	
(8) = (4) − (7)	Net value of lost trade		$32,664,776	$61,433,000	$1,683,350	$32,399,850
	Difference between WTO and EU–US					−0.81%
	Average					
			Edible Beef Offal (EBO)			
(1)	Volume of lost trade	mt	65,568	70,989	45,253	
(2)	Adjustment factor		81.6%	100%	75%	
(3)	Price	$/mt	$1,689	$1,689	$1,684	
(4) = (1) × (2) × (3)	Value of lost trade		$90,367,391	$119,900,000	$56,795,838	

(Continued)

Table 3.2. (*Continued*)

		WTO (DSB)	US	EU	Average of US & EC estimate
(5)	from promotion	—	$20,100,000	—	
(6)	Value of current imports	$2,460,759	—	$2,460,759	
(7)	Adjustment factor	75%		100%	
(8) = (6) × (7)	Adjusted value of current imports	$1,845,569	—	$2,460,759	
(9) = (4) + (5) − (8)	Gross value of lost trade	$88,521,822	$140,000,000	$54,335,079	
(10)	Adjustment Factor (pet food)	95%		95%	
(11) = (9) × (10)	Net value of lost trade	$84,095,731	$140,000,000	$51,618,325	$85,809,163
	Difference between WTO and EU–US Average				2.04%
	Total (EBO + HQB)	$116,760,507	$201,433,000	$53,301,675	$117,367,338
	Difference between WTO and EU–US Average				0.52%

and Pacific States, and the manner in which the most-favoured-nation (MFN) quotas under Article XIII were allocated. The arbitrators were of the view that, in the first instance, they had to determine whether or not the banana regime of the EC was consistent with the WTO Agreements. Their argument was that, in doing so, a breach of the WTO agreement would automatically imply nullification and impairment. Once this had been established, which it was, the arbitrators proceeded to quantify the nullification and impairment to establish the level of concessions to be suspended.

In proceeding with the estimate of nullification and impairment, the arbitrators stated that they were "of the view that the benchmark for the calculation of nullification or impairment of US trade flows should be losses in US exports of goods to the EC and losses of US service suppliers in services exports in or to the EC."[10] This statement makes clear that the benchmark is the trade effect of the offending measure.

Although the benchmark is clear, the arbitrators were faced with an important issue: the range of WTO-consistent measures that could be implemented to meet the same objective as the offending measure. Four such measures were identified in this case. Each of these is listed in Table 3.3 along with a corresponding estimate of the counterfactual trade effect as provided by the United States.

The arbitrators' decisions did not contain any information on how to decide which counterfactual would best serve their mandate. The range of values estimated by the United States is significant, with a difference of \$292.9 million dollars. Furthermore, the final decision of the arbitrators was based on a different scenario than the ones that were requested. The arbitrators simply state that:

> We have evaluated the various counterfactuals and we have decided to choose, as a reasonable counterfactual, a global tariff quota equal to 2.553 million tonnes (subject to a 75 Euro per tonne tariff) and unlimited access for ACP bananas at a zero tariff (with the ACP tariff preference being covered as now by a waiver).

---

[10] Para. 6.12.

The arbitrators estimate the counterfactual trade effect of this regime compared to the existing regime to be $191.4 million a year, which was the value of their final award.

Another issue in estimating the trade effect of a WTO-consistent measure is the definition of that measure. No WTO case has been as simple as that depicted in Table 3.3. In that case, a WTO-inconsistent measure is assumed to be a higher price, or tariff on import. In the Bananas arbitration, the EC makes the point that, at least in that case, a number of options are available to an offending Member to bring its policies into WTO conformity (Table 3.3).

(iii) *United States–Remote Gambling*

The Appellate Body's conclusion, which upheld the findings of the original panel report, that the United States has committed itself in their schedule to granting full market access in gambling and betting services. Furthermore, the Body decided that the United States acts inconsistently with GATS Article XVI:1 and XVI:2 (a) and (c) by maintaining certain inconsistent limitations on market access.

Table 3.3. Estimated impact on EC imports from the US under different counterfactuals.

Counterfactual regime	Estimated value
A tariff-only regime, without tariff quotas but including an ACP tariff preference (with effects calculated for a range of tariff rates from 75 Euro per tonne to the out-of-quota bound rate)	$326.9 million
A tariff-quota system with licence allocations based on the first-come, first-served method	$619.8 million
The complete allocation of a tariff-quota system (with traditional ACP quotas reduced to actual past trade performance) with country-specific allocations to all substantial and non-substantial ACP and non-ACP suppliers	$558.6 million
The base US counterfactual, which, as noted above, assumed a continuation of an 857 700 tonne quantity for ACP imports and an expansion of the MFN tariff quota to 3.7 million tonnes	$362.4 million

The Appellate Body modified the panel report with regard to GATS Article XIV and found that the United States provided evidence and demonstrated that the "Wire Act, the Travel Act, and the Illegal Gambling Business Act are measures necessary to protect public morals and maintain public order, in accordance with GATS Article XIV (a),"[11] but that the "Interstate Horsing Act" does not apply equally for "foreign and domestic service suppliers of remote betting services for horseracing and, therefore, [the United States] has not established that these measures satisfy the requirements of the chapeau."[12]

After the reasonable period of time to implement the recommendations and rulings of the DSU (11 months and 2 weeks), the Antigua-requested compliance panel found that the United States had failed to comply with the recommendations and did not "bring its measures into conformity with its obligations under GATS."[13] Hence, following Article 22.2 DSU, Antigua requested authorisation to suspend the application to the United States of concession and elated obligations under GATS and the TRIPS Agreement.

In this case, because of its unprecedented origin as the first under violation of GATS articles, the arbitrators were forced to use a new approach based on the "trade effect." Additionally, they were faced with data mostly consisting of proxies.

Faced with the "radical[ly] different approaches" of Antigua and the United States, the arbitrators had to use their own approach to estimate the level of nullification and impediment based on the revenue loss resulting from the WTO-inconsistent measure of the United States restricting Antigua's access of remote gambling services on horseracing.

The arbitrators took into account four steps: establishing a workable assumption about Antigua's revenues from remote gambling services exports to the United States; adjusting the revenues for the apparent impact of competing suppliers; determining a plausible share of

[11]WT/DS285/ARB, page 9 (1.2).
[12]WT DS285/AB/R, para. 373.
[13]WT/DS285/13.

betting services on horseracing in Antigua's total revenues from remote gambling; and appreciating the developments in the United States of market demand for gambling services on horseracing.

Because no real data on Antigua's revenues on remote gambling were available, the arbitrators used two different data sets as the underlying database to estimate Antigua's revenue loss on remote gambling exports to the United States, accepting Antigua's claim that the United States contributed 80 percent of its total number of recipients of remote gambling services. The first was the Quarterly eGaming Statistics Report of the private gambling consultant group Global Betting and Gaming Consultants. Between the turning-point year of 2001 and 2006, the arbitrators estimated the average loss in annual revenues from the United States marked for Antigua to be approximately US$304 million; see Table 3.4.[14]

The second data set, based on information on revenue per employee from publicly listed companies and data on employment in the remote

Table 3.4. Antigua's remote gambling revenues in million US dollars.

	Global revenues	Difference to year 2001	80% revenues	Difference to year 2001
2001	1630		1304	
2002	1693	−63	1354	−50
2003	1185	445	948	356
2004	1145	485	916	388
2005	1138	492	910	394
2006	1086	544	869	435
Average		381		**304**

Source: GBGC, October 2007.

[14]The arbitrators recognized that part of this loss was from the WTO-inconsistent measure of the United States and part to increasing competition in the market of remote gambling to Antigua. Furthermore, the arbitrators found Antigua's pre-2002 growth to be extreme. Thus, it is assessed that an expected growth would only be with decelerated rates. Hence, s-curve growth would be more appropriate than constant growth assumptions by Antigua.

Table 3.5. Revenues per employee, selected companies in US dollars.

	Party-gaming	Youbet	Betfair	888	Sportingbet	Unibet	Betcorp	Average
2001		82,895						
2002	266,372	342,105						
2003	356,876	807,463			410,810	360,490	229,886	
2004	825,240	804,938	425,299	258,206	470,563	524,934	155,686	
2005	719,426	837,736	460,808	305,869	560,964	650,895	118,069	
2006	918,453	305,817	295,830	393,885	749,645	737,052	167,777	
Average w/o extr.	617,273	530,159	369,800	319,320	547,996	568,343	167,855	**445,821**
Average	633,847	565,081	361,282	305,869	515,764	587,915	161,732	**447,356**

Note: To adjust for the average without extreme values, the arbitrator removed from the calculations the two years with the highest and lowest revenues. US dollars have been used as the base currency, using the average exchange rate of the respective year according to the IMF International Financial Statistics, November 2007.
Source: Antigua response to question 21 by the Arbitrator, pp. 18–19 and Exhibit AB–17.

Table 3.6. Revenues per employee (in US dollars) and number of employees (in total).

	Number of employees Antigua remote gambling	80% of number of employees	Difference of number of 80% employee to year 2001	Average revenues per employee times employee difference (dollars)
2001	1014	811		
2002	328	262	549	244,666,459
2003	431	345	466	207,930,824
2004	492	394	418	186,174,769
2005	628	502	309	137,669,465
2006	442	354	458	204,007,601
Average				196,089,823

Note: Small errors in the numbers of employees are due to rounding. For the present calculations, average revenues per employee of US$445,821 have been used.
Source: Antigua response to question 21 by the Arbitrator, pp. 18–19 and Exhibit AB-17.

gambling sector provided by Antigua, was used to conduct a rough test of the order of magnitude of the remote gambling revenues of Antigua; see Table 3.5. As indicated in Table 3.6, the data reveal an average annual value of US$446,000 per employee and US$447,000 per employee, given the exclusion of extreme cases. Multiplying the value by the difference between the number of employees in 2001 and 2002 and each year to 2006 — adjusted by 80 percent, which is the assumed market share of the US — and taking the average in those years gives an average annual revenue loss of about US$196 million.[15]

Following these estimates, the arbitrators adjusted the average annual loss in revenues from remote gambling since 2001 for competing suppliers. They interpreted Antigua's underperformance since

[15]The use of the Levenberg–Marquardt algorithm, which lets a logistic curve of the pre-2002 revenue data fit the saturation point k converging to US$1411 million as the value of the benchmark, would have given an annual loss of US$411 million. The arbitrators did not follow this approach because of the lack of the impact of competition as well as possible increases in US demand directly.

2002 in terms of its regional share in global remote gambling revenues as a loss in Antigua's competitiveness and that, therefore, as Antigua would have lost revenue even in the absence of the US measure, only part of this revenue loss can be imputed to the measure of the United States.

By doing so, the arbitrators compared the revenue of Antigua with its regional competitors in Central/South America and the Caribbean and found the regional contribution to have shrunk each year to reach about half its 2001 value in 2006. Taking this into account — a decline in its contribution to the global regional market share for each year 2002–2006 — the average annual revenue loss is reduced from US$304 and US$198 million to US$164 and US$128 million, respectively.

Because the United States measure only affects remote gambling in horseracing, in the third step, the arbitrators further adjusted the estimated revenue losses in remote gambling. They estimated the share of remote gambling in horseracing in total remote gambling by using the world's total amount in remote gambling and found that the share of gambling in horseracing has declined from 13 percent in 2001 to just 9 percent in 2006 while the total amount was about the same. Applying the average share of 11 percent, the revenue loss by Antigua from gambling in horseracing is estimated to be approximately US$18 and US$14 million, respectively.[16]

In the fourth and last step, the arbitrators investigated the growth of demand in the United States' non-remote gambling market and decided to use United States data on pari-mutuel net receipts in the non-remote gambling market from BEA statistics on consumption expenditure.[17] Additionally, the United States provided data for the non-remote gambling market from 1995–2006 that includes

[16]The arbitrators had the choice between two strategies to identify the unknown share of gambling on horseracing in Antigua's exports of remote gambling services to the United States. The GBGC data set combining remote and non-remote revenues from gambling on horseracing in various regions of the world, and the world share.

[17]Arbitrators accepted that the data may be influenced by a degree of substitution from remote to non-remote gambling on horseracing owing to the impact of the US measure on foreign suppliers.

Table 3.7. Online revenues from world, by country/group.

	C&Sam&Car rev. (million dollars)	World rev. (million dollars)	C&Sam&Car share in world rev. (percent)	A&B share in world rev. (percent)	A&B share in C&Sam&Car rev. (percent)	A&B contrib. to C&Sam&Car share in world rev. compared to 2001 (percent)
2001	2,397	3,530	68	46	68	**100**
2002	2,639	4,380	60	39	64	**94**
2003	2,676	5,650	47	21	44	**65**
2004	3,095	8,930	35	13	37	**54**
2005	3,232	11,890	27	10	35	**52**
2006	3,152	15,320	21	7	34	**51**

Note: C&Sam&Car denotes the Central and South American and Caribbean region; A&B refers to Antigua and Barbuda; rev. means revenues.
Source: GBGC, October 2007.

Table 3.8. Antigua's revenue loss, adjustment for competition.

	GBGC			Revenues per employee		
	Revenue loss (million dollars)	Contrib. A&B to 2001 share (percent)	Revenue loss adjusted (million dollars)	Revenue loss (million dollars)	Contrib. A&B to 2001 share (percent)	Revenue loss adjusted (million dollars)
2002	−50	94	−48	245	94	231
2003	356	65	232	208	65	135
2004	388	54	211	186	54	101
2005	394	52	204	138	52	71
2006	435	51	221	204	51	103
Average	304		**164**	196		**128**

Source: GBGC, October 2007 and Antigua response to question 21 by the Arbitrator, pp. 18–19 and Exhibit AB-17.

a breakdown of pari-mutuel net receipts, 90 percent of which are accounted for by betting on horseracing; see Table 3.7. Accordingly, over the period 2001–2006, expenditures in that segment grew on average by 5 percent per annum.[18] Applying the resulting compound growth rate to the amounts calculated in the third step results in an average annual revenue loss for Antigua of about US$23 million or US$18 million, respectively.

Because of the uncertainties discussed above, the arbitrators awarded the average of US$21 million; see Table 3.8.

3.4.2. *Government transfer cases*

Government transfer cases differ from trade-restrictive cases in that they involve behind-the-border policies. This means that in addition to the quantification difficulties, which arise from an analysis of trade-restrictive measures, there is the difficulty of identifying and quantifying the transmission mechanism between the transfer of funds and international trade values. The classic case of this type is export subsidies: a government provides funds to a firm in order to export. The effects of this subsidy are similar to the analysis of trade-restrictive measures, except in this case, the market is for exports and the effect of WTO compliance is to raise the price of exports. The overall effect is then determined by the increase in price and the relative elasticities of supply and demand.

Four cases have been adjudicated by WTO arbitrators that involve such policies, three under the SCM Agreement and one under the Anti-Dumping Agreement. Two of the three SCM cases were quite specific, involving a single company producing a single product. The third case, the FSC case, involved an across-the-border subsidy.

As explained in the previous section, the approach taken by the arbitrators in the aircraft cases and the FSC case was to use the value of the subsidy to meet their mandate. The effect of this approach is to change the role of economists to that of accountants and calculate the total

---

[18]The arbitrators point out that the same would be true if applying a linear trend over the time frame.

value of the subsidy. Important concepts in this methodology include estimating the total per unit value of the subsidy and the number of products affected by that subsidy. The product of these two variables is then the award.

The arbitrators in the FSC case adopted a similar approach and awarded the value of the subsidy. However, in contrast to the two aircraft cases, the FSC arbitrators introduced an analysis of the trade effects of the subsidy to ensure that their award could not be argued as being "inappropriate." By doing this, the FSC arbitrators introduced a number of important issues pertaining to modelling in general and the specific issue of modelling government transfer cases. The general issues are discussed in Section 3.5. The specific issues relate to the pass-through effect of the funds through domestic firms to affect the international market.

The concept of pass-through was also important in determining the award in the CDSOA case in which revenue collected from anti-dumping and countervailing duties are disbursed to petitioning firms. Modelling this measure is almost identical to that of trade-restrictive measures as discussed above. The difference is that in the previous cases, the cost of imports is increased because of the WTO-inconsistent measure. In this case, it is the price of domestic goods that is reduced. In both cases, the important thing to note from an economist's perspective is that there is a relative price change in favour of domestic goods.

A variety of expenditure options face a firm when it receives funds from the government. If these funds are untied, then in the absence of specific information, it is not clear that firms will use them to advantage in the international market. Certainly, as explained by the arbitrators in the CDSOA case, an assumption that they would not be put to any use is not credible. On the other hand, a 100 percent usage of the funds is also not credible.

3.4.3. *United States — continued dumping and subsidy offset act of 2000*

In this case, the United States Continued Dumping and Subsidy Offset Act of 2000 was deemed to be inconsistent with the Agreement on

Anti-Dumping and the SCM Agreement. Specifically, the panel and Appellate Body upheld that the Act, which transferred money collected from anti-dumping and countervailing duties to petitioning firms, was a "specific action against dumping or a subsidy."

Since this was a violation of GATT articles, the equivalency between the level of nullification or impairment and the level of suspensions had to be upheld. The complaining parties in this case were of the view that the total value of disbursed revenues met this standard. The United States, as the defending party, took the view that the amount disbursed did not bear any relation to the level of nullification or impairment. In their view, nullification or impairment as specified in Article 22.4 of the DSU was the trade effect of the measure.

The US then argued that the estimated trade effect of the disbursements would be zero, since the disbursed funds could be used for a range of purposes, many of which would not deter imports. This position created an interesting dilemma for the arbitrators, since it made clear the distinction between the finding of a breach and the effect of a breach. A finding of a breach results in a presumption that there has been nullification or impairment, but the trade effect of that breach could be zero. By making this distinction, the US opened up the possibility that the final award by an arbitrator could be zero. The arbitrators agreed to this difference by stating that the finding of a breach was the "precursor" to quantification: they were not the same thing.

The arbitrators accepted the US argument that the trade effects of the measure was the appropriate measure of nullification and impairment. However, in the actual process of modelling the effects of the disbursement, the arbitrators were not convinced that the total effect of the measure would be zero. The US relied heavily on the concept of pass-through for their argument. Pass-through in this instance is the same as that adopted by the arbitrators in the FSC case, who stated that:

> [P]ass-through relates to the degree to which a company uses a subsidy it receives to lower the price of the product that it exports. At one extreme the company may choose to apply the full amount of the subsidy to the price of its products,

> thereby lowering its price. At the other, it may choose not to lower the price of the product.[19]

The US argued that this value was zero, since the funds disbursed by the government were not tied to any specific performance by the firm. In response to this argument, the arbitrators in the CDSOA case stated that:

> The United States' position that the pass-through factor is zero is highly unrealistic. A factor of zero would presume that no recipient of a CDSOA payment would ever use the funds in any way that could have a price effect. While this may be the case for some firms, it would seem impossible that it would always and inevitably be the case for all firms, since as a basic rationale of economics, firms are expected to use their money efficiently, and at least some will use that money to lower their prices.

The arbitrators also held a strong view against the assumption that the entire transfer to firms would result in a reduction of imports, essentially concluding that a value of 100 percent would be equally implausible.[20] The implication of the arbitrators' assessment about pass-through was that the true value lay between 0 percent and 100 percent. In the absence of concrete information, the arbitrators opted for

---

[19] *US–FSC (Article 22.6–US)*, footnote 97.

[20] "The Requesting Parties' argument of full pass-through is based on the presumption that every firm receiving CDSOA payments in every case would fully use those payments to finance price reductions on the products subject to the anti-dumping or countervailing duty order in question. This would seem to be quite unlikely in reality. In particular, while some firms may use CDSOA receipts in this way, the programme leaves recipients free to use the funds as they wish. Furthermore, many or most firms producing a product that is subject to an anti-dumping or countervailing duty order also produce other products (often, many other products). Thus, it is possible for CDSOA benefits to be applied to products that are not subject to orders. In addition, some recipient firms may use their payments to train their workers, to upgrade their technology or machinery, or to expand their capacity and/or production. While using the funds in these sorts of ways clearly will have supply side effects that may have eventual consequential effects on prices, these price effects will be inter-temporal. Finally, some firms may, as the United States argues, not use the funds in any way that would have price effects."

a range between 25 percent as a lower bound and 100 percent as an upper bound.

Since the measure in question was the annual disbursement of tariff revenue, which depended upon a number of factors, the Requesting Parties were of the view that the level of suspensions should not be static but should vary according to the level of disbursements. This view was accepted by the arbitrators, who did not see a conflict between a varying level of suspensions and the use of trade effects to proxy nullification or impairment. Therefore, their modelling approach was to estimate a coefficient that could be multiplied against the annual level of disbursements to obtain the annual level of the suspension of concessions.[21]

The model used by the arbitrators was based on a model submitted by the Requesting Parties. It is defined as the product of four variables: the value of the subsidy, a measure of the *ad valorem* price reduction caused by the CDSOA disbursements (i.e., pass-through), a substitution elasticity of imports, and import penetration. This basic relationship of the trade effect is expressed as follows:

$$\text{Trade effect} = (\text{value of disbursements}) * [(\text{pass-through}) \\ *(\text{import penetration}) * (\text{elasticity of substitution})]$$

The term in the square brackets is the arbitrators' trade effect coefficient. For a given expenditure of CDSOA disbursements that is deemed to affect trade, the product of that expenditure and the coefficient provides the overall trade effect. The above relationship is written in more formal terms as:

$$\text{Reduction in imports} = \alpha^{*}\eta^{*}S^{*}R$$

[21] As mentioned above, we consider that an appropriate way to assess the trade effect of a law operating, in economic terms, like a domestic subsidy was to endeavour to establish an economic model. This model, when applied to the facts of this case, would identify a coefficient that, when multiplied by the amount of disbursements over a given period, would produce a figure corresponding to a trade effect that could reasonably be deemed to correspond to the level of nullification or impairment for that period.

where

- α, is a parameter that reflects the value of the pass-through effect of the disbursement and takes on values $0 < \alpha < 1$;
- η is the elasticity of substitution $\eta = \left(\frac{\Delta M/M}{\Delta P_q/\Delta P_q}\right)$;
- S is the total value of the payments expressed as a margin of the price reduction on domestic production financed by payments and can be expressed as $S = \Delta P_q^* Q$;
- R is the ratio of the value of imports to the value of domestic shipments in the markets in question and can be expressed as $R = \left(\frac{P_m M}{P_q Q}\right)$.

The relationship between the level of the transfer and the amount of imports that it deters depends on two variables for which data are readily available and two for which there is a range of views about their values. The value of the payments and the import penetration value are provided by national governments. Values for the other two variables, however, are subject to much debate. As mentioned above, the pass-through value could range from 0 to 1. Furthermore, the values of elasticities could vary not only in aggregate, but also across sectors.

Table 3.9 presents a summary of the elasticities submitted by the various parties to the arbitrators. The values are across industrial sectors. On the low end of the scale is an average of 2.67 and on the high end 5.17.

Table 3.9. Summary of elasticities submitted to the arbitrators.

	GTAP	USITC GTAP	Requesting parties NAIC	US product low*	US product mid-point*	US product high*
Mean	2.68	3.09	2.67	2.83	3.99	5.17
Median	2.8	2.80	2.8	3	4	5
Std. Deviation	0.8	1.18	0.79	0.87	0.92	1.12
Minimum	1.8	1	1.8	1	2	3
Maximum	5.2	5	5.2	5	6.5	8
Count	41	41	31	65	65	65

Table 3.10. Summary of trade effects.

	Low	Medium	High
	2001		
25 percent	0.22	0.27	0.33
50 percent	0.43	0.54	0.65
75 percent	0.65	0.81	0.98
100 percent	0.87	1.09	1.30
	2002		
25 percent	0.25	0.31	0.37
50 percent	0.50	0.62	0.74
75 percent	0.74	0.93	1.12
100 percent	0.99	1.24	1.49
	2003		
25 percent	0.22	0.28	0.34
50 percent	0.45	0.56	0.67
75 percent	0.67	0.84	1.01
100 percent	0.89	1.12	1.34

The lack of precision in the pass-through and elasticity estimates resulted in the arbitrators taking a very general approach to estimate the trade coefficient. For pass-through, they decided that an appropriate range would be between 0.25 and 1.0. This range was combined with three values for the substitution elasticity. An annual value of the coefficient was then calculated using these two ranges for the years 2001–2003; see Table 3.10. The arbitrators then took an average of these three values.

Using this methodology the arbitrators estimated the trade coefficient to be 0.72[22] ("in example there was an effective pass-through effect of 72 percent").[23] By awarding a coefficient instead of an actual

[22]The coefficient can also be interpreted readily in economic terms — in essence, the arbitrators have concluded that every dollar collected by the US government from anti-dumping revenues and returned to petitioning firms would reduce the value of US imports by 0.72.

[23]Georgiev and van der Borght (2006).

dollar amount, the arbitrators broke new ground by linking the annual effect of the inconsistent measure to the retaliation. Therefore, the level of retaliation, in dollar amounts, would not necessarily be the same for each year or for each complaining member to the dispute.

3.4.4. *United States — tax treatment for "Foreign Sales Corporations" — recourse to arbitration by the United States under Article 22.6 of the DSU and Article 411 of the SCM Agreement*

The US–FSC case is analytically similar to the US–CDSOA case in the sense that it involves a government transfer. Where the cases differ is in the impact of trade. The FSC case is an export subsidy case, therefore, the trade effect is through an increase in exports, whereas with the CDSOA case the funds were used to compete with imports. Modelling the effects of export subsidies, therefore, requires similar analytical tools; pass-through of the subsidy, various elasticities and the value of trade.

One key difference between an export subsidy case and a government support case is the value assigned to pass-through. As noted earlier, the US argued that in cases where government transfers to firms are untied it is unclear as to whether or not any of the funds are put towards enhancing the firm's competitive position. Clearly, this cannot be the case for a measure that is tied specifically to whether or not a firm exports its products.

The tied nature of the measure, therefore, rules out zero as a possible value for pass-through. This, however, only means that a lower bound has been established and does not provide any precision when the arbitrators interpret their mandate to be one of awarding a specific value. Although the arbitrators did not make their modelling efforts specific in their award, they did note that a study of a program similar to that of the FSC, the Domestic International Sales Corporation Act, found the pass-through value to be 75 percent.

In response to this finding, the US argued that the pass-through value has probably decreased since then for at least two reasons based on the evidence of the types of firms taking advantage of the FSC program. First, if firms are operating on the positively sloped segment of their average cost curve, an increase in production could result in an increase in costs that may not be compensated by the subsidy. Second, if firms in an industry have market power, they would not necessarily have an incentive to lower prices.

Taken together, these two reasons argue that the more anti-competitive the market, the lower the pass-through effect would be. The arbitrators in this case examined evidence from the parties on the nature of competition in international markets and concluded that competition had increased in the past 30 years. Interestingly, in support of their argument, the arbitrators cite that average import taxes have declined since the 1970s because of the implementation of the results from the Tokyo and Uruguay rounds of multilateral negotiations.

3.4.5. *Trade indeterminate cases*

An economic analysis of the trade effects of withdrawing a measure is relatively straightforward if information exists about the measure and data for the relevant parameters are available. In US 1916, a difficulty arose when it was clear that no data were available about the effects of the measure: it had only been used in one instance and not against the EC, which was one of the complaining parties.

WTO arbitrators had to make a decision on a qualitative award. The request for suspension by the EC was not of a specific value; it was to implement legislation that would "mirror" the effects of the offending measure. Because no value was specified, the arbitrators had the difficult dilemma of distinguishing between zero effects and unquantifiable effects. If the effect could not be quantified, then could a qualitative award be granted?

3.5. The Role of Economists in WTO Arbitration Cases

There is undoubtedly a role for economists in adjudicating WTO dispute cases, for the simple reason that they are the best placed to determine the causes and consequences of the international flow of goods and services. In reviewing the different arbitration cases a number of different areas where economists can contribute have been identified. This section divides these areas into two parts — assisting arbitrators in interpreting their mandate, and in the area of quantification.

3.5.1. *Defining the mandate*

The term "nullification or impairment of benefits" is sufficiently vague to allow arbitrators considerable latitude in its interpretation. To date, arbitrators appear to have confined the interpretation to the direct trade effects that would arise and its resulting revenues in the case of violations against GATS if an offending measure is brought into conformity with WTO rules. Part of the rationale for this approach lies in the difficulty of meaningfully quantifying a broader definition. WTO provisions are designed to create and maintain an open and stable trading system. How a member benefits from that system will depend on a number of complementary measures and domestic policies. By focusing only on foregone trade and resulting revenues as a measure of benefits arbitrators are not focussing on benefits *per se*, but on the means by which benefits are conferred. This would be the case, at least from the economist's perspective, since they typically focus on welfare as a measure of benefits. However, although easy to identify theoretically, benefits are very difficult to quantify in practical terms.

There also appears to be some convergence with the interpretation of the mandate for arbitration under the SCM Agreement and considerable discretion is given to arbitrators to define their award. Despite this latitude, arbitrators have consistently awarded the value of the subsidy as the "appropriate countermeasure."

There are, therefore, two dimensions to the issue of arbitral awards. The first is an award based on the impact of a measure and the second is an award based on the measure itself. The evaluation and exposition of the various arbitration cases in the previous section showed that awards based on trade effects can be readily interpreted by economists because they implicitly take into account the concept of opportunity costs.

As shown in Figure 3.1, this is accomplished by using changes in product prices.

Although awards based on the value of the measure appear to be increasingly common for prohibited subsidy cases, none of the awards to date have been clear as to the rationale for this approach. Two cases did examine the impact of the measure to see if the conclusion of such an analysis could question the use of the value of the measure, but stopped well short of advocating the impact as the principal benchmark for meeting their mandate.

Trade effects analysis in prohibited subsidies cases, therefore, has an insurance element to it. It is used just in case an award based on the value could be interpreted as being inappropriate and disproportionate. This approach raises an interesting issue with respect to economic analysis. Each of the three cases consisting of export subsidies have awarded 100 percent of the subsidy, yet one case involving a government transfer of funds to a firm to compete against imports was awarded 72 percent of the subsidy. Yet in export subsidy cases and the US–CDSOA case (the government transfer case), the arbitrators acknowledged that the upper end of the range of trade effects *exceeded* the value of the transfer. This fact on its own would imply that more economic research is required to deliver a more precise range that could support the precedence that arbitral awards in government transfer cases should be either the value of the measure, or less.

3.5.2. *Quantification*

Two aspects of quantification have been identified: the value of the WTO-inconsistent measure and the impact of that measure in terms of its trade effects.

Whereas economists have the potential to make an analytical contribution to interpreting a mandate, their quantitative skills can make a significant, if not crucial, contribution in estimating the overall value of the award.

Government transfer cases have consistently awarded the value of the transfer as the level of suspensions or the appropriate measure. In these cases, there is almost no role for economic analysis, since the arbitrators have argued that this value would be sufficient to meet their mandate. Economists in these types of cases would, for the most part, be used as accountants to simply add up the total value of the measure.

In the two aircraft cases, the quantitative task consisted of aggregating the total government support and dividing by production to obtain the per unit subsidy. Estimating the value of the government support was important in the US–FSC case, since government data were not available for the reference period. In this case, an estimate had to be made using the latest available year and then forecasting the level for the reasonable period. The key variable in these types of estimations is the discount rate used to increase the value. Not surprisingly, views differ on the values of the discount rate. In the end, the FSC arbitrators noted that both the US estimation method and the EC estimation resulted in figures that were almost identical to the requested amount. In addition, since their task was only to decide if the estimated amount was reasonable, there was no absolute requirement for precision.

A related issue that this paper has not dealt with is whether the awarded amount should serve the specific objective of inducing compliance. The reason for this omission is that no clear guidance can be distilled from the various arbitration cases about this objective. Nevertheless, it is obvious that any award that is so low as not to be taken into account by a respondent as part of its obligation to the trading system would seem odd. This is precisely what happened in Canada Aircraft when Canada announced they would not bring their measure into conformity even with the arbitral award. Faced with the problem of non-compliance, the arbitrators grossed up the calculated value of their award by 20 percent. The arbitrators admitted that this increase was purely symbolic in nature but that it set the precedent that the value of the award may not always be sufficient.

Economic analysis could be incorporated into such circumstances since contract enforcement is at stake. Certainly, the amount of information required to calculate an award that induces compliance but is not punitive may make the process prohibitive. But, at the very least, an analytical approach to the question needs to be taken. Simply adding

20 percent, or *X* percent, to an award as a symbolic gesture will not be sufficient to consider whether or not the mandate provided to the arbitrator has actually been fulfilled.

The second area of quantification holds the most promise for economists to make a contribution. As was seen in the previous sections, the legal precedent that the trade effect of an inconsistent measure is taken to be the level of nullification and impairment is now almost universally accepted. This means that the task of arbitrators in Article 22.6 cases of the DSU will be the quantification of the effects of the measure.

One of the messages from this section is that the general economic approach to quantifying nullification or impairment need not change. Standard empirical difficulties, such as the range in the values of the various elasticities, will always be a problem, but this is an area where economists can continue to work to improve their reliability. In some ways, the legal process has made the task of economists a bit easier, since it is clear that the indirect effects of a measure are usually not taken into account when estimating nullification or impairment. In this regard, there is absolutely no scope for computable general equilibrium analysis.

The most important aspect of quantification is whether or not it can lead to a robust result. By definition, arbitration is the last part of the legal process, with no room for appeal. Therefore, any award made by an arbitrator must at the very least pass the proverbial "laugh test." The United States took a very strong view against modelling in the FSC case and went so far as to say that modelling is so unreliable that it should be rejected completely. They further argued that the value of the subsidy could be taken as a "proxy" for the trade effect. This would, in effect, assume that a \$1.00 export subsidy would result in a \$1.00 increase in exports.

In response to this argument, the FSC arbitrators were strong in their condemnation of relying on *ad hoc* approaches. While they recognised that modelling had inherent difficulties, they believed that it could still be useful to the arbitration process. A similar point was made by the arbitrators in the CDSOA case and also in US

1916, even though quantification of the measure was deemed to be unreliable.

Robustness is not an easy standard to define, let alone meet. For example, the arbitrators awarded a coefficient of 0.72 in the CDSOA case using industry data over three years. There is no doubt that others would disagree with such a precise value and, using the same data that were available to arbitrators, would estimate a higher or lower coefficient. Additional work on substitution elasticities and the effects of pass-through could assist the WTO legal process greatly, especially in government transfer cases.

3.6. Summary

By definition, legal texts based on economic foundations, such as the WTO Agreements and national competition policies, require the use of economics to ensure their proper interpretation and application. This paper has focused on the role of economics in arbitration cases brought to the WTO. This particular stage in the WTO's quasi-judicial process is extremely important since it is the last and thus leaves parties to the dispute with no right to appeal. Therefore, with such finality, there is an important obligation on the part of the arbitrators to ensure that their interpretation of WTO law is legally consistent and legally robust. The principal point of this paper is that economic analysis can help in this regard in at least two ways. First, through assisting the arbitrators to interpret their mandate, and second, through using economic tools to quantify the effects of the inconsistent measure.

These two conclusions were developed and argued by reviewing existing arbitration cases. Both these elements can be found in almost every case, leading to the overall conclusion that economists have played a role in adjudicating cases that have reached the arbitration stage in WTO disputes. Furthermore, this role is not limited to simply quantifying the effects of the measure, once a legal interpretation of the guiding principles has been completed. Economic analysis, therefore, is not only a necessary part of the WTO arbitration process: its role is complementary to and not sequential to legal analysis.

References

Anderson, K (2002). Peculiarities of retaliation in the WTO dispute settlement. *World Trade Review*, 1, 123–134.

Bagwell, K and R Staiger (2002). *The Economics of the World Trading System*. Cambridge MA: MIT Press.

Bernstein, J and D Skully (2004). Calculating trade damages in the context of the World Trade Organisation's Dispute Settlement Process. *Review of Agricultural Economics*, 25, 385–398.

Brown, CP and M Ruta (2008). The Economics of Permissible WTO Retaliation, World Trade Organization, Staff Working Paper ERSD-2008-04.

Breuss, F (2004). WTO Dispute Settlement: An economic analysis of four EU–US mini-trade wars. Memo, Vienna Institute for Economic Research.

Georgiev, D and K van der Borght (eds) (2006). *Reform and Development of the WTO Dispute Settlement System*. London: Cameron May.

Lawrence, R (2003). *Crimes and Punishment: Retaliation under the WTO*. Washington DC: Institute for International Economics.

Chapter 4

The Impact of Manufacturing Protection on Agricultural Incentives in Australia*

Kym Anderson

Bijit Bora's interests covered a wide range of trade policy concerns, including manufacturing protectionism in Australia (e.g., Bora and Pomfret, 1995). During many of the years Sir Robert Menzies and Malcolm Fraser served as Prime Minister, protectionism took the form mainly of tariffs on imports (plus quantitative import restrictions), and most of those imports were manufactured goods. In the early years of Australia's Federation, tariffs were not as high as those in the United States, but by 1930 they were and came down considerably more slowly than US rates thereafter (Fig. 4.1). Indeed, following World War II they were higher than in any high-income country except New Zealand.

Partly as a consequence, during the first four decades after World War II, Australia's GDP per capita grew slowly relative to other high-income countries. In the past 20 or so years, by contrast, the

*This chapter draws on Anderson and Garnaut (1987), Anderson and Findlay (1995), Anderson (2001) and Anderson, Lloyd and MacLaren (2007).

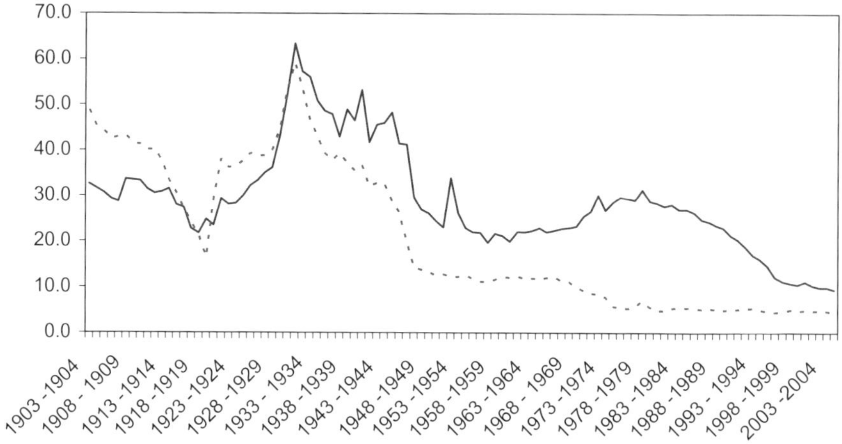

Fig. 4.1. Australian (solid line) and US (broken line) import tariff rates, 1903–04 to 2005–06 (tariff revenue as percent of value of dutiable imports).
Source: Lloyd (2007).

Australian economy has out-performed most other high-income countries, with its per capita income growing half as fast again as the OECD average. This marked difference between recent and earlier relative performance has been attributed to major economic policy reforms that have occurred since the 1970s and, in particular, to the belated opening of the Australian economy to the rest of the world. Having been more protectionist than all other OECD countries except New Zealand for most of the 20th century (Anderson and Garnaut, 1987), and having largely stood aside from the industrial trade policy reforms agreed to by other Contracting Parties to the General Agreement on Tariffs and Trade (GATT) in the first seven rounds of multilateral trade negotiations (1947–1979), Australia has since undergone a remarkable degree of domestic microeconomic reform and opening up of its current and capital accounts. This liberalisation has reversed the downward trend in its trade share of GDP, although no more than the average of other high-income countries (Fig. 4.2).

Manufacturing protectionism in effect amounted to anti-trade and anti-primary sector biases in the government's industry assistance

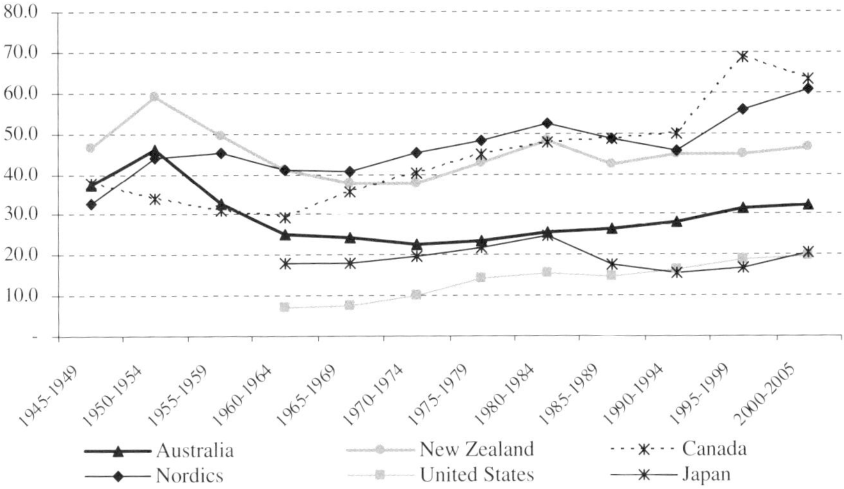

Fig. 4.2. Merchandise exports plus imports as a share of GDP, Australia and other high-income countries, 1945 to 2005 (percent, five-year averages).
Note: 'Nordics' refers to the weighted average for Denmark, Finland, Norway and Sweden, using mid-period imports as the weights for each five-year period.
Source: Mitchell (2003a,b,c), World Bank (2006).

policies. How extensive were those biases, and to what extent did they reduce agricultural incentives? What has happened to the export orientation of the various farm industries in the wake of the reform process? And how does the overall pattern of distortions that has evolved for Australia compare with that of other high-income countries?

This chapter provides answers to these empirical questions using a new set of estimates of distortions to agricultural incentives. After a brief synopsis of structural changes to the Australian economy over the past half century, it describes the build-up first of manufacturing protection and some agricultural subsidies and then, from the 1970s, the dismantling of those interventions. This is supported by a six-decade time series of nominal rates of protection provided for both agriculture and manufacturing. The chapter then contrasts those rates with new comparable estimates for other high-income countries.

4.1. Structural Changes Since 1950

Australia's long history of industrial protectionism resulted in a smaller share of its GDP being traded than would be normal for an economy of its size (Fig. 4.2).[1] It also ensured a bigger manufacturing sector than would have emerged under free trade, which was possible in its full-employment setting only at the expense of other sectors. The sectoral share of GDP held by manufacturing in the early 1960s was close to the OECD average of around 30 percent, even though Australia has always had few people relative to its rich endowments of agricultural land and mineral resources and so has a weak comparative advantage in manufacturing.

The removal of the ban on key mineral raw material exports in the early 1960s and the tariff reforms of the 1970s and 1980s gradually corrected Australia's pro-manufacturing policy bias. Between 1960 and 2005, the share of GDP from manufacturing fell much more rapidly for Australia than for the average OECD country, to just 11 percent, while the share of the mining sector initially trebled (Anderson, 2001). The share of Australian exports from mining also more than trebled between the early 1960s and the early 1980s, helped by the dramatic rises in energy raw material prices in the second half of that period — as it was again in 2007–08 (Table 4.1). It was not only natural resource-based exportables that Australia's anti-trade policies had discouraged, however. Export industries *within* the manufacturing sector and services exports were also discouraged. Together, those two sectors contributed only one-twelfth of Australia's exports in the early 1950s, and even by 1980 their combined contribution was barely above one-quarter. However, by 1990 their share had risen to one-third and by 2005 to 44 percent, or 22 percent each, thus exceeding the share for agriculture for the first time (Table 4.1).

Even though those changes lowered agriculture's relative contribution to exports, the share of exports in the gross value of farm

---

[1]The smaller shares for the large economies of Japan and the United States are to be expected, but even for those economies the share of GDP traded was rising during the 1960s and 1970s when it was falling slightly in Australia.

Table 4.1. Sectoral composition of GDP, employment and exports in Australia, 1950–51 to 2007–08 (percentage shares, at current prices).

	Agriculture	Mining	Manufacturing	Services	Total
GDP					
1950–54	22	2	29	47	100
1960–64	16	2	28	54	100
1970–74	9	3	26	62	100
1980–84	5	6	20	69	100
1990–94	3	5	15	78	100
2007–08	2	7	10	81	100
Employment					
1962–63	10	1	26	63	100
1972–73	7	1	24	68	100
1982–83	6	1	19	74	100
1993–94	5	1	14	80	100
2007–08	3	1	10	85	100
Exports	Agriculture	Mining	Other merchandise	Services	Total
1950–51	86	6	3	5	100
1962–63	66	8	13	13	100
1972–73	44	28	12	16	100
1982–83	39	34	11	16	100
1993–94	26	41	14	19	100
2005–06	21	35	22	22	100
2007–08	13	47	18	22	100

Source: ABARE (2008) and, for GDP before the 1960s, Mitchell (2003c) and Butlin (1962).

production nonetheless increased considerably, from around 55 percent in the mid-1970s to 75 percent now (ABARE, 2008). Moreover, that growth in farm exports came from an increasing range of farm products, as farmers diversified beyond traditional wheat, wool and sheepmeat enterprises to beef, cotton, sugar, dairy products, wine and canola (Fig. 4.3).

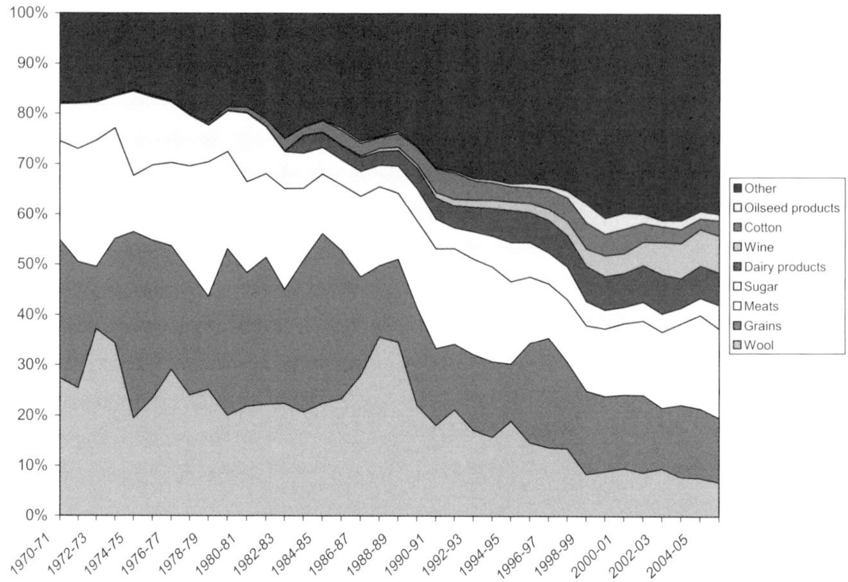

Fig. 4.3. Commodity composition of agricultural and food exports, Australia, 1970–71 to 2005–06 (percent).
Source: Compiled from data from ABARE (2008 and earlier years).

4.2. Methodology for Measuring Distortions to Incentives

It is *relative* prices and hence relative rates of government assistance that affect producers' incentives. In a two-sector model an import tax has the same effect on the export sector as an export tax (the Lerner (1936) Symmetry Theorem), and this carries over to a model that also includes a third sector producing only nontradables (Vousden, 1990, pp. 46–47). This understanding led Gruen (1968) to point out that raising assistance to agriculture in the presence of high assistance to manufacturing could increase rather than reduce national economic welfare.[2] Thus it is necessary to estimate the average nominal rate of assistance

[2] A policy debate followed Gruen's famously unpublished 1968 paper, with some arguing for tariff-compensating farm assistance to continue until manufacturing tariffs were brought down (e.g., Harris *et al.*, 1974; Harris, 1975) and others (e.g., Lloyd, 1975;

(NRA) for each of the tradable sectors of the economy. The NRA is the percentage by which government policies have raised gross returns to producers above what they would be without the government's intervention. It is based on NRA estimates for individual industries, derived either from domestic to border price comparisons (as with agriculture) or from applied import tariffs (as with manufacturing pre-1968), or by drawing on detailed knowledge of government interventions or lack thereof (as with manufacturing post-1968 and non-farm primary production). The sectoral NRAs allow a calculation of a Relative Rate of Assistance (RRA) to agriculture as compared with other tradable sectors, defined as:

$$\text{RRA} = 100[(1 + \text{NRAag}^t/100)/(1 + \text{NRAnonag}^t/100) - 1]$$

where NRAag^t and NRAnonag^t are the average percentage NRAs for the tradables parts of the agricultural and non-agricultural sectors, respectively. Since the NRA cannot be less than −100 percent if producers are to earn anything, so too must the RRA. If this measure is below zero, it provides an internationally comparable indication of the extent to which the policy regime has an anti-agricultural bias, and conversely when the RRA is positive.

4.3. Measuring Nominal Rates of Assistance (NRAs)

We describe the sources of non-agricultural NRAs, then those for agriculture.

4.3.1. *Non-agricultural tradable commodities*

The Productivity Commission has not provided systematic NRA estimates for mining for every year, but for those years that it has done so in recent decades the values are extremely small, varying within the range of −1 to +1 percent. We therefore simply assume that the

---

Warr, 1978) pointing out the political economy dilemmas and other problems this could raise.

sector's NRA has been zero since 1960 when the ban on exports of iron ore and coal was lifted. We also assume it is zero for other primary products (forestry and fishing), as they are not subject to government interventions other than for resource and environmental conservation reasons (and in any case they represent a very small fraction of even just the tradables' share of GDP).

Estimates of the NRA for manufacturing for the period before 1968–69 (referring to the fiscal year beginning 1 July), when Tariff Board estimates begin, rely on tariffs only. Between 1952 and 1960 there were also protective quantitative restrictions on imports of manufactures (ostensibly for balance of payments reasons in the presence of fixed exchange rates — see Moffatt, 1962; 1970), but since there are no estimates of the protective effects of those import licences, their impact on the average NRA for non-agricultural tradables is assumed to be exactly offset by the negative impact of the ban on key mining exports in those years.[3]

Since Australia's imports pre-1970 were almost exclusively manufactures, customs revenue as a percentage of the value of all merchandise imports provides a reasonable proxy for the country's nominal rate of tariff protection for manufacturing. Annual estimates of that indicator are provided by Lloyd (2008), along with estimates referring to only dutiable imports, using data from the Australian Bureau of Statistics (ABS, previously the Commonwealth Bureau of Census and Statistics).

These series relate to customs duties only and so do not include assistance resulting from non-tariff measures, apart from anti-dumping, countervailing and revenue ("primage") duties. They do include an adjustment for refunds and drawbacks of customs duties, and primage

[3]Before the 1950s, the relatively low international prices of mineral and energy products (World Bank, 2000), combined with the very high cost of transporting bulky coal and iron ore from Australia to the North Atlantic's industrial hub, means that the export ban was probably redundant. In the 1950s the ban signalled Australia's unwillingness to provide industrial raw materials to Japan — a foreign policy stance that was reversed after the signing of the Australia–Japan trade agreement in 1957 (Crawford, 1968). For more on mining policies, see Doran (1984), and on mineral taxation in particular, see Groenewegen (1983).

duties where applicable, which is important because these added significant protection to Australian producers of many goods. They also include duties levied on excisable goods, and refer to actual rates levied on imports, thereby combining MFN, preferential and concessional tariffs on final goods and intermediate or capital inputs. As those inputs that were not competitive with Australian-produced goods were admitted duty free under by-law and concessional import schemes, the series has long been regarded as less useful than the series of the average tariff on dutiable imports only. Thus the best available series measuring the average nominal protection resulting from the Australian tariff over the period to 1968–69 (after which more comprehensive Productivity Commission estimates are available) is the tariff on dutiable imports, where averages are calculated using import weights.

For the period since 1968–69, the Productivity Commission (and its predecessors, the Industries Assistance Commission and the Industry Commission) provide estimates of both nominal and effective rates of assistance to manufacturing, for industry sub-categories down to the four-digit level. In addition to tariffs, these cover subsidies, bounties and discriminatory sales taxes. Initially they did not cover quantitative restrictions, local content plans, etc. (Industries Assistance Commission, 1976, p. 4), but these are included from 1982–83.

The average NRAs for the whole non-agricultural tradables sector is calculated assuming only (and all) service sectors produce non-tradables, and a zero NRA for non-agricultural primary sectors. For manufacturing, the Productivity Commission NRA output estimates from 1968–69 are used (ignoring their estimates of net assistance via primary factor and intermediate input markets, which in the past decade would have lowered them by about one-fifth), while for earlier years the dutiable import tariff averages estimated by Lloyd are used. While the latter may overstate assistance to the sector in so far as some competing imports come in duty free, that is assumed to be offset by the numerous non-tariff barriers to imports that were in place before 1970. For the two years of overlap in the two series in the late 1960s, they are almost identical (at 23 percent). The manufacturing sector's share of non-agricultural tradables output is assumed to be in proportion to its share of GDP from manufacturing plus non-agricultural primary activities.

That share times the manufacturing NRA provides the estimated NRA for total non-agricultural tradables.

4.3.2. *Agricultural commodities*

The Industries Assistance Commission began calculating estimates of the nominal rates of assistance for major agricultural commodities beginning with the fiscal year 1970–71. This series has been continued by the Industry Commission and the Productivity Commission.[4] There are four breaks in the series as each sub-series is benchmarked to the reference years 1970–71, 1983–84, 1990–91 and 1996–97. There are some differences between periods in the estimation methodologies used. For example, the first three series were compiled on an agricultural commodity basis, while for the latest (1996–97 benchmarked) series the Productivity Commission moved to an ANZSIC industry-based classification of activities, in line with the methodology used for the manufacturing sector industries (see Productivity Commission, 2002c, Methodological Annex A). For this reason, the series for individual activities other than dairy, poultry and pig farming are not available from 1999–2000. Almost all other farm industries had zero nominal assistance by then and we have assumed this continued, which is consistent with PSE estimates for Australia by the OECD (2006). Two exceptional farm products were rice and oranges, and their small 1999–2000 NRA values are assumed to continue to 2004–05 (rice at 1.7 percent and oranges at 0.6 percent).[5]

Before 1970–71, the only comprehensive series available is that published in Lloyd (1973, pp. 149–58), which was prepared by the Bureau of Agricultural Economics. Those authors followed one of the methods used by Harris (1964) in his pioneering paper on agricultural protection in Australia, as explained in Lloyd (1973, Appendix Notes). They cover the major agricultural commodities for which data were available

[4] On the history and workings of this transparency agency and the policy reform process in which it has actively participated since it superseded the Tariff Board in 1973, see Productivity Commission (2003).

[5] For rice, this is very close to the calculations made by the OECD (2006).

at the time for the years 1946–47 to 1970–71.[6] The Lloyd/BAE series and the PC series use essentially the same methods. Commodities are designated as either export- or import-competing and then direct estimates of the implicit price changes to producers resulting from agricultural assistance are made and expressed as a percentage of the export or (in the case of tobacco and cotton pre-1970) the import parity price.

The two series report estimates for one year in common, 1970–71, which provides a check on the comparability of the two series. The estimates for that year are very close, with the exceptions of tobacco and eggs. In blending the two series of estimates, the Productivity Commission's are used from 1970–71 (see Table 4.2).

For the industries covered by the Commission but not by Lloyd, "guesstimates" have been made for the years before 1970, based on the policy descriptions in Edwards (2006) and the references cited therein. The only guesstimate of significant size is for wine grapes, of which the NRA is assumed to equal Lloyd's estimate for dried vine fruit up to 1970. All the other industries had either no assistance (maize, oats, rapeseed, soybean, bananas, olives, wool, beef, sheepmeat, pigmeat, chicken meat) or a very small weight in the total gross value of farm production. For the latter category, NRAs are assumed to be: apples at 6 percent, oranges at 25 percent and potatoes at 8 percent for the 1950s and 1960s, and zero for all three crops prior to 1950–51.

To obtain the weighted averages for agriculture as a whole, as shown in Table 4.3, we first assumed that the NRA was zero for products not covered by the above estimates and guesstimates. This is reasonable since those not covered are mostly small horticultural industries that are not subject to market interventions (apart from quarantine restrictions, which are in place purportedly for reasons of health rather than economic protection). Gross value of production at undistorted prices are used as weights, calculated by dividing that value at domestic producer prices — or, equivalently, the NRAs — by (1 + NRA/100).

[6]For milk before 1970–71, we took a simple average of the Lloyd/BAE estimates for butter and cheese to get the milk NRA shown in Table 4.2 for those years. The Lloyd/BAE and the PC series for the main distorted commodities are reported by individual commodity and year in the Appendix to Anderson *et al.* (2008).

Table 4.2. Nominal rates of assistance to covered farm products, Australia, 1946 to 2007. (percent, for fiscal years starting 1 July).

	1946–49	1950–54	1955–59	1960–64	1965–69	1970–74	1975–79	1980–84	1985–89	1990–94	1995–99	2000–04	2005–07
Exportables	**−7.5**	**0.9**	**6.4**	**7.0**	**10.0**	**7.6**	**3.6**	**4.6**	**5.6**	**4.8**	**3.0**	**0.0**	**0.0**
Rice	−3.2	−1.1	11.4	15.0	14.8	22.0	20.4	15.2	10.6	2.5	2.3	1.7	1.9
Wheat	−24.2	−8.4	1.9	6.1	10.1	7.2	−0.4	2.6	3.8	2.1	1.1	0.0	0.0
Barley	−14.1	−5.8	4.1	3.1	4.4	0.0	0.0	0.0	0.0	0.0	0.0	0.0	0.0
Oats	0.0	0.0	0.0	0.0	0.0	0.0	0.0	0.0	0.0	0.0	0.0	0.0	0.0
Grapes, total	10.5	4.5	5.6	9.7	18.7	39.7	19.2	21.3	18.3	13.3	4.9	0.0	0.0
Sugar	−8.2	0.7	12.8	15.9	32.8	7.6	−6.2	4.6	12.4	5.8	1.7	0.0	0.0
Cotton	0.8	2.0	26.7	52.1	73.9	53.4	17.6	4.4	2.0	0.0	0.0	0.0	0.0
Wool	0.0	0.0	0.0	0.0	0.0	6.0	1.4	1.0	1.0	5.4	0.7	0.0	0.0
Beef and veal	0.0	0.0	0.0	0.0	0.0	1.4	1.8	1.4	1.2	0.3	0.0	0.0	0.0
Mutton and lamb	0.0	0.0	0.0	0.0	0.4	1.6	1.8	1.4	1.8	0.9	0.0	0.0	0.0
Pigmeat	0.0	0.0	0.0	0.0	0.0	0.0	0.0	0.0	0.0	0.0	0.0	0.0	0.0
Milk	2.1	18.7	46.9	43.1	74.5	32.8	35.8	32.2	39.6	23.8	19.3	0.0	0.0
Apple	na	na	6.0	6.0	6.0	9.0	5.4	3.4	1.2	0.4	0.1	0.0	0.0
Sunflower	na	na	na	na	na	na	na	5.6	1.4	0.0	0.0	0.0	0.0
Import-competing products	**0.0**	**10.1**	**13.4**	**12.5**	**13.1**	**18.3**	**11.6**	**8.0**	**3.7**	**1.8**	**0.4**	**0.1**	**0.0**
Maize	0.0	0.0	0.0	0.0	0.0	0.0	0.0	0.0	0.0	0.0	0.0	0.0	0.0
Sorghum	0.0	0.0	0.0	0.0	0.0	0.0	0.0	1.6	2.0	0.0	0.0	0.0	0.0
Oilseeds	0.0	0.0	0.0	0.0	0.0	0.0	0.0	0.0	0.0	0.0	0.0	0.0	0.0
Tobacco	0.0	34.2	51.0	46.9	51.3	250.0	122.2	56.4	37.6	48.5	19.8	0.0	0.0
Poultry	0.0	0.0	0.0	0.0	0.0	0.0	0.0	0.0	0.0	0.0	0.0	0.0	0.0
Banana	na	na	0.0	0.0	0.0	0.0	0.0	4.8	1.0	0.1	0.0	0.0	0.0
Olive	na	na	0.0	0.0	0.0	0.0	0.0	0.0	0.0	0.0	0.0	0.0	0.0
Orange	na	na	25.0	25.0	25.0	25.8	32.8	38.2	13.0	2.7	0.7	0.6	0.6
Soybean	na	na	0.0	0.0	0.0	0.0	0.0	0.0	0.0	0.1	0.0	0.0	0.0
Non-tradables	**−1.2**	**12.6**	**31.4**	**41.6**	**78.1**	**25.3**	**19.5**	**24.2**	**12.2**	**1.8**	**0.2**	**0.0**	**0.0**
Eggs	−1.7	14.7	43.7	61.8	141.2	35.0	26.0	35.8	18.4	3.4	0.4	0.0	0.0
Potatoes	0.0	8.0	8.0	8.0	8.0	7.2	7.2	8.0	3.2	0.0	0.0	0.0	0.0

(Continued)

Table 4.2. *(Continued)*

	1946–49	1950–54	1955–59	1960–64	1965–69	1970–74	1975–79	1980–84	1985–89	1990–94	1995–99	2000–04	2005–07
Wted. ave. of covered products	**−7.0**	**1.8**	7.8	8.5	12.3	8.8	4.6	5.4	5.7	4.4	2.6	0.0	0.0
Domestic market support	na	na	1.4	1.6	2.5	1.0	0.8	0.9	0.5	0.4	0.2	0.0	0.0
Border market support	na	na	6.5	7.0	9.8	7.8	3.9	4.6	5.2	4.0	2.5	0.0	0.0
Dispersion of covered products	7.4	12.2	17.3	21.3	36.1	54.0	27.9	16.9	12.2	10.9	5.8	0.4	0.4
% coverage (at undistorted prices)	91	84	82	86	87	84	85	86	75	82	80	80	80

Note: Weighted averages, with weights based on the unassisted value of production (actual figures back to 1966, and the average for 1966–69 for earlier years). Dispersion of NRAs is their standard deviation of the simple five-year average of the annual standard deviation around the weighted mean.

Source: Anderson, Lattimore, Lloyd and MacLaren (2008).

Table 4.3. Nominal rates of assistance to agricultural relative to non-agricultural industries in Australia, 1946 to 2007 (percent, for fiscal years starting 1 July).

	1946–49	1950–54	1955–59	1960–64	1965–69	1970–74	1975–79	1980–84	1985–89	1990–94	1995–99	2000–04	2005–07
Covered products	−7.0	1.8	7.8	8.5	12.3	8.8	4.6	5.4	5.7	4.4	2.6	0.0	0.0
Non-covered products	0.0	0.0	0.0	0.0	0.0	0.0	0.0	0.0	0.0	0.0	0.0	0.0	0.0
All agriculture (excl. NPS)	−6.4	1.5	6.3	7.4	10.7	7.6	3.9	4.6	4.4	3.7	2.1	0.0	0.0
All importables	na	na	3.8	4.5	4.9	7.4	4.9	3.5	1.2	0.8	0.2	0.0	0.1
All exportables	na	na	5.7	6.4	9.3	7.0	3.3	4.2	4.8	4.3	2.6	0.0	0.0
All nontradables	na	na	31.4	41.6	78.1	25.3	19.5	24.2	12.2	1.8	0.2	0.0	0.0
TBI	na	na	0.02	0.02	0.04	0.00	−0.02	0.01	0.04	0.03	0.02	0.00	0.00
Non-product specific (NPS)	0.6	1.2	1.8	2.1	2.0	2.1	1.4	1.1	0.9	0.7	0.8	0.5	2.2
Inputs	na	na	na	na	na	na	1.2	0.7	2.0	3.0	3.3	2.8	2.8
Other	na	na	na	na	na	na	1.4	1.1	−1.1	−2.3	−2.5	−2.3	−0.6
All agriculture (incl. NPS)	−5.7	2.7	8.1	9.5	12.7	9.4	5.3	5.8	5.3	4.4	2.9	0.5	2.2
Decoupled payments	0.0	0.0	0.0	0.0	0.0	0.0	0.0	0.9	1.4	1.2	1.2	2.3	2.6
All agri. (incl. NPS & dec)	−5.7	2.7	8.1	9.5	12.7	9.4	5.4	6.6	6.6	5.6	4.1	2.8	4.8
All ag tradables (inc NPS)	−5.9	2.3	7.3	8.4	10.9	8.9	4.9	5.2	5.1	4.5	3.0	0.5	0.2
All nonag tradables	28.0	23.5	19.6	20.7	20.7	16.8	12.0	11.1	8.2	5.3	2.6	2.0	2.0
RRA	−26.3	−17.1	−10.3	−10.2	−8.2	−6.8	−6.4	−5.3	−2.9	−0.7	0.4	−1.5	−1.8

Notes:
[1] Before including Non-Product Specific (NPS) assistance.
[2] Total of assistance to primary factors and intermediate inputs divided to total value of primary agriculture production at undistorted prices (%).
[3] The Relative Rate of Assistance, RRA $= 100[(1 + \text{NRAag}^t/100)/(1 + \text{NRAnonag}^t/100) - 1]$, where NRAag^t and NRAnonag^t are the average percentage NRAs for the tradables parts of the agricultural and non-agricultural sectors, respectively.

Source: Anderson, Lattimore, Lloyd and MacLaren (2008).

The fourth row of Table 4.3 includes "non-product-specific" assistance (including all assistance via factor and intermediate input markets, even though some of that is in fact product specific), estimates of which are taken from the Productivity Commission for the period from 1970. We assume them to have been 1.8 percent of the gross value of farm production in 1969, 2 percent in 1960, 0.5 percent in 1946, with linear interpolations between those years.

4.4. NRA Estimates and the Evolution of Policies

In addition to reporting the NRA estimates, this section provides a brief history of policies up to the early 1970s and then of changes thereafter, particularly when the reforms accelerated in the mid-1980s. As there were relatively few agricultural subsidies or farm import barriers (other than quarantine restrictions) through most of the past six decades, the story is more about the *indirect* anti-agricultural bias that resulted from the protection of manufacturing. Nonetheless, coverage of policies that directly distorted various agricultural markets post-World War II is included.

4.4.1. *Before the early 1970s*

The long history of industrial protectionism has its roots from before the Australian Federation in 1901. Tariff revenue in the first decade of federation accounted for one-fifth of government revenue. That is very high for what at the time was one of the world's highest-income economies, as that share typically falls as per capita income rises. It is twice that of the Nordic countries, for example, even though their per capita incomes were barely half of Australia's (Mitchell, 2003a,c). Tariffs on manufactures rose steadily in the decades that followed, from a little less than 30 percent on average in the first quarter of the century to more than 50 percent in the next 20 years. They were supplemented by quantitative import restrictions first imposed in the late 1930s as "wartime measures", and by import licences after World War II. They rose even further in the 1960s when they substituted import licences as the latter were mostly removed in 1960 (with minor exceptions).

This trend during the 1950s and 1960s contrasted strongly with what other high-income countries were doing, which was lowering tariffs on manufactures as part of multilateral trade negotiations under the General Agreement on Tariffs and Trade (GATT).[7] Hence, by the early 1970s, Australia's average manufacturing tariff exceeded that of most other OECD countries (Anderson and Garnaut, 1987).

Meanwhile, the government intervened in numerous markets for farm products, but the subsidies and protection they provided to agricultural industries were only a modest offset to the indirect disincentives caused by the manufacturing protection. In the immediate post-World War II period, Australia's agricultural programs were directly taxing the farm sector. Most were removed by the end of the Korean War, when farmers were enjoying a boom in export prices that spurred the highest inflation in Australia since the gold-rush era in the 1850s. Farm assistance then rose gradually and by the end of the 1960s the nominal rate of assistance averaged 17 percent. The standard deviation of agricultural NRAs rose even more than the mean, indicating increasing misallocation of resources within the agricultural sector (second to last row of Table 4.2).

A striking feature of the agricultural assistance was that it applied to export industries almost as much as to import-competing ones (Fig. 4.4). Assisted export industries in Australia included wheat, manufactured dairy products, sugar and dried vine fruit. The schemes often contained so-called home consumption price schemes whereby domestic consumers were forced to pay more than the export price (Sieper, 1982; Edwards, 2006). Those schemes, which required the pooling of domestic and export returns, could only be implemented with the support of Australia's state governments. Other policy measures included fertiliser and fuel subsidies, income tax incentives, rural credit measures, involvement in and subsidies for agricultural research and extension, and public investment in land and water development

---

[7]The GATT came into effect in 1948. Even though Australia was a founding signatory, it chose not to join the commitments to cut manufacturing tariffs, claiming (disingenuously) that it was still a developing country, but also out of frustration with the unwillingness of other GATT contracting parties to commit to lowering their agricultural protection rates (Arndt, 1965; Snape, 1984; Anderson, 1999; Capling, 2001).

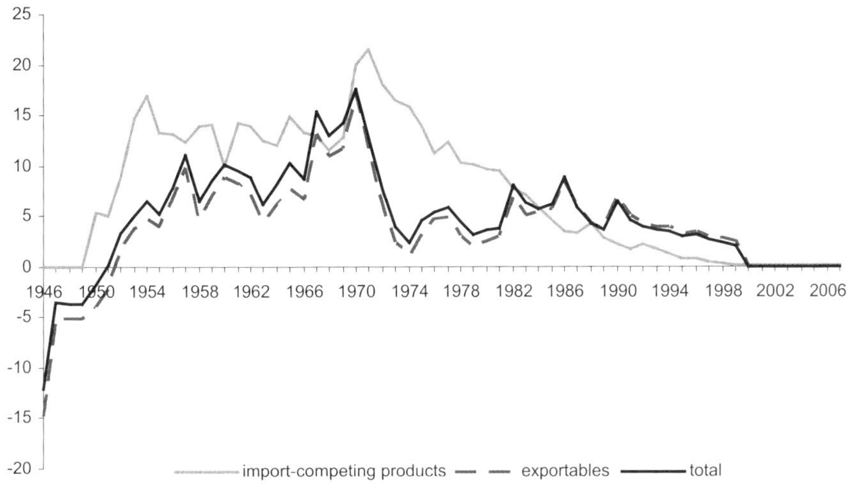

Fig. 4.4. Nominal rates of assistance to exportable, import-competing and all agricultural industries, Australia, 1946–47 to 2007 (percent).
Note: The total NRA can be above both the exportable and importable averages because assistance to non-tradables (e.g., eggs) and non-product-specific assistance are also included.
Source: Anderson, Lattimore, Lloyd and MacLaren (2008).

and rural infrastructure. But combined, all those non-product-specific measures added the equivalent of no more than 2 percent to Australian farmers' gross income as of the early 1970s (row 4 of Table 4.3).

The net effect of both farm and non-farm policies on agricultural incentives is summarised as the Relative Rate of Assistance (RRA) in Table 4.3 and Fig. 4.5. In the 1940s the negative effect on incentives from agricultural policies was trivial compared with that from non-agricultural ones, mostly import protection for manufacturers. Together those policies effectively reduced farmers' gross returns by around 40 percent in the mid-1940s (Fig. 4.5). Price stabilisation and other agricultural policies gradually provided direct assistance to Australian farmers over the 1950s and 1960s when manufacturing protection remained steady, such that the RRA went from −26 percent during 1946–49 to just under −10 percent by 1965–69. Of that change, about two-thirds resulted from changes in non-agricultural policies and only one-third from changes in direct assistance to farmers.

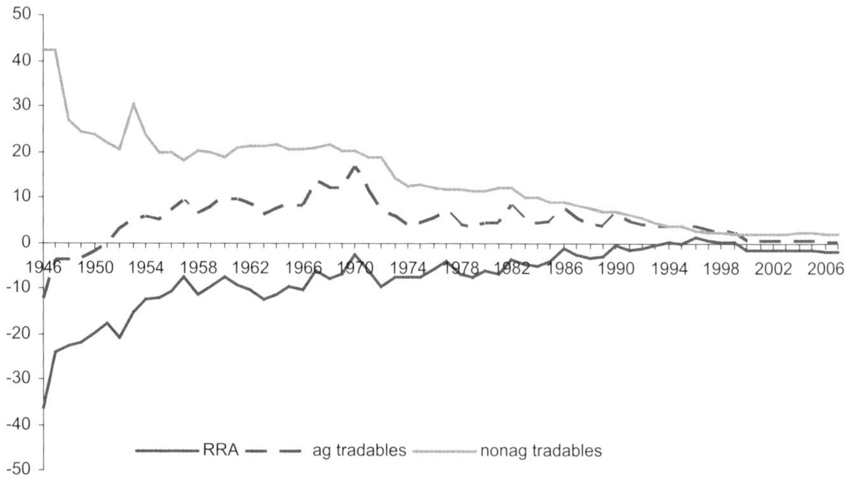

Fig. 4.5. Nominal rates of assistance to manufacturing, all non-agricultural tradables, all agricultural tradable industries, and relative rate of assistance, Australia, 1946–47 to 2004–05 (percent).
Note: The RRA is defined as $100^*[(100 + NRAag^t)/(100 + NRAnonag^t) - 1]$.
Source: Anderson, Lattimore, Lloyd and MacLaren (2008).

Meanwhile, by the late 1960s the home consumption price schemes were imposing tax equivalents of over 100 percent on Australian consumers of butter, cheese, sugar and eggs (Lloyd, 1973, Table 4.10.6).

4.4.2. *Reforms from the early 1970s*

Disenchantment with Australia's interventionist trade and related economic policies gradually spread in the 1960s, but tariff reductions did not begin until the 1970s. A 25 percent across-the-board cut in July 1973, preceded by some minor cuts in 1970–71, started the reform process. Apart from temporary reversals for cars and textiles, the process was accelerated in the 1980s and continued through the 1990s. Over those three decades the average nominal rate of assistance to Australian manufacturing fell from 23 to 3 percent, and the effective rate from 36 to 5 percent. In the 1990s alone, both the mean and the standard deviation of Australia's import tariffs on goods halved. This brought the average tariff for manufactures down to 4.2 percent in 1999.[8] The only manufacturers with significant tariff protection now are motor vehicles and parts, and textiles, clothing and footwear. Excluding them, the average effective rate of assistance to Australian manufacturing is now less than 3 percent (Productivity Commission, 2000a).[9]

Australia's agricultural subsidies and regulatory interventions have also been virtually eliminated over those 35 years. The average nominal rate of assistance to the farm sector fell from 16 percent in the early 1970s to less than 2 percent this decade, and the standard deviation has fallen from almost 60 percent to less than 1 percent. The process was piecemeal and gradual,[10] often involving a series of partial steps, but it was persistent. It began in 1972 with partial reforms to manufacturing milk and then two to four years later with cotton and tobacco, while it took another decade before supports for rice and eggs began to be dismantled, and almost a further decade for cuts to grape industry assistance. It was not without at least one significant reversion, with the introduction of the reserve price scheme for wool in 1973 that took until the early 1990s to unravel.[11]

---

[8]This average is still higher than for other OECD countries (World Bank, 2006), and Australia's WTO-bound tariffs average more than twice the applied rates. However, Australia uses non-tariff import barriers less frequently than other OECD countries, apart perhaps from anti-dumping duties (Productivity Commission, 2000a, 2000b, 2004).

[9]Tariffs on motor vehicle imports fell from 40 to 15 percent over the 1990s and were cut again to 10 percent in 2005; for clothing the decline over the 1990s was from 55 to 25 percent, and for footwear from 45 to 15 percent, with cuts to 17.5 and 10 percent in 2005, respectively. Further cuts, to as little as 5 percent, are scheduled for 2010 (Productivity Commission, 2000a, Table 4.4.4).

[10]By contrast, the reductions in manufacturing protection were more systematic: the 1973 across-the-board tariff cut, a Tariff Review program begun in 1971 by the Tariff Board and subsequently conducted by its successors (the Industries Assistance/Industry/Productivity Commission), and the pre-announced phased reductions in tariffs on textiles, clothing and footwear and motor vehicles and parts from 1988.

[11]The wool price stabilisation scheme operated conservatively until 1987, when the government transferred to growers the power to set the reserve price. Growers promptly raised that reserve price — which operated on the world market — by 71 percent. Predictably this encouraged growers to expand wool production and international buyers to reduce purchases (since the Australian Wool Corporation would then

Just two farm groups were still benefiting significantly from government programs in the latter 1990s: tobacco and milk producers, each with an NRA of more than 20 percent in 1997. Deregulation of tobacco marketing arrangements began in 1995 and was completed in 2000, bringing effective assistance to tobacco-growing down from 30 to 2 percent over that period. From 1 July 2000, the remaining impediments to a free domestic market in fluid milk began to be dismantled. An untied, one-off grant (providing a one-off total of around $1.94 billion or $170,000 per dairy farm) has been paid to dairy farmers as compensation, funded by a consumer levy on fresh milk at the retail level over the eight years to 2008.[12]

Thus, distortionary government assistance to both manufacturing and agriculture, and hence the overall anti-trade and anti-agricultural biases, have now all but disappeared in Australia, after being in place for more than seven decades. In the past 35 years it was non-agricultural policy reforms that overwhelmingly contributed to the improvement of farmers' incentives, with the decline in manufacturing protection large enough to more than offset the decline in direct assistance to farmers from the late 1960s. Farmers have benefited also from reform to the service sectors. Banking, post and telecommunications, ports, higher education, health, and rail, air and sea transport have been opened up; there has been progressive outsourcing of many government services; and substantial reforms to competition policy and practice, including privatisation and the corporatisation and demonopolisation of numerous government enterprises, are well advanced.[13] Moreover, following

stockpile wool and thereby save the buyer the cost of storage). The scheme collapsed in 1991 and the AWC had to dispose of its 4.75 million bales, at some expense to the government and at great expense to woolgrowers (Richardson, 2001).

[12]Contrary to some pessimistic forecasts at the time, dairy output has continued to increase: production from those leaving the industry (17 percent of producers departed during the first three years) has been more than compensated by output and productivity improvements on remaining farms (Harris, 2005a,b). The retail price of milk fell after deregulation as the supermarkets were able to exercise buying power with the milk processors which, in turn, were able to exert downward pressure on the farm-gate price, which was no longer supported by State governments.

[13]In addition, a comprehensive program of review of government regulations at all levels in Australia has been under way since the mid-1990s, with the aim of reducing/

the floating in 1983 of the Australian dollar, foreign investment began to flow more freely. That complemented financial sector reform and contributed to foreign direct investment, equity and foreign currency transactions growing at several times the pace of GDP. Even labour markets that were previously highly unionised have undergone considerable reform. Households have gained substantially from these widespread reforms, including consumers of food who for the past decade have faced an average tax equivalent of just 2 percent on their food purchases (compared with the OECD average of between 23 and 36 percent over that period, measured at the farm-gate level; see OECD, 2006).

4.5. Prospects for Further Policy Reform

Notwithstanding the huge amount of reform over the past two decades, a number of important agricultural policy issues remain on the table, in particular in the resource and environmental areas. Three are mentioned briefly, by way of illustration.

The first involves food and agricultural import restrictions for the protection of plant, animal and human health. The economic protection of farmers from import competition has not been fully captured in the Productivity Commission's NRA estimates for Australia, especially for horticultural products. Some of that protection may well be warranted on externality grounds, but some (such as a complete ban on imports of certain fruits from all countries) may be excessive from a national welfare viewpoint. The Australian government is slowly examining whether various measures are excessively restrictive, but mainly in response to pressure from other WTO Members seeking greater market access. Typically, consumer costs are not included in such assessments,

---

removing regulations that unjustifiably impede economic activities (Productivity Commission, 2000b). For an independent assessment of Australia's domestic microeconomic reforms, see Forsyth (2000). Recent research on barriers to trade in a wide range of services in almost 40 countries found that services markets in Australia, relative to those in the other countries in the study, are now ranked as either very liberal (banking, distribution services, telecoms, engineering professional services) or at worst just moderately restrictive (other professional services, maritime services); see Productivity Commission (2000c, pp. 50–61).

nor are all the cheaper ways of reducing any costs associated with the importation of disease (James and Anderson, 1998).

Second, Australia so far has not allowed the commercial growing of genetically modified (GM) varieties of farm products, with the sole exceptions of cotton and carnations. While the national Office of the Gene Technology Regulator has approved the commercial growing of GM canola, state governments have placed moratoriums on plantings. GM food can be sold only if strict labelling standards are adhered to (FSANZ, 2007). These restrictions may or may not be in the economy's and consumers' interests, depending on their impact on market access abroad for Australian farm products and on human health and the environment at home (Anderson and Jackson, 2005), but emotion has played more of a role at the state level in formulating these policies than has sound technical and economic analysis in the growing of GM crops.

Third, environmental and resource policies have become very important in Australian agriculture. Within this area, water policy was already becoming a major economic and political issue but was brought to a head in Australia during 2006 following the country's worst recorded drought. There has been substantial reform in recent years, but much remains to be done to make the most of this resource, particularly in rural Australia where more than two-thirds of it is used. More efficient pricing of that resource may lead to substantial reallocations of resources within the agricultural sector, with possible declines in Australian production of cotton, rice and milk as horticultural industries (and urban areas) bid away water from those farmers.[14]

The remaining big frontier for policy reform that would boost farm incomes in Australia is the dismantling of agricultural subsidies and import protection abroad. A successful conclusion to the Doha Round negotiations in the WTO provides the greatest promise for achieving that outcome: on a per capita basis, Australians — especially their farmers — would be among the major beneficiaries of a significant agricultural reform outcome from that round. According to

[14]The impact of past under-pricing of water for agriculture on farm returns has not been incorporated in the NRA estimates reported in this paper. Nor does the OECD include it in its PSE calculations.

global Linkage Model results reported in Anderson, Martin and van der Mensbrugghe (2006, Table 13), removing all merchandise trade barriers and agricultural subsidies globally would raise agricultural value added or net farm incomes in Australia and New Zealand by 26 percent. Even using the GTAP Model, whose supply response elasticities are lower than in Linkage, a similar study by Anderson and Valenzuela (2007, Table 4) reports agricultural value added in Australia and New Zealand would rise by 15 percent, compared with a rise of just 2 percent in value added in non-agricultural industries. Because milk is the most protected farm product abroad, the gains in Australia would be somewhat less than in New Zealand, and the impact within rural Australia is heavily skewed to dairy-intensive locations (Anderson, Giesecke and Valenzuela, 2010).

4.6. Comparison with Other High-Income Countries

How does the overall inter-sectoral distortions pattern that has evolved in Australia contrast with that in other high-income countries? Comparable new estimates of the relative rate of assistance are now available for all the other major high-income countries from 1955. All have followed a similar path to Australia's in the sense of raising their relative rates of assistance to farmers as their national incomes have risen, but — except for New Zealand — from higher bases and to higher levels than Australia, and more so the weaker their comparative advantage in agriculture.[15]

By contrast, in the United States the RRA averaged around zero between 1955 and 1975, grew to about 4 percent for the next 20 years, and then, since the 1996 Farm Bill, has been about half that but still

[15] New Zealand assistance to non-agricultural producers of tradables (mostly manufacturers) has been even higher than in Australia since 1955, while assistance to farmers has been less except for a period of high farm subsidies from 1975 to 1989. New Zealand's RRA is lower than Australia's except in the 1980s but, like Australia, New Zealand has virtually completely reformed its sectoral assistance policies affecting tradables, and has had an RRA close to zero since 2000 (Anderson *et al.*, 2008).

positive. In Western Europe, the advent of the Common Agricultural Policy, together with similar national support programs in countries prior to their joining the European Union or its predecessors, led to its already high RRA in the latter 1950s (around 20–35 percent) more than doubling in the early 1960s. It remained high through the rest of the 20th century. Because of the use of variable import levies and export restitutions aimed at stabilising domestic food prices, it fluctuated inversely with international prices (so was lower in the mid-1970s and early and late 1980s, and peaked in the mid-1980s when international food prices reached their lowest in real terms for the century). In Japan, the RRA rose from less than 40 percent before the mid-1960s to above 60 percent a decade or so later and to more than 100 percent from the mid-1980s.

Figure 4.6 summarises these estimates, showing that the RRA tends to be higher not only with higher per capita income but also with

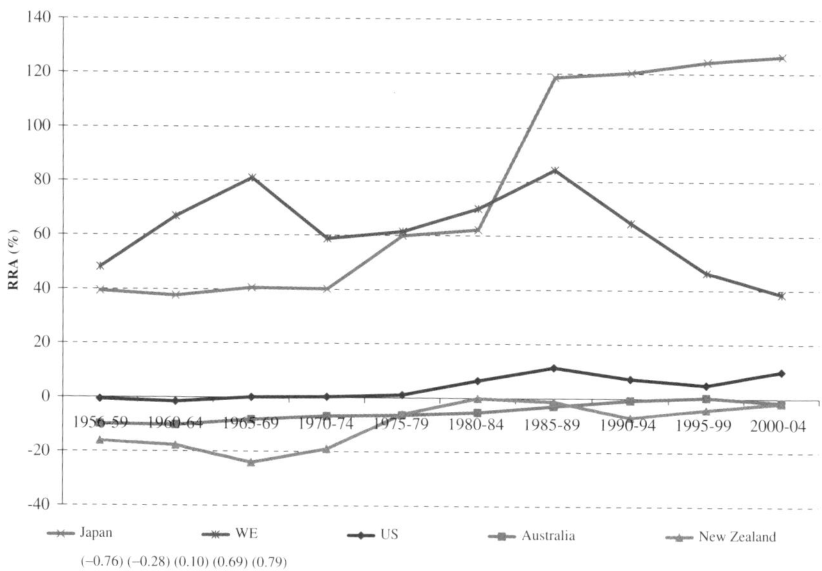

Fig. 4.6. Relative rates of assistance to agriculture, Australia and other high-income countries, 1956 to 2004.
Note: The RRA is defined as $100^*[(100 + \text{NRAag}^t)/(100 + \text{NRAnonag}^t) - 1]$.
Sources: Anderson, Lattimore, Lloyd and MacLaren (2008), Gardner (2008), Honma and Hayami (2008), Josling (2008).

weaker agricultural comparative advantage. While there is a hint of a structural break to the growth of agricultural protection around the time of the Uruguay Round Agreement on Agriculture coming into force in 1995, no other OECD country except New Zealand has made as dramatic a reduction in agricultural assistance — in terms of driving the RRA towards zero — as Australia.

4.7. Conclusion

Even without undertaking historical economy-wide modelling, the results presented above provide some clear answers to the empirical questions posed at the start of this chapter. First, the anti-trade and anti-primary sector biases in Australia's industry assistance policies were very extensive during the first 25 post-war years. The disincentives this generated for farmers have been falling progressively every half decade since the 1940s, however, and are now virtually zero (third to last row of Table 4.3).

Second, the timing of cuts to sectoral assistance, which gradually reduced those biases over the long term, were such that there were nonetheless numerous reversals in the relative rate of assistance for short periods when farm assistance cuts preceded cuts in manufacturing tariffs (bottom line in Fig. 4.5).

Third, the variation of industry assistance rates within the agricultural sector rose between the 1950s and the 1970s, when the standard deviation rose from less than three times to more than six times the weighted mean. That increase in variance probably reduced the second-best welfare contribution of those programs in their offsetting of manufacturing assistance during that period. However, the variation has progressively fallen since the 1970s and is now, like the mean, virtually zero (second last row of Table 4.2).

Fourth, the structure of assistance within the agricultural sector has not been as biased against the export industries as it has in many other countries. True, the average NRA for exportables was below that of import-competing farm industries every half decade from World War II to the early 1980s. However, several major export industries (rice, sugar, cotton, grapes) enjoyed assistance rates above the sectoral average and, after the early 1980s, exporters enjoyed a higher average rate of assistance than import-competing farm industries (Table 4.2). Despite this, the reforms were accompanied by a marked increase in the export orientation of numerous farm industries, as reflected in Fig. 4.3.

Fifth, Australia (along with New Zealand) is unusual in having cut its agricultural and trade policies to the point of virtually zero nominal and relative rates of assistance. This case study thus shows that removing even the largest and longest-lasting farm subsidies is politically possible. Even where that was done by providing generous adjustment assistance, such transition support was time-bound. Dairy adjustment assistance was able to be financed simply by delaying the rewards to domestic consumers and thereby creating a gap between the producer and consumer price, rather than through outlays from (and hence resistance by) the treasury (see Harris, 2005b).

This case study offers hope that good policy analysis and advisory institutions can alter the political economy sufficiently to allow removal of price distortions. More than that, it illustrates the growth dividend that can come from reforming such policies. Having now dismantled virtually all its import protection and agricultural subsidy policies, and having undertaken major domestic macro- and microeconomic reforms over more than two decades, the fruits of that undertaking are being reaped, including in the form of farm productivity growth.

It needs to be borne in mind that Australian farmers have not been immune from the standard "small farm problem" that requires them to "get big or get out" as the economy develops. It is true that their farm sizes were large relative to those in most other market economies in the early post-World War II years, and that the "wool boom" of the early 1950s provided massive incomes for woolgrowers. Nonetheless, as wages grew elsewhere in the economy, the need to adjust was felt strongly in Australia just as elsewhere; and it manifested itself in the same way, that is, with farmers funding agricultural research and adapting and adopting as appropriate the new technologies it generated, and with the number of farms and farmers declining steadily to lower the labour intensity of the sector even as output expanded.

Several aspects of Australia's reform success are worth underlining. One is that it helps if assistance to non-agricultural sectors is cut at the same time. In Australia those other micro- and macroeconomic reforms made it easier for farmers to adjust and raise their productivity. This is relevant for those many developing countries that still have industrial protection and behind-the-border restrictions on domestic non-farm market activities. For other high-income countries, where manufacturing protection rates are already low and the macro economy is well managed, the reduction of high agricultural supports would be more painful unless coupled with adjustment assistance measures.

Second, adjustment to cuts in agricultural assistance is easier the greater the heterogeneity within the agricultural sector. This can take at least two forms. Heterogeneity in rates of industry assistance within the sector, as captured by the standard deviation of farm industry NRAs shown near the bottom of Table 4.2, ensures that as high rates of assistance are lowered, resources will find it profitable to move to lightly assisted farm industries. Such transfers are far easier than transferring mobile resources to other sectors, and involve much less reduction in the value of sector-specific assets, particularly farm land. For Australia, the standard deviation was very high when the cuts in farm assistance began in the early 1970s, whereas for a country such as Norway, where the support levels are very similar across farm industries (OECD, 2006), there would be much less scope for adjustment within the sector.

The other form of heterogeneity has to do with firm efficiency *within* each industry. If some farmers are much more efficient than others, then a cut in assistance to that industry typically leads to the less efficient being bought out by the more efficient (who often are also the more export-oriented). The productivity effects of that could be substantial (Melitz, 2003; Baldwin, 2005; Gopinath, Sheldon and Echeverria, 2007). In the case of the Australian dairy industry, that force indeed seems to have been powerful (Harris, 2005a), and it may help to explain the rapid rise since the 1980s in the share of production exported by a number of Australia's agricultural industries, including beef, canola, wine and cotton (Fig. 4.3).

The third important aspect of Australia's reform success has to do with the scope and quality of public institutions that can facilitate the development of policy advice, provide policy coordination and administer policy changes. Australia's legal, accounting and media systems ensure relatively transparent and informed policy debate, and assist in resolving a host of firm-level complications that arise during policy implementation. The lesson for those wishing to emulate the Australian reform experience, especially in a developing country context, is to not underestimate the importance of long-term investments in the development of strong, pro-market, transparent, corruption-free institutions.

References

ABARE (2008). *Australian Commodities Statistics 2008*. www.abare.gov.au [15 December 2008].

Anderson, K (1999). The WTO agenda for the new millennium. *Economic Record*, 75(228), 77–88.

Anderson, K (2001). Australia in the international economy. In *Reshaping Australia's Economy: Growth with Equity and Sustainability*, J Nieuwenhuysen, PJ Lloyd and M Mead (eds.), pp. 33–49. Cambridge and New York: Cambridge University Press.

Anderson, K (ed.) (2009). *Distortions to Agricultural Incentives: A Global Perspective, 1955–2007*. London: Palgrave Macmillan and Washington DC: World Bank.

Anderson, K and C Findlay (1995). Policies affecting primary sectors. In *Australia's Trade Policies*, R Pomfret (ed.), pp. 74–90. London, Melbourne and New York: Oxford University Press.

Anderson, K and R Garnaut (1987). *Australian Protectionism: Extent, Causes and Effects*. Boston, London and Sydney: Allen and Unwin.

Anderson, K, J Giesecke and E Valenzuela (2010). How would global trade liberalization affect rural and regional incomes in Australia? *Australian Journal of Agricultural and Resource Economics*, 54 (forthcoming).

Anderson, K and LA Jackson (2005). GM crop technology and trade restraints: Economic implications for Australia and New Zealand. *Australian Journal of Agricultural and Resource Economics*, 49(3), 263–281.

Anderson, K, R Lattimore, P Lloyd and D MacLaren (2008). Distortions to agricultural incentives in Australia and New Zealand. Agricultural Distortions Working Paper 09, September. Washington DC: World Bank. Since published (without its Appendix) in K Anderson (ed.) (2009). *Distortions to Agricultural Incentives: A Global Perspective, 1955–2007*, pp. 221–256. London: Palgrave Macmillan and Washington DC: World Bank.

Anderson, K, PJ Lloyd and D MacLaren (2007). Distortions to agricultural incentives in Australia since World War II. *Economic Record*, 83(263), 461–482.

Anderson, K, W Martin and D van der Mensbrugghe (2006). Distortions to world trade: Impacts on agricultural markets and incomes. *Review of Agricultural Economics*, 28(2), 168–194.

Anderson, K and E Valenzuela (2007). Do global trade distortions still harm developing country farmers? *Review of World Economics/Weltwirtschaftliches Archiv*, 143(1), 108–139.

Arndt, HW (1965). Australia — developed, developing or midway? *Economic Record*, 41(95), 418–440.

Baldwin, RE (2005). Heterogeneous firms and trade: Testable and untestable properties of the Melitz Model. NBER Working Paper 11471, National Bureau of Economic Research, Cambridge MA.

Bora, B and R Pomfret (1995). Policies affecting manufacturing. In *Australia's Trade Policies*, R Pomfret (ed.), pp. 91–111. Melbourne: Oxford University Press.

Butlin, NG (1962). *Australian Domestic Product, Investment and Foreign Borrowing, 1861–1938/39*. Cambridge: Cambridge University Press.

Capling, A (2001). *Australia and the Global Trade System: From Havana to Seattle*. Cambridge: Cambridge University Press.

Crawford, JG (1968). *Australian Trade Policy, 1942–66: A Documentary History*. Canberra: ANU Press.

Doran, CR (1984). An historical perspective on mining and economic change. In *The Minerals Sector and the Australian Economy*, LH Cook and MG Porter (eds.), pp. 55–84. Boston, London and Sydney: Allen and Unwin.

Edwards, GW (2006). Fifty years of agricultural policy. Presented at the 50th Annual Conference of the Australian Agriculture and Resource Economics Society, Sydney, 8–10 February.

Forsyth, P (2000). Microeconomic policies and structural change. In *The Australian Economy in the 1990s*, D Gruen and S Shrestha (eds.), pp. 235–267. Sydney: Reserve Bank of Australia.

FSANZ (2007). Assessing the safety of new foods and technologies. Canberra: Food Standards Australia New Zealand. www.foodstandards.gov.au/foodmatters/gmfoods/assessingthesafetyof387.cfm [15 December 2008].

Gardner, B (2008). Distortions to agricultural incentives in the United States and Canada. Agricultural Distortions Working Paper 62. Washington DC: World Bank. September. Since published (without its Appendix) in K Anderson (ed.) (2009). *Distortions to Agricultural Incentives: A Global Perspective, 1955–2007*, pp. 177–220. London: Palgrave Macmillan and Washington DC: World Bank.

Gopinath, M, I Sheldon and R Echeverria (2007). Firm heterogeneity and international trade: Implications for agricultural and food industries. IATRC Trade Policy Issues Paper #5, March. www.iatrcweb.org [15 December 2008].

Groenewegen, PD (1983). Australian taxation policy. In *Surveys of Australian Economics*, Vol. 3, FH Gruen (ed.), pp. 191–249. London and Sydney: Allen and Unwin.

Gruen, FH (1968). Welfare economics, the theory of the second best, and Australian agricultural policy. Mimeo, Monash University, Clayton, Vic.

Harris, D (2005a). *Industry Adjustment to Policy Reform: A Case Study of the Australian Dairy Industry*, RIRDC Publication No. 05/110, Canberra: Rural Industries Research and Development Corporation.

Harris, D (2005b). *Rural Industry Adjustment to Trade Related Policy Reform*, RIRDC Publication No. 05/173, Canberra: Rural Industries Research and Development Corporation, December.

Harris, SF (1964). Some measures of levels of protection in Australia's rural industries. *Australian Journal of Agricultural Economics*, 8(3), 124–144.

Harris, SF (1975). Tariff compensation: Sufficient justification for protection to Australian agriculture? *Australian Journal of Agricultural Economics*, 19(3), 131–145.

Harris, SF, JG Crawford, FH Gruen and N Honan (1974). *The Principles of Rural Policy in Australia: A Discussion Paper*. Canberra: Australian Government Publishing Service.

Honma, M and Y Hayami (2008). Distortions to agricultural incentives in Japan, Korea and Taiwan. Agricultural Distortions Working Paper 35. Washington DC: World Bank. September. Since published (without its Appendix) in K Anderson (ed.) (2009). *Distortions to Agricultural Incentives: A Global Perspective, 1955–2007*, pp. 67–114. London: Palgrave Macmillan and Washington DC: World Bank.

Industries Assistance Commission (1976). *Assistance to Manufacturing Industries in Australia 1968–69 to 1973–74*. Industries Assistance Commission, Canberra.

Industry Commission (1995). *Assistance to Agricultural and Manufacturing Industries*. Canberra: Industry Commission.

James, S and K Anderson (1998). On the need for more economic assessment of quarantine/SPS policies. *Australian Journal of Agricultural and Resource Economics*, 42(4), 525–544.

Josling, T (2008). Distortions to agricultural incentives in Western Europe. Agricultural Distortions Working Paper 61. Washington DC: World Bank. September. Since published (without its Appendix) in K Anderson (ed.) (2009). *Distortions to Agricultural Incentives: A Global Perspective, 1955–2007*, pp. 115–176. London: Palgrave Macmillan and Washington DC: World Bank.

Lerner, AP (1936). The symmetry between import and export taxes. *Economica*, 3(11), 306–313.

Lloyd, PJ (1973). *Non-tariff Distortions of Australian Trade*. Canberra: Australian National University Press.

Lloyd, PJ (1975). Tariff compensation: An undesirable policy. *Australian Journal of Agricultural Economics*, 19(3), 146–153.

Lloyd, PJ (2008). 100 Years of tariff protection in Australia. *Australian Economic History Review*, 48(2), 99–145.

Melitz, M (2003). The impact of trade on intra-industry reallocations and aggregate industry productivity. *Econometrica*, 71(6), 1695–1725.

Mitchell, BR (2003a). *International Historical Statistics 1750 to 2000: Europe*, 5th edition. Cambridge: Cambridge University Press.

Mitchell, BR (2003b). *International Historical Statistics 1750 to 2000: The Americas*, 5th edition. Cambridge: Cambridge University Press.

Mitchell, BR (2003c). *International Historical Statistics 1750 to 2000: Africa, Asia and Oceania*, 5th edition. Cambridge: Cambridge University Press.

Moffatt, G (1962). The Australia import licencing system: 1952–1960. *Australian Economic Papers*, 1(1), 119–138.

Moffatt, G (1970). *Import Control and Industrialization.* Melbourne: Melbourne University Press.

OECD (2006). *Agricultural Policies in OECD Countries: Monitoring and Evaluation 2005.* Paris: Organization for Economic Cooperation and Development.

Productivity Commission (2000a). *Review of Australia's General Tariff Arrangements.* Canberra: Productivity Commission.

Productivity Commission (2000b). *Regulation and its Review 1999–00.* Canberra: Productivity Commission.

Productivity Commission (2000c). *Trade and Assistance Review 1999–2000.* Canberra: Productivity Commission.

Productivity Commission (2003). *From Industry Assistance to Productivity: 30 Years of 'the Commission'.* Canberra: Productivity Commission.

Productivity Commission (2004). *Trade and Assistance Review 2003–04.* Canberra: Productivity Commission.

Richardson, B (2001). The politics and economics of wool marketing, 1950–2000. *Australian Journal of Agricultural and Resource Economics*, 45(1), 95–115.

Sieper, E (1982). *Rationalising Rustic Regulation.* Sydney: Centre for Independent Studies.

Snape, RH (1984). Australia's relations with GATT. *Economic Record*, 60(168), 16–27.

Vousden, N (1990). *The Economics of Trade Protection.* Cambridge and New York: Cambridge University Press.

Warr, PG (1978). The case against tariff compensation. *Australian Journal of Agricultural Economics*, 22(2), 85–98.

World Bank (2000). *Global Commodity Markets: A Comprehensive Review of Price Forecasts.* Washington DC: World Bank.

World Bank (2006). *World Development Indicators.* Washington DC: World Bank.

Chapter 5

India and the Global Demand for Commodities: Is there an Elephant in the Room?*

Michael Francis and Corinne Luu†

5.1. Introduction

India is big: on the basis of purchasing power parity (PPP), India is the fourth largest economy in the world, after the United States, China and Japan. India has been growing at a rapid clip, averaging 8.6 percent growth over the past five years.[1] It is also a significant contributor to world growth, adding slightly less than half a percentage point to the world growth of 4.9 percent in 2007.[2] India now accounts for 4.6 percent of world GDP and 15.7 percent of Asia's GDP.[3] It also

*We have benefitted from comments and suggestions from Jocelyn Jacob and Larry Schembri. The views expressed in this paper are those of the authors.
†International Department, Bank of Canada. Correspondence to: mfrancis@ bankofcanada.ca
[1]This is based on a PPP measurement of GDP growth (IMF, 2008).
[2]In 1980, India contributed 0.08 percentage points to world growth of 2.0 percent (IMF, 2008).
[3]India made up 2.2 percent of world GDP and 13.1 percent of Asian GDP in 1980. Asia is defined here as Bangladesh, Bhutan, Cambodia, China, Fiji, Hong Kong SAR, India, Indonesia, Japan, Kiribati, Lao People's Democratic Republic, Malaysia, Maldives,

has a substantial population base, housing 17 percent of the world's population (World Bank, 2007). At first glance, these indicators would suggest that India's role in the world economy and in the global demand for commodities should be substantial. But India is different.

In this paper, we address why India is different and the implications this has had for its commodity demand since economic reforms commenced in the early 1990s. For instance, policies in India have had a distortionary impact on the expansion path of its economy, putting the service sector at the forefront and probably reducing India's demand for metals. Specific sectoral policies, such as its self-sufficiency policies in agriculture, have also altered India's demand for food commodities and its supplies of those commodities to international markets. Furthermore, India's trade policies have been restrictive and it continues to maintain high tariff rates and a relatively low share of trade in GDP.[4] As a result, unlike China and the four Asian Tigers, India's growth is largely driven by domestic demand, with net exports adding very little, and at times negatively, to overall growth. On the whole, these policies have probably affected India's demand for commodities, either (i) directly, by changing the relative prices paid for commodities and by altering India's domestic and international supplies, or (ii) indirectly, by distorting the sectoral composition of India's growth. Therefore, while India is large, its impact on world commodity demand has been distorted and constrained by policy.

This paper assesses India's impact on world markets for food and non-food (metals and energy) commodities. With the exception of energy, it appears that India has had only a modest impact on international commodity demand, in part because of the distortionary role of policy. However, recent trade data point to a more substantive

---

Myanmar, Nepal, Pakistan, Papua New Guinea, the Philippines, Samoa, Singapore, the Solomon Islands, South Korea, Sri Lanka, Thailand, Tonga, Vanuatu and Vietnam.

[4]For example, based on an openness measure defined as the sum of exports and imports of goods and services as a percentage of GDP, India is relatively closed at 45 percent in 2005, compared with 69 percent, 82 percent and 63 percent for China, Korea and Indonesia, respectively (World Bank, 2007). Furthermore, India's most favoured nation (MFN) tariff rates are relatively high, at an average 19.2 percent, compared with 9.9 percent, 12.1 percent and 6.9 percent for China, Korea and Indonesia, respectively (WTO, 2007).

role for India in world commodity demand since 2004, particularly for metals. Continued structural reforms could lead to a more important role for manufacturing in the Indian economy, potentially increasing its demand for metals and energy. The outlook for India's food demand will depend on several factors, including population growth, diet diversification and policy reform (e.g., initiatives to increase the production of non-cereal agricultural commodities, to better reflect average diets).[5] Therefore, while it appears that India's impact on international commodity markets so far has been smaller than expected, structural changes and demographic forces could lead to a more dramatic rise in India's demand for commodities.

This chapter is organised as follows: Section 5.2 provides an overview of India's pattern of economic growth and the resultant implications for India's commodity demand. Section 5.3 discusses the consequences of India's growth and domestic policies for commodity demand, focusing on India's external demand for metals (Section 3.1), energy commodities (Section 3.2) and food (Section 3.3). Section 5.4 provides a brief summary of the key findings of this chapter.

5.2. India is Big but its Growth is Different

To assess India's impact on global commodity demand, one must understand the underlying sources of growth in India that motivate its demand for commodities and its supplies to the international market. This section examines the composition of India's growth, since metals demand, for example, depends on the size of the industrial sector (and the intensity of metals production), as described further in Section 5.3.1.

India's pattern of development does not quite fit the typical pattern of modern economic growth as posited by Kuznets (1959). According to that view, manufacturing should become an engine of growth during the early stages of development as "surplus" labour is moved out of agriculture and into high-value-added industries, boosting the share of

[5] This change in agricultural production could lead to a reduction in cereals production, which would likely, in turn, reduce India's supplies of cereals to the international market.

manufacturing in total output.[6] In India, although the manufacturing sector did grow, its share in overall GDP has increased only marginally over the past 50 years (Fig. 5.1), and currently accounts for 16 percent of GDP (World Bank, 2007). Services, however, account for an increasing share of output, while the share of agriculture has declined. India's service sector grew by an average 8.0 percent 2000–2005, compared with a growth rate of 7.1 percent in the industrial sector, with the service sector accounting for 54.4 percent of GDP (World Bank, 2007). This pattern of development contrasts with other emerging market economies, such as China, whose growing manufacturing sector has been the main stimulus for economic growth.[7]

Figure 5.2 shows the predicted expansion path of the economy for a wide range of countries; the size of industry per capita is plotted on the horizontal axis and the size of other sectors (agriculture and services) per capita is plotted on the vertical axis from 1980 to 2005,

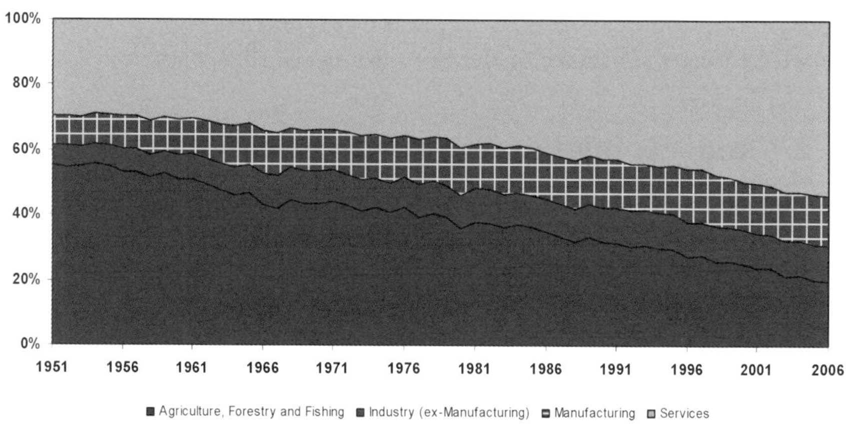

Fig. 5.1. Sectoral breakdown of India's nominal GDP.
Source: ISI Emerging Markets.

[6]Later, as GDP per capita increases, the share of the manufacturing sector in the GDP would eventually stabilise or begin to decline, as Chenery (1960) and Chenery and Taylor (1968) note, and the service sector share would likely rise.
[7]China's industrial sector grew by an average 10.5 percent in 2000–2005, and currently accounts for 47.5 percent of GDP. This compares to an average growth rate of 10.0 percent in the service sector, which accounts for 39.9 percent of GDP.

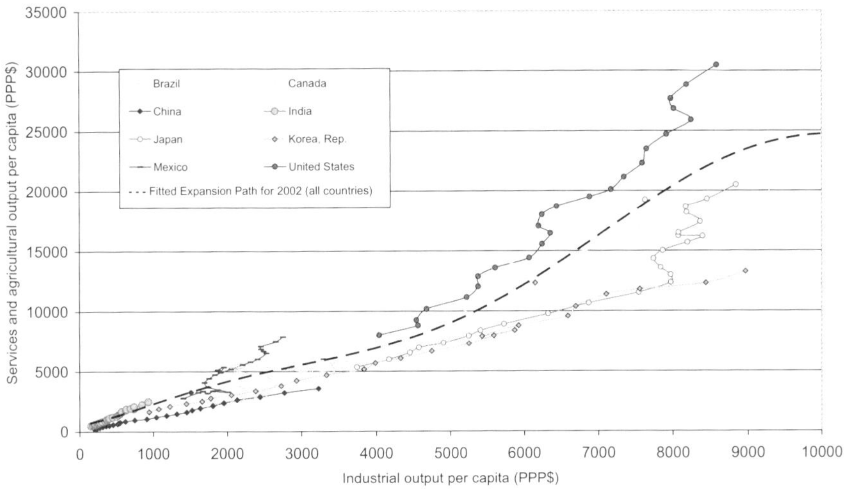

Fig. 5.2. Economic development and economic structure, 1980–2005.
Source: WDI; IMF (2008); Bank of Canada staff calculations.

with the dashed curve denoting the fitted expansion path.[8] According to Fig. 5.2, the share of industry in total output tends to rise until it reaches a per capita GDP of $10,200 (PPP$), after which other sectors of the economy (agriculture and services) outpace overall GDP growth, causing the industry share to fall.[9] From this figure it appears that while India is in its early development stage, its expansion path is consistent with what would be expected for a country with its per capita GDP, but with a slight bias towards agriculture and services. However, per capita GDP is not the only determinant of the expected share of industry in GDP. Economic theory, such as the Heckscher–Ohlin model, would suggest that the endowment of primary factors of production

[8]This is based on predicted values for 84 countries in 2002.

[9]At this point, per capita industrial output grows at the same rate as per capita GDP. An interesting feature of the data is that, over time, countries diverge from the fitted expansion path shown in Fig. 5.2. Economies such as China and Korea have tended to specialise in industry, while other economies, such as Mexico and Turkey, have tended to become more specialised in the non-industrial sectors (agriculture and services). One possible reason for this is trade liberalisation and specialisation according to comparative advantage.

also determines the pattern of production.[10] To account for this, we ran a simple cross-sectional ordinary least squares (OLS) regression that regressed the natural log of the value-added shares of agriculture, industry, manufacturing and services on per capita GDP, as well as country size (in square kilometres), population (all in logs) and an India dummy.

The results are provided in Table 5.1. India stands out, with a lower share of manufacturing and a higher share of services, in total

Table 5.1. Sectoral shares in total value added and India.[1]

	Agriculture[2]	Industry[3]	Manufacturing	Services
India dummy	0.05	−0.13	−0.43	0.22
	(0.14)	(0.09)	(0.13)***	(0.07)***
Ln per capita GDP	−0.76	0.12	0.21	0.13
	(0.05)***	(0.02)***	(0.04)***	(0.02)***
Ln size (sq. km)	0.12	0.07	−0.15	−0.04
	(0.06)**	(0.02)***	(0.04)***	(0.02)**
Ln population	−0.08	−0.01	0.25	0.01
	(0.05)	(0.02)	(0.04)***	(0.02)
R^2	0.78	0.25	0.37	0.37
Obs.	135	134	116	134

Notes:
1. Estimation involves a simple cross-sectional OLS regression for 2005. Dependent variables are in logs and robust standard errors are in parentheses. In general, 134 countries were used in the estimation, with the exception of manufacturing, which had 116 countries, and agriculture, which had 135 countries.
2. Dependent variables are in natural logs.
3. Industry includes mining, manufacturing, construction, electricity, water and gas.
*, ** and *** denote significance at the 10, 5 and 1 percent levels, respectively.

[10]For example, a country that has a relatively abundant supply of labour may specialise more heavily in labour-intensive manufacturing, and a country with a large land mass may produce more agricultural output as a share of total value added, since the price of the abundant factor input would be relatively low.

value added.[11] In particular, India's manufacturing sector is 35 percent smaller and its service sector 24 percent larger than would be expected.[12] To the extent that the service sector is less energy- and metals-intensive than manufacturing, India's impact on world commodity markets may be less than expected.

As a highly populated country, India is one of the largest consumers of commodities in the world, but it is also one of the poorest, with a relatively low per capita consumption for most food commodities (Table 5.2).[13] In the following section, we examine demand and supply factors that determine India's impact on the global commodity markets. In particular, we attempt to understand the extent to which India's metals, energy and food markets are driven by fundamental economic forces on the one hand, and the influence of domestic public policy on the other.

5.3. Metals

5.3.1. *India's demand for metals*

In general, the demand for non-food, non-energy commodities such as metals is derived from the process of transforming raw materials into goods for consumption and investment, which suggests that the demand for these commodities is proportional to the level of output in the economy. Thus, we posit that a country's commodity demand, C,

[11] This method is similar to that used by Kochhar *et al.* (2006), with updated PPP weights and data (however, our analysis includes the log of population, to control for a country's endowment of labour). The analysis included between 116 and 135 countries, depending on data availability. Performing the analysis for 2004, to allow for more data points, leaves the regression results largely unchanged.

[12] Agriculture is 4 percent larger than would be expected (Table 5.1); however, this result is statistically insignificant.

[13] This is the case for most commodities, with the exception of cereals, for which its share in world consumption is proportional to its share in world population.

Table 5.2. Shares of world population and commodity consumption.[1]

		Brazil	China	India	United States
Population		3%	22%	19%	5%
Food	Meat	6%	29%	2%	15%
		1.9[2]	*1.3*	*0.1*	*3.0*
	Cereals	2%	24%	19%	4%
		0.7	*1.1*	*1.0*	*0.7*
	Fruit	5%	17%	11%	9%
		1.5	*0.8*	*0.6*	*1.8*
	Vegetables	1%	48%	10%	5%
		0.3	*2.2*	*0.6*	*1.0*
	Milk	4%	4%	15%	16%
		1.4	*0.2*	*0.8*	*3.2*
Metals	Aluminium	2%	23%	3%	19%
		0.8	*1.0*	*0.2*	*3.9*
	Copper	2%	23%	2%	14%
		0.6	*1.0*	*0.1*	*2.8*
	Nickel	2%	15%	1%	10%
		0.6	*0.7*	*0.1*	*2.0*
	Steel	2%	31%	4%	10%
		0.5	*1.4*	*0.2*	*2.0*
Energy	Coal	0%	38%	8%	20%
		0.1	*1.7*	*0.4*	*3.9*
	Gas	1%	2%	1%	24%
		0.2	*0.1*	*0.1*	*4.8*
	Oil	3%	9%	3%	27%
		0.8	*0.4*	*0.2*	*5.3*

Notes:
1. In this table, the world is defined as a subset of countries that accounts for only 91% of the actual world population. Data are for 2005, except in the case of food, which are for 2002.
2. For each country/commodity pair, the share of world consumption relative to share in world population is shown in italics. A figure greater (less) than 1 implies that the share in world consumption is larger (smaller) than the population; a figure equal to 1 implies that the share in world consumption is proportional to the population.
Source: WDI; FAO; BP World Energy Statistics; *World Metals Yearbook*; IMF (2008); UN population database; Bank of Canada staff calculations.

depends on income, Υ, and metals intensity, c:[14]

$$C = c\Upsilon. \tag{5.1}$$

Although simple, Eq. (5.1) seems to explain the level of metals demand relatively well. This is illustrated by Figs. 5.3a–d, which show the relationship between GDP and commodity demand for steel, aluminium, copper and nickel for a cross-section of countries. The data are in logs, so the slope of the line of best fit through the data can be viewed as a proxy for the elasticity of commodity demand with respect to GDP. The line of best fit through the cross-section of the data (for 2001) indicates that, as would be predicted by Eq. (5.1), the elasticity of commodity demand is close to one for all four commodities in cross-section, but there is some variation.

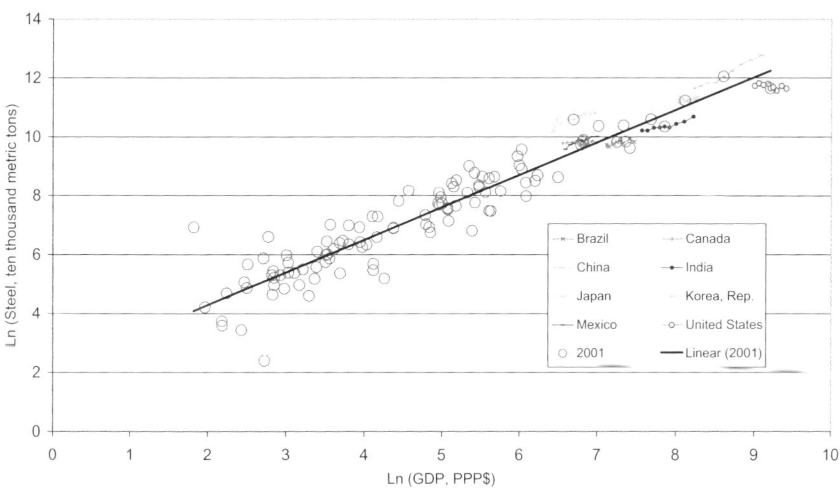

Fig. 5.3a. Steel consumption relative to GDP, 1997–2005.
Note: The fitted line is based on values for a cross-section of countries in 2001. The time series is shown only for select countries.
Source: International Iron and Steel Institute (2007); IMF (2008); WDI.

[14]We later use this same framework, with modifications, to examine the demand for other commodity groups.

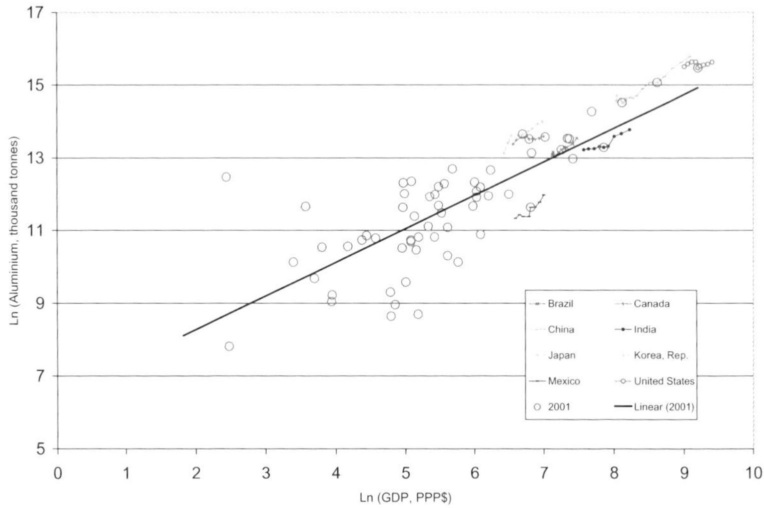

Fig. 5.3b. Aluminium consumption relative to GDP, 1996–2005.
Note: The fitted line is based on values for a cross-section of countries in 2001. The time series is shown only for select countries.
Source: *World Metals Yearbook*, IMF (2008); WDI.

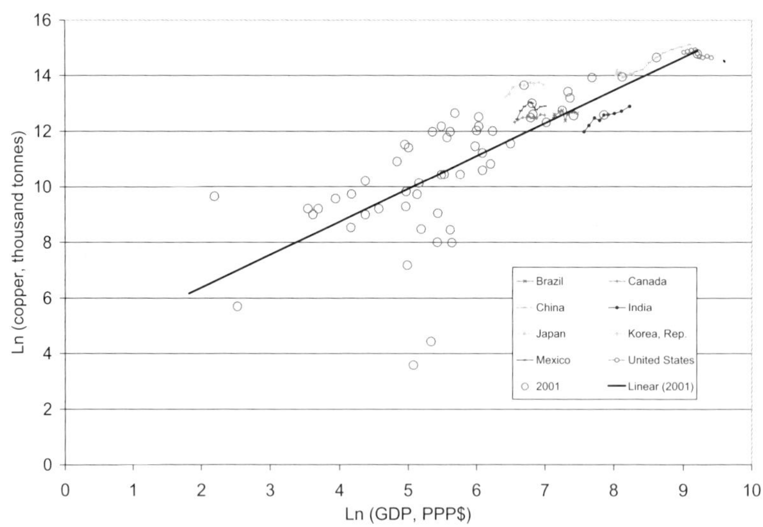

Fig. 5.3c. Copper consumption relative to GDP, 1996–2005.
Note: The fitted line is based on values for a cross-section of countries in 2001. The time series is shown only for select countries.
Source: *World Metals Yearbook*, IMF (2008); WDI.

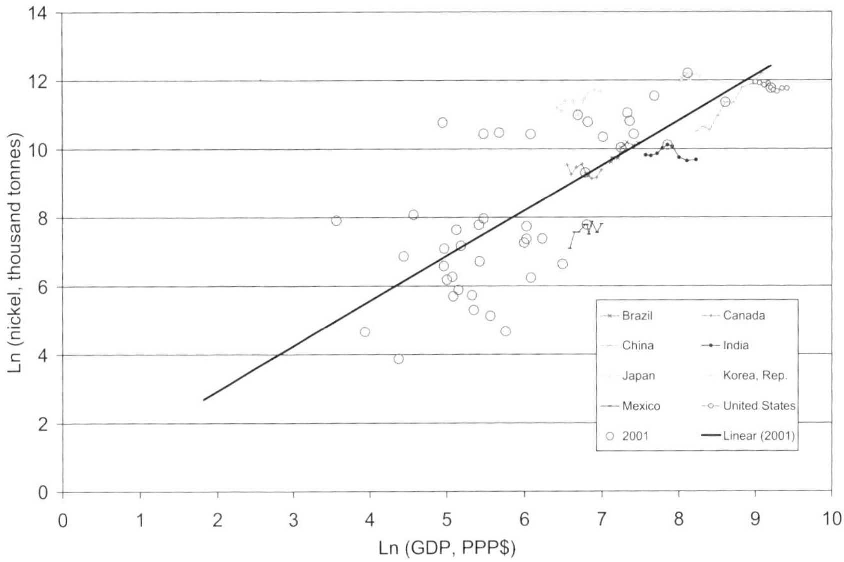

Fig. 5.3d. Nickel consumption relative to GDP, 1996–2005.
Note: The fitted line is based on values for a cross-section of countries in 2001. The time series is shown only for select countries.
Source: *World Metals Yearbook*, IMF (2008); WDI.

One reason for such variation is that the commodity intensity, *c*, can vary in a systematic way with income. Importantly, at the level of an individual economy, if commodity-intensive sectors of the economy are growing faster (slower) than other sectors, then the commodity intensity in the economy as a whole will rise (fall) with GDP, meaning that the elasticity of commodity demand will be greater (lesser) than one. In reality, in countries with low levels of per capita GDP, it is typically the case that growth in industry (construction, manufacturing and mining) exceeds the rate of economy-wide growth. As shown in Fig. 5.2, the share of industry in GDP tends to rise until a per capita GDP of $10,200 (PPP$) is reached, after which other sectors of the economy (agriculture and services) outpace overall GDP growth, causing the industry share to fall.

Assuming that services and agriculture do not demand metals as an intermediate input, the observed variation in industry share should be sufficient to generate the well-known inverted U-shape in commodity intensity as per capita GDP increases. According to the relationship in Fig. 5.2, we would expect that *c* would rise with the share of industry in GDP until reaching a peak for countries with a GDP per capita of approximately \$10,000, and that it would then decline thereafter, before possibly rising again at higher levels of income. In our sample, the commodity intensity of metals generally peaks at a higher level of per capita GDP (Figs. 5.4a–d). For example, for steel, *c* reaches a peak at a per capita GDP of around \$15,000 (Fig. 5.4a).

The most likely explanation is that the commodity intensity in industry is affected not only by the share of industry in GDP, but by the commodity intensity in the industrial sector itself, which may be a function of the level of development. In Figs. 5.5a–d, which plot the commodity intensity in *industry* against per capita GDP, this appears to be the case: for example, the steel intensity in industry peaks at a per capita GDP of just over \$20,000. Thus, for steel, one would expect that for a less-developed country with a per capita GDP of below \$10,000, metals

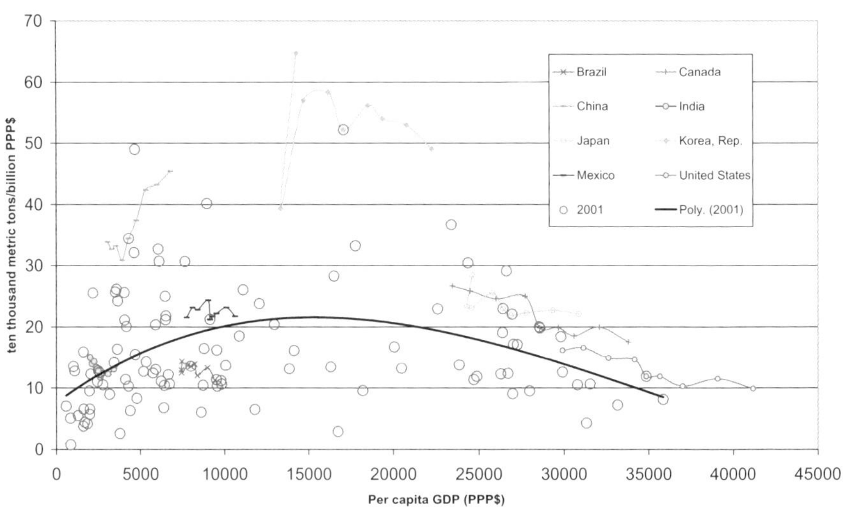

Fig. 5.4a. Steel intensity in GDP and per capita GDP, 1997–2005.
Note: The fitted line is based on values for a cross-section of countries in 2001. The time series is shown only for select countries.
Source: International Iron and Steel Institute (2007); IMF (2008); WDI.

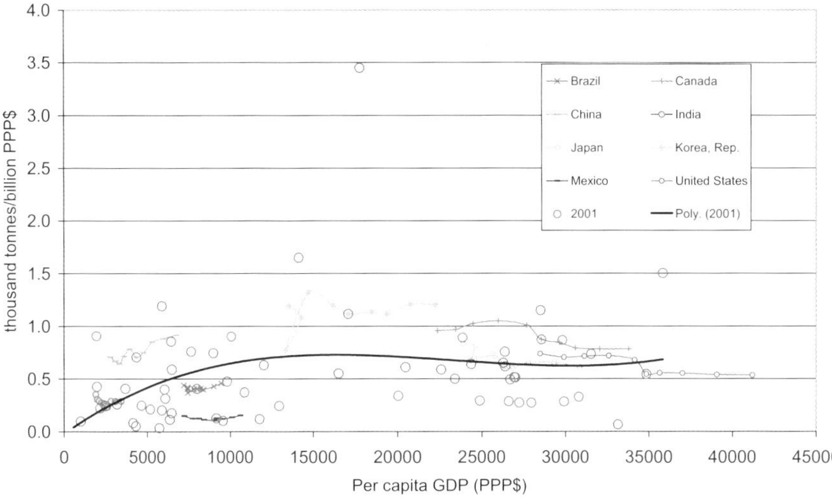

Fig. 5.4b. Aluminium intensity in GDP and per capita GDP, 1996–2005.
Note: The fitted line is based on values for a cross-section of countries in 2001. The time series is shown only for select countries.
Source: *World Metals Yearbook*, IMF (2008); WDI.

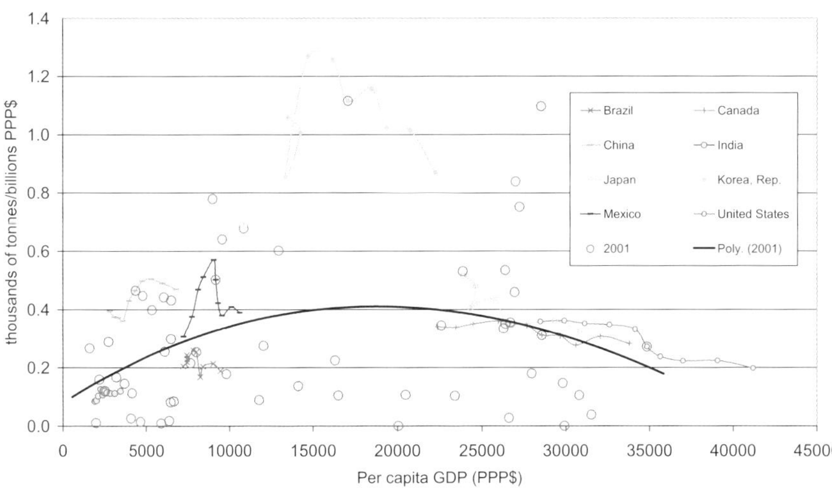

Fig. 5.4c. Copper intensity in GDP and per capita GDP, 1996–2005.
Note: The fitted line is based on values for a cross-section of countries in 2001. The time series is shown only for select countries.
Source: *World Metals Yearbook*, IMF (2008); WDI.

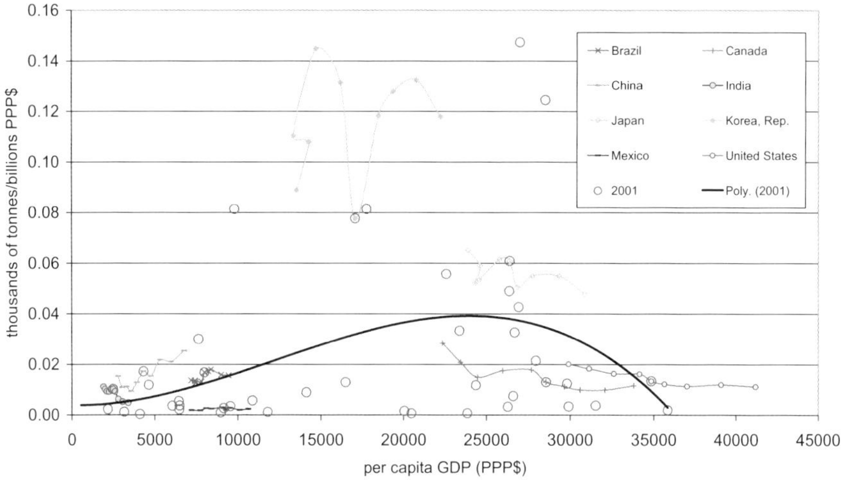

Fig. 5.4d. Nickel intensity in GDP and per capita GDP, 1996–2005.
Note: The fitted line is based on values for a cross-section of countries in 2001. The time series is shown only for select countries.
Source: *World Metals Yearbook*, IMF (2008); WDI.

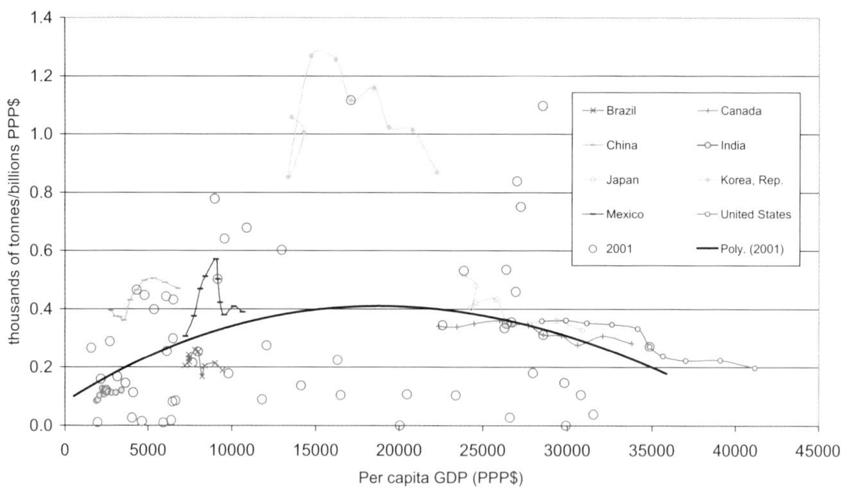

Fig. 5.5a. Steel intensity in industry and per capita GDP, 1997–2005.
Note: The fitted line is based on values for a cross-section of countries in 2001. The time series is shown only for select countries.
Source: International Iron and Steel Institute (2007); IMF (2008); WDI.

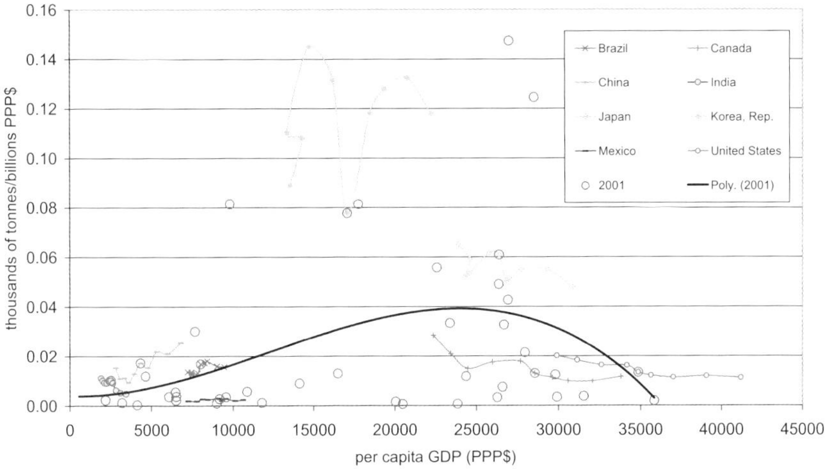

Fig. 5.5b. Aluminium intensity in industry and per capita GDP, 1996–2005.
Note: The fitted line is based on values for a cross-section of countries in 2001. The time series is shown only for select countries.
Source: *World Metals Yearbook*, IMF (2008); WDI.

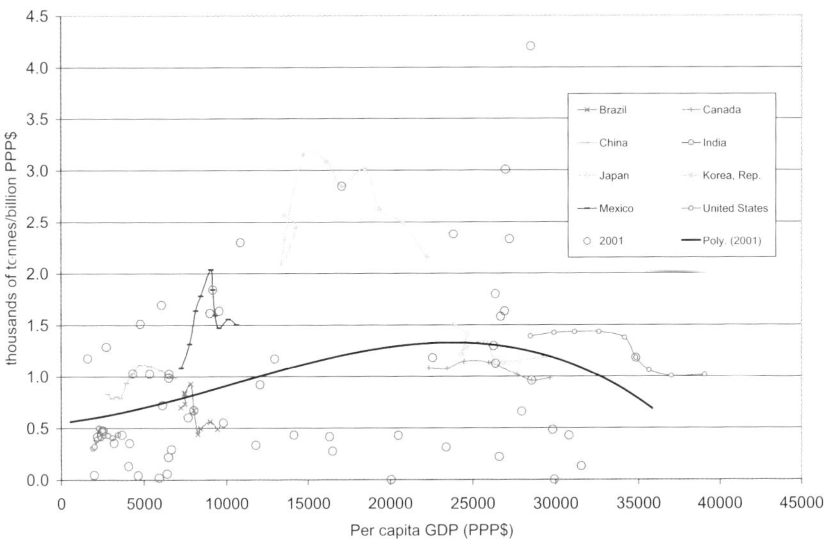

Fig. 5.5c. Copper intensity in industry and per capita GDP, 1996–2005.
Note: The fitted line is based on values for a cross-section of countries in 2001. The time series is shown only for select countries.
Source: *World Metals Yearbook*, IMF (2008); WDI.

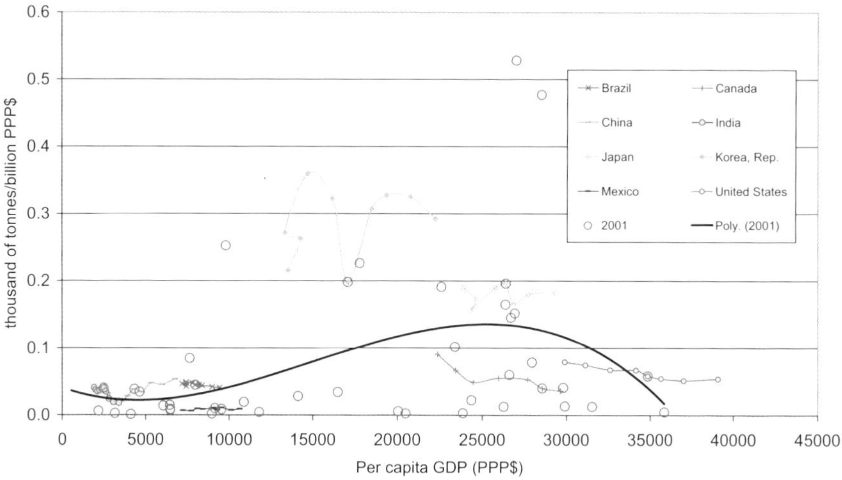

Fig. 5.5d. Nickel intensity in industry and per capita GDP, 1996–2005.
Note: The fitted line is based on values for a cross-section of countries in 2001. The time series is shown only for select countries.
Source: *World Metals Yearbook*, IMF (2008); WDI.

demand should rise, both because industry will expand with economic development and because industry will become more metals intensive.

From Fig. 5.2, it seems that India's expansion path is largely consistent with what would be expected for a country with its per capita GDP.[15] India's consumption of metals (Figs. 5.4 and 5.5) appears to be in line with what is expected of a developing economy with its level of per capita GDP, except for copper, for which India seems to have a low level of demand relative to per capita GDP. In this regard, India's commodity demand does not appear to be unusual.

Table 5.3 shows the contribution to global metals demand by Brazil, China, India and the United States for the period 1996–2005. China's contribution was dramatic and makes for an interesting contrast with India. The table shows that China's commodity demand has resulted

[15]However, as discussed above, per capita GDP is not the only determinant of the expected share of industry in GDP, and once factors such as endowments are accounted for, India's share of industry is smaller than predicted.

Table 5.3. Cross-country shares in global increase in metals demand, 1996–2005.[1]

		Aluminium	Copper	Nickel	Steel[2]
	% change in global consumption	**53.0%**	**35.2%**	**44.2%**	**44.4%**
	due to real GDP growth	68.8%	68.8%	68.8%	59.3%
	due to other	−15.7%	−33.5%	−24.5%	−15.0%
Brazil	**Share of global increase**	**2.4%**	**1.9%**	**2.6%**	**0.5%**
	due to GDP	2.2%	2.8%	1.9%	2.0%
	due to other	0.2%	−0.9%	0.7%	−1.6%
	due to growth in industrial activity	4.3%	5.3%	3.2%	4.1%
	due to commodity intensity in industry	−1.9%	−3.4%	−0.6%	−3.6%
China	**Share of global increase**	**45.7%**	**59.4%**	**37.8%**	**68.7%**
	due to GDP	31.6%	46.4%	18.7%	44.7%
	due to other	14.1%	13.0%	19.1%	24.0%
	due to growth in industrial activity	31.6%	46.5%	18.7%	44.7%
	due to commodity intensity in industry	14.1%	13.0%	19.1%	23.9%
India	**Share of global increase**	**3.4%**	**6.2%**	**−0.6%**	**4.7%**
	due to GDP	5.7%	3.6%	4.9%	7.3%
	due to other	−2.3%	2.6%	−5.5%	−2.6%
	due to growth in industrial activity	5.6%	3.5%	4.3%	7.4%
	due to commodity intensity in industry	−2.2%	2.7%	−5.0%	−2.7%

(Continued)

Table 5.3. *(Continued)*

		Aluminium	Copper	Nickel	Steel[2]
United States	**Share of global increase**	**7.0%**	**−8.1%**	**2.2%**	**−3.1%**
	due to GDP	29.0%	37.1%	14.9%	17.8%
	due to other	−21.9%	−45.2%	−12.7%	−20.9%
	due to growth in industrial activity	20.5%	26.3%	10.7%	12.8%
	due to commodity intensity in industry	−13.5%	−34.4%	−8.5%	−15.9%

Notes:
1. This table breaks down the proportion of the increase in metals demand from a particular country that is the result of GDP growth (or industrial growth) and other factors. It assumes that, if nothing else in the economy changed, then metals consumption would have to increase one-for-one with GDP (or industrial) growth (it assumes income elasticity of metals demand equals 1). The residual, probably owing to the metals intensity in industry, accounts for the unexplained portion.
2. The analysis for steel was for the period 1997–2005, in contrast to aluminium, copper and nickel, which covered 1996–2005, because of data availability on steel demand.
Source: *World Metals Yearbook*; WDI; IMF (2008); Bank of Canada staff calculations.

from a combination of growth in economic activity and an expansion in demand from other factors, including a growing metals intensity in the industrial sector.[16] For steel, China accounted for 68.7 percent of the global increase in demand, of which about two-thirds can be attributed to growth in the Chinese economy. In comparison, India's metals demand has risen by a much lesser extent. For steel, 4.7 percent of world incremental demand can be attributed to India, but GDP grew faster than India's steel consumption, meaning that, had nothing changed in the structure of the Indian economy, its steel demand would have accounted for 7.3 percent of the global increase in demand. However, India's declining steel intensity in industry meant that its share in the global increase in steel demand was 2.7 percent lower than otherwise would have been the case. In contrast, increased steel intensity in industry in China contributed 24 percent to the increase in global demand.

With the exception of copper, the same can be said to be true for India's demand for the other key metals. Expansion in the economy and economic activity increased India's demand, but declining commodity intensity in industry caused India's demand to contract.[17] Only for copper did increased commodity intensity in industry contribute to demand growth. This is not surprising since it may reflect a catching up to cross-country norms (Figs. 5.4c and 5.5c).

The falling demand for metals as a share of industry size in India probably reflects the declining importance of the two most metal-intensive sectors: the basic metal and alloy sector and the metal products and parts sector. But that is being offset by the growing importance of the machinery and transportation equipment sectors, which have consistently outgrown the rest of the industrial sector. During the past two years, however, all four of the metal-intensive sectors have posted strong growth, suggesting that, over that period, the commodity intensity in industry may have risen (Fig. 5.6); we consider this in

---

[16] In the following analysis, we assume that the income elasticity of metals demand is equal to 1.

[17] Intensity refers to metals usage per unit of output, and should be interpreted as output "efficiency".

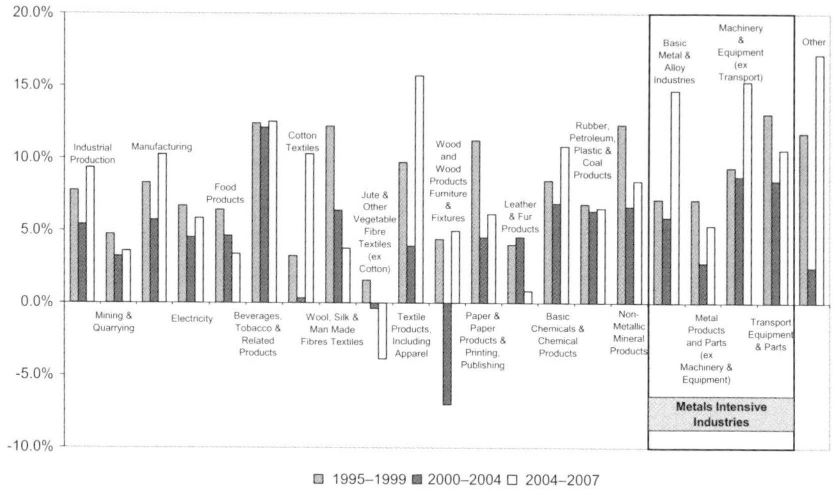

Fig. 5.6. India's industrial production growth by sector.
Source: ISI Emerging Markets.

more detail in Section 5.3.1.3 when we examine India's metals trade.[18] Unfortunately, we do not have comparable metals-consumption data for these years to determine how much India's consumption might have increased as a result.

5.3.2. *India's metals production*

In 1996, India accounted for only 0.3 percent of world refined copper production, but by 2005 its share had increased to over 3 percent. This increase accounted for 12 percent of the global increase in refined copper production during the period (World Bureau of Metal Statistics, 2007). That said, India's mine production of copper ores is less than 0.5 percent of world production, and between 1998 and 2007 this production fell by 22 percent.[19] This suggests that India is, in net terms, increasing its overall demand for copper ore in world markets,

[18]This expansion of metals-intensive industries is likely related to dereservation, which is described in more detail in Section 5.3.1.3.

[19]Statistics on India's mine production of bauxite, copper ore and iron ore are taken from the ISI Emerging Markets database (ISI Emerging Markets, 2008).

but increasing the relative supply of refined copper.[20] For aluminium, between 1996 and 2005, India's production accounted for 3.3 percent of the incremental increase in world production, closely matching the increase in consumption. But India's production of bauxite (aluminium ore) rose by 107 percent, with India's share of global bauxite production rising from 4.6 percent to 6.8 percent.

India's iron ore production has also increased dramatically, growing by 152 percent between 1998/99 and 2006/07. During the same period, steel production increased by 110 percent, accounting for 6.1 percent of the global increase in steel output. There are no readily available production statistics for nickel.

5.3.3. *Role of policy and implications for India's metals trade*

Public policy has played a major role in reducing India's demand for metals by directly intervening in the manufacturing sector, regulating the factors of production and creating an unfriendly business climate. Together, these elements of policy have hindered the expansion of the manufacturing sector, thereby reducing India's demand for metals commodities.

Even after India dismantled its industrial licensing system in the early 1990s, the manufacture of a wide range of goods continued to be heavily regulated by its small-scale industry policy. This policy (often referred to as small-scale reservation) required firms in most manufacturing industries to limit capital spending and the size of their labour forces (amongst other things).[21] As recently as 2002, around 800 items were reserved for production by these small-scale industries. As we discuss below, although this policy is being phased out, it prevented Indian firms from achieving minimum efficient scale and inhibited their growth.

In addition to India's reservation policies, its labour market restrictions are numerous and complex, and reduce firms' incentives to

[20] This is evident in India's pattern of trade for copper, as shown in Fig. 5.7b and discussed further in Section 5.3.1.3.

[21] These restrictions were lifted only if 50 percent of production was exported.

expand employment. One example of labour market policies is the Industrial Disputes Act of 1982, which made it necessary for firms employing more than 100 workers to seek government approval for layoffs, retrenchments and closures.[22] Besley and Burgess (2004) find that labour regulations in India have altered the pattern of manufacturing growth. In particular, Indian states that amended the Industrial Disputes Act in a pro-worker direction experienced lower levels of investment, employment, productivity and output in manufacturing.

As well as the excessive regulatory burden, the business environment faced by manufacturing firms is rather poor. Inadequate infrastructure and the costs of dealing with bureaucracy are two factors that contribute to this problem. For example, according to the Worldwide Governance Indicators (World Bank, 2008), India remained below the cross-country median in terms of the regulatory quality of its government in 2007, receiving a percentile rank of 46.1.[23] Moreover, India also has relatively low control over corruption, receiving a percentile rank of 47.3.[24] These two factors tend to be mutually reinforcing over time, contributing to the creation of an unfriendly business environment in India.

Furthermore, infrastructure improvements were likely to have been more forthcoming in the case of services than they were in the manufacturing sector. For instance, the telecom reforms, which were initiated in the mid-1990s, led to a large increase in fixed-line subscribers, which was augmented by the availability of mobile technology. In India, the number of fixed-line and mobile phone subscribers per 1000 people increased from six in 1990 to 128 in 2005.[25] In the case of electricity,

---

[22]This policy not only increased firing costs but also promoted corruption within the bureaucracy.

[23]This means that India's regulatory quality was better than 46 percent of the countries surveyed in 2007. This is an improvement over 1996, when India received a percentile rank of 39.5 (World Bank, 2008).

[24]This compares to a percentile rank of 39.3 in 1996 (World Bank, 2008).

[25]Direct measures of the quality of the telecom infrastructure in India are generally lagging or unavailable. According to the World Development Indicators (World Bank, 2006), the number of telephone faults per 1000 mainlines declined from 222 in 1995 to 126 in 2002.

which is more important for manufacturing, reforms were relatively unsuccessful (Virmani, 2004). In particular, transmission and distribution losses as a percentage of total electricity output increased from 19 percent in 1995 to 26 percent in 2004 (World Bank, 2006). Over this period, electricity production increased by an average annual rate of 6.7 percent; however, after accounting for these increasing transmission and distribution losses, the effective growth in electricity output was a more moderate 5.1 percent per year (World Bank, 2006; Bank of Canada staff calculations). This growth in electricity production was below India's average annual GDP growth of 6.1 percent over this period (or manufacturing growth of 6.6 percent), which may have constrained total output growth (ISI Emerging Markets, 2008). Not surprisingly, the 32 percent of managers surveyed ranked electricity as a major business constraint in India in 2006, relative to a cross-country average of 18 percent (World Bank, 2006).[26] In addition, India's transportation infrastructure is poor. One example is India's port system, which has experienced an increase in delays in recent years. The average pre-berthing waiting time increased from 4.86 hours in fiscal year 2003/04 to 11.17 hours between April and October 2007, and over the same period the average turnaround time increased from 3.45 days to 3.79 days. This compares to an average turnaround time of 10 hours in Hong Kong (Ministry of Finance, 2008). This congestion can be partially explained by the poor road–rail connectivity of ports, and highlights one of the many limitations of infrastructure that hinder manufacturing in India (thereby reducing its metals demand).[27]

In the past five years, however, structural changes, including the decline in small-scale reservation and lower restrictions on the inflow of foreign direct investment, have eased constraints that limited the expansion of the manufacturing and industrial sectors. For example, since October 2004, more than 650 industries have been "dereserved",

[26]This average was obtained by taking the last available survey result for 73 countries over the period 2004–2006. Looking only at 2006, where 26 countries were surveyed, the average was higher, at 27 percent.
[27]For more discussion of India's infrastructure, see Ministry of Finance (2008).

many of which are metals intensive, ranging from cutlery (dereserved in May 2006) to steel furniture (dereserved in February 2008). It is not unreasonable to expect that this dereservation policy partly explains the growth in metals-intensive industries shown in Fig. 5.6, and that it has led to an increased demand for metals in India in the past three to four years, which is reflected in India's rising import demand (and moderating export supplies).

India's import demand for metals commodities depends on the particular metal commodity being imported, given India's ore endowments and industry's metals intensity. India is relatively well endowed with bauxite and iron ores, and is a net exporter of both. However, it is a net importer of copper ores and refined nickel (Figs. 5.7a–d).[28]

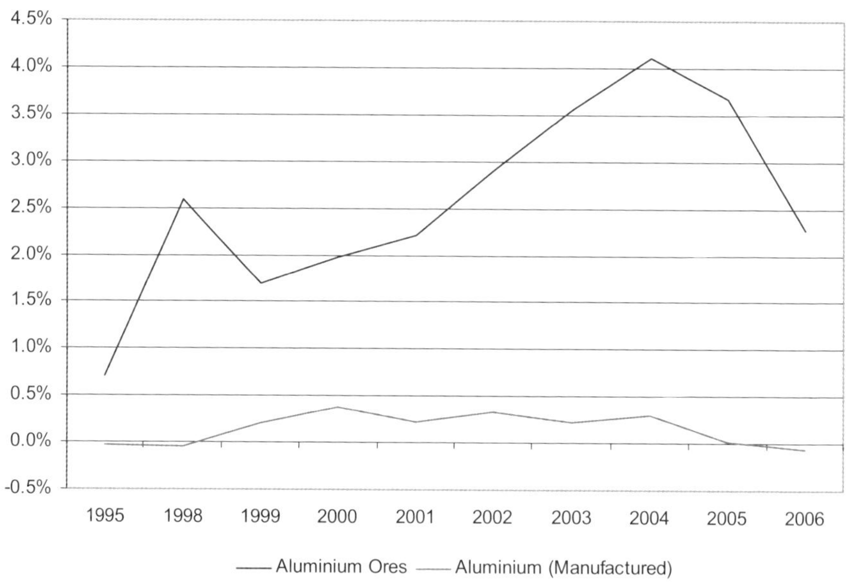

Fig. 5.7a. India's net exports of aluminium (percent of world trade).
Source: UN COMTRADE; Bank of Canada staff calculations.

[28]Another metals commodity, gold, is demanded fairly heavily in India, likely reflecting rising domestic demand (as a result of an increase in per capita incomes). Gold may be consumed, but it may also act as a store of value for Indian households. In particular, India's net imports of gold have increased from 3 percent of world trade in gold in 1995 to 28 percent in 2006.

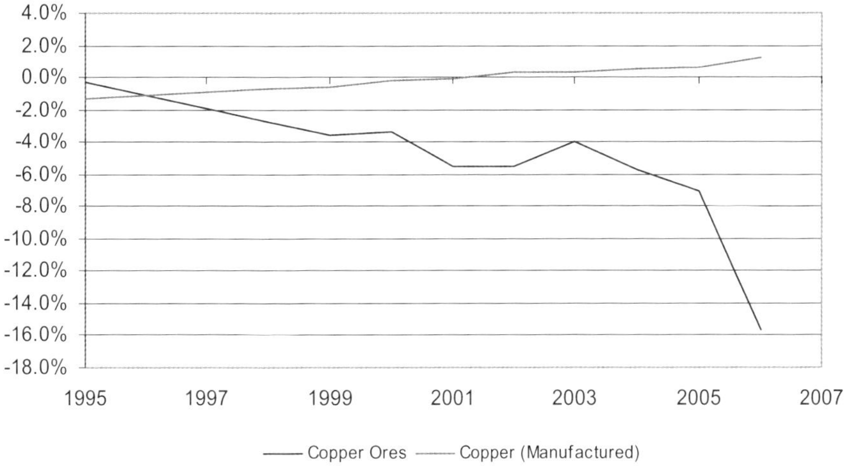

Fig. 5.7b. India's net exports of copper (percent of world trade).
Source: UN COMTRADE; Bank of Canada staff calculations.

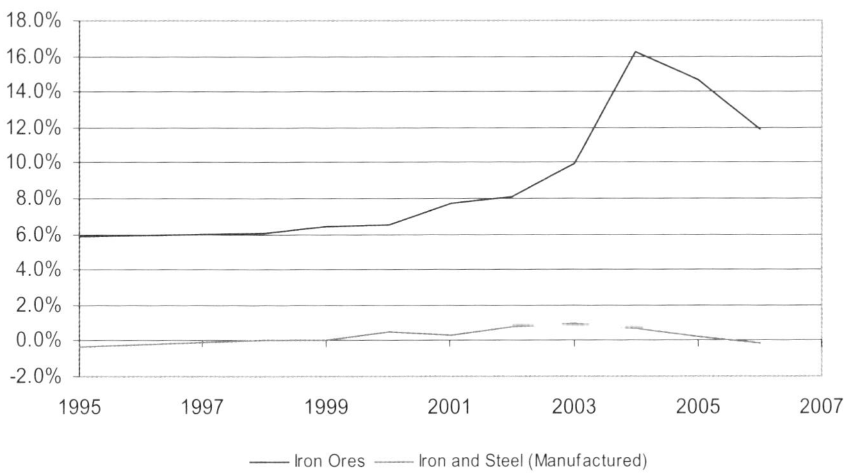

Fig. 5.7c. India's net exports of iron and steel (percent of world trade).
Source: UN COMTRADE; Bank of Canada staff calculations.

India's net exports of aluminium ores increased from 0.7 percent of world trade in 1995 to a peak of 4.2 percent in 2004; however, India's net exports have since moderated, probably reflecting rising domestic metals consumption, consistent with the expansion of India's industrial

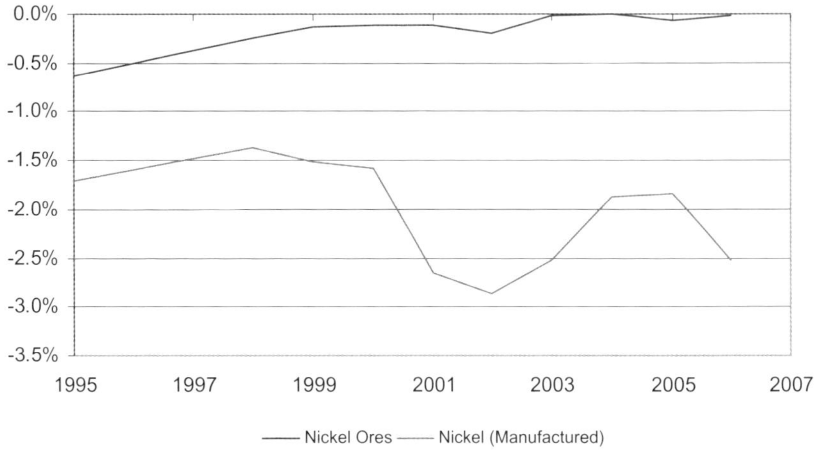

Fig. 5.7d. India's net exports of nickel (percent of world trade).
Source: UN COMTRADE; Bank of Canada staff calculations.

sector (following dereservation) (Figs. 5.3b, 5.4b and 5.5b). This effectively removed roughly 1.7 percent of world trade in aluminium ores from world markets (from 2004–2006), as India's net exports fell to 2.5 percent of world trade in 2006.[29] This development is reflected in India's net exports of iron ores: between 1995 and 2004, India's domestic production outstripped consumption, leading to a rise in its net exports of iron ores from 6 percent of world trade in 1995 to over 16 percent in 2004. However, India's net exports of iron ores then moderated, effectively removing roughly 4 percent of supplies from world markets.[30]

India is a net importer of copper ores, accounting for roughly 15 percent of world trade in 2006, a rise from the roughly balanced trade in copper ores in the early 1990s.[31] This is also probably related to

[29] Domestic refining of aluminium has largely kept pace with consumption growth, with India essentially maintaining balanced trade in refined aluminium over this period (Fig. 5.7a).

[30] India's net exports of iron ores moderated to 12 percent of world trade in 2006, or from roughly US$397 billion in 2004 to US$324 billion in 2006.

[31] India is also a net importer of nickel; however, its net imports have changed little over the past 15 years as a share of total world trade of nickel, accounting for roughly 2.5 percent of world trade.

Table 5.4. Population and income growth: The contribution of selected countries to the increase in global food consumption, 1991–2002.

Global consumption between 1991–2002		Meat	Cereals	Fruit	Vegetables	Milk
	Increase (tonnes/day)	181,997	170,327	265,205	767,240	228,459
	Percentage change	45%	8%	40%	77%	25%
Contribution from:						
	Population increase	15%	15%	15%	15%	15%
	Income increase	30%	−7%	25%	62%	10%
Contribution to global consumption growth by:						
Brazil	**Share of Global Increase**	**8.3%**	**5.2%**	**2.0%**	**0.7%**	**7.2%**
	due to population growth	2.3%	4.8%	2.8%	0.3%	3.1%
	due to income growth	6.0%	0.5%	−0.8%	0.3%	4.1%
China	**Share of Global Increase**	**52.7%**	**−43.0%**	**41.3%**	**74.3%**	**12.1%**
	due to population growth	5.6%	43.4%	2.5%	4.8%	1.0%
	due to income growth	47.2%	−86.4%	38.8%	69.5%	11.1%

(Continued)

Table 5.4. (*Continued*)

Global consumption between 1991–2002		Meat	Cereals	Fruit	Vegetables	Milk
India	**Share of Global Increase**	**1.8%**	**29.7%**	**13.6%**	**8.3%**	**26.3%**
	due to population growth	1.3%	49.1%	5.5%	3.5%	12.0%
	due to income growth	0.4%	−19.4%	8.1%	4.8%	14.3%
United States	**Share of Global Increase**	**9.3%**	**7.0%**	**4.1%**	**2.3%**	**11.6%**
	due to population growth	6.2%	6.3%	4.1%	1.5%	11.0%
	due to income growth	3.1%	0.6%	0.0%	0.9%	0.5%

Note:
This table breaks down the proportion of the increase in food demand from a particular country that can result from population growth and other factors. It assumes that, if nothing else in the economy changed, then food consumption would have to increase one-for-one with population growth. The residual, probably owing to diet diversification, which results with income growth, accounts for the unexplained portion.
Source: FAO; WDI; IMF (2008); Bank of Canada staff calculations.

the expansion of industry in India, and increased copper intensity (Table 5.4, which partially reflects a catch-up to international norms (Figs. 5.3c, 5.4c and 5.5c). Therefore, while India's past demand for metals was possibly muted because of government policies that have restricted the expansion of the manufacturing sector, India's demand has increased in the past couple of years and will probably continue to rise with structural change, improvements in infrastructure and the increased pace of economic reform.

5.4. Energy

5.4.1. *Demand for energy commodities*

Unlike metals, energy is consumed by all sectors of the economy, with varying intensities. In general, energy consumption is positively correlated with GDP (Figs. 5.8a–c). As a large economy, India is a large

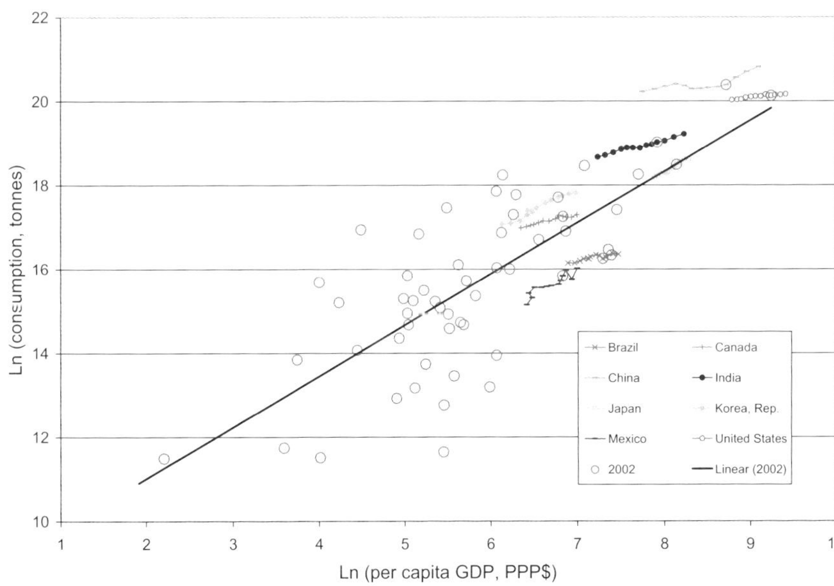

Fig. 5.8a. Cross-country coal consumption and per capita GDP, 1993–2005.
Note: The fitted line is based on values for a cross-section of countries in 2002. The time series is shown only for select countries.
Source: BP World Energy Statistics, IMF (2008); WDI.

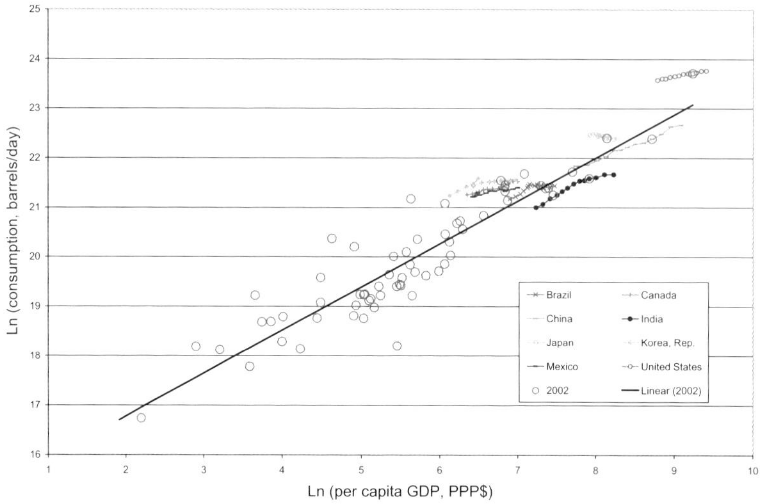

Fig. 5.8b. Cross-country oil consumption and per capita GDP, 1993–2005.
Note: The fitted line is based on values for a cross-section of countries in 2002. The time series is shown only for select countries.
Source: BP World Energy Statistics, IMF (2008); WDI.

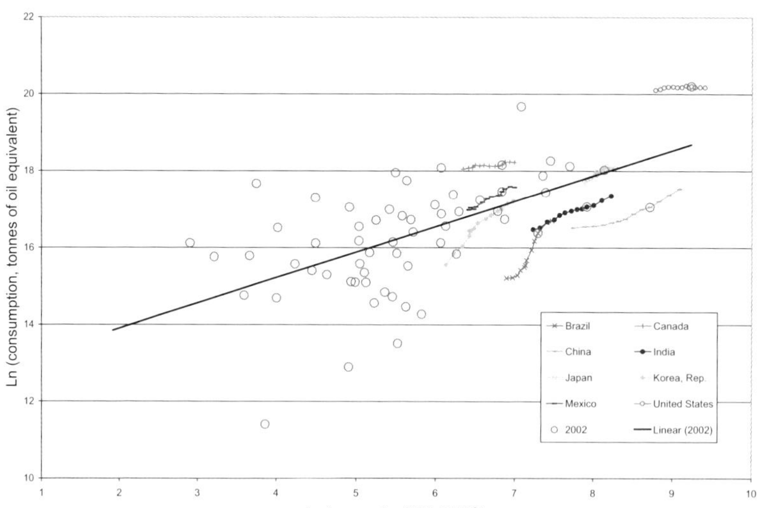

Fig. 5.8c. Cross-country gas consumption and per capita GDP, 1993–2005.
Note: The fitted line is based on values for a cross-section of countries in 2002. The time series is shown only for select countries.
Source: BP World Energy Statistics, IMF (2008); WDI.

consumer of energy commodities, being the third largest consumer of coal and the fourth largest consumer of oil. However, India is a relatively low energy-intensity economy, using 0.16 kg of oil-equivalent (kgoe) energy per unit of GDP (PPP based) compared with the world average of 0.21; as a poor country, India's per capita consumption is also low (Table 5.5).

Over time, as is the case with other countries, India's energy intensity has been declining as productivity improvements and capital accumulation raise the level of output that can be produced with a given amount of energy. In Figs. 5.9a–c, this negative relationship between energy and per capita GDP is apparent for nearly every country, for coal, oil and gas, although the use of gas has increased in some countries over time. But there is no obvious relationship with energy intensity and per capita GDP for the cross-section of countries, since the amount

Table 5.5. Comparative energy consumption statistics (2003).

	TPES1 per capita (kgoe/person)	**TPES/GDP** (kgoe/$2000, PPP)
China	1,090	0.23
Australia	5,630	0.2
Brazil	1,094	0.15
Denmark	3,852	0.13
Germany	4,210	0.17
India	439	0.16
Indonesia	753	0.24
Netherlands	4,983	0.18
Saudi Arabia	5,805	0.46
Sweden	5,751	0.21
United Kingdom	3,906	0.14
United States	7,835	0.22
Japan	4,052	0.15
World	1,688	0.21

Note: Total primary energy supply (TPES) is measured in kilograms of energy equivalent (kgoe).
Source: Planning Commission (2005).

of output per unit of energy used can vary from country to country for a variety of reasons, including different endowments, productivity and economic structure. Figures 5.9a–c also reveal that India generally uses coal more intensively as an energy source than most other countries, and oil and gas less intensively.

Table 5.6 shows the increase in the consumption of energy commodities globally and for Brazil, China, India and the United States. We find that, for the world economy, energy consumption has been growing more slowly than GDP. The first line of the table shows the growth in gas, oil and coal consumption between 1996 and 2006. The second line shows how much of this increase resulted from income growth, if

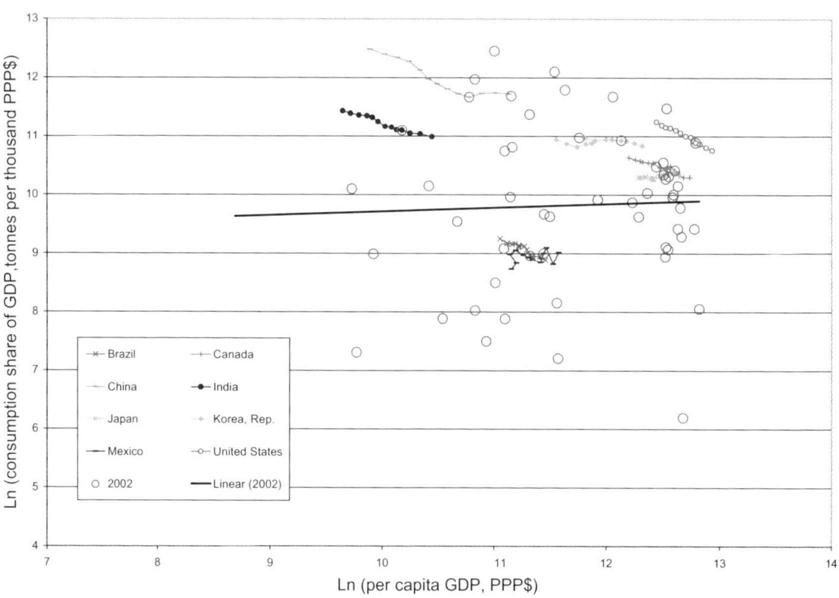

Fig. 5.9a. Cross-country coal consumption as a share of GDP and per capita GDP, 1993–2005.

Note: The fitted line is based on values for a cross-section of countries in 2002. The time series is shown only for select countries.

Source: BP World Energy Statistics, WDI; IMF (2008).

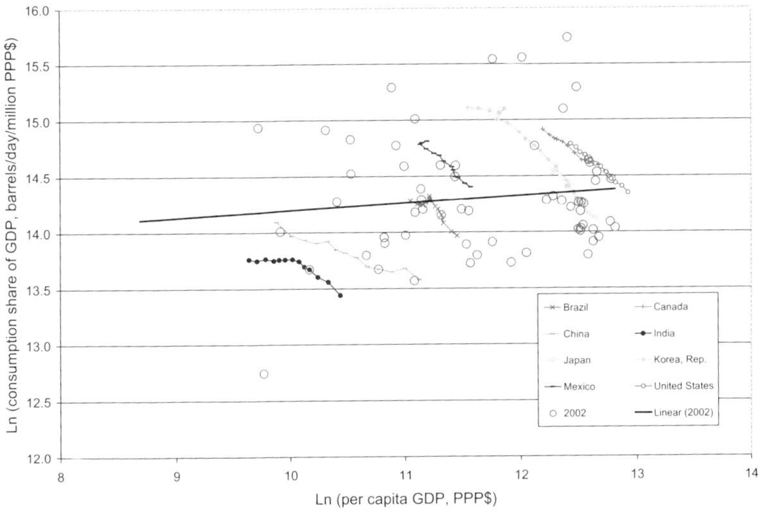

Fig. 5.9b. Cross-country oil consumption as a share of GDP and per capita GDP, 1993–2005.
Note: The fitted line is based on values for a cross-section of countries in 2002. The time series is shown only for select countries.
Source: BP World Energy Statistics; WDI; IMF (2008).

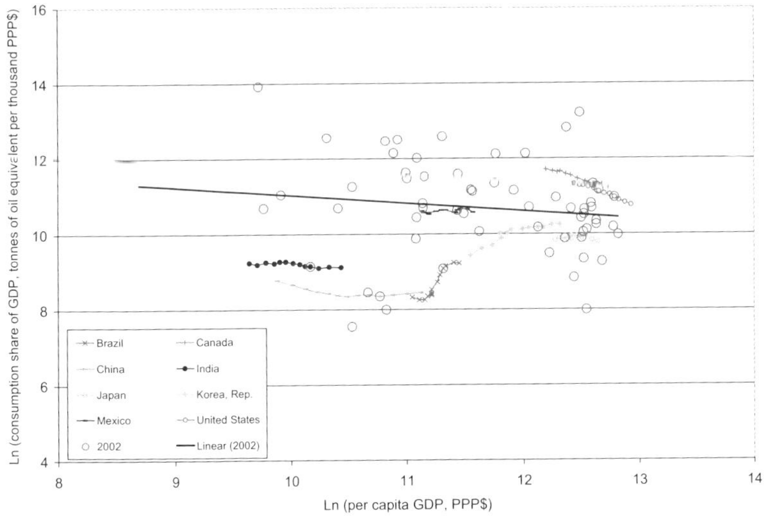

Fig. 5.9c. Cross-country gas consumption as a share of GDP and per capita GDP, 1993–2005.
Note: The fitted line is based on values for a cross-section of countries in 2002. The time series is shown only for select countries.
Source: BP World Energy Statistics; WDI; IMF (2008).

Table 5.6. Cross-country change in energy consumption, 1996–2006.

		Consumption change between 1996 and 2006		
		Gas consumption	Oil consumption	Coal consumption
	% change in global consumption	**24%**	**17%**	**31%**
	due to real GDP growth	83%	83%	83%
	due to other	−59%	−67%	−52%
Brazil	**Share of world incremental increase**	**3%**	**2%**	**0%**
	due to income	1%	10%	1%
	due to other	2%	−8%	−1%
China	**Share of world incremental increase**	7%	**34%**	**64%**
	due to income	7%	66%	203%
	due to other	0%	−33%	−139%
India	**Share of world incremental increase**	**4%**	**8%**	**12%**
	due to income	5%	20%	29%
	due to other	−2%	−12%	−17%
United States	**Share of world incremental increase**	**−4%**	**20%**	**5%**
	due to income	84%	113%	51%
	due to other	−87%	−92%	−46%

Note: This table breaks down the proportion of the increase in energy demand from a particular country that is the result of GDP growth and other factors. It assumes that, if nothing else in the economy changed, then energy consumption would have to increase one-for-one with GDP growth. The residual, probably owing to the energy intensity in the economy, accounts for the unexplained portion.
Source: BP World Energy Statistics; Bank of Canada staff calculations.

energy intensity did not change.[32] Thus, since incomes rose by 83 percent, energy consumption resulting from income growth would have had to increase by 83 percent. On the next line is the contribution of the combined increases in employment of other factors and productivity gains that caused the demand for gas to fall by 59 percent, which offset most of the income effect and resulted in an increase in global gas consumption of 24 percent. Interestingly, the largest offsetting impact was on oil, probably because of substitution towards other forms of energy (coal, gas and biofuels) as a result of elevated oil prices.

The second part of Table 5.5 shows the share of the global increase due to Brazil, China, India and the United States. For each country, the first line shows the share of the global increase that can be attributed to that country. For example, India accounted for 8 percent of the increase in global oil consumption between 1996 and 2006. Had other factors remained unchanged, India would have contributed 20 percent to world demand due to income growth. However, India's oil intensity declined and this change in energy usage removed 12 percent from the global energy demand.

Two interesting features stand out in Table 5.5. First, for India, the offsetting effects have been relatively large for oil and coal. It appears that this might partly be due to substitution towards gas, a trend that India appears to share with Brazil and China. Second, compared with the world as a whole, the offsetting effects for all the energy commodities are smaller for India than for the world. One possible interpretation of this result is that, compared with the rest of the world, during the past 10 years, India has increased its reliance on energy as a factor of

[32]This analysis assumes an income elasticity of energy demand equal to 1. Other studies that estimate the long-run income elasticity of energy demand yield results around or just above 1. For example, Krichene (2002) estimates the long-run income elasticity of oil and natural gas demand to be 1.2 and 1.5, respectively. A study by Pesaran, Smith and Akiyama (1999), which examines 12 Asian countries (including India and China), finds the long-run income elasticity of energy demand to be 1.18. However, empirical estimates of the short-run income elasticity of energy demand tend to be below 1: Krichene (2007) finds the short-run income elasticity of natural gas and crude oil demand to be around 0.4.

production, becoming *relatively* more energy intensive. This is not surprising, since India's consumption of energy commodities appears to be relatively low compared with the size of its population.[33]

On the production side, India accounts for approximately 1 percent of the global production of oil, and has 0.5 percent of proved reserves. Likewise, for gas, India accounts for 1.1 percent of global production and 0.6 percent of world gas reserves. India, however, has significant coal deposits and accounts for 6.6 percent of global production and 10.6 percent of global coal reserves, making it the third largest producer of coal (behind the United States and China, which together produce 60 percent of the world's coal).

5.4.2. *Policies governing the energy sector*

Government regulation and control in India's energy sector is widespread, complex and distorting, and the industry lacks competition. Typically, prices are set directly either by the government (as is also the case for the bulk of gas under the Administered Price Mechanism [APM]) or by publicly owned companies. Currently, there is a dual price system for gas; 60 percent of the gas sold in India (excluding all imported liquefied petroleum gas [LPG] and gas extracted by new joint ventures) is sold under the APM and is used to produce fertiliser and to run some vehicles such as rickshaws and taxis. In 2006, APM prices were about 28 percent of the world LPG spot price and one-sixth of the contracted import price.[34] The remaining 40 percent is sold at market rates.

The prices of (non-gas) petroleum products were also determined by the APM before 2002. Since then prices have, in theory, been set

---

[33]In particular, India accounts for 1.5 percent, 3.3 percent and 7.9 percent of global gas, oil and coal consumption, respectively, despite having one-sixth of the world's population.

[34]LPG and kerosene are sold at subsidised rates to poor households in an attempt to reduce the use of firewood and dung, which have adverse health consequences. In reality, higher-income households are the main beneficiaries of subsidised LPG, and corruption diverts kerosene earmarked for the poor for cooking to alternative uses (Planning Commission, 2005).

according to the import parity principle, where international prices are used as a benchmark to set domestic prices. However, in practice the public sector oil companies, which dominate the sector, collectively fix prices at the refinery gate and retail outlets (Planning Commission, 2005). Through this channel of ownership and control, the Government of India has frequently deviated from the import parity principle and effectively fixed the price of domestic crude as well as the price of petroleum products at the retail level.[35] This has created significant losses for the state-owned oil companies, amounting to 0.52 percent of GDP in 2006, which continue to rise (IEA, 2007; IMF, 2008). These losses have been partially financed through the issuance of bonds that have been guaranteed by the Government of India. Ironically, the state and central governments also levy significant taxes on gasoline, and in 2006 the after-tax price of gasoline was 30 percent higher in India than the OECD average (IEA, 2007).

There are also substantial pricing distortions in the electricity sector. It is estimated that, owing to agricultural subsidies, theft and excessive transmission losses, unpaid-for electricity is equal to 40 percent of total electricity throughput (Planning Commission, 2005). To cover these losses, industrial, commercial and large domestic consumers pay highly inflated prices. Moreover, because the utilities are so unprofitable, production capacity is low, transmission networks are poorly maintained and power outages are common.[36] For these reasons, private investment in power generation has been permitted and takes place when the consumer is a captive large industrial producer (such as an auto manufacturer).[37] In addition, millions of households and businesses use small diesel generators to supplement public production during outages.

As a result of the inefficiencies caused by distorting public policies, the costs of energy provision are probably higher, and therefore energy

[35]According to the IMF, petroleum product prices would have to be increased by 40 to 45 percent to be in line with international prices, with the largest adjustments required for kerosene and LPG (IMF, 2006).

[36]In many parts of India electricity is unavailable for up to 14 hours per day (IEA, 2007).

[37]This means that an energy producer must sell only to a designated firm.

consumption is probably lower, than would otherwise be the case. Meanwhile, the distorting influence of subsidies has probably produced an excessive allocation of energy to agriculture and some other uses, such as auto rickshaws and taxis, at the expense of other sectors (such as the manufacturing and service sectors).

5.4.3. *Trade implications for energy*

India's external demand for energy commodities has increased substantially in recent years. As Fig. 5.10 shows, India has been a net importer of fuels and lubricants and this energy trade deficit has increased from 2 percent of world trade in the mid-1990s to roughly 3 percent in 2006. While India is a small net exporter of refined petroleum products, it increasingly relies on crude oil imports to meet domestic demand, importing roughly 70 percent of domestic consumption, up from around 44 percent in 1990 (IEA, 2007). These imports of crude oil (India's largest energy import) have increased dramatically since 2003, with some moderation in the past couple of years. This rise in crude

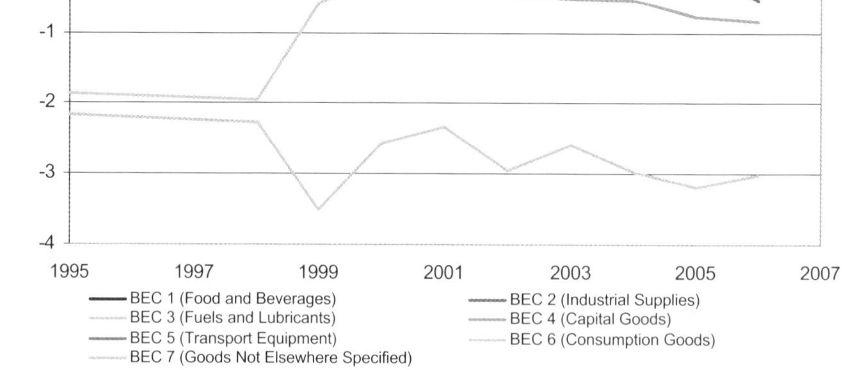

Fig. 5.10. India's net exports of various goods and commodities.
Note: World trade refers to the total imports reported by all countries.
Source: UN COMTRADE; Bank of Canada staff calculations.

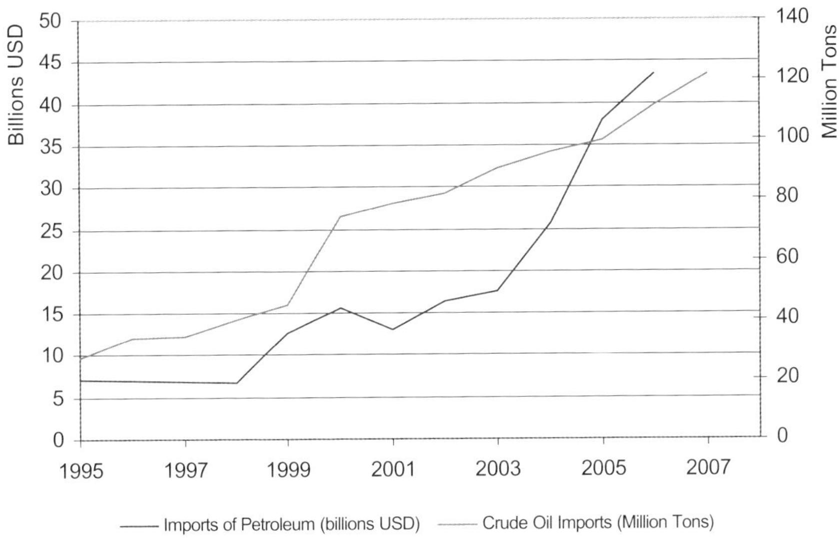

Fig. 5.11. India's imports of petroleum.
Source: UN COMTRADE; Ministry of Finance (1999, 2001, 2007, 2008).

oil imports may have been related to policy changes, since tariffs on petroleum were reduced from around 27 percent in the mid-1990s to 10 percent in 2000.[38] In fact, as Fig. 5.11 shows, there was a large increase in the volume of crude oil imports in 2000. Nevertheless, increases in global oil prices played a dominant role: the volume of imports rose an average 7.8 percent per year from 2001 to 2006, compared with a nominal increase in imports (based on a US dollar measure) of 46.3 percent. In real terms, India's impact on global petroleum demand looks relatively moderate, with India's net imports accounting for over 3 percent of world trade in petroleum in 2006, compared with 2.5 percent in 1995 (Fig. 5.12). Going forward, India will probably play a larger role in crude oil demand as industry and household consumption rise. In particular, as Fig. 5.13 shows, India's per capita

[38]Most recent data put applied MFN tariffs on petrol and diesel at 7.5 percent in June 2006 (WTO, 2007).

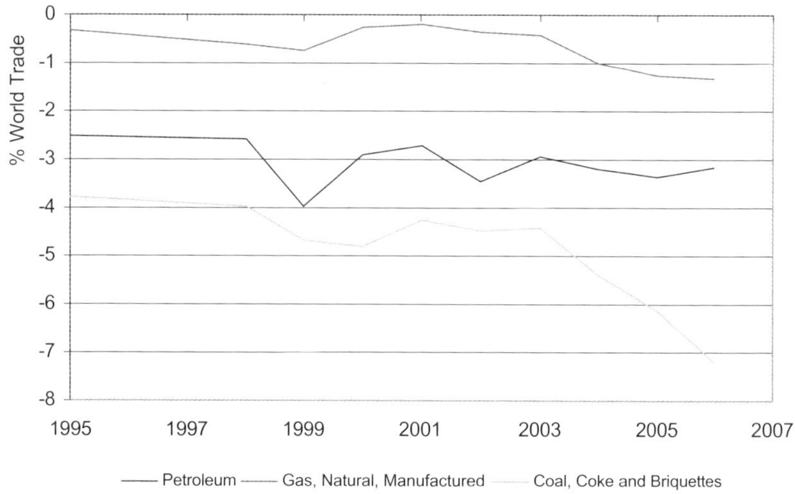

Fig. 5.12. India's net exports of energy commodities.
Source: UN COMTRADE.

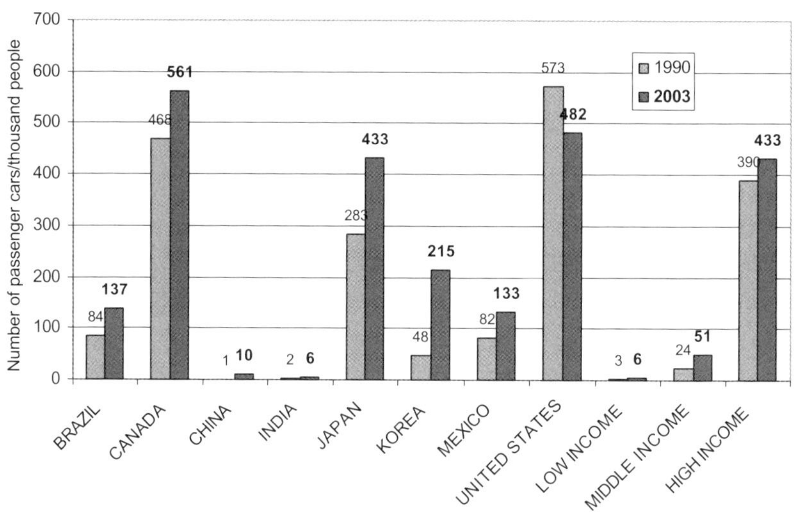

Fig. 5.13. Passenger car ownership by income levels.
Note: Passenger cars refer to motor vehicles, other than two-wheelers, intended for the carriage of passengers to seat no more than nine people. Low income refers to a gross national income (GNI) per capita of $825 (PPP$) or less, middle income refers to a GNI per capita of over $825 and below $10,066, and high income refers to a GNI per capita of $10,066 and over in 2004.
Source: World Bank (2006).

vehicle ownership is relatively low (at 6 per 1000 people in 2003), and consistent with a low-income country. However, as per capita incomes rise, increased vehicle ownership will increase India's dependence on imported oil.[39]

Imports of coal, coke and briquettes have increased in tandem with petroleum imports, but represent a much lower share of India's energy import bill. However, while India probably had a modest impact on relative crude oil import demand and therefore prices, its trade deficit as a share of total trade in coal products was much larger — and has increased at a faster pace from 2003 — than for other energy commodities. In particular, net imports of coal, coke and briquettes accounted for over 7 percent of world trade in these commodities in 2006, up from less than 4 percent in 1995, which would have placed significant upward pressure on coal prices over this period (Fig. 5.12). Coal imports now account for 12 percent of India's domestic usage (IEA, 2007). This increase in the import of coal probably reflects the growing needs of the iron and steel industry, requiring imports of higher-quality coking coal, since domestic coal resources are of lower quality.[40] This growth in coal import demand could also reflect, in part, the switch from oil to coal as a source of energy, since the increase in coal imports corresponds well with the increase in the world price of oil. Coal accounted for 39 percent of India's total primary energy demand in 2005, and with industrial activity expected to grow significantly in coming years, India's demand for coal will probably increase.[41]

India's net imports of gas (natural and manufactured) have increased from 0.5 percent of world trade in the mid-1990s to roughly 1.3 percent in 2006. This increase is related to deliberate government initiatives to diversify India's fuel mix (IEA, 2007). For example, India's permission to import liquefied natural gas (LNG) as of February 2004

---

[39] Increased efficiency in the electricity sector could lead to a reduced reliance on diesel generators, which could lead to a reduction in India's demand for oil. Therefore, the total effect of India on world oil demand is less clear.

[40] The iron and steel industry imports almost 50 percent of its coking coal needs (IEA, 2007).

[41] In 2005, industry accounted for 28 percent of final energy demand in India.

resulted in an increase in imports of LNG that accounted for 17 percent of total gas demand in 2005 (IEA, 2007). Gas now accounts for roughly 5 percent of primary energy demand, up from 3 percent in 1990 (IEA, 2007). Overall, India's energy needs are likely to accelerate, which, given limited domestic resources, will fall more heavily on import demand.

5.5. Food

5.5.1. *India's demand*

The two most important factors driving a country's total demand for food commodities are: first, per capita GDP, which largely determines per capita consumption and diet diversification and, second, population, which determines overall consumption for the country as a whole.[42] For both factors, recent changes in India have been dramatic. Since 1991, India's per capita GDP has nearly tripled while at the same time its population has increased by 34 percent, from 838 million to 1.12 billion people (IMF, 2008). Together, these two factors have shaped not only India's consumption of food commodities, but the world's.

Food is typically considered a normal good, with demand rising with income; however, there is variation according to the food group and per capita GDP. For example, Fig. 5.14 shows that cereals (primarily wheat and rice) are an important part of diets in low-income countries, whereas meat and dairy products are more important in relatively rich economies.[43] This implies that a disproportionately high share of cereals consumption relative to population can be expected in low-income countries, while a disproportionately large share of meat and dairy consumption will occur in rich countries. In this context, India's pattern

---

[42]Other economic factors are also important, such as price, income distribution and the degree of urbanisation, which affect food preferences, but we assign them a secondary role in this paper and focus on population and income.

[43]Figure 5.4 does not provide an exhaustive list of food groups (for example, fish has become an increasingly important part of diet, especially in richer countries, but is excluded from the table).

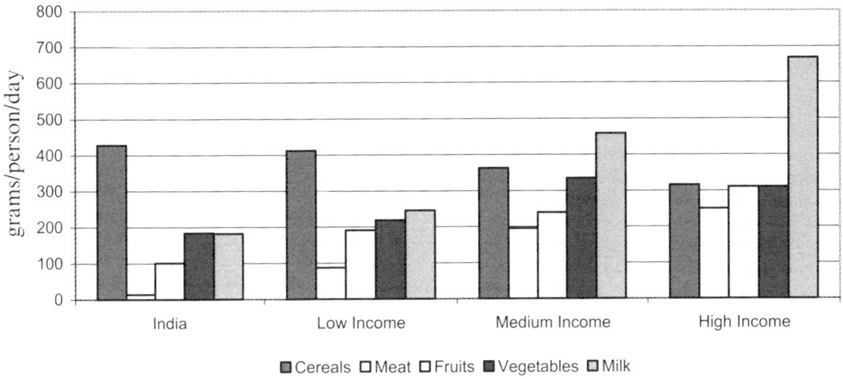

Fig. 5.14. Consumption of major food groups per capita by income levels.
Source: FAO.

of food consumption is consistent with what would be expected from a low-income country, with a relatively high consumption of cereals and a low consumption of fruits, vegetables, milk products and meat. But given that India's share of the world population is close to 17 percent, it nevertheless accounts for a substantial share of world food consumption in all categories except meat (Table 5.2). Strikingly, the United States consumes 15 percent of global meat while having only 5 percent of the global population.[44]

Figures 5.15a–e, which display scatter plots of food consumption relative to per capita income for various countries, show similar relationships. The slope of the fitted curve can be loosely interpreted as an estimate of the cross-sectional Engel curve, which generally varies with income and is positive for most food groups except cereals at

[44]The data for cereals consumption pertain to human consumption and exclude the demand for livestock feed. Rice is generally not used as feed, but other grain feeds represent a significant source of overall demand. Globally, 17 percent of wheat production is used for feed, and for coarse grains (corn, sorghum, barley, oats, rye and millet) the share used for feed in 2005/06 was 64 percent. Thus, meat and dairy consumption create an important derived demand for cereals, which is not examined here.

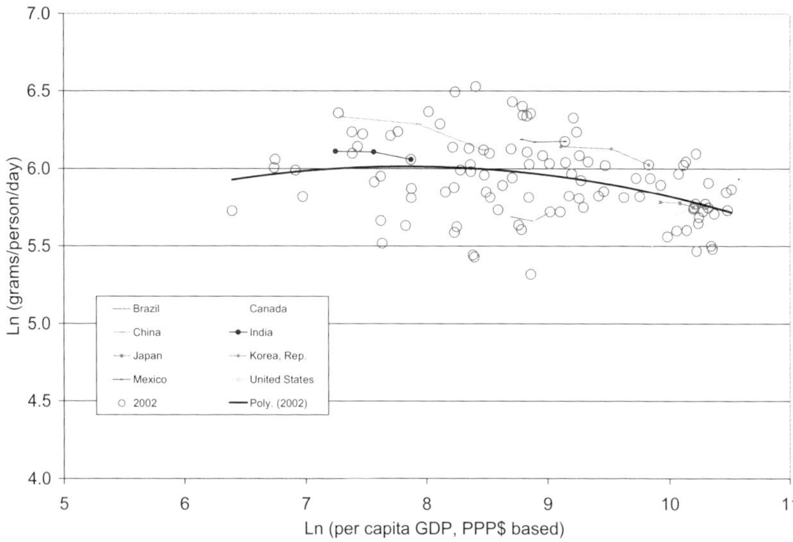

Fig. 5.15a. Per capita cereals consumption, 1991–2002.
Note: The fitted line is based on values for a cross-section of countries in 2002. The time series is shown only for select countries.
Source: FAO; IMF (2008); WDI.

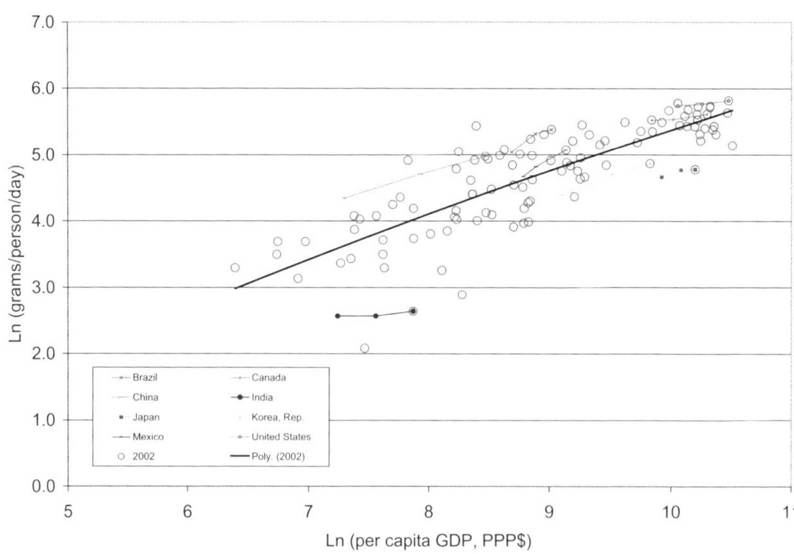

Fig. 5.15b. Per capita meat consumption, 1991–2002.
Note: The fitted line is based on values for a cross-section of countries in 2002. The time series is shown only for select countries.
Source: FAO; IMF (2008); WDI.

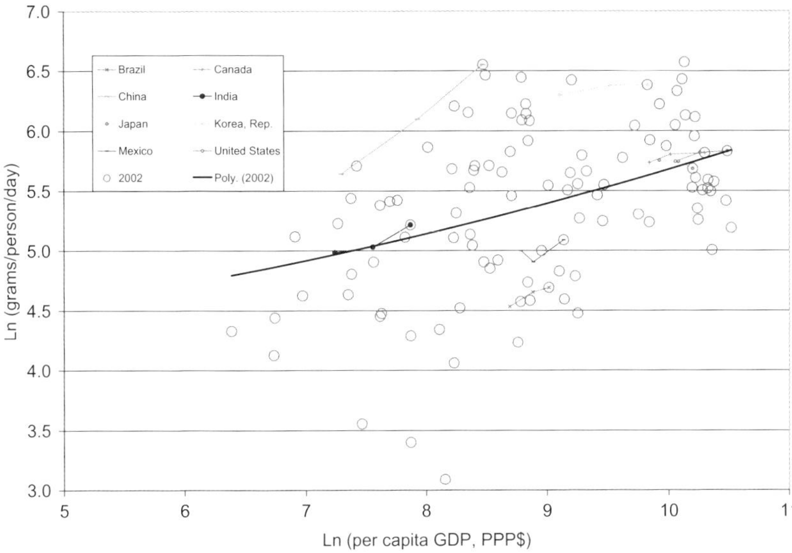

Fig. 5.15c. Per capita vegetable consumption, 1991–2002.
Note: The fitted line is based on values for a cross-section of countries in 2002. The time series is shown only for select countries.
Source: FAO; IMF (2008); WDI.

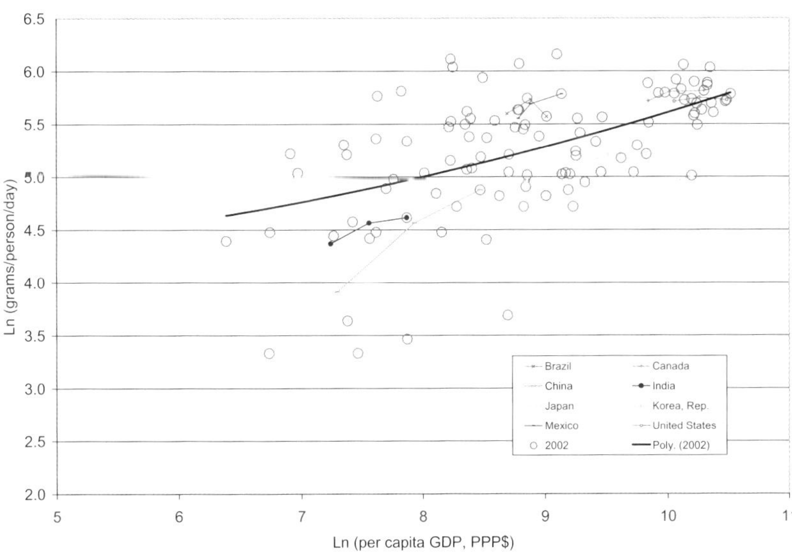

Fig. 5.15d. Per capita fruit consumption, 1991–2002.
Note: The fitted line is based on values for a cross-section of countries in 2002. The time series is shown only for select countries.
Source: FAO; IMF (2008); WDI.

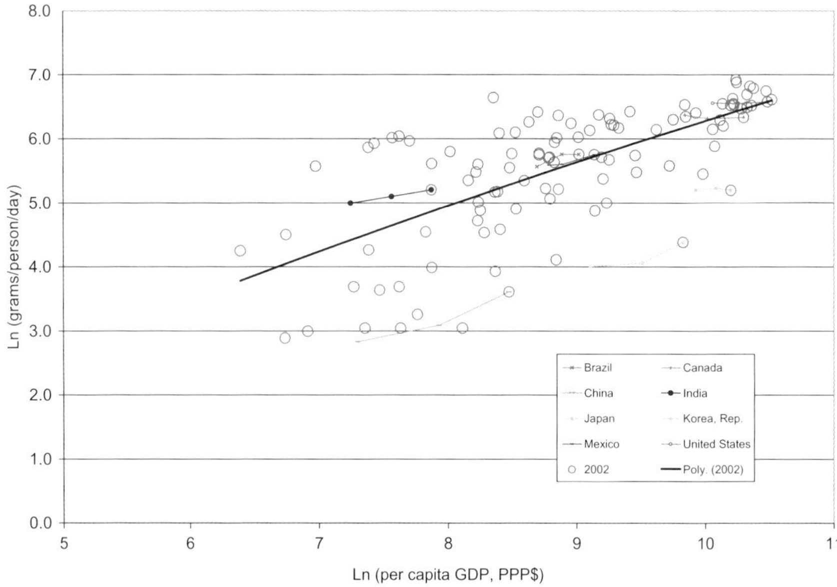

Fig. 5.15e. Per capita milk consumption, 1991–2002.
Note: The fitted line is based on values for a cross-section of countries in 2002. The time series is shown only for select countries.
Source: FAO; IMF (2008); WDI.

higher income levels.[45] Interestingly, for cereals, the data suggest that per capita consumption declines when per capita GDP is approximately $2600 (PPP$), which India surpassed in 2003. As Fig. 5.15a shows, in the earlier part of the 1990s, India's per capita cereals consumption was about 10 percent above what would have been expected of a country with its income, but that consumption was falling in the latter part of the 1990s. Much the same is true for milk products. However, given its per capita income, India appears to underconsume other food commodities, including fruits, vegetables and meat. For meat, this finding can be explained partly by cultural and religious factors, but it is perhaps

[45]A detailed analysis would estimate income elasticities using a more sophisticated approach, accounting for variations in relative prices, income distribution, demographics such as the age structure of the population, etc.

surprising that the consumption of fruit is approximately 30 percent less than what would have been expected given India's income.

Although India's rising real income is a key factor motivating its food demand, to put India's changing consumption patterns into a global perspective we also consider the influence of population growth. The top portion of Table 5.6 shows the global increase in food consumption for the five key food groups, and the importance of population and income growth (including other factors). Globally, consumption of all food groups increased between 1991 and 2002, but the most dramatic increase was for vegetables, which increased by 77 percent, followed by meat at 45 percent, fruits at 40 percent, milk at 25 percent and cereals at just 8 percent. Not surprisingly, rising income (and other factors) was the most important factor affecting the consumption of vegetables, meat and fruit, whereas population growth was more important for milk (accounting for 60 percent of the overall increase in milk consumption).[46] For cereals, rising population more than accounted for the increase in demand, while rising income, which is associated with falling per capita consumption of cereals, reduced consumption.

Table 5.6 shows two striking features regarding India. First, India's consumption of cereal and milk accounted for 30 percent and 26 percent, respectively, of the overall increase in global consumption between 1991 and 2002.[47] The reason for India's relatively large cereal consumption (and, to a lesser extent, milk consumption) is that, in these two categories, India had somewhat unusually high levels of per capita consumption in general (as is evident in Figs. 5.15a and 5.15e), which was magnified by India's strong population growth during this period.[48]

[46]For global food consumption (as well as the individual country breakdowns), the increase in food consumption is attributed one-for-one to an increase in population, since there are more people to feed, assuming that per capita consumption is unchanged. Then the residual is attributed to changes in per capita consumption, likely largely related to changes in per capita income.

[47]Note that consumption should not be equated with demand, since, according to the US Department of Agriculture, 17 percent of global wheat demand and 64 percent of global coarse grains demand is for feed.

[48]At the other extreme, because of India's low consumption of meat, India accounted for just 1.8 percent of the global increase in meat consumption, most of which was concentrated in poultry consumption.

For example, in the case of cereals, the overall increase in India's demand is more than fully accounted for by its population growth (accounting for 50 percent of the increase in global cereal consumption during this period). However, India's income growth has reduced global consumption (by 19 percent of the global increase), owing to a negative income elasticity at higher levels of per capita GDP.[49]

This decrease in the per capita consumption of cereals in India appears to be driven by per capita rice consumption, though similar effects appear to be setting in for wheat. In particular, per capita consumption of rice peaked at 87 kilos per year per person in 1991, when per capita GDP was $1400, and it subsequently declined to 77 kilos per person per year by 2006, as per capita GDP reached $3800 (Fig. 5.16).

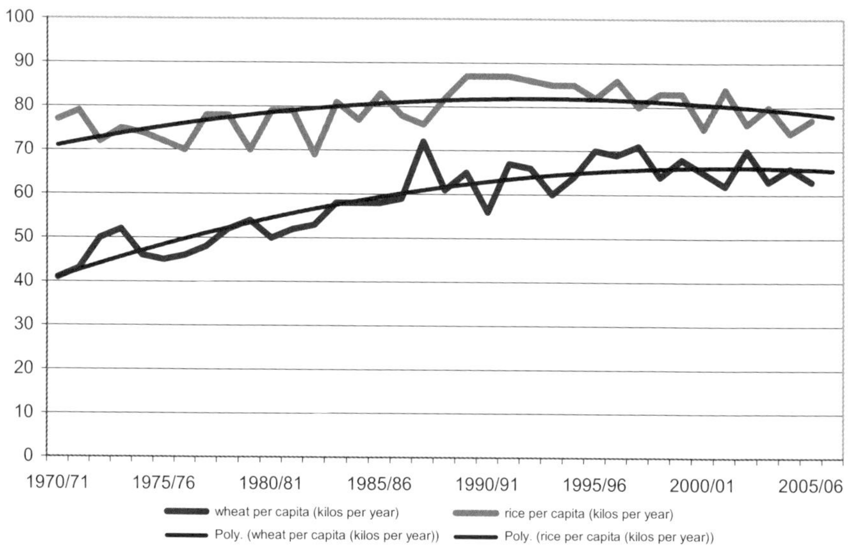

Fig. 5.16. Wheat and rice consumption (kilos per year per capita).
Source: Jha, Srinivasan and Landes (2007).

[49]The overall findings are the same for China, except that its slower rate of population growth (11.2 percent versus India's 21 percent), and its much greater increase in per capita income (160 percent versus 52 percent) means that China, in net terms, reduced its consumption of cereals. Thus, in both cases, rising incomes have acted as a drag on consumption as households have diversified their diet.

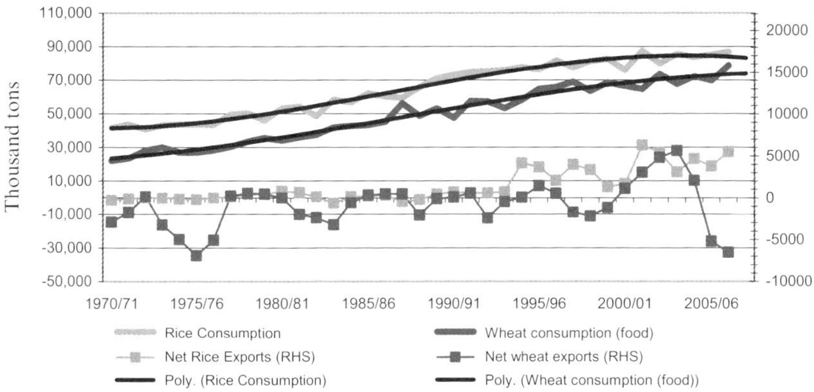

Fig. 5.17. India's rice and wheat consumption and net exports, 1970/71–2006/07. *Source*: Jha, Srinivasan and Landes (2007).

As a result, India's total rice consumption, while still increasing because of population growth, has levelled off significantly.[50] For wheat, India's per capita consumption appears to have peaked at around 70 kilograms per person per year in 2003, resulting in slower aggregate growth in wheat consumption than in the past (Fig. 5.17). The findings for wheat and rice suggest that income growth and diet diversification are becoming increasingly important factors in food commodity demand in India.

5.5.2. *India's production*

Since 1990, as the area under cultivation increased (Table 5.7), India increased rice production by 26 percent and wheat production by 36 percent. This has generally outpaced its consumption, albeit only slightly in the case of wheat. As a result, although India's share of global rice production has stayed roughly constant over this time (at just over 20 percent of the world total), it has become a consistent exporter of rice and an intermittent exporter of wheat. The area under cultivation for crops such as soybeans, rape and mustard seed, and sunflowers

[50]In 2005/06, India's consumption of rice accounted for 20.4 percent of global consumption.

Table 5.7. Share of cultivated area (percent) for major crops and change in share, 1990 and 2007.

	1990[1]	2007[1]	Percentage point change[2]
Rice	27%	27%	0
Coarse cereals	24%	18%	−6
Wheat	15%	18%	3
Pulses	15%	15%	0
Cotton	5%	6%	1
Soybean	1%	5%	4
Rapeseed and mustard	3%	4%	1
Groundnut	6%	4%	−2
Sugarcane	2%	3%	1
Sunflower	1%	1%	1
Potato	1%	1%	0

Notes:
1. May not sum to 100% because of rounding.
2. This refers to the percentage point change between 2007 and 1990.
Source: ISI Emerging Markets; Bank of Canada staff calculations.

(collectively referred to here as oilseeds) has also grown rapidly since 1990. However, crop yields for oilseeds increased by only 0.1 percent per year, whereas respective crop yields for rice and wheat increased by 1.6 percent and 1.7 percent per year, respectively, during the same period (Connell, Hirad and Jahan, 2004). The rapid rise in oilseed production, despite the poor rate of increase in crop yields, probably in part reflects the increasing demand for biofuels. But it also reflects government policy implemented in the late 1980s that aimed at achieving self-sufficiency in oilseeds.[51] Indeed, it is almost impossible to understand India's agricultural food production (and consumption) without giving some consideration to India's agricultural and food policies.

[51]Although, according to the Ministry of Finance, India has yet to become self-sufficient in oilseed production (Ministry of Finance, 2007).

5.5.3. *India's domestic agricultural and food policies*

Three objectives guide India's agricultural and food policy framework: food self-sufficiency, maintenance of adequate returns for farmers, and stable prices for consumers (particularly the poor). On the consumption side, it is likely that India's relatively high consumption of cereals has been partly a result of its public distribution system (PDS), which provides subsidies for major food staples (primarily rice and wheat).[52] Since 1997, below-poverty-line (BPL) households have received subsidised food and are granted ration cards that allow them to purchase a ration at below market prices.[53] Other consumers purchase at prices that are meant to reflect market prices. However, there have been problems with this targeted public distribution system (TPDS), with some states issuing more BPL ration cards than households in the state, and a large increase in the total cost of the subsidy occurred in the first few years after the introduction of the TPDS (Planning Commission, 2005).

On the production side, there are three main pillars of farm support: minimum support prices (MSP) for key agricultural products (mostly wheat and rice), direct subsidies for farm inputs, and a highly interventionist trade policy. The MSP scheme targets major field crops, of which rice and wheat are the most important.[54] Under the scheme, the Government of India announces minimum prices based on a broad range of economic factors, including the rental cost of the land, an imputed value of family labour and a return to management and international prices; the Food Corporation of India (for wheat and rice) intervenes when the market price falls below the announced minimum. In recent years, the MSP for rice and wheat have risen relative to the market prices (Fig. 5.18).

Input subsidies are the second pillar of support for India's farmers. These subsidies are principally for electricity, water and fertilisers, but

[52]Other goods provided through the PDS include sugar, imported edible oil, kerosene and soft coke.

[53]The PDS (in various forms) has been in place since December 1942.

[54]Other crops (including pulses and oilseeds as well as horticultural and perishable commodities) are covered by similar schemes (for a summary see WTO, 2007).

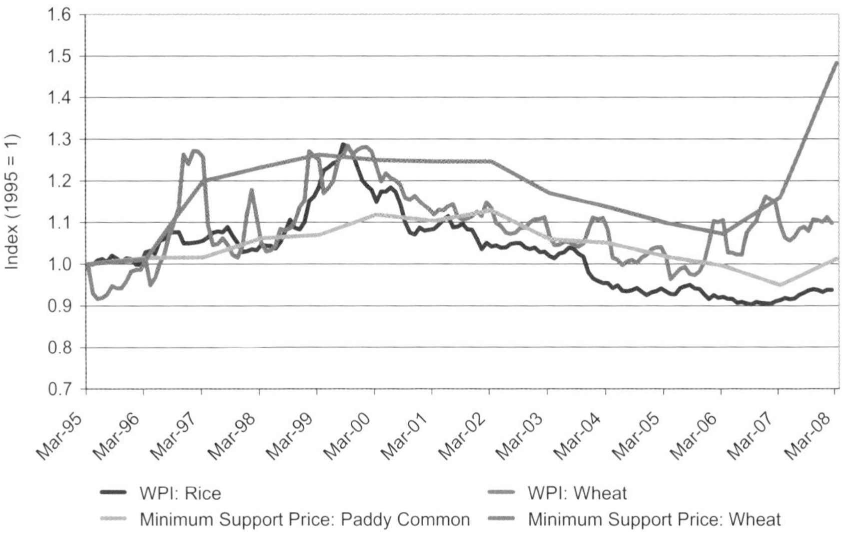

Fig. 5.18. Wheat and rice prices (relative to the wholesale price index).
Source: ISI Emerging Markets.

subsidies for pesticides and seeds are also provided. Electricity subsidies, which primarily cover the cost of pumping water for irrigation at zero marginal cost to the farmer, are typically the most significant, costing an estimated 292 billion Indian rupees (INR) (0.7 percent of GDP) in 2007/08, up from INR59 billion in 1991/92.[55] Because of these subsidies, in 2001/02, 41 percent of India's total cultivated area (75 million hectares) was irrigated, including 54 percent of the rice crop and 88 percent of the wheat crop, which makes Indian agriculture one of the most irrigation-dependent agricultural sectors in the world. For instance, around 2001, 21 percent of the world's irrigated areas were found in India, although India accounted for just 12 percent of the world's arable land (Connell, Hirad and Jahan, 2004). The combined cost of the PDS and farming subsidies has risen through time,

[55] In addition, farmers generally do not pay the economic costs of water used in irrigation (these include the costs of maintaining the irrigation networks and the opportunity cost of the water itself). The cost of this subsidy is difficult to assess, because it does not appear directly on government budgets, but it probably has a significant impact on agricultural production.

peaking at 1.1 percent of GDP in 2002/03 and declining thereafter (in 2006/07 it was 0.6 percent of GDP) (Ministry of Finance, 2008). Fertiliser subsidies are also large, at an estimated 1.1 percent of GDP in 2007/08 (and they are expected to more than double in 2008/09) (Paswan, 2008). The food and input subsidies combined accounted for 2.3 percent of GDP, or 12 percent of agricultural output, in 2007/08 (Fig. 5.19).

It is not difficult to see how the production subsidies could be inefficient. Since the MSP schemes compensate for production costs, they also tend to remove the incentives for farmers to minimise these costs and improve efficiency. The main beneficiaries of MSP schemes are rice and wheat farmers, and, although rice and wheat crop yields are relatively high, it would appear that this is partly because rice and wheat producers benefit disproportionately from the electricity and water subsidies. As a consequence, Indian agricultural production is probably overconcentrated in rice and wheat. Furthermore, for the

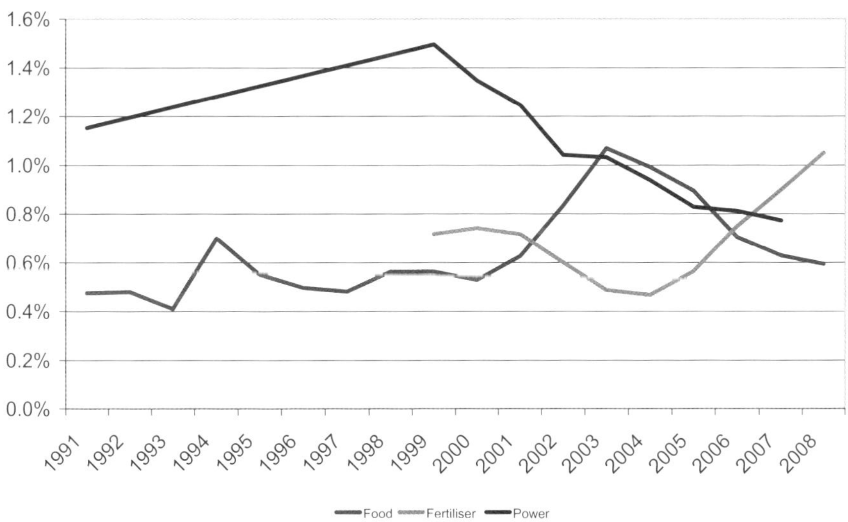

Fig. 5.19. India's agricultural subsidies (percent of GDP).

Note: Food subsidy estimate includes subsidies to consumers and excludes sugar subsidy. 2008 is a budget estimate. Years are fiscal years ending 31 March.

Source: India Ministry of Finance, *Economic Survey* (various years); Department of Fertilizers.

agricultural sector as a whole, such policies could reduce the incentive for farm labour to migrate to other higher-value-added industries.

5.5.4. *External policies and India's agricultural trade*

India commenced agricultural trade liberalisation in earnest in 1994 when it lifted its export ban on rice. Since then, it has become the world's second largest rice exporter, with net exports accounting for roughly 14 percent of the world rice trade in 2006 (Fig. 5.20).[56] The ban on wheat exports was removed in 1995, and the gradual process of dismantling India's system of export licences and quotas began. Under the more liberal trade regime, India has maintained its position as a modest exporter of food and beverages, accounting for 0.14 percent of global trade in 2006 (Fig. 5.10). Nevertheless, some exports continue to be restricted via prohibitions, licensing and other (often ad hoc) restrictions. For example, between 2006 and 2008, export restrictions (including outright bans and government-imposed minimum export

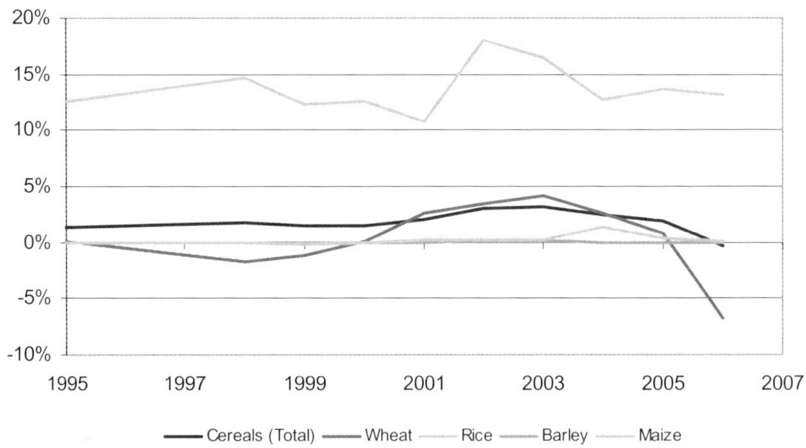

Fig. 5.20. India's net exports of cereals (percent of world trade).
Source: UN COMTRADE; Bank of Canada staff calculations.

[56]This is related to the increase in agricultural production, subsidies and rising per capita income over this period.

prices) on a range of agricultural products were imposed (including pulses, sugar and rice).[57] In addition, India manipulates the exports of grain by controlling the price mechanism. For example, during 2007, when facing rapidly rising global prices and domestic inflationary pressures, the MSP for rice was increased by 11.2 percent, which permitted the Food Corporation of India (FCI) to divert grain sales from the export market.

On the import side, the Government of India actively manages its applied tariff within the range determined by its high bound tariff rates. For example, the World Trade Organization (WTO, 2007) reports that the simple average applied tariff for agriculture was close to 41 percent in 2006/07, compared with the average bound rate for agriculture of 117 percent.[58] As a consequence, there is ample scope for the government to raise the applied tariff on an item as it sees fit. Furthermore, India's tariff rates tend to reflect the needs of the domestic economy: they are lower when domestic food prices become relatively high for consumers, and higher when prices are low, to ensure stable prices for farmers. However, these changes in tariff rates have a destabilising influence on world markets, adding a positive (negative) boost to prices during times of excess world demand (supply).[59]

[57] A listing of the notifications pertaining to changes in trade policy (including those imposed on agricultural commodities) is available at the Directorate General of Foreign Trade's website under the "Notifications" heading (http://dgft.delhi.nic.in/).

[58] Bound tariff rates are the maximum tariff rates that can be charged by a country according to the country's schedule of concessions at the WTO. This compares to average MFN agricultural tariff rates of 15.4 percent in China, 8.2 percent in Indonesia and 16.0 percent in Canada (WTO, 2007). However, this may reflect, in part, India's lower usage of quotas, which averaged 0.7 percent of agricultural commodities (six-digit Harmonized System classifications), compared with 5.0 percent in China, 0.9 percent in Indonesia and 12.4 percent in Canada (WTO, 2007).

[59] These policy changes are reflected, for example, in its net exports of wheat. During 2002–2005, India exported wheat because the FCI had built up excessive stocks, but by 2006 these stocks were largely depleted. As a result, the government decreased the import duty on wheat from a standard tariff rate of around 50 percent to zero, and India moved from being a net exporter of wheat from 2000–2005, when global prices were relatively low, to a net importer of wheat in 2006, when prices were relatively high. India's net imports reached around 7 percent of world trade in wheat in 2006

Evidence of the distortionary influence of policy on India's agricultural trade can be found by looking at cross-country import demand and export supplies of cereals (as a percent of GDP) as a function of per capita income, population and land endowment, as well as trade restrictiveness parameters. Using data for 2005 (and a simple OLS estimation), we find that India's imports of cereals are lower than would be the case for other countries with similar endowments and level of income (Table 5.8).[60] At the same time, India's exports of rice and

Table 5.8. Is India different? India's food imports and exports as a share of GDP.

	Cereals	Dairy	Meat	Oilseeds	Fruit	Vegetables
(a) Imports[1]						
Ln per capita GDP	−0.89	−0.34	0.15	0.06	0.29	−0.03
	(0.12)***	(0.13)**	(0.24)	(0.12)	(0.13)**	(0.12)
Ln area	−0.33	−0.19	−0.15	−0.23	−0.07	−0.16
	(0.07)***	(0.09)**	(0.12)	(0.06)***	(0.07)	(0.08)**
Ln population	−0.05	−0.24	−0.45	0.23	−0.27	−0.13
	(0.09)	(0.12)**	(0.17)**	(0.08)***	(0.09)***	(0.09)
Ln mean tariff rates	0.42	−0.28	−0.37	0.09	−0.34	−0.16
	(0.18)**	(0.17)	(0.38)	(0.15)	(0.18)*	(0.19)
India dummy	−6.19	−3.43	−4.74	−2.49	1.85	1.15
	(0.31)***	(0.42)***	(0.72)***	(0.38)***	(0.30)***	(0.33)***
Landlocked	−0.52	−0.21	−1.13	0.02	−0.34	−0.01
	(0.23)**	(0.27)	(0.53)**	(0.28)	(0.26)	(0.26)
Island	−0.27	−0.45	−1.00	−0.74	−0.83	−0.18
	(0.33)	(0.32)	(0.45)**	(0.25)***	(0.21)***	(0.29)
R^2	0.74	0.41	0.37	0.17	0.47	0.25
Obs.	94	95	93	92	95	95

(Continued)

while maintaining net exports of other cereal commodities (Fig. 5.20). Recent bans on rice exports have also had a destabilising effect.

[60]This involves a simple cross-sectional OLS regression for 2005, which involves regressing the natural log of the share of various food exports (imports) in GDP, on per capita GDP (PPP$), the country size (in square kilometres), the population, all in logs, and on trade restrictiveness parameters. The trade restrictiveness parameters included are the mean tariff rate (in logs), which accounts for the openness of India (and other countries) to world trade more generally; a dummy if the country is landlocked, to account for transportation costs; and a dummy if the country is an island.

Table 5.8. (*Continued*)

	Cereals	Dairy	Meat	Oilseeds	Fruit	Vegetables
(b) Exports[1]						
Ln per capita GDP	0.09	0.48	0.99	−0.18	−0.47	−0.37
	(0.34)	(0.35)	(0.35)***	(0.24)	(0.35)	(0.22)
Ln area	0.15	−0.01	0.55	0.07	−0.18	−0.12
	(0.20)	(0.18)	(0.19)***	(0.18)	(0.19)	(0.16)
Ln population	0.36	−0.11	−0.48	0.25	0.26	0.34
	(0.28)	(0.24)	(0.24)**	(0.17)	(0.22)	(0.17)*
Ln mean tariff rates	−1.37	−1.07	−0.65	−0.28	−0.41	−0.45
	(0.56)**	(0.59)*	(0.54)	(0.39)	(0.49)	(0.39)
India dummy	2.03	1.98	4.08	−0.94	−0.86	−0.93
	(0.85)**	(0.71)***	(0.84)***	(0.54)*	(0.70)	(0.59)
Landlocked	0.90	−0.13	0.96	−0.52	−1.81	−0.22
	(0.68)	(0.61)	(0.73)	(0.74)	(0.72)**	(0.51)
Island	−0.53	−0.53	−0.03	−0.24	−0.73	−0.26
	(0.78)	(0.73)	(0.72)	(0.58)	(0.68)	(0.60)
R^2	0.16	0.29	0.30	0.06	0.11	0.07
Obs.	111	112	109	116	118	116

Notes:
1. The estimation involves a simple cross-sectional OLS regression for 2005. Dependent variables are in logs and refer to imports (or exports) as a percent of GDP. Robust standard errors are in parentheses.
*, ** and *** denote significance at the 10, 5 and 1 percent levels, respectively.

wheat to the world market (a function of the same parameters employed for import demand) are larger than would be expected given its endowments and openness. This probably reflects India's agricultural policy distortions.

For other food commodities we find the reverse. Generally, for food commodities that are probably less affected by policy restrictions (e.g., having lower tariff rates), such as fruits and vegetables, India appears to export less and import more than would be expected.[61] Therefore,

Caution should be exercised in interpreting these estimates, since only one year (2005) is used in the estimation because of data availability.

[61] For example, average tariffs on cereals were roughly 53 percent, compared with 33 percent for "edible vegetables and certain roots and tubers" in 2006/07 (WTO, 2007).

increases in domestic demand for these commodities probably translate more readily into increases in import demand. These results also probably reflect the price distortions created by government policies (i.e., subsidies on the production of cereals), which encourage farmers to grow cereals instead of fruits and vegetables.[62]

Overall, India's imports of agricultural products remain modest, having fallen from 7.6 percent of total merchandise imports in 2000/01 to 4.9 percent in 2005/06 (WTO, 2007). India remains a net exporter of food commodities overall, although its food trade surplus has moderated from 0.8 percent of world trade in food and beverages in 2000 to 0.2 percent in 2006 (Fig. 5.10). Nonetheless, on the margin, India has recently contributed more to increases in demand for food commodities than it has for supply, since its contribution to international supplies (as measured by the total exports of a food commodity) has moderated (Figs. 5.20 and 5.21). This has been the case for fruits and vegetables, dairy and (more recently) cereals; however, India probably has had the opposite effect on meat supply and demand.[63]

5.6. Conclusion

As a rapidly growing, large but poor economy, India's impact on global commodity markets is being shaped by some broad-based economic forces: India's population growth is increasing its demand for agricultural commodities, particularly for wheat and rice, but its per capita

---

[62]This may also reflect cultural and religious factors. As Figs. 5.15c–e show, respectively, vegetable, fruit and milk consumption are higher in India than was the case in China at a similar GDP per capita, which may reflect the impact of differing tastes between countries. India also maintains import prohibitions on certain agricultural products for health and religious reasons. For example, imports of beef and beef products, fats and oils of animal origin are restricted on moral grounds. These import restrictions on meat, in addition to India's relatively low per capita income, have led India to become a net exporter of meat (Fig. 5.21).

[63]This low level of meat and fish imports probably reflects the relatively low average per capita income levels.

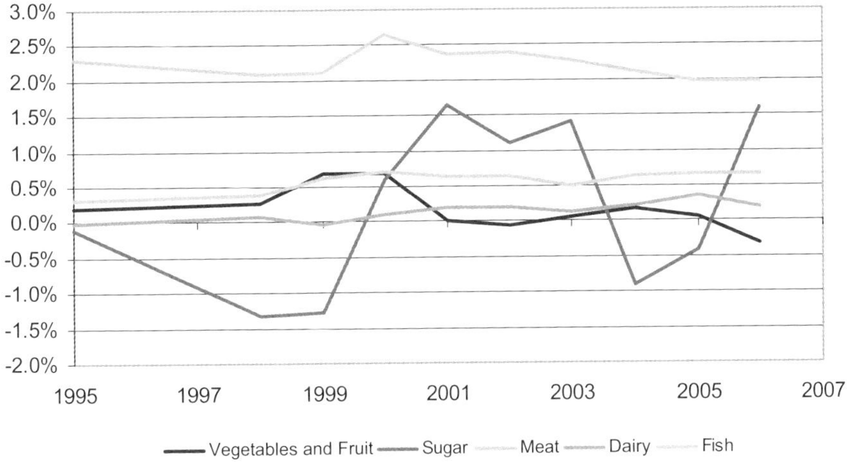

Fig. 5.21. Net exports of food commodities (percent of world trade).
Source: UN COMTRADE; Bank of Canada staff calculations.

income growth is leading to a diversification of diet away from cereals and to fruit, vegetables and dairy. Furthermore, its rapid GDP growth is naturally leading India to consume more energy commodities and metals, albeit to a lesser extent. But economic policies are at work that have distorted market outcomes: for example, the manufacturing sector has been held back in the past by small-scale reservation, which has limited India's demand for metals, and price distortions in agriculture have shifted production towards cereals rather than being reflective of average diets. Continued policy reforms are likely to diminish the distorting influence of India's domestic and trade policies. Recent evidence of some dereservation in manufacturing appears to coincide well with an increase in metals demand as the growth in manufacturing output has risen. India's demand for energy and metals should rise as some rebalancing occurs in its economic structure. However, the outlook for India's demand for food commodities is less clear; it depends on the ongoing diversification of diet in India, and whether policies, including subsidies and price controls, continue to exert an influence on domestic production.

References

Besley, T and R Burgess (2004). Can labor regulation hinder economic performance? Evidence from India. *Quarterly Journal of Economics*, 119(1), 91–134.

Chenery, H (1960). Patterns of industrial growth. *American Economic Review*, 50, 624–654.

Chenery, H and L Taylor (1968). Development patterns: Among countries and over time. *Review of Economics and Statistics*, 50, 391–416.

Connell, P, S Hirad and N Jahan (2004). Indian agriculture: Trends, trade and policy reforms. *Australian Commodities*, 11(4), 611–629.

IEA (2007). *World Energy Outlook 2007*. Paris: International Energy Agency.

IMF (2006). India: Selected issues. IMF Country Report No. 06/56.

IMF (2008). World economic outlook. April. http://www.imf.org/external/pubs/ft/weo/2008/01/index.htm.

International Iron and Steel Institute (2007). *Steel Statistical Yearbook 2007*. Brussels: IISI Committee on Economic Studies.

ISI Emerging Markets (2008). CEIC data. http://www.ceicdata.com.

Jha, S, PV Srinivasan and M Landes (2007). Indian wheat and rice sector policies and the implications of reform. USDA Economic Research Report No. 41.

Kochhar, K, U Kumar, R Rajan, A Subramanian and I Tokatlidis (2006). India's pattern of development: What happened, what follows? IMF Working Paper No. 06/22.

Krichene, N (2002). World crude oil and natural gas: A demand and supply model. *Energy Economics*, 24(6), 557–576.

Krichene, N (2007). An oil and gas model. IMF Working Paper No. 07/135.

Kuznets, S (1959). *Six Lectures on Economic Growth*. Glencoe, Illinois: Free Press.

Ministry of Finance (1999). Economic Survey 1998–1999. http://indiabudget.nic.in/es1998-99/esmain.htm.

Ministry of Finance (2001). Economic Survey 2000–2001. http://indiabudget.nic.in/es2000-01/esmain.htm.

Ministry of Finance (2003). Economic Survey 2002–2003. http://indiabudget.nic.in/es2002-03/esmain.htm.

Ministry of Finance (2007). Economic Survey 2006–2007. http://indiabudget.nic.in/es2006-07/esmain.htm.

Ministry of Finance (2008). Economic Survey 2007–08. http://indiabudget.nic.in/es2007-08/esmain.htm.

Pesaran, MH, RP Smith and T Akiyama (1999). *Energy Demand in Asian Developing Economies*. Oxford University Press: Oxford.

Planning Commission (2005). *Performance Evaluation of Targeted Public Distribution System (TPDS)*. PEO Report No. 189. New Delhi: Government of India.

Virmani, A (2004). Economic reforms: Policy and institutions. Some lessons from Indian reforms. ICRIER Working Paper No. 121.

World Bank (2006). *World Development Indicators*. Washington DC: World Bank Institute.

World Bank (2007). *World Development Indicators*. Washington DC: World Bank Institute.

World Bank (2008). *Governance Matters: Worldwide Governance Indicators, 1996–2007*. Washington DC: World Bank Institute.
World Bureau of Metal Statistics (2007). *World Metal Statistics*. Ware, UK: World Bureau of Metal Statistics.
WTO (2007). *Trade Policy Review: India*. Geneva: World Trade Organization.

Chapter 6

Foreign Direct Investment in China: Trends, Characteristics and Impacts

Chunlai Chen

6.1. Introduction

Foreign direct investment (FDI) in China has been one of the most successful aspects of China's economic reform and opening up to the outside world. The gradual liberalisation of restrictions on FDI since 1979 and the government's commitments to further opening up, particularly the commitments to the WTO in trade and investment liberalisation, have greatly improved the overall investment environment in China. Foreign firms have been attracted by the huge domestic market and pool of relatively well-educated, low-cost labour, which have made China one of the most attractive destinations for FDI in the world.

During the last three decades China has attracted a huge amount of FDI inflows and, by the end of 2008, had attracted a total of over US$880 billion FDI inflows, making it the largest FDI recipient among developing countries. This large amount of FDI inflows has contributed substantially to China's economic development. FDI is playing an increasingly important role in China's economy in terms of capital formation, employment creation, labour training, export promotion, technology transfer, productivity growth, competition and integration with the world economy.

The following overview of FDI in China is structured as follows. The next section reviews the growth of FDI inflows into China, evaluates China's performance in attracting FDI inflows, and discusses the impact of FDI inflows into China on other countries, particularly on other Asian economies. Section 3 analyses the characteristics and discusses the determinants of FDI inflows into China in terms of the composition of FDI sources and the regional and sectoral distribution of FDI inflows. Section 4 examines the impact of FDI on China's economy in the aspects of capital formation, employment and international trade. Section 5 discusses technology transfer and spillover effects of FDI. The final section summarises the main findings of the study.

6.2. Growth Trend of FDI Inflows into China

During the past three decades, China has attracted a large amount of FDI inflows. As shown in Fig. 6.1, the growth of FDI inflows into China from 1979 to 2008 can be broadly divided into three phases: the experimental phase from 1979 to 1991, the boom phase from 1992 to 2001, and the post-WTO phase from 2002 to 2008.

During the experimental phase, FDI inflows into China were at a very low level but grew steadily. In the second phase, FDI inflows at first increased sharply but slowed after 1997 and actually declined in 1999 and 2000 mainly because of the Asian financial crisis, and then had a moderate recovery in 2001. After entry into the WTO, with the implementation of the WTO commitments and broader and deeper liberalisation in trade and investment, China's economy grew rapidly. As a result, FDI inflows presented an increasing trend, increasing from US$46.88 billion in 2001 to US$83.52 billion in 2007,[1]

[1] In 2005, China for the first time published the data of FDI inflow into its financial sector — US$12.1 billion in 2005, US$6.5 billion in 2006 and US$8.72 billion in 2007. Therefore, data for FDI inflows from 2005 to 2007 include FDI inflows into the financial sector.

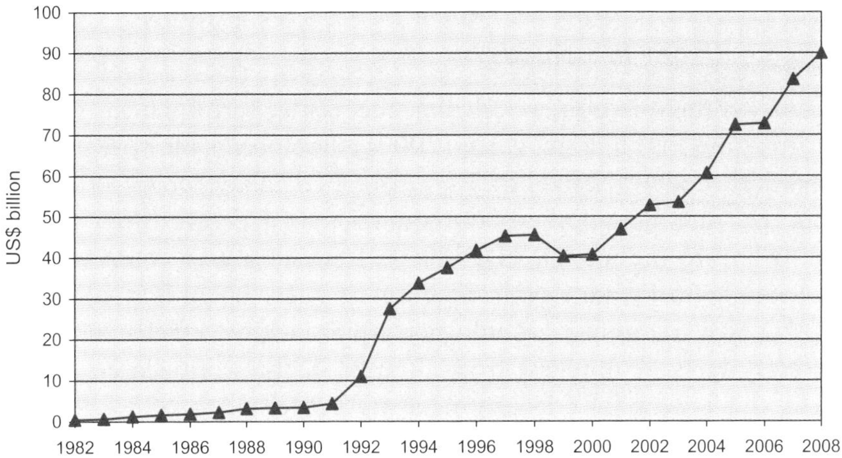

Fig. 6.1. FDI inflows into China (at current price).
Note: Data for 2008 are author's estimation and do not include FDI inflows into the financial sector.
Sources: National Bureau of Statistics of China (NBS) (various issues), *China Statistical Yearbook*, Beijing: China Statistics Press.

with an annual growth rate of 10.1 percent. For the first 11 months of 2008, FDI inflows reached US$86.42 billion, increasing by 26.29 percent over the same period last year (*People's Daily Online*, 2008). By estimation, FDI inflows into China could reach US$90 billion in 2008;[2] however, because of the global financial crisis, it is expected that they will slow down in 2009 (*China Daily*, 2008).

Undoubtedly, China has been very successful in attracting FDI inflows, particularly after its WTO accession. However, this success has caused increasing concerns that China has attracted more FDI inflows from the world than it should and has thus crowded out FDI inflows into other countries, particularly into other Asian developing countries.

[2]Because of the global financial crisis, FDI inflows into China declined from US$6.72 billion in October to US$5.32 billion in November, a decrease of 21 percent. Assuming FDI inflows in December will decline by the same rate, therefore, we estimate that FDI inflows into China in December 2008 would be US$4.2 billion.

6.2.1. *Has China attracted more FDI inflows from the world?*

To answer this question, we calculate the relative performance of China in attracting FDI inflows. Chen (2000a) developed a multi-regression empirical model to establish a norm of FDI inflows from all source countries into a developing host country for the period 1987–1998.[3] According to the model, FDI inflows from all source countries into developing host countries is a function of a developing host country's market size, economic growth, per capita income, efficiency wages, illiteracy rates, remoteness from the rest of the world, level of FDI stock and its economic development strategy. Using the simplified version of the empirical model developed by Chen (2000a), Chen (2002) estimated FDI inflows into China for the period 2001–2010. Against the empirical norm and the model's prediction, we can examine the relative performance of China in attracting FDI inflows.

We define the relative performance of China in attracting FDI inflows as the percentage ratio of the difference between the actual FDI inflows and the FDI inflows predicted by the model. According to the definition, a positive figure indicates that actual FDI inflow is more than the model's prediction, and the larger the figure the better the relative performance of China in attracting FDI inflow. In contrast, a negative figure indicates that actual FDI inflow is less than what China could receive based on its location variables, and the smaller the figure, the poorer its relative performance in attracting FDI inflows. If the figure is zero, then the amount of FDI inflows attracted by China is exactly equal to the amount of FDI that China should receive.

Using the model's prediction and the actual FDI inflows, we calculated the relative performance of China in attracting FDI inflows for the period 1987–2008. In aggregate, from 1987 to 2008 China attracted 2.4 percent (US$21.11 billion) more FDI inflows than its potential based on its location variables. Therefore, although China is the largest FDI recipient among the developing countries, after controlling for its

[3]The empirical model is a multi-regression model with pooled data. The data set contains 32 developing countries for a period of 12 years from 1987 to 1998.

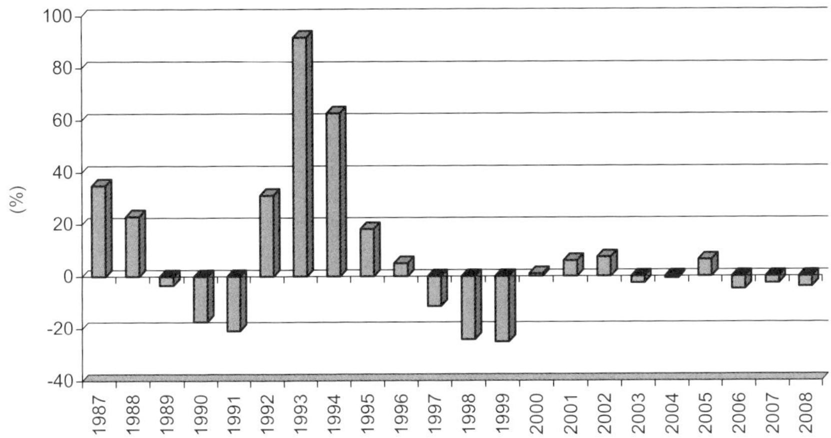

Fig. 6.2. China's annual relative performance in attracting FDI inflows, 1987–2008.
Source: Author's calculation.

huge market size, fast economic growth, low labour costs, relatively well-educated human resources, and other economic and geographical characteristics, China's relative performance in attracting FDI inflows is at a level only moderately above its potential.

From a dynamic point of view, as shown in Fig. 6.2, China's relative performance in attracting FDI inflows fluctuated greatly during the 1980s and 1990s. It attracted more FDI inflows than its potential in 1987 and 1988 but from 1989 to 1991 received less FDI inflows than it might have expected.[4] The unprecedented surge in FDI inflows into China from 1992 is attributed mainly to the implementation of a series of open-door policies in the early 1990s.[5] As a result, China received much more FDI inflows than its potential from 1992 to 1996. However, from 1997 to 1999 it received less FDI inflows than its potential, mainly because of the negative impact of the Asian financial crisis and a number of economic and policy factors in China.[6] Since

[4]China's poor performance in attracting FDI inflows from 1989 to 1991 was largely a result of foreign countries' reaction to the Tiananmen Square Incident.

[5]For details of China's FDI policy development from 1978 to the 1990s, see Chen (1997a), Chen and Bora (1997a) and Chen and Findlay (2003).

[6]For a detailed discussion of the factors, see Chen (2007a).

China's accession to the WTO, its relative performance in attracting FDI inflows has been stable around its potential. This is because of a series of factors in China, including macroeconomic stability, fast and steady economic growth, an improved investment environment, accelerated trade and investment liberalisation, social stability and increasing integration with the global economy.

The above analysis reveals that China's relative performance in attracting FDI inflows was only moderately above its potential. Therefore, even though China is the largest FDI recipient among the developing countries and has attracted a large amount of FDI inflows in absolute dollars, in terms of its huge market size, fast economic growth, low labour costs and other economic and geographical characteristics, it received only its fair share of FDI inflows, or at most marginally more than its potential. In fact, from 1987 to 2008, it attracted only US$21.11 billion more FDI inflows than its potential, accounting for only 2.4 percent of the total FDI inflows into China.

6.2.2. *Has China crowded out FDI inflows into other countries?*

China's success in attracting FDI inflows has raised increasing concerns that it has crowded out inflows into other countries, particularly into other Asian developing countries. A growing China can add to other countries' FDI inflows by creating more opportunities for production networking and raising the need for raw materials and resources, but at the same time its extremely low labour costs may lure multinationals away from other Asian sites when they consider alternative locations for low-cost export platforms. Theoretically, competition in any resource flow may occur when the resource in question is available in limited amounts. However, this "zero-sum" hypothesis is difficult to justify in the case of FDI. For example, FDI inflows accounted for only 14.8 percent of world gross fixed capital formation in 2007 (UNCTAD, 2008), and additional FDI resources can be easily diverted from domestic resources and other international capital inflows should investment opportunities arise.

As China emerged as a more and more important player in the world economy, particularly in attracting FDI inflows, an increasing number of empirical studies have focused on the effects of FDI into China on FDI into other countries, including, for example, Chantasasawat *et al.* (2004), Cravino *et al.* (2007), Eichengreen and Tong (2005), Mercereau (2005), Resmini and Siedschlag (2008), Wang *et al.* (2007) and Zhou and Lall (2005). While these studies all develop a model explaining determinants of bilateral FDI inflows augmented with the FDI into China, they differ in both the measurement of this variable and the estimation techniques.

Chantasasawat *et al.* (2004) use data for eight Asian economies (Hong Kong, Taiwan, the Republic of Korea, Singapore, Malaysia, the Philippines, Indonesia and Thailand) in addition to China over the period 1985–2001 and estimate equations for China's FDI inflows and other Asian countries' FDI inflows by two-stage least squares. They find that the level of China's FDI is positively related to the levels of these economies' inward FDI, and that the "China Effect" is generally not the most important determinant of the inward FDI of these economies. Policy and institutional factors such as openness, corporate tax rates and the level of corruption tend to be more important. Zhou and Lall (2005) and Wang *et al.* (2007) estimate panel models to investigate the effect of FDI into China on FDI into Asian economies and also find that, on average, FDI into China has raised rather than diverted FDI into neighbouring countries.

Mercereau (2005) developed an empirical model to investigate the impact of China's emergence on FDI inflows to Asia, using data from 14 Asian economies from 1984 to 2002. In contrast to the above studies, he does not find any positive relationship between China's FDI inflows and FDI inflows to other Asian economies. However, neither does he find much evidence that China's success in attracting FDI has been at the expense of other countries in the region, with the exception of Singapore and Myanmar. Low-wage economies that compete with China for low-wage investment do not appear to have been particularly affected. Low levels of education or scientific developments are not associated with increased crowding out by China either. Some economic fundamentals help to explain the allocation of FDI inflows among Asian countries, however, and countries might attract more FDI by improving these fundamentals.

Using a gravity model Eichengreen and Tong (2005) show that the emergence of China as a leading FDI destination has encouraged FDI inflows to other Asian countries via supply-chain production linkages. However, they find evidence that FDI inflows into China have substituted FDI inflows into European countries because of the negative effect of distance on supply-chain production linkages. In contrast, Resmini and Siedschlag (2008) estimate an augmented gravity model to analyse the effects of FDI into China originating in OECD countries on FDI into the European Union (EU) and other countries over the period 1990–2004. Their results suggest that on average, *ceteris paribus*, over the analysed period, FDI inflows into China have been complementary to FDI inflows into other host countries as well as into the EU. However, this complementary relationship is not constant across countries, being less strong inside than outside Europe. Also these complementarities follow a decreasing trend over the analysed period.

Finally, Cravino *et al.* (2007) examine the effect of foreign capital stock in China on the Latin American and Caribbean (LAC) countries and find no evidence of FDI diversion from OECD countries, in particular from the US, into China at the expense of the LAC countries. While the growth of capital stocks in China originating from the OECD, especially from the US, was faster than in LAC countries over the period 1990–1997, this relative growth has slowed since 1997.

From the above analysis of China's relative performance in attracting FDI inflows and the review of empirical studies on the effects of FDI inflows into China on FDI inflows into other countries, we may come to the following conclusions: First, although China has been the largest FDI recipient among developing countries and has attracted over US$880 billion FDI inflows into its economy in the last three decades, based on its location variables it has only received its fair share of global FDI inflows. Second, there is little evidence that China's success in attracting FDI inflows has crowded out FDI inflows into other countries. On the contrary, there is strong empirical evidence that, on average, FDI inflows into China have been complementary to FDI inflows into other host countries, especially to Asian economies and to China's neighbours.

6.3. Characteristics of FDI in China

FDI in China is characterised by an overwhelming dominance of developing source economies, high concentration in the eastern and southeastern coastal regions, and biased investment towards the manufacturing sector.

6.3.1. *Overwhelming dominance of developing source economies*

By the end of 2006, FDI in China was overwhelmingly dominated by the developing economies, which accounted for 73.99 percent of the total accumulated FDI inflows into China, while developed economies accounted for only 26.01 percent of the total. In terms of individual investors (see Fig. 6.3), FDI in China was dominated by four investors — Hong Kong, Japan, the United States and Taiwan — accounting for 41.84 percent, 8.48 percent, 7.95 percent and 6.47 percent of the total accumulated FDI inflows into China, respectively.

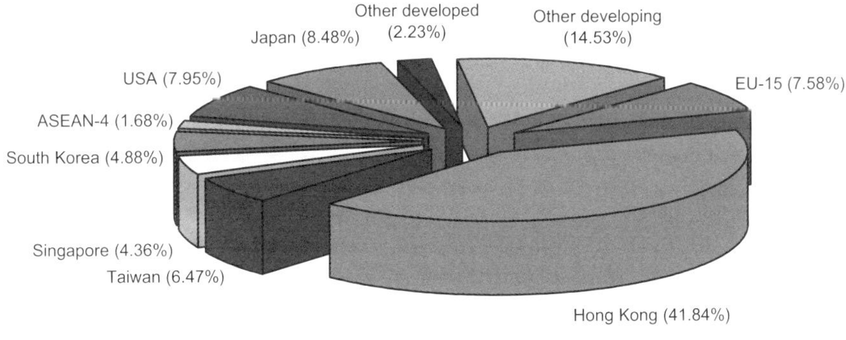

Fig. 6.3. Shares of accumulated FDI by source economies in China (1983–2006).
Note: The calculation is based on 2000 constant US dollar prices.
Sources: Calculated from National Bureau of Statistics of China (NBS) (various issues), *China Statistical Yearbook*, Beijing: China Statistics Press.

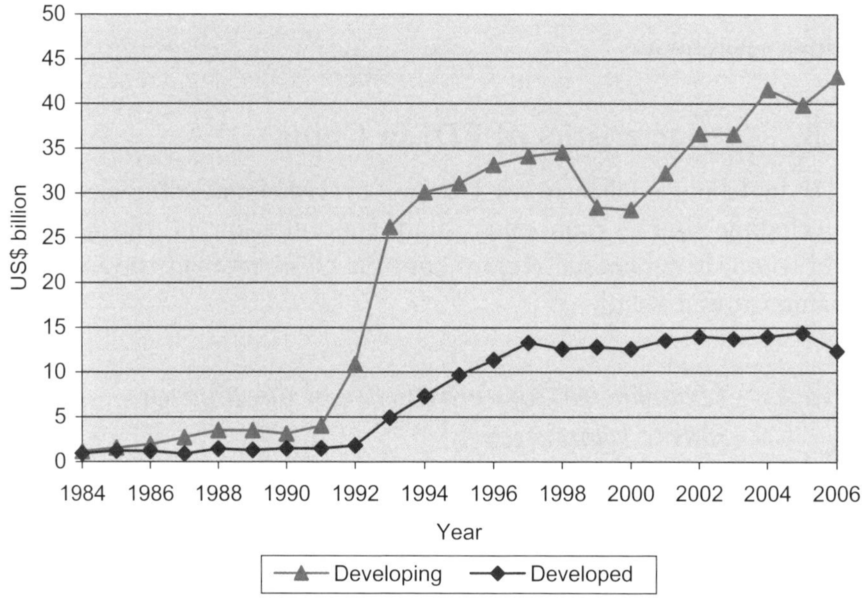

Fig. 6.4. FDI inflows into China by source countries and economies (at 2000 constant US dollar prices).
Sources: National Bureau of Statistics of China (NBS) (various issues), *China Statistical Yearbook*, Beijing: China Statistics Press.

After China's accession to the WTO, as shown in Fig. 6.4, developing economies increased investments in China substantially, growing from US$32.22 billion in 2001 to US$43.04 billion in 2006, with an annual growth rate of 5.96 percent. However, FDI inflows from developed economies increased only slightly during 2002–2005 and declined in 2006.

Why has China been so successful in attracting FDI inflows from developing economies, especially Hong Kong and Taiwan, but not from developed economies, especially European countries, even though they are the major investors for world FDI? Chen (1997b, 2000b, 2002) calculated an investment intensity index and conducted an empirical regression analysis of the investment relations between China and its major investors. This index reveals the relative importance of a country as a host for a source country's investment as compared to the rest of the world as a host for the same source country's investment, and is usually used as an indicator of investment relations between countries.[7]

The studies found that the investment intensity index for the major investors varies enormously. For the major investors from developing economies, including Hong Kong, Taiwan, Singapore, South Korea, Thailand, Malaysia, Indonesia and the Philippines, the indexes are all above 100 percent, indicating that these economies' investments in China have been more than the amount of their shares of investments in the world. In other words, China is more important as a host for these economies' investments compared to the rest of the world. In contrast, the investment intensity indexes for the major investors from developed countries are all below 100 percent, particularly for the European countries. However, among the developed countries, the investment intensity indexes of Japan, the United States, Australia and New Zealand are relatively high compared with those of the European countries, which reflect the regional biases of these countries' investments in the Asia–Pacific region.

The empirical regression analysis revealed that the investment intensities of the major investors in China are negatively related to the gaps of

---

[7]The equation of investment intensity index is as follows:

$$III_{ij} = \left(\frac{I_{ij}}{I_{*j}} \Big/ \frac{I_{i*}}{I_{**}} \right) \times 100$$

where:

III_{ij} = investment intensity index of i's investment in j;
I_{ij} = investment by i (source country) in j (host country);
I_{*j} = investment from the world in j;
I_{i*} = investment from i in the world;
I_{**} = total investment in the world.

The index measures the relative importance of country j as a host for country i's investment as compared to the rest of the world. It can be interpreted as a measure of the relative resistances to FDI flows between countries reflected by the variations in the investment intensity index. If the index is above 100 percent, it indicates that country i's investment in country j is more than the amount of its share of investment in the world. This implies that the relative resistance to FDI flows between country i and country j is lower than those between country i and the rest of the world.

economic and technological development levels and positively related to the levels of economic proximity between China and the major investors.

The domination of developing economies in FDI in China could be attributed to their economic development level and the nature and characteristics of their firms. Because developing economies have moderate technological and innovative capabilities and are at the mid-level of economic development, the ownership advantages possessed by their firms are more concentrated in the forms of labour-intensive production technology, standardised manufacture products and well-established export market networks. Obviously, China, being relatively abundant in labour resources and having a comparative advantage in labour-intensive activities, is an attractive location for the developing economies' investors to explore overseas investment opportunities, particularly for export-oriented FDI. In addition, Hong Kong, Taiwan and, to a lesser extent, Singapore, South Korea and the ASEAN-4 (Thailand, the Philippines, Malaysia and Indonesia) have high proximity with China. The common Chinese culture and language, extensive Chinese business networks,[8] and close geographical distance greatly reduce the costs of doing business in China for these investors and have led to and facilitated companies within these economies to venture into China. Therefore, it is expected that China will remain an important host country for investments from developing economies for a relatively long period.

There are many reasons for the low level of FDI inflows into China from the developed countries. Apart from the relatively large economic and technological development gaps and the low proximities between most developed countries and China, several other factors may hinder FDI inflows into China. First, firms from developed countries usually possess more advanced technology and production techniques. Since the legal network for protecting intellectual property rights in China is poor, these firms are reluctant to invest in China. Second, the services sector in developed countries is advanced and

[8]For more detailed analysis on overseas Chinese business networks see EAAU (1995).

has recorded the highest growth rates in global FDI over the last two decades. FDI in China's services sector has been restricted and most of the services industries were closed to foreign investments before China's accession to the WTO in 2001. Third, the large multinational enterprises (MNEs) are the main carriers of FDI from developed countries, and cross-border mergers and acquisitions (M&As) are an increasingly important means by which they carry out their FDI. However, cross-border M&As transactions by foreign investors in China have to date only been allowed in an experimental fashion with very strict restrictions. All of these factors have strong negative impacts on the investment decisions of the developed countries' investors who are considering investing in China. Not surprisingly, the result is that the magnitude and the intensity of investment from developed countries in China are very low compared with their total investments in the world.

Obviously, the current composition of FDI sources needs to be diversified if China wants to benefit more from FDI. The diversification of FDI sources is not only necessary for China to attract more FDI inflows, but is also very important to attract high quality FDI inflows. In general, enterprises from developed countries with high technological and innovative capabilities will possess more ownership advantages in the forms of high technology, product differentiation, managerial and entrepreneurial skills, and knowledge-based intangible assets. Because of these firm-specific ownership advantages, FDI from developed countries is more market oriented. The general implication is that host countries with larger market size, faster economic growth and a higher degree of economic development will attract more market-oriented FDI. China's huge domestic market, fast economic growth and increasing per capita income are very attractive to developed countries' investors, particularly to market-oriented FDI. Therefore, China has a great potential to attract FDI from developed countries. However, to realise its potential, it must fulfil its commitments to the WTO in trade and investment liberalisation, particularly in strengthening the protection of intellectual property rights, opening more economic sectors, especially the services sector, to FDI, and relaxing restrictions on cross-border M&As.

6.3.2. *Unbalanced regional distribution of FDI inflows*

Since China started to attract FDI, the regional distribution of FDI inflows into China has been very uneven and overwhelmingly concentrated in the east. While there have been some small fluctuations, the gap between the eastern region and the central and western regions in receiving FDI inflows has increased, especially since the early 1990s. As shown in Fig. 6.5, by the end of 2006, the eastern region[9] attracted 86.6 percent of the total FDI inflows into China while the central region[10] and the western region[11] received only 8.92 percent and 4.48 percent, respectively.

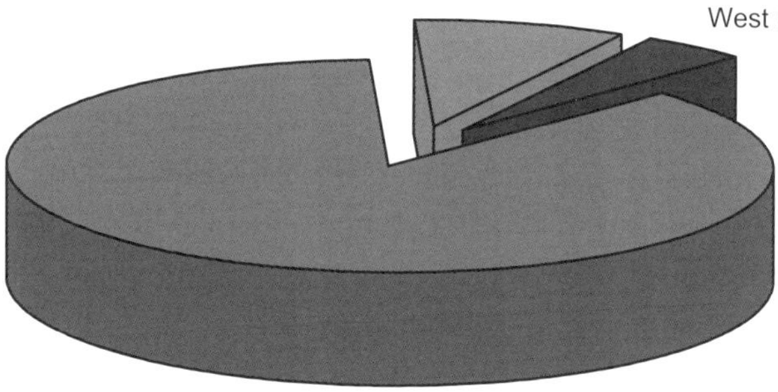

Fig. 6.5. Shares of accumulated FDI in China by regions (1983–2006).
Note: The calculation is based on 2000 constant US dollar prices.
Sources: Calculated from National Bureau of Statistics of China (NBS) (various issues), *China Statistical Yearbook*, Beijing: China Statistics Press; and Ministry of Commerce of China (MOFCOM) (various issues), *China Foreign Investment Report*, Beijing: MOFCOM.

[9]The eastern region includes Beijing, Tianjin, Hebei, Liaoning, Shanghai, Jiangsu, Zhejiang, Shandong, Fujian, Guangdong and Hainan.
[10]The central region includes Shanxi, Jilin, Heilongjiang, Henan, Hubei, Hunan, Anhui and Jiangxi.
[11]The western region includes Inner Mongolia, Guangxi, Chongqing, Sichuan, Yunnan, Guizhou, Tibet, Shaanxi, Gansu, Qinghai, Ningxia and Xinjiang.

With China's accession to the WTO it was expected that the trade and investment liberalisation would bring more benefits to the eastern region than to the rest of the country, especially than to the western region, and therefore that the economic growth in the eastern region would be higher and faster than that in the central and western regions. Consequently, it was expected that more FDI would flow into the eastern region and the uneven regional distribution of FDI inflows into China, especially between the eastern and the western regions, would be reinforced in the short run. As shown in Fig. 6.6, after China's entry into the WTO, FDI inflows continued to be concentrated in the eastern region and increased rapidly from US$39.40 billion in 2001 to US$50.04 billion in 2006. In contrast, on average, FDI inflows into both the central region and the western region declined during this period.

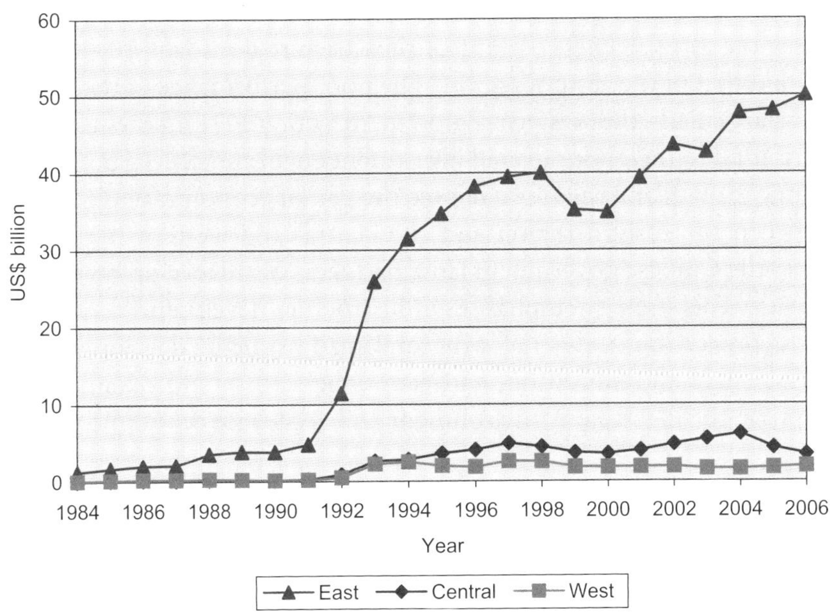

Fig. 6.6. FDI inflows into China by regions (at 2000 constant US dollar prices).
Sources: National Bureau of Statistics of China (NBS) (various issues), *China Statistical Yearbook*, Beijing: China Statistics Press, and Ministry of Commerce of China (MOFCOM) (various issues), *China Foreign Investment Report*, Beijing: MOFCOM.

Empirical studies reveal that this uneven regional distribution of FDI inflows within China is primarily caused by the differences in location determinants affecting FDI inflows (Chen, 1997b, 2000c, 2003). To determine if this situation could be improved in the near future, Chen (2003) calculated the inward FDI attractiveness index for China's provinces and regions.[12] The study reveals large differences among China's provinces and regions in the inward FDI attractiveness index. Because of their relatively more open and developed economy, closer connections with the outside world, better infrastructure, higher level of scientific research and technical innovation, and higher quality of labour forces, the most attractive provinces are Shanghai, Guangdong, Beijing, Tianjin, Jiangsu, Fujian, Zhejiang and Shandong, all in the east region.

Although there has been some improvement in the investment environment for FDI, the central and western regions still have very low FDI attractiveness in terms of location factors. On a comparable basis, the attractiveness to FDI of these two regions lags 10–15 years behind that of the eastern region. The poor performance of the central and particularly the western region in attracting FDI inflows is mainly attributed to their poor overall investment environment. To boost economic growth and therefore reduce the gap of economic development between the eastern region and the central and western regions, in 1998 the Chinese government launched the "West Development Strategy".[13] This strategy emphasises infrastructure development, environment protection, industrial structural readjustment, development of the sciences and education, and economic reform and openness. To improve the investment environment and accelerate economic growth

[12]The inward FDI attractiveness index is the average of the scores on 15 variables (including three dummy variables) for each province or region. The value of the index ranges from 0 to 1. The higher the value of the index, the more attractive a province or a region is to inward FDI.

[13]According to the West Development Strategy, the areas include 12 provinces, municipalities and autonomous regions — Sichuan, Chongqing, Guizhou, Yunnan, Gansu, Shaanxi, Qinghai, Ningxia, Xinjiang, Tibet, Guangxi and Inner Mongolia — and two prefectures — Enshi in Hubei Province and Xiangxi in Hunan Province.

in the western region, China has invested heavily in its infrastructure development.[14]

Undoubtedly the West Development Strategy and the further opening up of the central and western regions have provided great opportunities for foreign investors. However, because the inward FDI attractiveness index values are largely based on structural economic factors that tend to change slowly over time, it is unrealistic to expect that the central region and particularly the western region will attract large FDI inflows in the near future. Therefore, the eastern region will continue to attract most of the FDI inflows into China, and the uneven regional distribution of FDI inflows into China will persist.

6.3.3. *Sectoral distribution of FDI inflows*

By the end of 2006, the sectoral distribution of FDI in China was characterised by the concentration of FDI in the manufacturing sector. As shown in Fig. 6.7, this sector attracted 65.11 percent, the services sector attracted 32.16 percent and the primary sector attracted only 2.73 percent of total FDI inflows during the period 1997–2006.[15]

After China's accession to the WTO, as shown in Fig. 6.8, FDI inflows continued to be concentrated in the manufacturing sector. These increased from US$30.18 billion in 2001 to US$39.43 billion in 2004, but declined to US$35.23 billion in 2006. Studies of the impacts of China's accession to the WTO predicted that China's labour-intensive manufacturing industries, especially the textiles and clothing industries, would grow rapidly, led by the large expansion of exports

[14]The major infrastructure projects include, for example, investing 120 billion yuan in highway and road construction from 2000 to 2020; investing 100 billion yuan in large and medium-sized railway projects from 2000 to 2005; creating a hydro-electricity generation base in the western region and constructing a national electricity supply network to transport electricity from the western region to the eastern region from 2000 to 2015; investing 300 billion yuan in gas pipeline construction to transport natural gas from the western region to the eastern region from 2000 to 2007; and constructing more airports in the western region (Office of the West Development Leading Group of the State Council, 2000).

[15]Data for actual FDI inflows before 1997 by sector are not available.

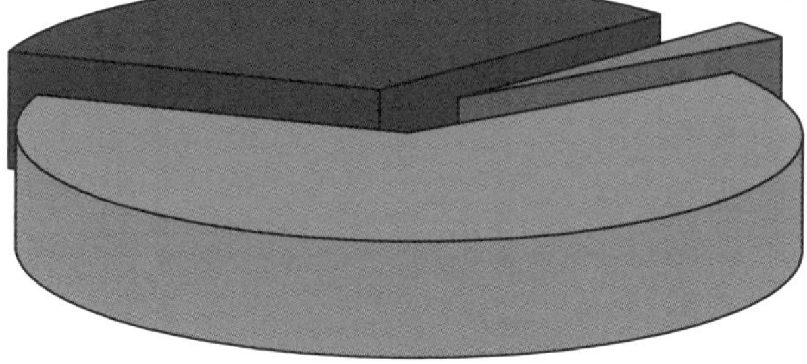

Fig. 6.7. Sectoral distribution of accumulated FDI inflows in China (1997–2006).
Note: The calculation is based on 2000 constant US dollar prices.
Sources: Calculated from National Bureau of Statistics of China (NBS) (various issues), *China Statistical Yearbook*, Beijing: China Statistics Press.

resulting from the reduction of import tariffs and the elimination of import quotas from the developed countries on the imports of China's labour-intensive manufactured goods.[16] It was expected that the introduction of foreign capital, technology and advanced equipment to upgrade labour-intensive industries would accelerate this process and therefore even more FDI would flow into China's manufacturing sector.

FDI inflows into the primary sector continued to decline after 2001. This is not surprising given the declining share of the agricultural sector in China's national economy and the rapid loss of overall comparative advantage in agricultural production in China (Chen, 2006). In addition, China's agricultural land tenure system and the traditional small-scale family-based agricultural production pattern have greatly limited the inflows of agricultural FDI with large-scale production and advanced technology. Therefore, China will not attract large amounts of FDI inflows into its agricultural sector without fundamentally changing its land tenure system and

[16]See, for example, McKibben and Wilcoxen (1998), Walmsley and Hertel (2000), UNCTAD (2000), Chen (2002).

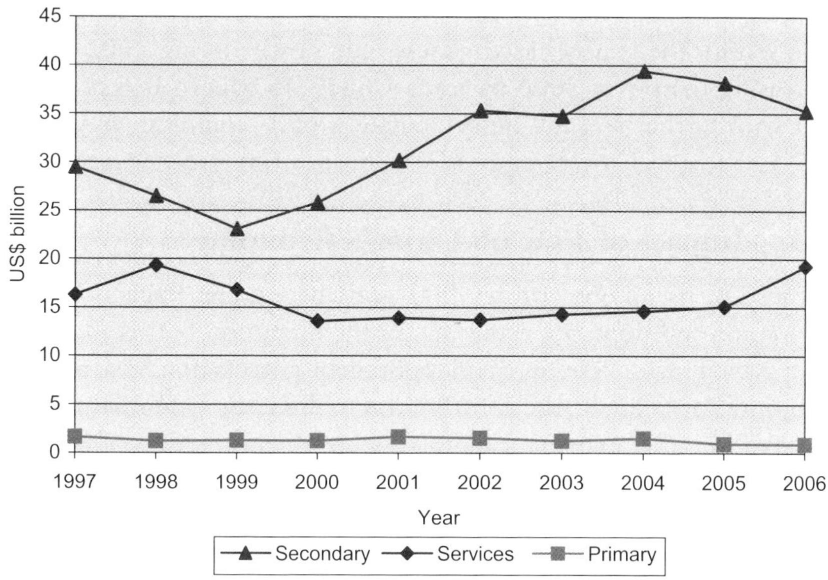

Fig. 6.8. FDI inflows into China by sectors (at 2000 constant US dollar prices).
Note: Excluding FDI inflows into finance services.
Sources: National Bureau of Statistics of China (NBS) (various issues), *China Statistical Yearbook*, Beijing: China Statistics Press.

dramatically reforming the traditional family-based small-scale farming pattern. On 19 October 2008, the Communist Party of China (CPC) Central Committee approved "The Decision on Major Issues Concerning the Advancement of Rural Reform and Development" (CPC, 2008) that allows farmers "to lease their contracted farmland or transfer their land-use rights". The policy is aimed at promoting farmland consolidation, thus creating farming economies of scale, improving agricultural productivity and increasing farmers' income. This policy change should have a positive impact on FDI inflows into China's agricultural sector.

While China made substantial commitments to the WTO to open its services sector to international trade and FDI, it took a step-by-step approach to implementing these. In most of the services sectors, especially in telecommunications, banking and insurance, wholesale and retail, storage, and transportation, China fulfilled its commitments three to five years after its accession to the WTO. As a result, FDI inflows into the services sector grew only slowly during 2002–2005, increasing sharply in 2006 to reach US$19.24 billion. It is expected that with further and full implementation of its commitments to the WTO, China will attract more FDI inflows into the services sector.

6.4. Impact of FDI on China's Economy

Because of its unique nature, FDI must have some impacts on the host countries' domestic economy. In the literature, FDI is shown to have played major roles in the development process of a host country economy, for example, the contribution to domestic capital formation, the creation of employment opportunities, the promotion of international trade, the transfer of technology, the role in economic restructuring, and the introduction of competition to the domestic economy. Over the past three decades, China has attracted huge amounts of FDI inflows and FDI firms have generated some important impacts on China's domestic economy.

6.4.1. *Capital formation*

Both in the general literature and in empirical evidence, FDI has been supposed, and has been proved, to have played major roles in the development process of a host country's economy, especially in the domestic capital formation of developing countries. To discover how important FDI inflows have been in China's domestic capital formation we analyse the ratio of FDI inflows in China's domestic gross fixed capital formation and the share of foreign capital in China's total investment in fixed assets for the period 1994–2006.[17]

FDI has provided important external finance to China's economic development. As shown in Fig. 6.9, in terms of domestic gross fixed capital formation, FDI inflows reached 17.3 percent of China's

---

[17] China unified its dual exchange rate system in 1994. As a result, the exchange rate of RMB to the US dollar depreciated sharply from 5.76 yuan per US dollar in 1993 to 8.62 yuan per US dollar in 1994. For consistency, data before 1994 were excluded from the analysis.

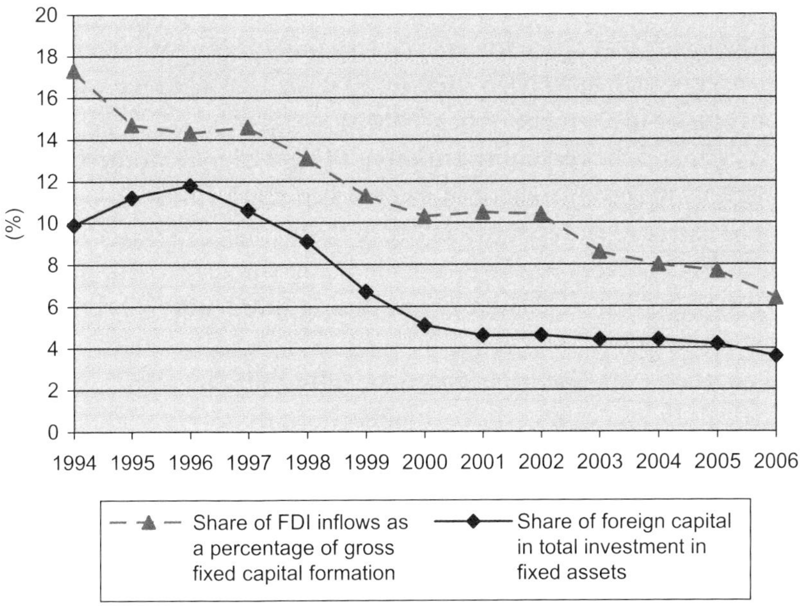

Fig. 6.9. FDI inflows as a percentage of gross fixed capital formation and foreign capital in total investment in fixed assets in China (1994–2006).
Sources: Calculated from National Bureau of Statistics of China (NBS) (various issues), *China Statistical Yearbook*, Beijing: China Statistics Press.

domestic gross fixed capital formation in 1994. However, the ratio of FDI inflows in China's domestic gross fixed capital formation then declined continuously, falling to 6.4 percent in 2006. The main reason for this decline is the much higher growth rate of China's domestic gross fixed capital formation as compared with that of FDI inflows. During 1994–2006, the annual growth rate of China's domestic gross fixed capital formation was 14.74 percent, while the annual growth rate of FDI inflows into China was 6.59 percent.

The above figures, however, may overestimate the real contribution of FDI to China's domestic gross fixed capital formation. In fact, total FDI inflows have not all been used as long-term fixed capital investment. There is evidence that investment in fixed assets made by FDI firms accounted for only a portion of the total FDI inflows into China each year. FDI firms' investment in fixed assets accounted for around

80 percent of the total FDI inflows into China in the late 1990s, and in earlier years was much lower. The remainder (around 20 percent) of FDI inflows may have been used by FDI firms as working capital and for inventory investment (Chen, 2002).

To evaluate the real contribution of FDI to China's domestic capital formation, we use the share of foreign capital in China's total investment in fixed assets. As shown in Fig. 6.9, the share reached the highest level of 11.8 percent in 1996, declined continuously to 4.6 percent in 2001, stabilised around 4.4 percent during 2002–2005 and fell below 4 percent in 2006.

The above analysis suggests that, although the share of FDI in China's domestic capital formation has been declining, for a large and fast-growing economy like China — the fourth largest economy in the world with an average annual GDP growth of around 10 percent for the last three decades — FDI has provided an important supplementary source of finance to China's domestic capital investment, thus contributing to its economic development.

6.4.2. *Employment opportunities*

In the developing countries, where capital is relatively scarce but labour is abundant, one of the most prominent contributions of FDI to the local economy is the creation of employment opportunities. In general, FDI involves direct and indirect employment effects in a host country's economy. Direct employment refers to the total number of people employed within the FDI firms. Indirect employment effects refer to the employment opportunities indirectly generated by FDI firms' activities in the host country's domestic economy. While indirect employment effects are very difficult to measure, the results of a series of country case studies conducted by the International Labour Organization (ILO) show that the indirect employment effects associated with inward direct investment may sometimes be as important, if not more, than the direct effects (Dunning, 1993).

Because of the difficulties in measuring indirect employment effects, we confine our analysis to the direct employment effect of FDI in China but acknowledge the importance of the indirect employment effects.

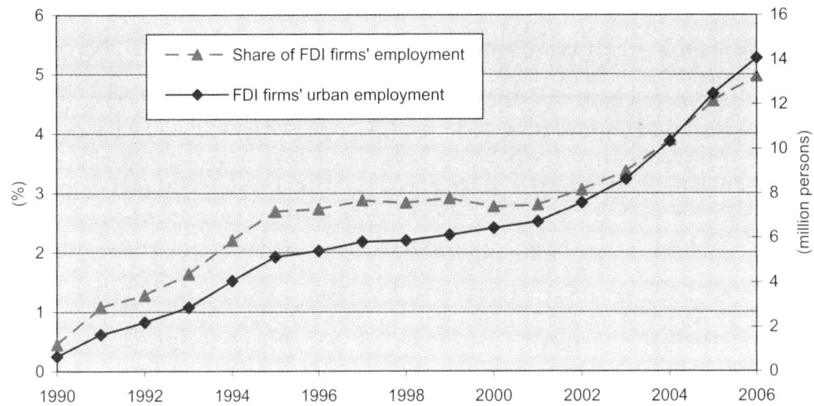

Fig. 6.10. FDI firms' urban employment in China (1994–2006).
Sources: Calculated from National Bureau of Statistics of China (NBS) (various issues), *China Statistical Yearbook*, Beijing: China Statistics Press.

Figure 6.10 shows that the urban employment of FDI firms in China increased significantly during 1990–2006: they employed 0.66 million workers or 0.45 percent of China's urban employment in 1990, which increased to 14.07 million workers or 4.97 percent of China's urban employment in 2006.

6.4.3. *Export promotion*

There is considerable evidence that FDI contributes to the growth of host countries' international trade. The most direct way to measure its impact on China's international trade growth is to examine the international trade performance of FDI firms. Table 6.1 presents the international trade performance of FDI firms from 1980 to 2006. In terms of the total trade value, FDI firms' trade increased spectacularly from US$0.04 billion in 1980 to US$236.71 billion in 2000 and further to US$1036.27 billion in 2006, with an annual growth rate of 47.82 percent. As a result, the importance of FDI firms in China's international trade has increased dramatically from only 0.11 percent in 1980 to 49.91 percent in 2000 and further to 58.87 percent in 2006.

China's policy has been deliberately biased towards export-oriented FDI and as a result, these firms have rapidly become major exporters.

Table 6.1. FDI firms' international trade performance (1980–2006).

	Value of FDI firms' trade (billion $US)			FDI firms as % of China's total		
Year	Total trade	Exports	Imports	Total trade	Exports	Imports
1980	0.04	0.01	0.03	0.11	0.05	0.17
1985	2.36	0.29	2.06	3.39	1.09	4.89
1990	20.12	7.81	12.31	17.43	12.58	23.07
1995	109.82	46.88	62.94	39.10	31.51	47.66
2000	236.71	119.44	117.27	49.91	47.93	52.10
2001	259.10	133.24	125.86	50.84	50.07	51.68
2002	330.24	169.99	160.25	53.20	52.21	54.29
2003	472.17	240.31	231.86	55.48	54.84	56.17
2004	663.18	338.61	324.57	57.44	57.07	57.83
2005	831.64	444.18	387.46	58.49	58.30	58.71
2006	1036.27	536.78	472.49	58.87	58.19	59.70

Sources: National Bureau of Statistics of China (NBS) (various issues), *China Statistical Yearbook*, Beijing: China Statistics Press; and National Bureau of Statistics of China (NBS) (various issues), *China Foreign Economic Statistical Yearbook*, Beijing: China Statistics Press.

As Table 6.1 shows, in 1980 the value of exports from FDI firms was US$0.01 billion, accounting for only 0.05 percent of China's total exports. By 2000, exports from FDI firms had reached US$119.44 billion, accounting for 47.93 percent of China's total exports, and by 2006 had reached US$536.78 billion, accounting for 58.19 percent of China's total exports.

Some empirical studies investigate the relationship between FDI and China's international trade. Using a gravity model, Chen (1997c, 1999) investigated the impact of inward FDI stock on China's provincial trade and China's bilateral trade for the period 1990–1993. He reports that inward FDI stock has a positive impact both on China's provincial trade and its bilateral trade with its 101 trading partners. The explanation for this finding is that, given the overwhelming dominance of developing source economies and their labour-intensive investment pattern, FDI in China is mainly export oriented and, therefore, has a positive impact on promoting China's international trade. Lardy (1995), Zhang and van den Bulcke (1999) and Hu and Ma (1999) also find a positive impact of FDI presence on China's export expansion.[18] Tse *et al.* (1997) and Sun and Parikh (2001), focusing on manufacturing industries in China, find a positive impact of inward FDI on China's exports. However, the role of FDI on exports changes across regions: it has a positive and significant impact on exports from the coastal and central regions, but its impact on exports from the western region is found to be insignificant.

Extending the analysis on the relationship between FDI inflows and China's international trade to an international framework, Liu, Wang and Wei (2001) use a gravity model with the panel data of bilateral trade for China and its 19 trading partners over the period 1984–1998 to examine the causal relationship between FDI inflows into China and China's imports and exports. They find that the growth of China's imports from a country/region causes the growth of FDI inflows from that home country/region, which in turn leads to the growth of exports from China to that home country/region. Li (2003) uses the panel data of bilateral trade and FDI inflows for China and its 75 trading partners over the period 1989–2000 to confirm the mechanism in Liu, Wang and Wei (2001). He finds that inward FDI has a larger predicted impact on China's imports than does outward FDI, and is highly dependent on FDI's motivation and region-specific characteristics. Using a similar method but a different dataset, Hu and Ma (1999) explore a more specific relationship between China's intra-industry trade with the rest of world and FDI inflow. They find that China has the prerequisite of intra-industry trade and that this is heavily driven by FDI inflows.

While the above empirical studies help to explain the relationship between FDI inflows and China's international trade, they do not explore how the entry of FDI firms may affect domestic firms' trade behaviour. This is an area for future study.

---

[18] I would like to thank Yu Sheng for providing the literature review.

6.5. Technology Transfer and Spillover Effects of FDI

Technology transfer is one of the primary motivations for developing countries to attract FDI. It is often hoped that such technology transfer will go beyond the actual projects undertaken by foreign investors and, through knowledge spillovers, will benefit domestic firms and increase their productivity. For the last three decades the Chinese government has designed specific policies and offered generous incentives to encourage foreign investors to introduce advanced technology, production know-how, marketing techniques and management skills in the hope that these technologies will spill over into China's domestic industries. However, have foreign investors brought advanced technologies into China and, if so, have these technologies spilled over into China's domestic firms?

6.5.1. *Has FDI brought advanced technologies into China?*

According to the theories of FDI, for a firm to invest overseas it must possess some ownership advantages, for example a product or a production process to which other firms do not have access such as a patent or blueprint. It could also be some specific intangible assets or capabilities such as technology and information, managerial, marketing and entrepreneurial skills, organisational systems and access to intermediate or final goods markets. Whatever its form, the ownership advantage confers some valuable market power or cost advantage on the firm sufficient to outweigh the disadvantages of doing business abroad (Dunning, 1993; Caves, 1996).

When foreign firms conduct FDI and start production, the ownership advantages they possess will be brought into the host country in which they operate. While it is difficult to directly measure the extent to which ownership advantages, such as technology and managerial skills, have been brought in by FDI firms, there are several ways to measure them indirectly. These include analysing the level of presence of FDI in domestic industries, analysing the industrial structure of FDI

Table 6.2. Level of presence of FDI firms in the manufacturing sector by total assets (%).

Industry	1995	2001	2006
Labour-intensive	25.18	31.44	34.96
Capital-intensive	11.74	15.78	24.09
Technology-intensive	22.04	33.44	44.28
Total	18.93	25.07	32.95

Sources: Calculated from National Bureau of Statistics of China (NBS) (various issues), *China Statistical Yearbook*, Beijing: China Statistics Press.

firms, and examining basic indicators of firm characteristics, including the size, physical capital intensity and labour productivity of both FDI firms and domestic firms.

In China's manufacturing sector, as shown in Table 6.2, FDI firms increased their level of presence substantially during 1995–2006. In aggregate, the level of presence of FDI firms in China's manufacturing sector increased from 18.93 percent in 1995 to 32.96 percent in 2006. Among the three industry groups — labour-intensive,[19] capital-intensive[20] and technology-intensive[21] — the level of presence of FDI firms in technology-intensive industries increased the most rapidly and dramatically, reaching 44.28 percent in 2006. FDI firms in labour-intensive industries also increased their level of presence substantially,

[19]Labour-intensive industries include food processing, food manufacturing, textiles, clothing and other fibre products, leather and fur products, timber processing, furniture manufacturing, printing, cultural, educational and sports goods, rubber products, plastic products, non-metal mineral products, metal products, and others.

[20]Capital-intensive industries include beverage manufacturing, tobacco processing, paper and paper products, petroleum refining and coking, chemical materials and products, chemical fibres, ferrous metal smelting, non-ferrous metal smelting, and transport equipment.

[21]Technology-intensive industries include medical and pharmaceutical products, general machinery, special machinery, electrical machinery and equipment, electronics and telecom equipment, and instruments and meters.

reaching 34.96 percent in 2006. While the level of presence of FDI firms in capital-intensive industries is still relatively low compared to those in the other two sectors, it increased to 24.09 percent in 2006. Given the ownership advantages of FDI firms, the large and rapid increase in their level of presence indicates an increasing and rapid transfer of technology of FDI firms to China's manufacturing sector, especially to technology-intensive industries.

In the last three decades, the composition of FDI inflows into China's manufacturing sector has changed from being heavily concentrated in labour-intensive industries towards more investments in capital-intensive and technology-intensive industries, which has led to significant changes of FDI firms' industrial structure in the manufacturing sector. As shown in Table 6.3, from 1995 to 2006, the share of labour-intensive industries declined while the share of capital-intensive industries, especially the share of technology-intensive industries, increased in the industrial composition of FDI firms in the manufacturing sector. The share of labour-intensive industries declined from 47.19 percent in 1995 to 30.17 percent in 2006, while the shares of capital-intensive and technology-intensive industries increased from 25.43 percent and 27.38 percent in 1995 to 31.40 percent and 38.43 percent in 2006, respectively. The changing industrial structure of FDI firms from the high concentration in labour-intensive industries towards more investments

Table 6.3. Industrial structure of FDI firms in the manufacturing sector by total assets (%).

Industry	1995	2001	2006
Labour-intensive	47.19	36.55	30.17
Capital-intensive	25.43	27.75	31.40
Technology-intensive	27.38	35.71	38.43
Total	100	100	100

Sources: Calculated from National Bureau of Statistics of China (NBS) (various issues), *China Statistical Yearbook*, Beijing: China Statistics Press.

in capital-intensive and technology-intensive industries is clearly an indication of increased technology transfer into China's manufacturing sector by FDI firms.

Because of their ownership advantages, FDI firms, compared with domestic firms, are supposed to be superior in some basic firm indicators, such as firm size, physical capital intensity and labour productivity. For industries with internal economies of scale, the size of the firm is very important for it to reap the benefits from such economies of scale. If the size of FDI firms is larger than that of domestic firms in the same industry, then they should be more technically efficient in production than domestic firms, thus indicating that FDI firms use more technically efficient methods in their production. Physical capital intensity is the capital-to-labour ratio. Usually FDI firms have higher capital-to-labour ratio than do domestic firms in the same industry. This higher capital-to-labour ratio may represent a more technologically advanced production method that requires high capital intensity. Labour productivity is the value-added per worker. A higher figure of value-added per worker represents a higher productivity of the firm. Because of their distinctive ownership advantages, FDI firms are usually expected to have higher productivity compared with domestic firms.

Chen and Bora (1997b), Chen (2002) and Chen and Findlay (2004) find that, compared with domestic firms, FDI firms have larger firm size, higher physical capital intensity and higher labour productivity in China's manufacturing sector. From a dynamic perspective, Chen (2007b) finds that FDI firms on average are superior to domestic firms in terms of firm size, capital-to-labour ratio and labour productivity. However, the level of superiority of FDI firms over domestic firms weakened, particularly in labour-intensive industries, during 2001 to 2005.

Table 6.4 presents the ratios of firm size, capital-to-labour ratio and labour productivity of FDI firms to domestic firms in China's manufacturing sector for the years of 1995, 2001 and 2006.

As Table 6.4 shows, in terms of size, FDI firms on average are larger than domestic firms, which is particularly apparent in technology-intensive industries. This suggests that FDI firms are more able than

Table 6.4. Ratios of firm indicators of FDI firms over domestic firms in China's manufacturing sector.

Industry	1995	2001	2006
Firm size			
Labour-intensive	2.73	1.25	1.87
Capital-intensive	1.48	0.64	1.11
Technology-intensive	2.24	1.27	2.35
Total	2.00	1.07	1.80
Capital-to-labour ratio			
Labour-intensive	2.56	1.32	0.97
Capital-intensive	2.80	1.94	1.59
Technology-intensive	3.04	1.53	1.07
Total	2.38	1.30	1.00
Labour productivity			
Labour-intensive	2.48	1.38	0.88
Capital-intensive	2.50	2.25	1.52
Technology-intensive	4.17	2.17	1.28
Total	2.46	1.60	1.02

Sources: Calculated from National Bureau of Statistics of China (NBS) (various issues), *China Statistical Yearbook*, Beijing: China Statistics Press.

domestic firms to capture economies of scale and that FDI firms are more technically efficient in their production.

FDI firms on average had a higher capital-to-labour ratio than domestic firms in the same industry in 1995 and 2001. However, during the period 2001–2006, the gap between FDI firms and domestic firms in terms of capital intensity reduced substantially. In particular, for labour-intensive industries, the capital-to-labour ratio of FDI firms fell below that of domestic firms. But in capital-intensive and technology-intensive industries the capital-to-labour ratio of FDI firms remained higher than that of domestic firms, suggesting that FDI firms in capital-intensive and technology-intensive industries possess superior ownership advantages and have more advanced production methods.

In 1995 and 2001, FDI firms on average had higher labour productivity than domestic firms. However, the superiority of FDI firms in labour productivity over domestic firms has been weakening and in 2006, labour productivity in FDI firms on average was only marginally higher (2 percent) than that in domestic firms. In labour-intensive industries, labour productivity in FDI firms has fallen below that in domestic firms (12 percent lower). However, in capital-intensive and technology-intensive industries, although the gap between FDI firms and domestic firms in labour productivity has narrowed, labour productivity in FDI firms was still 52 percent and 28 percent higher than that in domestic firms, respectively.

Overall, there is evidence that FDI firms have introduced advanced technologies and modern corporate management skills into China's economy. Over the past three decades, advanced equipment and technical projects have been introduced by FDI firms, which have not only filled some technological gaps between China and the outside world, but have also helped in the development of many new products in China.

6.5.2. *Has FDI generated spillovers to China's domestic firms?*

The above analysis does not explore whether the advanced technologies and modern management skills brought by FDI firms have been transferred to and absorbed by domestic firms. To answer this question, the common practice is to examine the spillover effects of FDI firms on domestic firms' productivity. The general argument is that because of their ownership advantages, FDI firms are expected to generate some positive spillover effects on domestic firms' productivity.

The spillover effects of FDI can occur through three channels. The first channel is through domestic firms' imitation or learning by doing from FDI firms. Because FDI firms' advantages in productivity have the nature of public goods and cannot be fully internalised, domestic firms can copy the production technologies of FDI firms operating in the local market through observation and can learn FDI firms' management skills through hiring workers trained by FDI firms, thus achieving a rapid increase in their productivity (Rugman, 1986). The second channel is through the increased competition caused by the presence of FDI firms in the domestic market. If the entry of FDI firms leads to more competition in the host country market, domestic firms may be forced to improve their productivity by using their existing resources more efficiently or by searching for new technologies (Blomstrom and Kokko, 1998; Aitken and Harrison, 1999). The third channel is through forward and backward industrial linkages between FDI firms and domestic firms (Javorcik, 2004; Blalock and Gertler, 2008). For example, foreign-invested firms have incentives to make their local suppliers in upstream sectors improve the quality and decrease the price of intermediate goods by transferring technology and sharing with them technical know-how with respect to management and quality control, thus directly increasing domestic firms' productivity in upstream industries.

A growing number of empirical studies have focused on the impact of spillover effects of FDI on domestic firms' productivity.[22] In the case of China, earlier studies using data at the industry level generally find a positive correlation between foreign presence and domestic firms' average productivity in the same industry. For example, Liu (2002), using data on 29 manufacturing industries from 1993 to 1998 in Shenzhen Special Economic Zones, finds that FDI has large and positive spillover effects on the productivity of the manufacturing industry. Using panel data for 26 provinces and 4 administrative cities for the period 1995–2000, Cheung and Lin (2004) examine the spillover effects of FDI on the innovation activity of domestic firms and find that inward FDI has significant and positive effects on the number of patent applications filed by domestic firms. However, these studies may overestimate the impact of FDI firms on domestic firms' productivity because of the problems of causality/endogeneity and the productivity aggregation, such that the average productivity at the industry level usually contains the productivity of FDI firms (Javorcik, 2004).

[22] I would like to thank Yu Sheng for providing the following literature reviews.

To overcome these econometric problems, some recent studies use firm-level data to examine the impact of FDI on domestic firms' productivity in China. However, their results are inconclusive.

In terms of horizontal spillover effects, Hu, Jefferson and Qian (2005) use the unbalanced panel data of large and medium-sized enterprises of 29 two-digit manufacturing industries for the period 1995–1999 to examine FDI's horizontal spillover effects and find that FDI does not facilitate the transfer of market-mediated foreign technology. Lin, Liu and Zhang (2008) use a large unbalanced panel dataset covering all state-owned enterprises and private enterprises above the designated size of 71 three-digit manufacturing industries for the period 1998–2005 to examine the impact of FDI on domestic firms' productivity and find that the horizontal spillover effects of FDI firms are generally insignificant. Du, Harrison and Jefferson (2008), using the same panel data but for 60 three-digit manufacturing industries, find similar results.

In terms of different sources of FDI, Abraham, Konings and Slootmaekers (2006) use unbalanced panel data covering 17,645 plants to examine FDI's horizontal spillover effects on China's domestic firms' productivity. By distinguishing different sources of FDI, they find that FDI originating from Hong Kong, Macao and Taiwan (HMT) tends to generate positive spillover effects whereas that from other countries/regions (non-HMT) generates negative effects. However, Lin, Liu and Zhang (2008) find that HMT-invested firms may generate negative horizontal effects while non-HMT-invested firms tend to bring positive horizontal spillovers and that their impact could cancel out at the aggregate level.

In terms of domestic firms' absorptive ability, Girma, Gong and Gorg (2006) find that FDI spillover effects are more likely to be positive for those state-owned enterprises that export, invest in human capital or research and development, or have prior innovation experience. Liang (2008) finds that FDI spillover effects increase with domestic firms' absorptive ability measured with their knowledge stock, such as firms' previous experience and investment in research and development and human capital.

In terms of backward and forward linkages, Lin, Liu and Zhang (2008) find significant positive backward and forward spillovers at the aggregate level, but that the horizontal spillover effects become negative and insignificant. Du, Harrison and Jefferson (2008) find a modest positive relationship between domestic firms' productivity and FDI presence in the downstream industries, but the horizontal spillover effects are insignificant.

Overall, the many attempts to explore the spillover effects of FDI on China's domestic firms' productivity have produced inconclusive results and further studies are still needed.

6.6. Conclusion

This chapter has analysed the growth trend of FDI inflows into China, evaluated China's performance in attracting FDI inflows, examined the impact of China's success in attracting FDI inflows on other countries, analysed the composition of FDI sources and the regional and sectoral distribution of FDI in China, and examined the major impacts of FDI on China's economy. The following summarises the main findings of the study.

China has been very successful in attracting FDI inflows, particularly after its WTO accession. This success can be attributed to several major factors. Among these, China's increasingly liberalised FDI regime, much improved investment environment both in infrastructure and in legal framework, potentially huge and fast-growing domestic markets, increasing per capita income, relatively well-educated and low-cost labour force, and extensive connections with overseas Chinese business communities in Asia and around the world have played important roles.

China's success in attracting FDI inflows has not been at the expense of other countries. First, although China has been the largest FDI recipient among developing countries and has attracted over US$880 billion FDI inflows into its economy in the last three decades, based on its location variables, it only received its fair share of global FDI inflows. Second, there is little evidence that China's success in attracting FDI inflows has crowded out FDI inflows into other countries. On the contrary, there is strong empirical evidence that, on average, FDI inflows into China have been complementary to FDI inflows into other countries, especially to Asian economies and to China's neighbours.

FDI inflows into China have been overwhelmingly dominated by developing economies, particularly by the Asian Newly Industrialising Economies (Hong Kong, Singapore, the Republic of Korea and Taiwan) and the ASEAN-4. The study finds that the domination of these economies in FDI inflows into China could be attributed to their economic development level, the nature and characteristics of their firms, and the high proximity with China. It is expected that China will remain a very important host country for investments from developing economies for a relatively long period.

Obviously, the current composition of FDI sources in China needs to be diversified if it wants to benefit more from FDI. The diversification of FDI sources is not only necessary for China to attract more FDI inflows, but is also very important to attract high quality FDI inflows. China's huge and growing domestic market, fast economic growth and increasing per capita income are very attractive to developed countries' investors, particularly to market-oriented FDI. Therefore, China has great potential to attract FDI from developed countries. However, to realise this potential, it must work hard to fulfil its commitments to the WTO in trade and investment liberalisation, particularly in the areas of strengthening protection of intellectual property rights, opening more economic sectors, especially the services sector, to FDI, and relaxing restrictions on cross-border M&As.

The regional distribution of FDI inflows into China has been very uneven and highly concentrated in the eastern region. The study reveals that this uneven regional distribution of FDI inflows can primarily be attributed to the regional differences in location determinants. The attractiveness of the eastern region is its relatively more open and developed economy, closer connections with the outside world, better infrastructure, higher levels of scientific research and technical innovation, and a higher quality labour force. Compared with the eastern region, although there has been some improvement in the investment environment, the central and western regions still have very low FDI attractiveness in terms of location factors. On a comparable basis, the attractiveness to FDI of the central and western regions lags 10–15 years behind that of the eastern region. Therefore, the eastern region will continue to attract most of the FDI inflows into China, and the uneven regional distribution of FDI inflows will persist.

The sectoral distribution of FDI in China was characterised by the concentration of FDI in the manufacturing sector. China's huge pool of relatively well-educated and low-cost labour is very attractive to manufacturing FDI, which has made China the processing, manufacturing and assembling "factory" of the world. It is expected that FDI will continue to flow into China's manufacturing sector. FDI inflows into the services sector started to increase sharply in 2006 mainly as a result of China's fulfilment of its commitments to the WTO to open this sector. It is expected that with further and full implementation of these commitments, China will attract more FDI inflows into the services sector. FDI inflows into the primary sector have been very low and have declined since 2001. China's agricultural land tenure system and the traditional small-scale family-based agricultural production pattern have greatly limited the inflows of agricultural FDI. However, we expect that the new land reform policy may have a positive impact on FDI inflows into China's agricultural sector.

The fast growth and high inflows of FDI have greatly contributed to the Chinese economy in terms of capital formation, employment creation and export promotion. As a result, FDI has played an increasingly important role in the Chinese economy. This study reveals that FDI has introduced advanced technologies and modern corporate management skills. However, empirical studies find no clear evidence that FDI has produced strong positive spillover effects on China's domestic firms' productivity.

References

Abraham, F, J Konings and V Slootmaekers (2006). FDI spillovers, firm heterogeneity and degree of ownership: Evidence from Chinese manufacturing, Working Paper, Catholic University Leuven. http://www.econ.kuleuven.be/ew/academic/intecon/home/workinggroupseminars/files/fdi%20spillovers%20china.pdf [15 December 2008].

Aitken, B and A Harrison (1999). Do domestic firms benefit from foreign direct investment? Evidence from Venezuela. *American Economic Review*, 89(3), 605–618.

Blalock, G and P Gertler (2008). Welfare gains from foreign direct investment through technology transfer to local suppliers. *Journal of International Economics*, 74(2), 402–421.

Blomstrom, M and A Kokko (1998). Multinational corporations and spillovers. *Journal of Economic Surveys*, 12(2), 247–277.

Caves, R (1996). *Multinational Enterprise and Economic Analysis*, 2nd Ed. Cambridge: Cambridge University Press.

Chantasasawat, B, K Fung, H Iizaka and A Siu (2004). Foreign direct investment in China and East Asia. http://www.hiebs.hku.hk/working_paper_updates/pdf/wp1135.pdf [4 December 2008].

Chen, C (1997a). The evolution and main features of China's foreign direct investment policies. Chinese Economies Research Centre Working Paper No. 15, University of Adelaide.

Chen, C (1997b). Provincial characteristics and foreign direct investment location decision within China. Chinese Economies Research Centre Working Paper No. 16, University of Adelaide.

Chen, C (1997c). Foreign direct investment and trade: An empirical investigation of the evidence from China. Chinese Economies Research Centre Working Paper No. 11, University of Adelaide.

Chen, C (1999). The impact of FDI and trade. In *Foreign Direct Investment and Economic Growth in China*, Y Wu (ed.), pp. 71–99. Cheltenham, UK: Edward Elgar.

Chen, C (2000a). The location determinants of foreign direct investment in developing countries — with special reference to comparing China's performance in attracting FDI with other developing countries. Research Paper to the MOFTEC/OECD co-operation programme on FDI and presented in the OECD/MOFTEC joint seminar in Beijing, May.

Chen, C (2000b). Composition and characteristics of the major source countries in China. Research Paper to the MOFTEC/OECD co-operation programme on FDI and presented in the OECD/MOFTEC joint seminar in Beijing, May.

Chen, C (2000c). Provincial distribution of foreign direct investment in China. Research Paper to the MOFTEC/OECD co-operation programme on FDI and presented in the OECD/MOFTEC joint seminar in Beijing, May.

Chen, C (2002). Foreign direct investment: Prospects and policies. In *China in the World Economy: The Domestic Policy Challenges*, OECD (eds.), pp. 321–358. Paris: OECD.

Chen, C (2003). Location determinants and provincial distribution of FDI. In *China: New Engine of World Growth*, R Garnaut and L Song (eds.), pp. 189–216. Canberra, Australia: Asia Pacific Press.

Chen, C (2006). Changing patterns in China's agricultural trade after WTO accession. In *The Turning Point in China's Economic Development*, R Garnaut and L Song (eds.), pp. 227–255. Canberra, Australia: Asia Pacific Press.

Chen, C (2007a). Foreign direct investment in China: Trends and characteristics after WTO accession. In *China — Linking Markets for Growth*, R Garnaut and L Song (eds.), pp. 197–224. Canberra, Australia: Asia Pacific Press.

Chen, C (2007b). Changes of Foreign Direct Investment in China's manufacturing after WTO accession. ACESA 2007 Conference, 13–14 July, Australian National University, Canberra, Australia.

Chen, C and B Bora (1997a). Foreign investment and internationalization. In *China Embraces the Market: Achievements, Constraints and Opportunities*, pp. 179–224. Canberra, Australia: East Asia Analytical Unit, Department of Foreign Affairs and Trade.

Chen, C and B Bora (1997b). The internationalisation of China and its implications for Australia. Chinese Economies Research Centre Working Paper No. 5, University of Adelaide.

Chen, C and C Findlay (2003). Australia's FDI policy experience: Implications for China. Research report submitted to A Policy Study under the Economics and Foreign Trade Training (EFTT) Project. Canberra, Australia: AusAid.

Chen, C and C Findlay (2004). The impact of foreign direct investment on China's economy. In *China's Third Economic Transformation — The Rise of the Private Economy*, R Garnaut and L Song (eds.), pp. 102–117. London and New York: RoutledgeCurzon.

Cheung, K and P Lin (2004). Spillover effects of FDI on innovation in China: Evidence from the provincial data. *China Economic Review*, 15(2), 25–44.

China Daily (2008). FDI inflows begin to slow amid global crisis, 13 November. http://www.chinadaily.com.cn/bizchina/2008-11/13/content_7200011.htm [2 December 2008].

Communist Party of China Central Committee (CPC) (2008). The Decision on Major Issues Concerning the Advancement of Rural Reform and Development, 19 October. http://www.gov.cn/jrzg/2008-10/19/content_1125094.htm (in Chinese) [9 December 2008].

Cravino, J, D Lederman and M Olarreaga (2007). Foreign direct investment in Latin America during the emergence of China and India: Stylized facts. World Bank, Policy Research Working Paper 4360. http://ideas.repec.org/p/wbk/ wbrwps/4360. html [4 December 2008].

Du, L, A Harrison and G Jefferson (2008). Testing for horizontal and vertical foreign investment spillovers in China: 1998–2005, Working Paper, presented to the International Workshop for FDI in China, Fudan University, Shanghai.

Dunning, J (1993). *Multinational Enterprises and the Global Economy*, Wokingham UK: Addison-Wesley.

East Asia Analytical Unit (EAAU) (1995). *Overseas Chinese Business Networks in Asia.* Canberra, Australia: EAAU, Department of Foreign Affairs and Trade.

Eichengreen, B and H Tong (2005). Is China's FDI coming at the expense of other countries? NBER Working Paper 11335. http://www.nber.org/papers/w11335 [4 December 2008].

Girma, S, Y Gong and H Gorg (2006). Can you teach the old dragon new trick? FDI and innovation activity in Chinese state-owned enterprises. CEPR Discussion Paper No. 5838.

Hu, X and Y Ma (1999). International intra-industry trade of China. *Review of World Economics*, 135(1), 82–101.

Hu, A, G Jefferson and J Qian (2005). R&D and technology transfer: Firm-level evidence from Chinese industry. *Review of Economics and Statistics*, 87(4), 780–786.

Javorcik, B (2004). Does foreign direct investment increase the productivity of domestic firms? In search of spillovers through backward linkages. *American Economic Review*, 94(3), 605–627.

Lardy, N (1995). The role of foreign trade and investment in China's economic transformation. *China Quarterly*, 144, 1065–1082.

Li, Y (2003) The impact of FDI on trade: Evidence from China's bilateral trade. *Journal of the Academy of Business and Economics*, 2(2), 1–11.

Liang, F (2008). Does foreign direct investment improve the productivity of domestic firms? Technology spillovers, industry linkages, and firm capabilities. Working Paper, UC Berkeley. http://faculty.haas.berkeley.edu/fenliang/research/spillover/FDIspillover.pdf [15 December 2008].

Lin, P, Z Liu and Y Zhang (2008). Do Chinese domestic firms benefit from FDI inflow? Evidence of horizontal and vertical spillovers. *Chinese Economic Review*, 15(1), 25–44.

Liu, X, C Wang and Y Wei (2001). Causal links between FDI and trade in China. *Chinese Economic Review*, 12(2–3), 190–202.

Liu, Z (2002). Foreign direct investment and technology spillover: Evidence from China. *Journal of Comparative Economics*, 30(3), 579–602.

McKibben, W and P Wilcoxen (1998). The global impacts of trade and financial reform in China. Asia–Pacific School of Economics and Management, Australian National University, Working Paper 98–3.

Mercereau, B (2005). FDI flows to Asia: Did the dragon crowd out the tigers? IMF Working Paper, WP/05/189, September. http://ssrn.com/abstract=888058 [4 December 2008].

Ministry of Commerce of China (MOFCOM) (various issues). *China Foreign Investment Report*. Beijing: MOFCOM.

National Bureau of Statistics of China (NBS) (various issues). *China Statistical Yearbook*. Beijing: China Statistics Press.

National Bureau of Statistics of China (NBS) (various issues). *China Foreign Economic Statistical Yearbook*. Beijing: China Statistics Press.

Office of the West Development Leading Group of the State Council (2000). Guojia Zhichi Xibu Dakaifa de Youguan Zhengce Cuoshi [State's relevant policies and measures on supporting the development of west areas].

People's Daily Online (2008). China's FDI declines in November 10 December. http://english.people.com.cn/90001/90776/90884/6551141.html [13 December 2008].

Resmini, L and I Siedschlag (2008). Is FDI into China crowding out the FDI into the European Union? http://www.etsg.org/ETSG2008/Papers/Siedschlag.pdf [4 December 2008].

Rugman, A (1986). *Inside The Multinationals: The Economics of International Markets*. New York: Columbia University Press.

Sun, H and A Parikh (2001). Exports, inward foreign direct investment (FDI) and regional economic growth in China. *Regional Studies*, 35(3), 187–196.

Tse, D, Y Pan and K Au (1997). How MNCs choose entry modes and form alliances: The China experience. *Journal of International Business Studies*, 28(4), 779–805.

United Nations Conference on Trade and Development (UNCTAD) (2000). *World Investment Report, Cross-Border Mergers and Acquisitions and Development*. New York and Geneva: United Nations.

United Nations Conference on Trade and Development (UNCTAD) (2008). *World Investment Report, Transnational Corporations and the Infrastructure Challenge*. New York and Geneva: United Nations.

Walmsley, T and T Hertel (2000). China's accession to the WTO: Timing is everything. Centre for Global Trade Analysis, Purdue University.

Wang, C, Y Wei and X Liu (2007). Does China rival its neighbouring economies for inward FDI. *Transnational Corporation*, 16(3), 35–60.

Zhang, H and D van den Bulcke (1999). The restructuring of the Chinese automotive industry: The role of foreign direct investment and impact of European multinational enterprises. CIMDA Discussion Paper No. 38, Center for International Management and Development, University of Antwerp.

Zhou, Y and S Lall (2005). The impact of China's surge on FDI in South-East Asia: Panel data analysis for 1986–2001. *Transnational Corporation*, 14(1), 41–65.

Chapter 7

The Changing Patterns of Trade and Investment in East Asia

Shujiro Urata

7.1. Introduction

The world has been witnessing East Asia's remarkably high economic growth in recent decades despite several setbacks including two crises — one in the late 1990s and the other currently under way. Favorable macroeconomic management, the availability of well-disciplined workers, active investment supported by abundant savings and, most importantly, foreign trade and foreign direct investment (FDI) are among the various factors that have contributed to this rapid economic growth. As shown clearly in Figs. 7.1 and 7.2, the importance of foreign trade and FDI in economic activities in East Asia increased remarkably from the mid-1980s, enabling East Asian economies to obtain technology, management know-how, raw materials and other items, which promoted economic growth, from foreign countries.

This paper examines the changing characteristics of foreign trade in East Asia that are masked by the aggregated picture shown in the figures.* Such an analysis discerns the ways, and also how and why,

*This paper draws on Urata (2007).

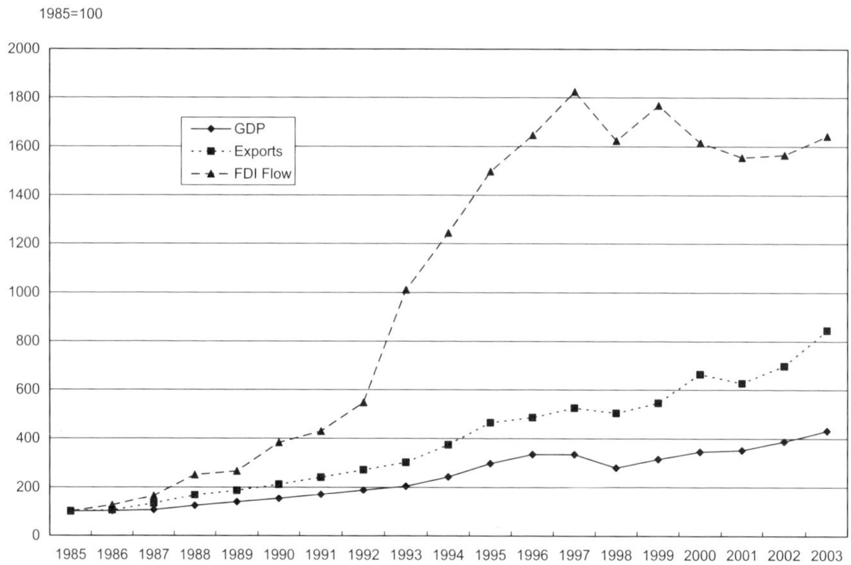

Fig. 7.1. Exports, FDI inflows, and GDP in developing East Asia ($, 1985=100).

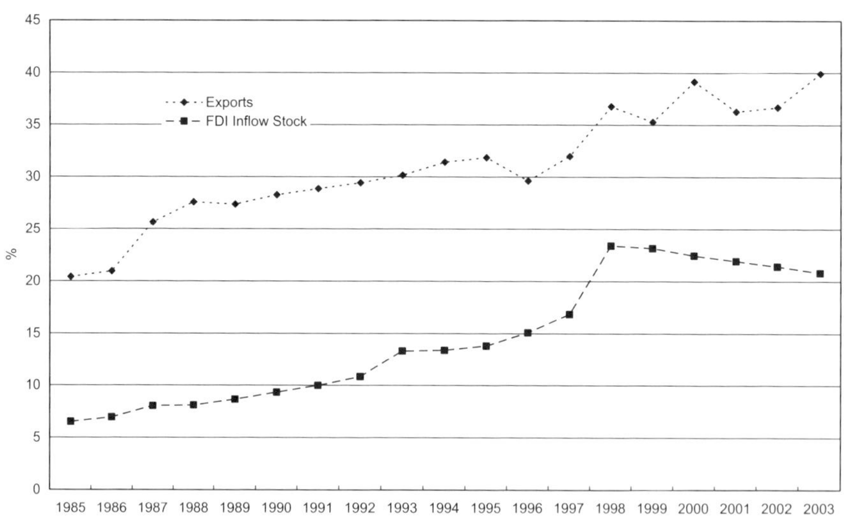

Fig. 7.2. Exports and FDI inflows stock as share of GDP in developing East Asia (%).

foreign trade contributed to the economic growth. Since foreign trade and FDI are closely related, this paper analyses them jointly; however, the focus is on foreign trade and therefore the discussions and analysis of FDI are limited.

The structure of the paper is as follows: Section 7.2 examines the changing patterns of foreign trade in East Asia from various perspectives, including geographical distribution of trading partners, commodity composition, comparative advantage, intra-industry trade and trade in parts. Section 7.3 sheds light on trade by multinational corporations (MNCs), a major promoter of FDI. Section 7.4 discusses trade policies in East Asia to discern the reasons for the rapid expansion of foreign trade and FDI. Finally, Section 7.5 presents some concluding remarks.

7.2. Changing Patterns of Foreign Trade in East Asia

7.2.1. *Rapid expansion of intra-regional trade in East Asia: Overall trade*

One notable characteristic of East Asian trade in recent years has been the rapid expansion of intra-regional trade, that is, trade between and among East Asian economies.[1] The share of total intra-regional exports and imports in East Asia respectively increased from 44.1 and 49.0 percent in 1990–94 to 49.0 and 54.6 percent in 2000–04 (Table 7.1). As a result of the rapid expansion of intra-regional trade, more than half of East Asia's trade (combining exports and imports) is now conducted within the region. It should be noted that East Asia is more important as an import source than as an export destination. This not only reflects the role of East Asia as a "factory" for the world market, as East Asia manufactures products for the world market with the parts and

[1] Many studies have identified rapid expansion of intra-regional trade in East Asia. See, for example, Petri (1993), Ng and Yeats (2003), Urata (2001, 2005a).

Table 7.1. Changing regional patterns of trade.

	Trading partners															
	East Asia		ASEAN		NIEs		China		Japan		EU		US		World	
	1990–94	2000–04	1990–94	2000–04	1990–94	2000–04	1990–94	2000–04	1990–94	2000–04	1990–94	2000–04	1990–94	2000–04	1990–94	2000–04
Exports																
East Asia	44.1	49.0	13.0	12.9	16.3	17.1	6.4	11.1	8.6	8.2	15.9	14.7	24.4	21.4	100.0	100.0
Indonesia	62.0	56.9	12.9	17.9	12.6	12.7	3.6	5.4	32.9	21.0	14.0	13.6	13.5	13.3	100.0	100.0
Malaysia	54.7	54.2	28.8	25.5	10.4	12.4	2.5	5.3	13.6	11.5	14.9	12.6	19.2	19.9	100.0	100.0
Philippines	36.1	53.7	7.8	16.5	9.7	16.7	1.2	4.2	17.4	16.4	18.3	17.5	38.1	24.0	100.0	100.0
Singapore	48.2	56.4	25.3	26.0	14.9	18.3	2.0	6.1	7.8	7.0	14.5	13.3	20.1	14.9	100.0	100.0
Thailand	41.7	48.3	15.8	19.8	8.3	10.3	1.5	5.3	17.3	14.7	19.0	15.5	21.7	19.4	100.0	100.0
Vietnam		49.0		15.9		9.3		9.6		15.7		19.4		12.3	100.0	100.0
China	60.5	45.3	5.9	7.1	39.2	24.2			15.8	14.3	11.3	16.0	13.5	21.1	100.0	100.0
Hong Kong	47.0	55.5	6.6	6.1	5.1	4.8	29.9	39.3	5.4	5.4	16.9	14.0	23.2	20.0	100.0	100.0
Taiwan	42.7	55.2	10.8	12.5	20.6	23.4	0.0	10.3	11.3	9.2	15.4	13.5	28.7	19.9	100.0	100.0
Korea	40.8	46.6	11.2	10.6	9.6	10.8	4.2	15.6	15.7	9.8	13.2	13.2	24.3	19.2	100.0	100.0
Japan	34.6	43.1	13.4	13.4	17.5	19.9	3.7	10.0			18.0	15.5	30.0	27.1	100.0	100.0

(Continued)

Table 7.1. *(Continued)*

	Trading partners															
	East Asia		ASEAN		NIEs		China		Japan		EU		US		World	
	1990–94	2000–04	1990–94	2000–04	1990–94	2000–04	1990–94	2000–04	1990–94	2000–04	1990–94	2000–04	1990–94	2000–04	1990–94	2000–04
Imports																
East Asia	49.1	54.6	11.7	14.6	11.8	13.2	9.2	13.8	16.8	13.3	13.9	11.5	16.9	12.5	100.0	100.0
Indonesia	48.4	52.8	9.4	21.4	12.2	9.5	3.4	7.8	23.4	14.5	21.3	12.2	12.3	8.9	100.0	100.0
Malaysia	58.9	62.5	19.9	23.8	10.5	13.2	2.3	7.3	26.4	18.3	14.4	11.8	16.4	15.9	100.0	100.0
Philippines	48.9	57.5	10.5	17.0	15.7	16.8	1.4	4.2	21.8	19.5	11.3	8.5	19.2	18.5	100.0	100.0
Singapore	55.3	56.4	20.5	24.5	10.7	11.1	3.1	7.7	21.4	13.4	13.1	12.1	15.9	14.4	100.0	100.0
Thailand	55.4	54.6	13.4	16.5	10.4	9.4	2.8	6.6	29.9	23.8	15.8	10.8	11.4	10.9	100.0	100.0
Vietnam		75.3		25.2		27.1		10.8		13.0		9.3		3.1	100.0	100.0
China	55.8	53.5	6.0	10.8	30.6	25.2			19.4	17.6	15.1	13.0	11.5	8.9	100.0	100.0
Hong Kong	73.8	78.4	8.2	11.3	13.2	12.1	36.4	43.4	16.0	11.7	10.2	8.6	7.8	5.9	100.0	100.0
Taiwan	45.2	55.0	8.9	13.9	5.5	8.2	1.1	7.3	29.8	25.7	14.4	10.6	22.0	15.1	100.0	100.0
Korea	39.2	45.7	8.0	10.7	2.3	4.3	4.3	11.1	24.9	19.9	13.3	10.6	22.4	15.0	100.0	100.0
Japan	30.5	42.2	13.9	15.3	9.7	9.3	7.5	18.1			14.6	12.6	22.9	16.7	100.0	100.0

components procured in East Asia, but also indicates the importance of non-East Asian markets for East Asia.[2]

The importance of intra-regional trade has increased for most East Asian countries, with the notable exception of China, whose trade with non-East Asian countries expanded faster from 1990–94 to 2000–04. Specifically, the share of East Asia for China's overall exports and imports declined from 60.5 and 55.8 percent to 45.3 and 53.5 percent over the period under study. A large decline in the importance of intra-regional exports mirrors a substantial increase in the importance of exports to the United States and the European Union.

Contrary to the declining importance of East Asia for China's trade, China has become an increasingly important country for other East Asian countries in their trade relationships. The share of East Asian exports from and imports to China increased substantially from 6.4 and 9.2 percent in 1990–94 to 11.1 and 13.8 percent in 2000–04. This increased importance is shared by all the East Asian economies under study. However, it should be noted that ASEAN and NIEs were similarly important in East Asia's trade in 2000–04. What is notable is the decline in the importance of Japan, the share of East Asia's exports from and imports to Japan declining from 8.6 and 16.8 percent in 1990–94 to 8.2 and 13.3 percent in 2000–04. The decline is largely attributable to the long economic recession in Japan.

7.2.2. *Rapid expansion of the machinery trade*

Rapid expansion of foreign trade by East Asian economies was accompanied by substantial changes in commodity compositions from 1990–94 to 2000–04 (Table 7.2). The changes are especially notable for exports, among which manufactures and, in particular, machinery increased notably. Among machinery, exports of office and telecommunications equipment and electrical machinery grew

[2]This observation on the role of East Asia as a factory of the world will be elaborated later by examining the nature of intra-regional trade in East Asia.

Table 7.2. Commodity composition of foreign trade for East Asian economies (percentage share of total).

	EA		ASEAN		NIEs		China		Japan		World	
	1990–94	2000–04	1990–94	2000–04	1990–94	2000–04	1990–94	2000–04	1990–94	2000–04	1990–94	2000–04
Export composition of East Asia (1)												
Agriculture	7.0	4.1	15.7	9.0	4.7	2.3	13.7	5.2	1.1	1.0	12.1	8.8
Raw materials	1.9	1.0	4.4	1.9	1.3	0.9	2.5	0.7	0.5	0.5	2.5	1.7
Food	5.1	3.1	11.2	7.1	3.4	1.4	11.2	4.5	0.6	0.5	9.6	7.1
Mining & fuels	5.4	5.1	16.5	12.6	2.1	3.5	6.4	4.1	1.3	1.7	9.9	11.3
Metalliferous ores and metal scrap	0.3	0.3	0.8	0.7	0.2	0.1	0.2	0.1	0.1	0.3	0.9	0.8
Mineral fuels	4.2	3.7	14.7	10.9	1.1	2.2	5.3	2.7	0.5	0.4	7.2	8.7
Non-ferrous metals	0.9	1.1	1.0	1.0	0.8	1.2	1.0	1.3	0.7	1.0	1.8	1.8
Total manufactures	86.1	88.7	65.2	75.6	92.7	93.2	78.5	90.1	95.8	93.0	74.9	76.9
Chemicals	5.0	6.5	3.8	6.2	5.2	6.8	5.3	4.6	5.6	7.8	9.0	10.4
Leather, rubber, travel goods, footwear	4.0	2.9	2.3	1.7	7.1	3.5	6.9	5.4	1.3	1.2	2.5	2.1
Wood, paper & furniture	2.3	2.0	4.6	3.3	2.2	1.5	2.0	3.3	0.8	0.6	3.5	3.2
Metal	4.6	4.3	1.7	1.6	5.7	5.1	4.4	5.1	5.5	5.0	5.1	4.6

(Continued)

Table 7.2. (*Continued*)

	EA		ASEAN		NIEs		China		Japan		World	
	1990–94	2000–04	1990–94	2000–04	1990–94	2000–04	1990–94	2000–04	1990–94	2000–04	1990–94	2000–04
Machinery	46.6	53.6	37.6	51.0	36.8	52.6	17.4	40.6	71.6	67.1	38.0	41.4
Power generator	1.9	1.7	0.9	0.9	0.9	1.0	0.8	1.1	3.9	3.9	2.5	2.6
Industrial & metalworking	6.8	6.3	3.1	3.0	4.7	4.9	2.6	3.8	12.8	12.6	8.3	7.1
Office & telecoms	15.9	19.4	19.5	22.0	14.4	21.6	6.3	22.3	17.7	12.2	7.9	10.2
Electrical	11.1	16.8	11.9	23.2	11.2	18.0	4.0	10.1	12.7	15.2	6.9	9.3
Autos	9.0	7.7	0.9	1.3	3.9	4.9	3.0	2.6	21.8	20.6	9.3	9.5
Other transportation	1.8	1.7	1.2	0.6	1.7	2.3	0.6	0.8	2.7	2.5	3.0	2.6
Textiles & garments	12.7	9.1	8.7	5.8	20.6	11.8	29.1	18.3	2.1	1.5	7.1	5.7
Other manufactures	11.0	10.2	6.6	6.0	15.0	11.9	13.4	12.8	9.0	9.8	9.7	9.3
Others	1.5	2.1	2.6	2.8	0.5	1.0	1.4	0.6	1.8	4.3	3.1	3.0
Total	100	100	100	100	100	100	100	100	100	100	100	100

(*Continued*)

Table 7.2. *(Continued)*

	Indonesia		Malaysia		Philippines		Singapore		Thailand		Hong Kong		Taiwan		Korea	
	1990–94	2000–04	1990–94	2000–04	1990–94	2000–04	1990–94	2000–04	1990–94	2000–04	1990–94	2000–04	1990–94	2000–04	1990–94	2000–04
Export Composition of East Asia (2)																
Agriculture	16.0	15.3	19.9	9.6	17.9	6.0	6.8	2.5	28.7	18.3	4.8	2.3	5.3	2.5	4.1	2.3
Raw materials	4.8	4.4	9.6	2.4	1.5	0.5	1.7	0.4	4.4	3.8	1.3	0.9	1.4	1.2	1.2	0.9
Food	11.2	10.9	10.3	7.2	16.4	5.5	5.1	2.1	24.3	14.6	3.5	1.4	3.9	1.3	2.8	1.4
Mining & fuels	36.8	29.1	13.4	11.0	7.6	2.9	14.7	9.8	1.2	3.6	1.9	1.5	1.7	3.4	2.6	5.8
Metalliferous ores and metal scrap	2.7	3.6	0.3	0.1	2.9	0.7	0.3	0.2	0.1	0.2	0.3	0.2	0.1	0.1	0.1	0.1
Mineral fuels	33.0	23.6	12.0	10.0	2.1	1.2	13.3	8.8	0.9	2.9	0.8	0.3	0.7	2.0	1.9	4.5
Non-ferrous metals	1.2	1.9	1.1	0.9	2.6	1.1	1.1	0.9	0.2	0.5	0.8	1.1	0.9	1.2	0.6	1.3
Total manufactures	46.5	54.8	66.1	78.2	45.9	83.0	76.9	84.3	68.6	74.8	92.5	94.7	92.8	94.0	92.7	90.9
Chemicals	2.5	5.4	2.1	4.7	2.7	1.2	6.2	9.7	2.6	6.1	5.4	4.8	4.8	7.5	5.4	8.5
Leather, rubber, travel goods, footwear	4.5	3.4	1.0	0.6	2.0	0.8	0.5	0.5	5.7	3.4	7.5	6.0	5.9	1.6	7.6	2.1
Wood, paper & furniture	14.9	10.9	4.0	3.7	3.8	1.5	1.3	0.5	2.4	2.8	1.8	1.5	3.9	1.8	1.1	1.2
Metal	1.5	1.7	1.6	2.0	1.0	0.5	1.9	1.2	2.0	2.8	3.0	2.4	7.1	8.4	8.5	5.8

(Continued)

Table 7.2. *(Continued)*

	Indonesia		Malaysia		Philippines		Singapore		Thailand		Hong Kong		Taiwan		Korea	
	1990–94	2000–04	1990–94	2000–04	1990–94	2000–04	1990–94	2000–04	1990–94	2000–04	1990–94	2000–04	1990–94	2000–04	1990–94	2000–04
Machinery	4.7	16.9	46.0	58.6	19.8	68.6	56.8	63.3	28.0	43.2	28.6	43.7	41.9	55.5	43.9	60.8
Power generator	0.1	0.8	0.9	0.7	0.1	0.2	1.7	1.1	0.7	1.8	0.9	1.3	0.6	0.5	1.1	1.0
Industrial & metalworking	0.3	1.1	2.5	2.4	0.4	1.2	5.4	4.7	3.0	3.9	3.8	2.9	7.0	6.9	3.5	5.6
Office & telecoms	2.4	9.4	20.4	29.6	6.3	22.4	32.7	25.6	13.3	17.5	12.9	21.4	18.1	21.7	12.9	21.7
Electrical	1.0	4.4	18.9	25.1	12.2	41.8	14.5	30.2	9.0	15.0	8.8	17.3	11.2	22.7	14.9	15.2
Autos	0.6	1.0	0.6	0.5	0.9	2.6	1.1	0.8	1.4	4.4	2.0	0.7	4.5	3.3	6.0	11.0
Other transportation	0.3	0.2	2.7	0.4	0.0	0.4	1.3	1.0	0.6	0.6	0.1	0.1	0.4	0.5	5.5	6.2
Textiles & garments	15.2	12.6	5.6	3.2	11.3	6.8	4.0	1.8	15.4	8.0	25.4	16.9	14.9	8.7	19.3	8.2
Other manufactures	3.3	3.9	5.7	5.4	5.4	3.5	6.2	7.3	12.6	8.4	20.8	19.3	14.5	10.5	6.9	4.4
Others	0.7	0.8	0.6	1.2	28.6	8.1	1.6	3.4	1.5	3.3	0.8	1.5	0.2	0.1	0.6	1.0
Total	100	100	100	100	100	100	100	100	100	100	100	100	100	100	100	100

(Continued)

Table 7.2. (*Continued*)

	EA		ASEAN		NIEs		China		Japan		World	
	1990–94	2000–04	1990–94	2000–04	1990–94	2000–04	1990–94	2000–04	1990–94	2000–04	1990–94	2000–04
Import composition of East Asia (1)												
Agriculture	12.9	8.9	8.5	6.9	9.9	6.2	9.3	7.7	23.3	15.6	12.0	9.1
Raw materials	4.3	2.5	2.5	1.6	3.8	1.8	4.4	4.0	6.8	3.1	2.9	1.9
Food	8.6	6.3	6.1	5.2	6.1	4.4	4.9	3.7	16.4	12.5	9.2	7.2
Mining & fuels	15.4	16.8	11.5	13.6	11.5	14.7	7.7	13.7	27.9	25.5	12.2	13.3
Metalliferous ores and metal scrap	1.7	1.8	0.7	0.5	1.2	1.2	1.9	3.3	3.3	2.4	1.1	1.0
Mineral fuels	11.3	12.7	9.0	11.5	8.0	11.1	4.1	7.8	21.2	20.7	9.1	10.5
Non-ferrous metals	2.4	2.3	1.8	1.6	2.3	2.4	1.7	2.6	3.4	2.4	2.0	1.8
Total manufactures	68.3	72.7	76.5	77.5	75.4	77.8	82.3	77.9	45.7	56.7	72.5	74.7
Chemicals	8.3	9.0	8.9	8.6	9.0	8.3	11.7	12.2	7.0	7.3	9.1	10.5
Leather, rubber, travel goods, footwear	2.3	1.9	1.1	1.0	3.6	2.8	1.8	1.2	1.9	2.0	2.4	2.1
Wood, paper & furniture	2.1	1.7	1.6	1.3	2.2	1.5	2.7	1.5	2.3	2.6	3.4	3.2
Metal	5.3	4.0	6.6	4.6	5.1	4.1	8.6	5.5	2.7	2.1	5.1	4.6

(*Continued*)

Table 7.2. *(Continued)*

	EA		ASEAN		NIEs		China		Japan		World	
	1990–94	2000–04	1990–94	2000–04	1990–94	2000–04	1990–94	2000–04	1990–94	2000–04	1990–94	2000–04
Machinery	34.3	41.8	47.6	52.9	34.4	42.6	42.0	45.0	16.9	27.6	36.0	39.5
Power generator	2.1	1.8	3.3	2.1	1.8	1.6	2.7	2.0	1.0	1.6	2.3	2.5
Industrial & metalworking	9.0	6.8	12.1	7.8	8.4	6.4	18.0	10.5	2.9	3.2	7.9	6.7
Office & telecoms	7.5	11.6	10.2	12.3	7.8	13.2	6.6	10.3	4.4	10.1	7.8	9.9
Electrical	9.7	18.1	14.5	25.9	11.4	19.3	5.6	18.6	4.1	8.8	6.8	9.5
Autos	3.7	2.3	4.1	2.9	3.3	1.5	5.7	2.3	3.0	2.9	9.0	9.0
Other transportation	2.3	1.2	3.4	1.9	1.8	0.8	3.3	1.5	1.5	1.0	2.2	1.9
Textiles & garments	7.3	5.4	3.7	2.9	10.0	7.0	9.4	4.4	6.6	6.5	6.8	5.5
Other manufactures	8.7	8.9	7.2	6.3	11.0	11.5	6.2	8.0	8.2	8.5	9.7	9.3
Others	2.9	1.6	3.5	2.0	3.2	1.3	0.7	0.7	3.1	2.2	3.3	2.9
Total	100	100	100	100	100	100	100	100	100	100	100	100

(Continued)

Table 7.2. (*Continued*)

	Indonesia		Malaysia		Philippines		Singapore		Thailand		Hong Kong		Taiwan		Korea	
	1990–94	2000–04	1990–94	2000–04	1990–94	2000–04	1990–94	2000–04	1990–94	2000–04	1990–94	2000–04	1990–94	2000–04	1990–94	2000–04
Import composition of East Asia (2)																
Agriculture	11.5	16.6	7.2	6.3	10.9	8.4	7.0	3.7	9.5	7.5	8.1	4.9	10.4	6.0	12.3	8.0
Raw materials	5.2	6.0	1.1	1.2	2.3	1.1	1.2	0.4	4.5	2.8	1.7	1.1	4.5	2.0	6.5	2.7
Food	6.3	10.6	6.1	5.1	8.5	7.3	5.9	3.3	4.9	4.7	6.4	3.8	5.9	4.0	5.8	5.3
Mining & fuels	11.7	23.1	6.8	8.4	15.3	12.9	13.9	14.7	10.8	15.1	3.4	3.8	13.3	15.9	22.2	28.2
Metalliferous ores and metal scrap	1.6	1.1	0.9	0.7	1.5	1.1	0.1	0.1	0.7	0.5	0.2	0.1	1.2	1.3	2.9	2.7
Mineral fuels	8.2	20.3	3.8	5.5	12.5	10.7	12.0	13.4	8.1	12.1	2.0	2.1	8.4	11.3	16.5	22.7
Non-ferrous metals	1.9	1.7	2 1	2.2	1.3	1.1	1.7	1.2	2.0	2.4	1.3	1.6	3.7	3.3	2.7	2.8
Total manufactures	75.6	59.5	82 0	82.0	59.1	78.1	77.5	80.1	76.6	75.3	85.4	90.6	71.2	76.5	64.1	61.9
Chemicals	14.2	16.8	7.5	7.3	10.2	7.9	7.0	6.1	10.1	10.7	6.7	5.9	12.3	11.6	9.7	8.9
Leather, rubber, travel goods, footwear	1.6	1.3	0.5	0.6	1.1	0.8	1.2	0.8	1.1	1.1	6.5	5.4	1.2	0.8	1.3	1.0
Wood, paper & furniture	1.0	1.2	1.9	1.6	1.4	1.6	1.7	1.0	1.2	1.0	2.7	1.9	2.3	1.4	1.6	1.2
Metal	7.5	6.6	6.7	4.6	6.4	3.8	4.2	2.8	9.9	7.9	3.3	2.8	7.5	4.8	5.8	5.2

(*Continued*)

Table 7.2. (*Continued*)

	Indonesia		Malaysia		Philippines		Singapore		Thailand		Hong Kong		Taiwan		Korea	
	1990–94	2000–04	1990–94	2000–04	1990–94	2000–04	1990–94	2000–04	1990–94	2000–04	1990–94	2000–04	1990–94	2000–04	1990–94	2000–04
Machinery	43.4	28.0	55.7	60.6	31.4	56.8	50.5	59.3	43.3	44.3	31.8	46.4	38.2	46.4	35.1	34.8
Power generator	5.1	2.7	2.7	2.0	3.2	1.1	3.1	2.2	3.2	2.2	1.1	1.6	1.6	1.3	2.9	1.7
Industrial & metalworking	21.1	11.6	13.2	7.0	7.5	4.7	8.4	7.4	13.8	8.9	4.6	3.5	9.6	10.0	13.0	7.3
Office & telecoms	3.5	2.8	8.1	11.2	4.8	13.5	16.6	17.1	7.1	9.8	11.6	20.6	5.0	8.7	4.5	6.7
Electrical	5.0	3.0	23.1	36.8	8.6	34.1	16.8	27.8	10.4	18.4	10.4	18.9	14.6	23.0	10.1	16.8
Autos	5.5	5.6	3.4	2.3	4.4	3.0	2.3	2.0	6.8	3.5	3.4	1.2	5.4	2.0	1.3	1.4
Other transportation	3.2	2.3	5.3	1.3	2.9	0.4	3.3	2.8	2.0	1.5	0.6	0.4	2.0	1.3	3.2	0.8
Textiles & garments	3.8	2.8	3.1	1.4	4.8	3.3	4.1	2.2	2.8	2.6	18.3	12.9	2.8	1.7	3.6	3.2
Other manufactures	4.0	2.9	6.5	6.1	3.7	3.9	8.8	7.9	8.2	7.6	16.1	15.5	6.8	9.7	7.1	7.7
Others	1.2	0.8	4.0	3.3	14.7	0.6	1.6	1.5	3.1	2.1	3.1	0.7	5.1	1.6	1.4	1.9
Total	100	100	100	100	100	100	100	100	100	100	100	100	100	100	100	100

particularly fast for ASEAN, NIEs and China.[3] For China, the share of office and telecommunications equipment in its overall exports increased remarkably from 6.3 to 22.3 percent, while the share of electrical machinery increased from 4 to 10.1 percent. Many ASEAN countries, with the exception of Indonesia, saw exports of office and telecommunications equipment and electrical machinery rise significantly to account for a combined share of 30–60 percent of their total exports.

Among manufactured exports, textiles and garments grew relatively slowly and experienced a decline in their share of total exports for East Asian developing economies, although their share is still high for China and the NIEs.

In contrast to these East Asian developing countries, Japan experienced no notable changes in export composition from 1990–94 to 2000–04. Unlike East Asian developing economies, with the exception of Korea, Japan registered a high share of automobiles in its exports.

A close examination of the export commodity composition of East Asian economies in 1990–94 and 2000–04 reveals increasing similarity among them, which can be seen by the increase in the correlation coefficient of the export composition between most pairs of economies (Table 7.3). Indeed, the decline in the correlation coefficient from 1990–94 to 2000–04 was found in only 3 cases out of 90 pairs. With regard to the magnitude of the index, the correlation coefficient was greater than 0.5 for only 12 exports to the world (7 to East Asia) out of 45 cases in 1990–94, but the number increased to 29 (31) in 2000–04. In this period, Indonesia is practically the only country that has a very different export product composition.

There are relatively smaller changes to the import composition of East Asian economies when compared to exports. The shares of manufactures remained around 70–80 percent throughout the period for East Asian developing economies, with the exception of Korea, where

---

[3]For the Philippines the share of others was high in 1990–94, mainly because the consignment trade was classified under others. In 2000–04 the consignment trade was classified under specific sectors such as office and telecommunications equipment, for the production of which the consignment trade was utilised.

Table 7.3. Similarity of export composition among East Asian economies.

	Indonesia	Malaysia	Philippines	Singapore	Thailand	China	Hong Kong	Taiwan	Korea	Japan
1990–94										
Indonesia	1.00	0.22	0.18	0.10	0.19	0.18	0.13	0.04	0.09	−0.06
Malaysia	0.24	1.00	0.63	0.49	0.42	0.08	0.34	0.44	0.60	0.35
Philippines	0.20	0.49	1.00	0.38	0.50	0.28	0.42	0.38	0.51	0.21
Singapore	0.21	0.49	0.42	1.00	0.35	0.10	0.28	0.57	0.49	0.39
Thailand	0.11	0.47	0.43	0.28	1.00	0.42	0.52	0.52	0.43	0.20
China	0.06	0.05	0.07	0.11	0.13	1.00	0.73	0.36	0.30	0.04
Hong Kong	0.05	0.48	0.27	0.40	0.38	0.36	1.00	0.62	0.50	0.23
Taiwan	0.02	0.43	0.29	0.31	0.37	0.22	0.74	1.00	0.59	0.40
Korea	0.08	0.63	0.48	0.51	0.37	0.22	0.63	0.63	1.00	0.55
Japan	−0.04	0.62	0.38	0.47	0.34	0.10	0.59	0.58	0.70	1.00
2000–04										
Indonesia	1.00	0.33	0.13	0.18	0.26	0.34	0.27	0.19	0.20	0.07
Malaysia	0.38	1.00	0.89	0.92	0.81	0.46	0.68	0.90	0.73	0.53
Philippines	0.13	0.94	1.00	0.93	0.69	0.33	0.58	0.84	0.67	0.51
Singapore	0.19	0.92	0.94	1.00	0.74	0.42	0.61	0.89	0.76	0.54
Thailand	0.24	0.83	0.75	0.76	1.00	0.55	0.69	0.80	0.67	0.49
China	0.18	0.46	0.41	0.46	0.55	1.00	0.79	0.53	0.48	0.27

(Continued)

Table 7.3. *(Continued)*

	Indonesia	Malaysia	Philippines	Singapore	Thailand	China	Hong Kong	Taiwan	Korea	Japan
Hong Kong	0.20	0.80	0.75	0.76	0.80	0.74	1.00	0.72	0.63	0.43
Taiwan	0.16	0.90	0.92	0.91	0.78	0.47	0.83	1.00	0.76	0.58
Korea	0.22	0.83	0.82	0.91	0.77	0.53	0.81	0.88	1.00	0.75
Japan	0.12	0.81	0.83	0.84	0.70	0.41	0.77	0.90	0.80	1.00
Change from 1990–94 to 2000–04										
Indonesia	0.00	0.11	−0.05	0.09	0.07	0.16	0.14	0.16	0.11	0.13
Malaysia	0.14	0.00	0.26	0.43	0.39	0.38	0.34	0.46	0.13	0.18
Philippines	−0.07	0.44	0.00	0.54	0.19	0.05	0.16	0.45	0.16	0.30
Singapore	−0.02	0.43	0.52	0.00	0.39	0.32	0.33	0.32	0.27	0.15
Thailand	0.14	0.36	0.33	0.48	0.00	0.13	0.18	0.29	0.24	0.30
China	0.12	0.42	0.34	0.35	0.42	0.00	0.06	0.18	0.18	0.23
Hong Kong	0.15	0.32	0.48	0.37	0.42	0.38	0.00	0.11	0.13	0.20
Taiwan	0.14	0.46	0.63	0.59	0.40	0.24	0.09	0.00	0.17	0.18
Korea	0.14	0.21	0.34	0.40	0.40	0.31	0.18	0.25	0.00	0.20
Japan	0.16	0.19	0.45	0.37	0.35	0.31	0.17	0.32	0.10	0.00

Note: The figures indicate the correlat.on coefficients of the compositional shares of exports for a pair of economies. The figures below the diagonal are with respect to total exports to East Asia, those above the diagonal are with respect to total exports to the world.

the corresponding shares stayed lower, at around 60 percent. Japan's import composition is similar to that of Korea, as the share of manufactures in total imports was significantly low at 57 percent in 2000–04 even after a rise from 46 percent in 1990–94.

Similar to the changes observed for exports, imports of machinery, in particular office and telecommunications equipment and electrical machinery, increased their shares in total imports in many East Asian economies, including Japan.

An examination of the changes in commodity composition of trade for East Asian economies from 1990–94 to 2000–04 revealed a shift in exports from non-manufactures to manufactures. Among the manufactures, a shift was observed from light manufactures such as textiles and garments, and wood, paper and furniture to more sophisticated manufactures such as machinery. The share of office and telecommunications equipment and electrical machinery increased notably. Although the changes in import composition were less dramatic, similar to the case of exports, the share of telecommunications equipment and electrical machinery increased substantially. These observations indicate rapid growth of intra-industry trade in telecommunications equipment and electrical machinery.

Before analysing intra-industry trade in East Asia, we examine similarities or differences between the export product composition of an economy and the import product composition of its trading partner. Such an analysis not only gives useful information on the extent of intra-industry trade but also provides useful information on the possible scope for the benefits of regional preferential trade agreements such as FTAs and customs unions. The trade complementarity index is computed for this purpose and the results shown in Table 7.4. The most interesting observation is an increase in the complementarity indices for most pairs of economies from 1990–94 to 2000–04. Out of 90 cases, the decline in complementarity indices was found in 19 cases. Increasing complementarity among the East Asian economies apparently contributed to increased intra-regional trade, as it provided scope for trade. It also indicates favourable prospects for the formation of FTAs in the region. According to Yeats (1998), for the previously failed arrangements the value of complementarity indices ranged from

Table 7.4. Trade complementarity index for East Asian economies.

Exporter		Importer										
		Indonesia	Malaysia	Philippines	Singapore	Thailand	Vietnam	China	Hong Kong	Taiwan	Japan	Korea
Indonesia	1990–94		21.4	35.7	32.1	26.5		25.2	41.1	26.8	42.4	31.4
	2000–04		34	36.8	38.5	42.6	36.9	38.7	45.9	39	49.6	43.5
	change		*12.6*	*1.1*	*6.4*	*16.1*		*13.5*	*4.8*	*12.2*	*7.2*	*12.1*
Malaysia	1990–94	29.8		47.5	59.3	41		35.8	47.1	45	41.8	43.9
	2000–04	29.2		60.7	66.8	51.6	31.7	51.6	56.9	55.3	46.2	48
	change	*−0.6*		*13.2*	*7.5*	*10.6*		*15.8*	*9.8*	*10.3*	*4.4*	*4.1*
Philippines	1990–94	32	44		46.2	40		37.7	50.7	45.9	48.1	41.3
	2000–04	21.4	59.5		57.6	43.3	26.4	40.6	48.5	46.7	39.9	39.4
	change	*−10.6*	*15.5*		*11.4*	*3.3*		*2.9*	*−2.2*	*0.8*	*−8.2*	*−1.9*
Singapore	1990–94	35.7	51.2	46.4		46.6		39.9	50.6	48.2	36.8	43.2
	2000–04	35	66.6	61.5		51.5	40	50.6	53.5	55.9	43.6	48.7
	change	*−0.7*	*15.4*	*15.1*		*4.9*		*10.7*	*2.9*	*7.7*	*6.8*	*5.5*
Thailand	1990–94	26.2	35	38.2	42.4			31.6	54.4	34.5	39.3	31.7
	2000–04	33.9	50.8	49.5	54.6		41.2	48.9	60.7	47.2	52.1	45.7
	change	*7.7*	*15.8*	*11.3*	*12.2*			*17.3*	*6.3*	*12.7*	*12.8*	*14*
Vietnam	1990–94											
	2000–04	27.5	21.2	26.9	26.1	30.1		23	40.5	25	43.2	33
	change											

(Continued)

Table 7.4. *(Continued)*

Exporter		Importer										
		Indonesia	Malaysia	Philippines	Singapore	Thailand	Vietnam	China	Hong Kong	Taiwan	Japan	Korea
China	1990–94	35.2	33.7	41.2	39.9	37.3			58.4	40.1	43.7	36.9
	2000–04	30.7	41.9	36.9	44.7	43.7	40.8		63.7	40.1	49.5	39.6
	change	*−4.5*	*8.2*	*−4.3*	*4.8*	*6.4*			*5.3*	*0*	*5.8*	*2.7*
Hong Kong	1990–94	32.9	39.8	46.7	50.7	42.5		43.1		40.5	44	39.3
	2000–04	27.8	47.2	46.5	53.7	53.1	36.8	49.4		44.8	48.4	48.8
	change	*−5.1*	*7.4*	*−0.2*	*3*	*10.6*		*6.3*		*4.3*	*4.4*	*9.5*
Taiwan	1990–94	33.7	42.9	44.1	50.4	44.8		43.4	60.1		34.4	36.9
	2000–04	32.1	56.5	54	59.1	56.5	40.8	57.4	58.6		40.6	48.1
	change	*−1.6*	*13.6*	*9.9*	*8.7*	*11.7*		*14*	*−1.5*		*6.2*	*11.2*
Japan	1990–94	45.2	54.1	50.8	58	55.7		47.2	46.5	50.7		45.2
	2000–04	41.5	52.1	43.4	52	55.5	42.7	54.8	47.4	52.6		50.4
	change	*−3.7*	*−2*	*−7.4*	*−6*	*−0.2*		*7.6*	*0.9*	*1.9*		*5.2*
Korea	1990–94	34.7	47.6	48.9	53.7	42.8		43.7	61	48.2	38.5	
	2000–04	38.1	51.6	47.4	55	51.9	43.8	53.1	57.9	48.9	42.3	
	change	*3.4*	*4*	*−1.5*	*1.3*	*9.1*		*9.4*	*−3.1*	*0.7*	*3.8*	

Note: Trade complementarity index between two countries k and j (Ckj) is defined as $Ckj = 100 - \sum(|mik - xij| \div 2)$.

7 to 22. In the case of East Asian economies in 2000–04, only 10 pairs of economies registered a value less than 30. It should be added that 7 out of these 10 cases involve Vietnam, implying that the scope for trade for East Asian economies with Vietnam is limited.

We saw in an earlier section that intra-regional dependence in East Asia is stronger with imports than exports. This is mainly because of machinery products, particularly office and telecommunications equipment and electrical machinery (Table 7.5). Except for Japan, East Asia's import dependence on other East Asian economies increased for these sectors.

7.2.3. *Pattern of comparative advantage for East Asian economies*

An analysis of the pattern of comparative advantage is useful for identifying commodities with relative competitiveness and also helps us to understand the factors determining trade patterns.

The commodity composition of exports and imports of an economy, which we analysed above, largely reflects the pattern of comparative advantage of the economy. However, the commodity composition is a very rough measure of comparative advantage because it does not take into account important information in measuring the pattern of comparative advantage such as the commodity composition of other economies. To overcome such a deficiency and to identify the sectors with comparative advantage, the concept of revealed comparative advantage (RCA) was developed.[4]

An examination of the computed RCAs for East Asian economies in Table 7.6, in which the manufactured products are classified into four and nine broad categories, reveals that many East Asian economies have

---

[4] Balassa (1965) developed the concept of "revealed comparative advantage". In our exercise $RCAij = [xij/Xj] \div [xwj/Xw]$, where xij and xwj are the value of j product exported by country i and the world, respectively, while Xwj and Xw are world exports of j product and total world trade, respectively. Product i is interpreted to have a comparative advantage if $RCAi$ is greater than unity.

Table 7.5. Changing regional patterns of trade for East Asia by commodity (%).

	East Asia		ASEAN		China		NIEs		Japan		EU		US	
	1990–94	2000–04	1990–94	2000–04	1990–94	2000–04	1990–94	2000–04	1990–94	2000–04	1990–94	2000–04	1990–94	2000–04
Destinations of East Asia's exports														
Agriculture	60.6	58.3	13.1	14.3	6.1	11.8	17.1	14.0	25.1	19.3	13.0	11.2	9.5	10.7
Raw materials	64.6	63.2	12.6	11.4	9.8	25.2	21.6	14.6	20.7	12.2	14.3	13.7	8.6	9.1
Food	59.1	56.7	13.2	15.2	4.8	7.4	15.5	13.8	26.7	21.6	12.5	10.3	9.9	11.2
Mining & fuels	80.7	76.9	19.9	20.5	7.5	12.4	20.3	24.5	33.3	20.3	2.7	3.7	5.6	4.5
Metalliferous ores and metal scrap	80.4	76.5	7.9	8.5	9.1	20.3	14.2	24.0	49.4	23.8	7.3	13.9	3.6	1.5
Mineral fuels	81.1	75.9	20.1	21.7	6.4	9.4	18.7	22.1	36.3	23.8	1.8	2.3	5.4	4.4
Non-ferrous metals	79.0	80.4	23.1	19.9	12.6	20.3	30.5	32.3	13.1	8.1	5.5	5.5	7.8	5.5
Total manufactures	40.5	46.9	12.5	12.3	6.4	11.1	16.0	16.7	5.8	7.0	16.9	15.5	26.7	22.9
Chemicals	64.4	63.9	18.6	15.1	14.8	22.8	26.0	21.5	5.4	4.9	12.2	11.9	11.0	11.3
Leather, rubber, travel goods, footwear	30.5	31.1	5.3	5.5	4.2	7.7	14.0	10.6	7.2	7.6	18.0	18.3	35.3	31.0
Wood, paper & furniture	56.4	45.6	8.8	8.1	11.6	8.3	19.6	14.0	16.7	15.5	12.2	13.0	20.2	27.8
Metal	54.3	54.6	18.4	15.8	10.0	13.4	17.3	19.0	9.1	6.8	9.3	10.9	19.5	18.7
Machinery	36.2	46.1	14.5	13.8	5.1	10.3	13.5	16.3	3.4	6.0	17.9	16.4	29.7	23.9
Power generator	42.4	42.4	19.5	16.9	6.3	9.9	12.7	11.1	4.3	4.8	11.9	12.8	28.1	27.9
Industrial & metalworking	54.7	52.3	21.3	16.0	10.7	15.0	20.6	17.9	2.5	3.7	11.3	13.2	18.2	18.3
Office & telecoms	28.8	41.9	11.1	10.4	4.3	9.7	9.8	14.1	3.7	7.8	24.6	20.9	34.7	27.2
Electrical	50.8	66.1	20.4	20.3	4.0	13.2	21.0	25.4	5.5	7.2	14.5	12.0	26.4	15.6
Autos	19.7	15.6	7.5	6.9	3.9	3.4	7.6	4.1	1.1	1.6	18.3	17.6	38.2	40.6
Other transportation	16.8	16.5	10.7	8.1	1.8	0.9	4.1	6.4	0.7	1.4	10.5	18.9	8.3	9.1
Textiles & garments	44.9	45.3	7.0	7.2	7.9	10.8	20.0	16.1	10.1	12.0	15.9	13.0	20.7	19.0
Other manufactures	37.5	42.9	8.9	8.4	4.8	8.9	17.0	17.8	7.0	7.9	19.8	17.0	29.0	27.1
Others	37.9	49.6	15.4	18.0	4.7	7.2	13.2	21.2	4.9	3.5	14.6	13.3	30.5	17.9
Total trade	44.1	49.0	13.0	12.9	6.4	11.1	16.3	17.1	8.6	8.2	15.9	14.7	24.4	21.4

(*Continued*)

Table 7.5. *(Continued)*

	East Asia		ASEAN		China		NIEs		Japan		EU		US	
	1990–94	2000–04	1990–94	2000–04	1990–94	2000–04	1990–94	2000–04	1990–94	2000–04	1990–94	2000–04	1990–94	2000–04
Source of East Asia's imports														
Agriculture	33.4	31.5	16.1	15.6	8.5	9.8	6.8	4.2	2.5	2.3	9.3	9.8	27.6	23.3
Raw materials	32.9	31.4	19.9	17.9	5.3	4.6	5.5	5.9	3.6	4.0	5.3	9.5	28.1	19.2
Food	33.6	31.5	14.2	14.7	10.1	11.9	7.5	3.5	1.9	1.7	11.3	10.0	27.3	24.9
Mining & fuels	29.7	27.4	21.8	17.0	3.7	4.0	2.8	5.0	3.0	2.6	2.8	1.8	6.2	2.5
Metalliferous ores and metal scrap	16.0	19.0	10.3	10.1	1.3	0.9	2.5	3.0	2.1	5.1	6.1	4.9	13.9	8.3
Mineral fuels	32.0	26.7	26.9	19.8	4.0	3.6	1.9	4.1	1.4	0.8	0.8	0.6	4.0	1.3
Non-ferrous metals	28.8	37.7	6.2	6.9	4.0	8.9	7.6	11.4	11.0	10.6	9.7	6.5	11.3	4.5
Total manufactures	57.4	64.0	8.8	14.0	10.7	16.7	14.9	16.2	23.0	17.2	17.1	13.9	17.0	13.5
Chemicals	38.9	49.9	5.9	11.7	3.8	4.9	12.1	17.2	17.1	16.1	24.1	20.6	23.0	16.5
Leather, rubber, travel goods, footwear	70.0	69.9	4.4	7.8	38.5	45.7	21.0	11.7	6.0	5.0	18.1	17.2	6.1	4.6
Wood, paper & furniture	60.8	65.1	29.1	26.7	8.0	20.6	13.3	11.4	10.5	6.6	16.0	16.2	15.1	10.3
Metal	55.4	64.7	4.2	5.5	6.1	12.7	15.1	20.4	30.0	26.0	12.7	10.4	5.9	4.8
Machinery	57.0	55.4	10.6	17.4	4.8	12.7	12.0	16.4	29.6	19.0	18.1	13.4	20.8	15.1
Power generator	44.6	44.4	5.0	9.6	4.4	10.4	5.3	6.0	29.9	18.4	22.0	22.4	27.7	23.7
Industrial & metalworking	50.8	52.3	3.9	5.8	1.5	5.2	11.7	11.3	33.6	30.1	29.0	25.9	15.1	16.6
Office & telecoms	71.5	75.6	21.0	22.2	10.9	24.5	13.4	16.5	26.2	12.5	7.4	7.4	18.6	10.1
Electrical	66.5	71.5	15.3	21.8	5.1	10.0	16.5	21.4	29.5	18.4	10.0	8.1	21.4	15.0
Autos	51.9	47.8	1.9	6.0	1.9	5.1	8.0	7.0	40.1	29.8	31.2	37.5	12.0	8.0
Other transportation	13.6	13.2	2.4	2.8	0.8	1.4	2.2	2.3	8.3	6.8	19.4	20.1	55.4	55.5
Textiles & garments	82.0	83.1	5.7	6.8	36.1	51.0	32.2	19.3	8.1	6.3	8.4	6.9	3.1	2.0
Other manufactures	53.6	58.4	6.2	7.3	16.1	21.1	12.8	12.5	18.5	17.5	16.5	14.4	17.7	16.5
Others	25.2	45.7	8.0	16.1	2.0	5.0	8.6	17.7	6.8	7.0	15.3	12.7	25.0	16.1
Total trade	49.1	54.6	11.7	14.6	9.2	13.8	11.8	13.2	16.8	13.3	13.9	11.5	16.9	12.5

Table 7.6. Revealed comparative advantage.

Reporters	Technology class/1	Period 1990–94	Period 2000–04	Reporters	Technology class/1	Period 1990–94	Period 2000–04
China & Hong Kong				Philippines			
A. Resources-based	a.1. Agro-based	0.53	0.45	A. Resources-based	a.1. Agro-based	1.40	0.60
	a.2. Fuel, mining	0.54	0.51		a.2. Fuel, mining	0.63	0.32
B. Low technology	b.1. Textiles, garments, shoes	4.00	3.33	B. Low technology	b.1. Textiles, garments, shoes	1.63	1.12
	b.2. Glass, iron, steel	1.65	1.64		b.2. Glass, iron, steel	0.78	0.34
C. Medium technology	c.1. Automotive	0.25	0.14	C. Medium technology	c.1. Automotive	0.09	0.28
	c.2. Process	0.74	0.73		c.2. Process	0.36	0.15
	c.3. Engineering	0.84	0.95		c.3. Engineering	0.31	0.46
D. High technology	d.1. Electrical, electronics	0.99	1.70	D. High technology	d.1. Electrical, electronics	1.19	3.60
	d.2. Engines, aircraft, optics	0.39	0.42		d.2. Engines, aircraft, optics	0.07	0.18
Indonesia				Singapore			
A. Resources-based	a.1. Agro-based	2.27	2.39	A. Resources-based	a.1. Agro-based	0.58	0.30
	a.2. Fuel, mining	0.93	1.11		a.2. Fuel, mining	2.08	1.68
B. Low technology	b.1. Textiles, garments, shoes	2.02	2.05	B. Low technology	b.1. Textiles, garments, shoes	0.45	0.28
	b.2. Glass, iron, steel	0.56	0.86		b.2. Glass, iron, steel	0.49	0.51
C. Medium technology	c.1. Automotive	0.06	0.11	C. Medium technology	c.1. Automotive	0.11	0.08
	c.2. Process	0.71	0.82		c.2. Process	0.67	0.79
	c.3. Engineering	0.13	0.41		c.3. Engineering	1.01	0.72
D. High technology	d.1. Electrical, electronics	0.18	0.61	D. High technology	d.1. Electrical, electronics	3.38	3.15
	d.2. Engines, aircraft, optics	0.09	0.07		d.2. Engines, aircraft, optics	0.40	0.52

(*Continued*)

Table 7.6. (*Continued*)

Reporters	Technology class/1	Period 1990–94	Period 2000–04	Reporters	Technology class/1	Period 1990–94	Period 2000–04
Japan				Thailand			
A. Resources-based	a.1. Agro-based	0.27	0.33	A. Resources-based	a.1. Agro-based	1.34	1.52
	a.2. Fuel, mining	0.47	0.55		a.2. Fuel, mining	0.65	0.74
B. Low technology	b.1. Textiles, garments, shoes	0.18	0.17	B. Low technology	b.1. Textiles, garments, shoes	2.36	1.44
	b.2. Glass, iron, steel	0.79	0.71		b.2. Glass, iron, steel	1.12	0.98
C. Medium technology	c.1. Automotive	2.38	2.22	C. Medium technology	c.1. Automotive	0.12	0.47
	c.2. Process	0.83	1.04		c.2. Process	0.51	0.81
	c.3. Engineering	1.65	1.67		c.3. Engineering	0.58	0.78
D. High technology	d.1. Electrical, electronics	2.11	1.37	D. High technology	d.1. Electrical, electronics	1.54	1.69
	d.2. Engines, aircraft, optics	0.65	0.82		d.2. Engines, aircraft, optics	0.20	0.21
S. Korea				Taiwan			
A. Resources-based	a.1. Agro-based	0.42	0.45	A. Resources-based	a.1. Agro-based	0.43	0.28
	a.2. Fuel, mining	0.57	0.94		a.2. Fuel, mining	0.34	0.46
B. Low technology	b.1. Textiles, garments, shoes	2.46	1.13	B. Low technology	b.1. Textiles, garments, shoes	2.17	1.20
	b.2. Glass, iron, steel	1.25	0.81		b.2. Glass, iron, steel	2.08	1.63
C. Medium technology	c.1. Automotive	0.53	1.18	C. Medium technology	c.1. Automotive	0.44	0.34
	c.2. Process	1.72	1.33		c.2. Process	1.07	1.38
	c.3. Engineering	1.03	1.11		c.3. Engineering	0.88	0.86
D. High technology	d.1. Electrical, electronics	1.84	2.02	D. High technology	d.1. Electrical, electronics	2.15	2.43
	d.2. Engines, aircraft, optics	0.24	0.22		d.2. Engines, aircraft, optics	0.24	0.62

(*Continued*)

Table 7.6. (*Continued*)

Reporters	Technology class/1	Period 1990–94	Period 2000–04	Reporters	Technology class/1	Period 1990–94	Period 2000–04
Malaysia				Vietnam			
A. Resources-based	a.1. Agro-based	2.28	1.48	A. Resources-based	a.1. Agro-based		0.63
	a.2. Fuel, mining	0.31	0.45		a.2. Fuel, mining		0.38
B. Low technology	b.1. Textiles, garments, shoes	0.69	0.47	B. Low technology	b.1. Textiles, garments, shoes		4.44
	b.2. Glass, iron, steel	0.61	0.64		b.2. Glass, iron, steel		0.69
C. Medium technology	c.1. Automotive	0.06	0.05	C. Medium technology	c.1. Automotive		0.10
	c.2. Process	0.37	0.70		c.2. Process		0.20
	c.3. Engineering	0.89	0.73		c.3. Engineering		0.20
D. High technology	d.1. Electrical, electronics	2.52	2.87	D. High technology	d.1. Electrical, electronics		0.30
	d.2. Engines, aircraft, optics	0.57	0.34		d.2. Engines, aircraft, optics		0.05

Note: Technology classification is based on Lall (2000).
Source: COMTRADE.

a comparative advantage in electrical and electronics products. Specifically, for 2000–2004 China, Japan, Korea, Malaysia, the Philippines, Singapore, Thailand and Taiwan have a comparative advantage in electrical and electronics products, as the values of the RCA for that product for these economies are greater than unity. What is noteworthy is that the RCA for China increased from 0.99 in 1990–94 to 1.70 in 2000–04, indicating that electrical and electronics products changed from having a comparative disadvantage to having a comparative advantage. Even though East Asian economies enjoy a comparative advantage in electrical and electronics products, which can be characterised as high-technology products, many East Asian developing economies are engaged in the assembly of these products, which requires labour-intensive rather than high-technology-intensive operations such as developing new products. This reflects the "inter-process" division of labour in East Asia, which we will discuss below.

Another product in which many East Asian economies have a comparative advantage is textiles and garments, and China, Indonesia, Korea, the Philippines, Thailand, Taiwan and Vietnam registered a value greater than unity. However, the degree of comparative advantage declined for all economies except Indonesia.

Indonesia, Malaysia and Thailand share a common pattern in having a comparative advantage in agriculture-based products, while Japan and Korea exhibit a similar pattern in having a comparative advantage in medium- to high-technology products. Medium-technology products include automotives and chemicals and industrial machinery, while high-technology products include electrical and electronics products.

Our findings on the pattern of comparative advantage for East Asian economies are mostly consistent with the expectation that it reflects the endowment of resources. Specifically, advanced economies abundantly endowed with well-educated human resources such as Japan and Korea have a comparative advantage in medium- and high-technology products, while developing economies abundantly endowed with low-wage labour such as ASEAN countries, China and Vietnam have a comparative advantage in low-technology products. Economies with abundant natural resources such as Indonesia and Malaysia have a comparative advantage in natural resource-based products. One important caveat to note is the case of developing economies that are shown to have a comparative advantage in high-technology products, i.e., electrical and electronics products. This seeming inconsistency may be a result of the development of the inter-process division of labour in East Asia, where labour-intensive processes in the production of high-technology products is conducted in low-wage developing economies. As we will see later, the main promoters of developing inter-process division of labour are MNCs from developed economies such as Japan and the US and developing economies from Korea and Taiwan, among others.

7.2.4. *Expansion of vertical intra-industry trade*

We saw earlier that the export composition of East Asian economies became similar in the 1990s as the share of machinery, in particular office and telecommunications equipment and electrical machinery, increased for most economies. We also observed similar increasing shares of machinery, in particular office and telecommunications equipment and electrical machinery, in the import composition for many East Asian economies. Furthermore, we confirmed the increasing complementarity of trading patterns between and among East Asian economies. These observations on changing export and import compositions appear to indicate the increase in intra-industry trade for East Asian economies.

To investigate the degree of intra-industry trade, the intra-industry trade (IIT) index is computed for the manufactured products for East Asian economies (Table 7.7).[5] As expected, many East Asian economies expanded their intra-industry trade with the rest of the world as well as with other East Asian economies. These trends are particularly notable for the machinery trade (SITC 7). The IIT index for East Asia with

---

[5] Intra-industry trade index (IIT) is computed as $IIT = 1 - [\sum\sum\sum|Xijk - Mijk| \div (Xijk + Mijk)]$ where $Xijk$ represents exports from industry i by country j to country k, and $Mijk$ represents corresponding import values. The greater the degree of intra-industry trade, the greater the value of IIT.

Table 7.7. Intra-industry trade in East Asia: Manufactured products (intra-industry trade index).

	Trading Partners																	
	East Asia			ASEAN			NIEs			China			Japan			World		
	1990–94	2000–04	Change	1990–94	2000–04	Change	1990–94	2000–04	Change	1990–94	2000–04	Change	1990–94	2000–04	Change	1990–94	2000–04	Change
Chemicals (SITC 5)																		
East Asia	0.64	0.64	0.00	0.42	0.53	0.11	0.45	0.50	0.05	0.33	0.26	−0.07	0.31	0.34	0.03	0.60	0.62	0.02
ASEAN	0.56	0.60	0.04	0.52	0.61	0.09	0.49	0.56	0.07	0.30	0.27	−0.03	0.26	0.51	0.25	0.46	0.58	0.12
Indonesia	0.27	0.51	0.24	0.27	0.43	0.16	0.26	0.42	0.16	0.09	0.19	0.10	0.14	0.41	0.27	0.25	0.47	0.22
Malaysia	0.35	0.51	0.16	0.43	0.51	0.08	0.28	0.44	0.16	0.22	0.17	−0.05	0.19	0.49	0.30	0.33	0.51	0.18
Philippines	0.36	0.19	−0.17	0.40	0.20	−0.20	0.16	0.13	−0.03	0.27	0.17	−0.10	0.21	0.12	−0.09	0.29	0.20	−0.09
Singapore	0.58	0.40	−0.18	0.25	0.31	0.06	0.45	0.33	−0.12	0.32	0.20	−0.12	0.32	0.49	0.17	0.55	0.51	−0.04
Thailand	0.26	0.39	0.13	0.34	0.35	0.01	0.24	0.31	0.07	0.13	0.21	0.08	0.17	0.24	0.07	0.23	0.38	0.15
Vietnam		0.13	0.13		0.12	0.12		0.12	0.12		0.07	0.07		0.17	0.17		0.13	0.13
NIEs	0.53	0.52	−0.01	0.44	0.51	0.07	0.42	0.45	0.03	0.26	0.22	−0.04	0.23	0.24	0.01	0.46	0.48	0.02
Hong Kong	0.39	0.38	−0.01	0.40	0.18	−0.22	0.22	0.14	−0.08	0.22	0.17	−0.05	0.18	0.06	−0.12	0.49	0.44	−0.05
Taiwan	0.43	0.43	0.00	0.36	0.54	0.18	0.18	0.19	0.01	0.03	0.19	0.16	0.18	0.21	0.03	0.32	0.41	0.09
Korea	0.49	0.49	0.00	0.24	0.35	0.11	0.16	0.20	0.04	0.26	0.18	−0.08	0.28	0.33	0.05	0.41	0.46	0.05
China	0.34	0.25	−0.09	0.27	0.22	−0.05	0.27	0.24	−0.03			0.00	0.36	0.26	−0.10	0.37	0.35	−0.02
Japan	0.29	0.35	0.06	0.26	0.42	0.16	0.20	0.24	0.04	0.40	0.32	−0.08			0.00	0.58	0.55	−0.03
Materials (SITC 6)																		
East Asia	0.76	0.79	0.03	0.41	0.53	0.12	0.72	0.69	−0.03	0.50	0.56	0.06	0.38	0.40	0.02	0.63	0.68	0.05
ASEAN	0.50	0.60	0.10	0.67	0.76	0.09	0.39	0.45	0.06	0.17	0.37	0.20	0.19	0.32	0.13	0.51	0.61	0.10
Indonesia	0.28	0.33	0.05	0.19	0.27	0.08	0.29	0.29	0.00	0.08	0.27	0.19	0.11	0.19	0.08	0.29	0.33	0.04
Malaysia	0.41	0.54	0.13	0.58	0.65	0.07	0.32	0.38	0.06	0.11	0.44	0.33	0.11	0.20	0.09	0.41	0.54	0.13
Philippines	0.18	0.27	0.09	0.30	0.41	0.11	0.13	0.22	0.09	0.11	0.13	0.02	0.13	0.20	0.07	0.22	0.33	0.11
Singapore	0.61	0.64	0.03	0.53	0.64	0.11	0.43	0.52	0.09	0.17	0.36	0.19	0.10	0.16	0.06	0.60	0.64	0.04
Thailand	0.33	0.49	0.16	0.46	0.48	0.02	0.45	0.47	0.02	0.14	0.32	0.18	0.12	0.26	0.14	0.44	0.52	0.08
Vietnam		0.19	0.19		0.29	0.29		0.18	0.18		0.12	0.12		0.20	0.20		0.24	0.24

(Continued)

Table 7.7. (*Continued*)

	Trading Partners																	
	East Asia			ASEAN			NIEs			China			Japan			World		
	1990–94	2000–04	Change	1990–94	2000–04	Change	1990–94	2000–04	Change	1990–94	2000–04	Change	1990–94	2000–04	Change	1990–94	2000–04	Change
NIEs	0.66	0.66	0.00	0.31	0.40	0.09	0.68	0.65	−0.03	0.51	0.59	0.08	0.45	0.47	0.02	0.59	0.63	0.04
Hong Kong	0.82	0.77	−0.05	0.47	0.43	−0.04	0.23	0.11	−0.12	0.48	0.60	0.12	0.22	0.23	0.01	0.81	0.81	0.00
Taiwan	0.44	0.45	0.01	0.27	0.33	0.06	0.18	0.15	−0.03	0.04	0.37	0.33	0.42	0.47	0.05	0.38	0.38	0.00
Korea	0.47	0.48	0.01	0.15	0.27	0.12	0.22	0.20	−0.02	0.38	0.41	0.03	0.38	0.43	0.05	0.45	0.47	0.02
China	0.51	0.52	0.01	0.19	0.35	0.16	0.57	0.54	−0.03			0.00	0.31	0.31	0.00	0.46	0.52	0.06
Japan	0.39	0.39	0.00	0.19	0.29	0.10	0.43	0.41	−0.02	0.31	0.30	−0.01			0.00	0.42	0.41	−0.01
Machinery & transport (SITC 7)																		
East Asia	0.93	0.93	0.00	0.61	0.76	0.15	0.65	0.80	0.15	0.51	0.68	0.17	0.29	0.50	0.21	0.67	0.74	0.07
ASEAN	0.66	0.86	0.20	0.87	0.87	0.00	0.70	0.74	0.04	0.53	0.63	0.10	0.28	0.53	0.25	0.63	0.79	0.16
Indonesia	0.19	0.38	0.19	0.48	0.35	−0.13	0.14	0.45	0.31	0.07	0.38	0.31	0.05	0.22	0.17	0.17	0.37	0.20
Malaysia	0.62	0.81	0.19	0.71	0.78	0.07	0.58	0.74	0.16	0.37	0.62	0.25	0.30	0.40	0.10	0.66	0.69	0.03
Philippines	0.41	0.68	0.27	0.40	0.66	0.26	0.41	0.69	0.28	0.10	0.55	0.45	0.26	0.60	0.34	0.50	0.75	0.25
Singapore	0.73	0.86	0.13	0.70	0.78	0.08	0.68	0.70	0.02	0.56	0.58	0.02	0.31	0.53	0.22	0.73	0.81	0.08
Thailand	0.50	0.69	0.19	0.74	0.69	−0.05	0.55	0.64	0.09	0.23	0.69	0.46	0.24	0.47	0.23	0.50	0.68	0.18
Vietnam		0.29	0.29		0.27	0.27		0.19	0.19		0.09	0.09		0.35	0.35		0.31	0.31
NIEs	0.79	0.88	0.09	0.66	0.70	0.04	0.75	0.85	0.10	0.50	0.68	0.18	0.31	0.50	0.19	0.70	0.76	0.06
Hong Kong	0.79	0.83	0.04	0.64	0.58	−0.06	0.67	0.57	−0.10	0.49	0.70	0.21	0.23	0.40	0.17	0.80	0.90	0.10
Taiwan	0.66	0.78	0.12	0.46	0.65	0.19	0.43	0.50	0.07	0.16	0.62	0.46	0.31	0.48	0.17	0.54	0.68	0.14
Korea	0.63	0.74	0.11	0.39	0.70	0.31	0.58	0.58	0.00	0.41	0.54	0.13	0.34	0.49	0.15	0.52	0.56	0.04
China	0.50	0.56	0.06	0.46	0.52	0.06	0.52	0.55	0.03			0.00	0.25	0.40	0.15	0.46	0.53	0.07
Japan	0.26	0.50	0.24	0.25	0.46	0.21	0.26	0.46	0.20	0.25	0.45	0.20			0.00	0.26	0.44	0.18

(*Continued*)

Table 7.7. *(Continued)*

	Trading Partners																	
	East Asia			ASEAN			NIEs			China			Japan			World		
	1990–94	2000–04	Change	1990–94	2000–04	Change	1990–94	2000–04	Change	1990–94	2000–04	Change	1990–94	2000–04	Change	1990–94	2000–04	Change
Other manufactured goods (SITC 8)																		
East Asia	0.82	0.79	−0.03	0.62	0.74	0.12	0.62	0.52	−0.10	0.28	0.28	0.00	0.31	0.34	0.03	0.57	0.69	0.12
ASEAN	0.68	0.78	0.10	0.70	0.76	0.06	0.60	0.64	0.04	0.26	0.40	0.14	0.36	0.49	0.13	0.48	0.57	0.09
Indonesia	0.32	0.39	0.07	0.09	0.27	0.18	0.33	0.56	0.23	0.07	0.26	0.19	0.17	0.14	−0.03	0.13	0.12	−0.01
Malaysia	0.54	0.75	0.21	0.53	0.67	0.14	0.48	0.67	0.19	0.18	0.41	0.23	0.43	0.54	0.11	0.42	0.57	0.15
Philippines	0.44	0.62	0.18	0.36	0.59	0.23	0.42	0.44	0.02	0.21	0.19	−0.02	0.20	0.50	0.30	0.18	0.34	0.16
Singapore	0.61	0.63	0.02	0.51	0.56	0.05	0.55	0.51	−0.04	0.20	0.33	0.13	0.41	0.44	0.03	0.72	0.76	0.04
Thailand	0.47	0.51	0.04	0.41	0.59	0.18	0.47	0.47	0.00	0.23	0.31	0.08	0.26	0.37	0.11	0.26	0.36	0.10
Vietnam		0.38	0.38		0.39	0.39		0.30	0.30		0.26	0.26		0.31	0.31		0.29	0.29
NIEs	0.72	0.61	−0.11	0.53	0.62	0.09	0.66	0.64	−0.02	0.33	0.33	0.00	0.30	0.38	0.08	0.48	0.72	0.24
Hong Kong	0.59	0.56	−0.03	0.54	0.58	0.04	0.56	0.62	0.06	0.33	0.31	−0.02	0.34	0.43	0.09	0.60	0.77	0.17
Taiwan	0.49	0.52	0.03	0.41	0.42	0.01	0.33	0.40	0.07	0.05	0.31	0.26	0.37	0.34	−0.03	0.29	0.45	0.16
Korea	0.34	0.56	0.22	0.52	0.52	0.00	0.49	0.64	0.15	0.43	0.42	−0.01	0.20	0.29	0.09	0.27	0.59	0.32
China	0.23	0.30	0.07	0.16	0.39	0.23	0.22	0.32	0.10			0.00	0.19	0.23	0.04	0.16	0.23	0.07
Japan	0.26	0.29	0.03	0.32	0.43	0.11	0.31	0.32	0.01	0.08	0.15	0.07			0.00	0.43	0.42	−0.01

Note: The intra-industry trade (IIT) index is computated by using trade data based on 3-digit SITC classification. The definition of the IIT index is given in the main text.

its trade with the world in machinery products was 0.74 in 2000–04, an increase from 0.67 in 1990–94. The level of the IIT index for machinery products is greater when compared to chemicals (SITC 5), materials (SITC 6) or other manufactured products (SITC 8). Intra-industry trade is especially active for intra-East Asia trade in machinery, where the IIT index is as high as 0.93 for the two periods under study.[6]

Wide variations can be observed for the IIT indices among different East Asian economies. Malaysia, the Philippines, Singapore, Thailand, Hong Kong, Taiwan and Korea registered a high IIT index for their machinery trade with East Asian economies, while Indonesia, Vietnam, China and Japan had only a limited degree of intra-industry trade. These patterns for the machinery trade are similar for other products in intra-industry trade.

Two types of intra-industry trade are identified. One is horizontal, where products of similar quality price but different design and other characteristics are traded. Such trade may occur between countries with similar income levels, where consumers have similar tastes but also demand variety. The other type is vertical, under which products of different quality and price are traded. An example of such trade involves standard colour televisions and high-definition televisions, which are of different quality and price. As such, vertical intra-industry trade takes place between developing and developed countries, where factor prices are very different.

A large part of intra-industry trade in East Asia can be characterised as vertical. Table 7.8 reports the results of the analysis to classify intra-regional trade in East Asia into three types: two types of intra-industry trade and inter-industry trade (or one-way trade).[7] The results show that the share of intra-industry trade increased considerably from 1990 to 2004, consistent with the earlier finding on the IIT index. A large

[6]IIT tends to increase when the level of aggregation increases in terms of the number of countries under one group, such as East Asia, rather than individual countries. It also increases when the level of product aggregation increases, say from SITC three digit to SITC two digit.

[7]See Fukao *et al.* (2003) for the classification of three types of trade. Six-digit HS classification is used for the analysis.

Table 7.8. Intra-industry trade within East Asia.

Year	Inter-industry trade	Horizontal intra-industry trade	Vertical intra-industry trade
1990	42.5	3.3	54.2
1991	40.8	3.7	55.5
1992	23.8	11.7	64.5
1993	34.6	14.1	51.3
1994	33.0	13.7	53.3
1995	31.8	14.1	54.2
1996	31.0	15.4	53.6
2000	27.4	16.1	56.5
2001	25.5	14.0	60.5
2002	21.6	19.9	58.5
2003	23.4	16.4	60.3
2004	21.3	15.1	63.5

Note: Aggregation is based on 6-digit HS1988. Computed using method proposed by Fukao, Ishido, and Ito (2003).
Source: UN-COMTRADE.

portion of this increase is in vertical intra-industry trade, although both horizontal and vertical trade increased.[8] Table 7.9 compares unit-export prices of selected products and gives examples of vertical intra-industry trade in East Asian economies. The figures show the pattern where unit prices and the level of economic development of the exporting countries are closely related, in particular that products from developed economies such as Japan are significantly higher than those from developing economies such as China.

A large share of vertical intra-industry trade in intra-regional trade in East Asia reflects substantial diversity in the level of economic development among the economies and the development of regional

[8]This finding is consistent with Fukao *et al.* (2003).

Table 7.9. Unit export prices of selected products from East Asian economies.

	1990–92	1993–95	1999–2001	2002–04	1990–92	1993–95	1999–2001	2002–04
	Woven fabrics of synthetic filament				Woven fabrics ≥85% synthetic staple			
China	0.7	1.1	0.7	0.8	0.6	0.7	0.5	0.5
Hong Kong		0.8	0.7	4.5		1.2	0.9	5.5
Indonesia	13.1	10.8	8.9	4.8	9.3	8.5	8.2	3.1
Japan	19.1	20.3	18.4	16.4	16.9	19.7	18.0	15.1
Korea	8.9	10.0	8.8	6.6	7.9	7.6	7.4	5.7
Malaysia	0.4	1.0	3.9	0.3	2.5	1.7	0.8	1.0
Philippines				2.5			5.5	3.3
Singapore	1.1	2.4	1.1	1.0	1.1	1.3	1.2	0.9
Thailand	0.8		6.9	4.0	0.8	2.0	10.7	5.9
Taiwan				4.7				4.6
	Men's or boys' shirts knitted/crocheted				Women's or girls' blouses knitted/crocheted			
China	2.3	2.5	2.1	2.3	2.0	2.4	1.9	2.0
Hong Kong		7.1	7.1	7.0		6.6	6.3	5.9
Indonesia	14.8	15.9	16.7	10.9	15.6	16.4	16.5	12.7
Japan	60.6	109.4	127.3	119.9	45.7	115.5	129.2	105.5
Korea	17.4	18.2	20.5	17.8	18.1	18.4	21.0	19.5

(Continued)

Table 7.9. *(Continued)*

	1990–92	1993–95	1999–2001	2002–04	1990–92	1993–95	1999–2001	2002–04
Malaysia	15.8		12.6	6.3	8.0		12.9	4.4
Philippines				11.5				10.7
Singapore	5.1	6.1	6.2	5.3	3.6	3.6	3.8	3.9
Thailand	4.5	5.3	6.4	5.4	4.0	4.3	4.5	4.3
Taiwan				17.3				17.4
	Footwear with leather, plastic soles (HS 6403)				Record players, other sound systems (HS 8519)			
China	6.0	5.7	5.2	5.3	5.6	11.1	13.6	18.5
Hong Kong		10.9	11.1	11.2		17.0	22.0	19.5
Indonesia	12.9	13.9	15.8	13.7	6.3	29.3	21.6	18.7
Japan	25.9	37.3		31.7	70.4	91.4	101.0	90.0
Korea	18.9	19.1	17.5	15.3	16.5	21.6	32.3	43.0
Malaysia	7.3	7.0	4.2	0.3	24.8	42.3	50.2	70.1
Philippines			13.8	10.4			57.1	97.2
Singapore	8.7	12.6	18.4	9.4	46.3	65.3	62.0	83.0
Thailand	10.1	11.9	13.4	10.8	17.0	43.3	5.1	24.8
Taiwan				17.8				22.1

Note: Unit export values are computed by using 5-digit HS classification.

production networks under which parts and components of different quality and characteristics are actively traded.

7.2.5. *Active intra-regional trade in machinery parts*

One notable characteristic of intra-regional trade in East Asia is the increasing and high importance of trade in machinery parts, as shown in Table 7.10. For office and telecommunications, electrical appliances and road vehicles, the share of parts in intra-East Asian trade increased from 1990–94 to 2000–04, although the magnitude of the shares differs among the products. Although the share of parts in the textiles and garments trade and for road vehicles is also high, it declined over time. Among the machinery sectors, the share of parts is highest for electrical appliances, followed by office and telecommunications equipment and then road vehicles. The importance of parts in intra-East Asian trade can be found by a comparison with trade with the US and the EU. East Asia's exports have a lower (higher) share of parts (finished products) in its trade with the US and the EU compared with intra-East Asian trade.

The pattern of intra-East Asian trade in parts differs by products and by economies. For electrical appliances, approximately 80 percent of East Asia's exports are parts and the remaining 20 percent are finished products regardless of their export destinations. The high share of parts in electrical appliances may be attributable to high shipping costs as white goods, which are a large portion of traded electrical appliances, are bulky and heavy. However, one exception is China, where the share of finished products in the export of electrical appliances is high, especially in exports to developed countries, possibly reflecting the very competitive (low) prices of Chinese products.

A similar pattern in China's electrical appliances trade can be found for East Asia's trade in office and telecommunications and textiles/apparel. East Asian economies import parts from other East Asian economies and export finished products to developed countries.

Our findings on the pattern of trade in parts and finished products in office and telecommunications, electrical appliances and textiles/apparel suggest the presence of triangular trade. Under triangular

Table 7.10. Parts trade for East Asian economies: Share of total (%).

	Export destinations															
	East Asia		ASEAN		NIEs		China		Japan		US		EU		World	
Exporting Regions	1990–94	2000–04	1990–94	2000–04	1990–94	2000–04	1990–94	2000–04	1990–94	2000–04	1990–94	2000–04	1990–94	2000–04	1990–94	2000–04
Office and telecommunications equipment: (SITC 759 + 764)/(SITC 75 + 76)																
East Asia	58.2	66.7	65.3	76.4	47.6	61.5	70.8	80.7	49.4	45.8	41.0	43.8	38.2	43.7	44.5	54.2
ASEAN	56.9	62.3	68.7	76.2	39.0	54.9	73.7	64.7	42.6	43.5	33.7	39.1	24.8	38.4	38.3	49.2
NIEs	69.4	75.0	65.0	81.1	69.3	73.3	79.5	81.7	56.5	51.6	41.3	56.6	36.2	52.3	46.9	64.9
China	39.0	56.6	44.1	72.1	36.5	58.5			51.1	42.3	40.2	34.8	32.7	36.5	37.1	46.2
Japan	53.3	71.7	60.6	74.0	50.0	61.1	42.9	88.5			46.0	42.1	47.9	43.8	48.1	51.6
Electrical and apparatus: (SITC 771 + 772 + 773 + 776)/SITC 77																
East Asia	81.2	85.4	84.3	88.1	79.0	84.6	68.5	83.8	86.7	83.1	73.1	69.7	64.7	70.0	74.2	79.3
ASEAN	87.1	91.8	85.6	89.8	87.5	95.1	69.2	90.3	89.8	90.3	90.7	93.1	87.8	93.7	86.6	91.6
NIEs	82.3	87.2	87.3	91.8	83.8	88.9	68.4	84.6	85.1	83.4	67.9	69.1	56.5	68.0	71.5	80.9
China	56.3	72.2	63.2	76.2	52.4	72.4			77.4	68.2	33.9	37.0	27.6	35.8	47.2	55.9
Japan	79.4	80.2	81.7	84.9	78.5	77.5	69.0	77.9			68.7	60.2	59.3	59.6	71.3	73.1

(*Continued*)

Table 7.10. *(Continued)*

	Export destinations															
	East Asia		ASEAN		NIEs		China		Japan		US		EU		World	
Exporting Regions	1990–94	2000–04	1990–94	2000–04	1990–94	2000–04	1990–94	2000–04	1990–94	2000–04	1990–94	2000–04	1990–94	2000–04	1990–94	2000–04
Road vehicles: SITC 784/(SITC 722 + 781 + 782 + 783 + 784)																
East Asia	48.7	53.9	45.0	48.8	63.2	58.4	20.6	46.4	94.9	92.7	21.5	19.5	13.2	18.8	23.3	23.6
ASEAN	67.7	78.1	58.3	68.5	56.7	89.0	64.9	86.0	91.4	87.3	97.7	98.3	19.0	40.2	55.8	58.5
NIEs	30.0	44.2	32.2	32.4	44.0	60.9	21.2	39.0	93.3	92.2	33.5	14.9	15.7	10.8	26.4	21.5
China	97.7	88.3	79.2	79.1	98.4	63.6			99.1	99.2	95.6	95.7		92.3	92.8	83.5
Japan	42.4	50.7	43.6	47.2	45.6	55.1	18.4	50.9			20.2	18.2	12.7	18.5	20.2	20.8
Textiles and apparel: SITC 65/SITC (65 + 84)																
East Asia	62.6	56.0	84.9	79.8	64.4	56.9	91.1	83.0	21.8	18.5	14.1	16.6	21.7	23.8	44.5	43.8
ASEAN	63.3	62.5	73.1	74.8	77.8	71.2	94.0	91.1	29.1	37.2	9.2	6.3	23.0	18.5	32.7	29.8
NIEs	75.4	76.2	91.2	86.9	93.3	88.5	90.8	80.0	19.5	22.9	10.7	14.4	13.8	16.9	47.2	53.4
China	37.3	32.4	76.3	62.3	40.8	42.6			23.1	15.4	24.0	25.4	31.4	29.0	35.5	33.5
Japan	93.6	93.6	97.0	97.0	92.2	84.2	94.3	98.3			82.7	85.7	82.0	85.1	91.3	92.5

Table 7.11. Triangular trade index.

Products	1990–94	2000–04
Manufacturing	0.103	0.173
Chemicals	0.053	0.092
Wood, paper & furniture	0.065	0.131
Metal	0.059	0.168
Power generator	0.054	0.081
Industrial & metalworking	0.065	0.099
Office & telecoms	0.025	0.164
Electrical	0.014	0.211
Autos	0.337	0.244
Textiles & garments	0.055	0.133

Note: For definition of the triangular trade index, see the main text.
Source: Author's computation.

trade, parts produced by Japan and the NIEs are exported to China and ASEAN countries to be assembled as finished products, which are then exported to North America and Europe. To examine this relationship, the triangular trade index is computed for the selected products.[9] The results in Table 7.11 show that triangular trade increased from 1990–94 to 2000–04 for many products, particularly machinery products.

East Asia's trade pattern in road vehicles is different from the patterns observed for electronics or textiles/apparel (Table 7.10) Similar to the case for office and telecommunications equipment and for electrical appliances, the share of parts in intra-East Asian trade is increasing, but unlike these products finished products account for a large share of road vehicle exports from Japan and the NIEs. Unlike office and telecommunications equipment and textiles/apparel, almost all

[9] Triangular trade index is defined as: [(Export of intermediate goods from Japan and NIEs to China and ASEAN) ÷ (Export of intermediate goods from Japan and NIEs to the world)] × [(Export of finished goods from China and ASEAN to the EU, US and Canada) ÷ (Export of finished goods from emerging EAs to the world)].

of Japan's imports in road vehicles from East Asia are parts and not finished products. This indicates a lack of competitiveness in assembling automobiles in East Asian developing economies *vis-à-vis* Japan. However, with improved technical capability, East Asian developing economies may improve competitiveness and successfully export finished products to Japan, just as they do other machinery products.

The findings in this Section indicate the developing role of East Asia as a world factory for electronics and electrical machinery and textiles, as they produce finished products by assembling the parts and components supplied by developed and developing economies and sell the finished products in the world market.

7.3. Foreign Direct Investment and Foreign Trade: Increasing Role of Multinational Corporations in International Trade

7.3.1. *Changing patterns of FDI inflows in East Asia*

We saw earlier that FDI inflows to East Asia have increased rapidly and remarkably since the mid-1980s. Several notable characteristics, which have implications on trade patterns in East Asia, can be found for these.

First, increasing intra-regional orientation is not the source of FDI inflows, unlike the case for international trade (Table 7.12). Out of eight countries for which the data on the sources of FDI inflows are available, only three — Indonesia, Thailand, and Korea — saw the increase in the share of East Asian FDI as a source of FDI inflows. Wide variations in the importance of East Asia as a source of FDI inflows should also be noted. Unlike the pattern observed for international trade, where intra-regional trade accounted for approximately 40–60 percent of total trade for all the East Asian economies, dependence on intra-regional FDI ranges from 99 percent for Thailand in 2000–04 to 22 percent for Singapore in 2000–04.

Second, somewhat similar to the pattern found for international trade, the machinery sector, especially the electrical and electronics sector, received substantial FDI in many East Asian economies (Table 7.13). In particular, the share of the electrical and electronics

Table 7.12. Sources of FDI inflows to East Asian developing economies (%).

	China (actualised)		Indonesia (approved)		Malaysia (approved)		Philippines (BOP)		Singapore (committed)		Thailand (BOP)		Korea (approved)		Taiwan (approved)	
	1995–99	2000–04	1995–99	2000–04	1995–99	2000–04	1995–99	2000–04	1995–99	2000–04	1995–99	2000–04	1995–99	2000–04	1995–99	2000–04
World	100	100	100	100	100	100	100	100	100	100	100	100	100	100	100	100
East Asia	73.1	61.6	38.3	41.7	45.4	36.4	48.5	37.5	29.0	21.6	52.0	99.1	26.3	26.5	34.8	31.0
Japan	8.3	8.6	14.7	9.7	18.6	11.6	25.4	24.3	29.0	21.6	26.5	42.1	8.8	13.5	17.2	15.2
East Asia ex Japan	64.8	52.9	23.6	32.0	26.8	24.9	23.1	13.3	0.0	0.0	25.5	57.0	17.6	13.0	17.7	15.8
China	0.0	0.0	0.1	10.2	0.7	4.4	2.7	0.0	0.0	0.0	0.0	0.5	0.2	2.9	0.0	0.0
Korea	3.6	6.7	2.9	3.1	3.2	4.5	1.6	0.1	0.0	0.0	0.9	1.2	0.0	0.0	0.5	1.4
Taiwan	7.4	6.2	4.8	0.7	7.7	4.2	2.6	0.2	0.0	0.0	3.6	5.2	0.1	1.0	0.0	0.0
Hong Kong	45.8	34.1	2.9	3.2	0.5	0.8	8.8	1.4	0.0	0.0	9.4	9.0	2.4	1.2	6.2	3.1
Singapore	6.1	4.2	6.9	9.6	14.2	9.8	6.2	10.8	0.0	0.0	10.6	37.7	4.8	2.3	7.5	8.8
Indonesia	0.2	0.3	0.0	0.0	0.5	0.4	0.0	0.1	0.0	0.0	0.2	0.1	0.0	0.0	0.1	0.0
Malaysia	0.8	0.6	4.5	4.9	0.0	0.0	1.2	0.6	0.0	0.0	0.5	1.2	10.0	5.4	0.3	2.4
Philippines	0.3	0.4	0.1	0.2	0.0	0.3	0.0	0.0	0.0	0.0	0.1	1.9	0.0	0.0	3.1	0.0
Thailand	0.6	0.4	1.3	0.2	0.0	0.5	0.0	0.1	0.0	0.0	0.0	0.0	0.0	0.1	0.0	0.1
Vietnam	0.0	0.0	0.0	0.0	0.0	0.0	0.0	0.0	0.0	0.0	0.0	0.0	0.0	0.0	0.0	0.0
Cambodia	0.0	0.0	0.0	0.0	0.0	0.0	0.0	0.0	0.0	0.0	0.0	0.1	0.0	0.0	0.0	0.0
Brunei	0.0	0.1	0.0	0.0	0.0	0.0	0.0	0.0	0.0	0.0	0.0	0.0	0.0	0.0	0.0	0.0
Myanmar	0.0	0.0	0.0	0.0	0.0	0.0	0.0	0.0	0.0	0.0	0.0	0.1	0.0	0.0	0.0	0.0
Laos	0.0	0.0	0.0	0.0	0.0	0.0	0.0	0.0	0.0	0.0	0.1	0.0	0.0	0.0	0.0	0.0
US	8.5	8.8	4.0	1.7	29.7	21.2	20.6	19.1	45.3	42.4	20.4	2.2	31.3	31.5	24.9	16.6
EU	7.7	7.0	24.0	17.0	9.1	30.3	18.7	4.8	23.2	30.8	17.3	−0.2	29.5	21.6	7.5	17.0

Note: The EU includes Italy, the UK, the Netherlands, France and Germany. In the case of Singapore, the EU refer to Europe.

Source: Country data sources.

Table 7.13. Sectoral distribution of FDI inflows (%).

	Malaysia (Approved)		Thailand (BOP)		Korea (Approved)		Taiwan (Approved)	
	1995–99	2000–04	1995–99	2000–04	1995–99	2000–04	1995–99	2000–04
Manufacturing	100	100	100	100	100	100	100	100
Food	2.5	3.5	7.3	7.3	11.9	4.4	3.2	3.4
Textiles	2.6	1.9	4.2	2.6	1.3	0.9	2.8	1.3
Wood	8.2	8.0	a	a	11.3	0.9	0.5	1.6
Metals	8.3	9.6	20.2	13.6	3.6	5.1	12.2	6.9
Chemicals	33.0	17.1	9.3	10.2	18.9	18.5	12.6	10.0
General machinery	2.2	1.7	25.9	32.2	8.7	13.2	3.1	5.3
Electric machinery	35.4	43.1	26.9	11.9	29.6	35.9	56.9	61.9
Transport machinery	2.9	6.5	b	b	8.8	12.6	5.3	4.0
Others	4.9	8.4	10.9	22.3	5.5	8.4	3.4	5.5
Manufacturing Share of total	na	na	39.6	53.5	49.4	36.4	48.6	35.0

Note: For Thailand, wood (a) is included in others and transport machinery (b) is included in general machinery.
Source: Country data sources.

sector is high in Taiwan, where more than half of FDI inflows in manufacturing were in that sector. The low share in Thailand is largely a result of the negative FDI value, or the withdrawal of FDI, in the electrical and electronics sector in recent years. Despite a declining trend in Thailand, the large amount of FDI inflows in the electrical and electronics sector in East Asia since the mid-1980s has led to a substantial increase in international trade in that sector, which we confirmed earlier.

7.3.2. *Foreign trade by multinational corporations*

MNCs have had a huge impact on East Asian economies through various forms, including generating production, fixed investment and employment. In particular, their impact on foreign trade has been substantial.[10] For example, the share of MNCs' exports in China's exports increased from 29 percent in 1994 to 55 percent in 2003, while the corresponding share for imports increased from 46 to 56 percent.[11] Although similar information for many other East Asian economies is not available, the contributions of MNCs to much of East Asia's trade are substantial, considering their increased position in East Asia and their well-developed global trading networks. Thus, it is important to investigate the trading patterns of MNCs in East Asia to gain a deeper understanding of the changing trade patterns. Because of the limited availability of necessary information, we examine the patterns of trade by Japanese MNCs.

Asian affiliates of Japanese MNCs have a strong export orientation compared with affiliates in other parts of the world, while the import orientation of Asian affiliates is similar to those elsewhere. In 2001, the share of exports in total sales for the Asian affiliates in the manufacturing sector was 52 percent, significantly higher than 14 percent for the affiliates in North America, while the shares of imports in total

[10]On the impacts of FDI on trade, see, for example, Urata (2001), Kawai and Urata (1998, 2004).
[11]*China's Statistical Yearbook*, various years.

procurements forthe affiliates in Asia and North America are similar at 54 and 50 percent, respectively.[12]

Among the different sectors, trade orientation is particularly high for the machinery sectors, with the highest orientation registered by the electrical and electronics sector. Indeed, in this sector 70 percent of total sales were destined for overseas, while 70 percent of total procurements came from overseas.

Several trade patterns, which were found in the earlier analysis of foreign trade in East Asia, can also be found in the trade patterns of Japanese MNCs'. First is the increase in the importance of intra-regional trade in East Asia for Japanese MNCs' trade. The share of exports to Asia (Japan and the rest of Asia combined) in total exports in manufacturing increased slightly from 79.6 percent in 1992 to 82.4 percent in 2001, and the corresponding share for imports rose from 90.9 to 95.5 percent (Table 7.14). These increases are remarkable since the degrees of intra-regional dependence in both exports and imports for the Asian affiliates of Japanese MNCs' were already very high in the early 1990s.

Several interesting changes are observed at sectoral levels. The high share of Japan in both the exports and imports of Asian affiliates in textiles reflect the strategy of Japanese textile producers to use Asia as a production base for the Japanese market. A substantial increase in the share of exports to Asia is found for transport machinery at the expense of exports to North America, probably reflecting the increased importance of the Asian market. A shift in the importance of the import source from Japan to the rest of Asia is found for electrical and electronics machinery, probably because of the improved competitiveness of these parts produced in other Asian economies.

Second is the emergence of a triangular trade in electrical and electronics products involving Asian affiliates of Japanese MNCs, wherein parts are imported from Asian economies, including Japan, to be assembled for finished products, which in turn are exported to North America and the EU.

---

[12]METI, Kaigai Jigyo Katsudo Kihon Chosa [A Comprehensive Survey of Overseas Activities of Japanese Firms] No. 32, 2004.

Table 7.14. Trading patterns of Asian affiliates of Japanese firms.

Exports	1992					2001				
	Exports to					Exports to				
	Total Asia	Japan	Other Asia	North America	Europe	Total Asia	Japan	Other Asia	North America	Europe
Manufacturing total	79.6	46.6	33.0	10.9	5.9	82.4	47.2	35.1	8.9	5.1
Food	58.1	49.1	9.1	5.7	3.7	83.3	38.4	44.9	5.6	4.4
Textiles	60.4	32.3	28.0	16.4	15.3	83.4	59.1	24.3	9.3	6.4
Wood and pulp	95.4	94.8	0.6	4.8	0.0	88.0	72.4	15.6	6.1	5.9
Chemical products	94.9	13.9	81.0	1.1	0.6	88.3	25.7	62.6	2.9	6.3
Iron and steel	73.8	14.5	59.3	20.7	6.2	83.9	13.1	70.9	12.8	1.9
Nonmetallic products	98.9	58.3	40.6	0.3	0.0	93.2	37.4	55.8	2.5	0.8
General machinery	74.3	50.2	24.0	4.5	20.9	87.8	61.7	26.2	3.7	2.6
Electric and electronics machinery	85.1	50.1	35.0	9.8	4.1	82.4	50.5	31.9	10.6	4.0
Electric machinery	na	na	na	na	na	68.6	42.8	25.8	20.7	6.5
Electronics machinery	na	na	na	na	na	86.4	52.7	33.7	7.6	3.3
Transport machinery	36.5	23.0	13.5	52.7	6.8	72.3	24.0	48.3	8.4	11.9
Precision instruments	85.1	82.1	3.0	8.2	6.0	92.2	69.8	22.4	5.2	2.2
Coal and petroleum products	0.5	0.0	0.5	99.5	0.0	95.5	71.1	24.4	0.0	2.3
Other manufacturing	70.1	43.9	26.2	12.1	13.1	82.2	62.7	19.5	11.8	4.4

(*Continued*)

Table 7.14. *(Continued)*

Imports	1992					2001				
	Imports from					Imports from				
	Total Asia	Japan	Other Asia	North America	Europe	Total Asia	Japan	Other Asia	North America	Europe
Manufacturing total	90.9	73.6	17.3	3.5	1.0	95.5	64.4	31.1	2.1	1.2
Food	97.9	16.1	81.8	1.1	0.4	77.5	32.9	44.6	9.0	0.9
Textiles	58.2	37.8	20.4	7.9	2.4	77.0	60.3	16.7	5.1	14.8
Wood and pulp	82.8	81.0	1.8	5.5	11.7	84.0	62.5	21.5	3.0	4.0
Chemical products	71.3	59.1	12.2	12.9	4.5	83.6	43.0	40.6	12.0	3.0
Iron and steel	98.0	66.6	31.4	0.0	0.0	98.5	86.6	11.9	0.0	1.3
Nonmetallic products	43.8	26.1	17.6	1.1	1.1	84.8	53.3	31.5	4.6	4.4
General machinery	95.9	93.7	2.2	3.3	0.8	98.9	88.5	10.4	0.8	0.3
Electric and electronics machinery	97.9	73.7	24.3	1.9	0.2	97.7	54.3	43.3	0.8	0.4
Electric machinery	na	na	na	na	na	98.5	55.6	43.0	0.4	0.9
Electronics machinery	na	na	na	na	na	97.5	54.0	43.4	0.8	0.3
Transport machinery	95.3	93.0	2.3	3.8	0.8	95.7	88.2	7.5	3.0	0.8
Precision instruments	97.1	91.5	5.6	2.9	0.0	99.5	84.5	15.0	0.1	0.4
Coal and petroleum products	85.1	51.4	33.8	14.9	0.0	91.6	4.1	87.5	2.3	0.6
Other manufacturing	81.4	66.4	15.0	9.7	5.1	94.8	72.7	22.1	1.1	3.7

Note: The figures indicate the share of sales to (procurements from) the respective regions in total sales (procurements).
Source: Computed from METI, Kaigai Jigyo Katsuodo Kihon Chosa, No. 5 and No. 34, [Comprehensive Survey of Overseas Affiliates of Japanese Firms], 1994 and 2004.

In light of the large increase in trade volume by the Asian affiliates of Japanese MNCs from 1992 to 2001, the two changes discussed above contributed to the increase in intra-regional trade and triangular trade involving East Asia.

A large portion of trade conducted by Asian affiliates of Japanese firms is intra-firm trade — trade between an MNC's parent firm in Japan and its affiliates in Asia, or trade between overseas affiliates (Table 7.15). For manufacturing as a whole, more than 70 percent of exports of Asian affiliates are destined for their affiliated firms regardless of destination. At 96 percent, the share of intra-firm exports in total exports is particularly high for their exports to Japan, which is understandable considering the strong linkage between the affiliates and their parent firms. The importance of intra-firm transactions is less for the Asian affiliates' imports from Japan and other Asian economies than it is for their exports. Slightly less than half of the Asian affiliates' imports from Japan come from their parent or other affiliated firms.

Coupled with the fact that 74 percent of the exports of a Japanese MNC's parent office are destined for its overseas affiliates and 56 percent of its imports are from overseas affiliates, our findings on Japanese MNCs' trade and intra-firm trade in Asia indicate that they have developed their own production and distribution networks in Asia by fragmenting their production processes into several sub-processes and by locating them in the least-cost country.[13] Furthermore, the high share of intra-firm trade by Japanese MNCs indicates the closed nature of the production and distribution network they have developed.

7.4. Changing Policy Environment: Liberalisation of Trade and FDI Policies[14]

The factors behind the notable expansion of foreign trade and FDI inflows in East Asia fall into two groups — domestic and external. The most important domestic factor was the liberalisation of both trade and

[13]METI, Kaigai Jigyo Katsudo Kihon Chosa [A Comprehensive Survey of Overseas Activities of Japanese Firms] No. 32, 2004.
[14]This section extends Urata (2005a).

Table 7.15. Intra-firm trade by Asian affiliates of Japanese firms, 2001 (%).

	Exports to				Imports from			
	Japan	Other Asia	North America	Europe	Japan	Other Asia	North America	Europe
Manufacturing total	96.0	70.2	73.8	80.9	46.7	65.9	98.9	93.9
Food	78.7	66.6	73.8	21.8	52.3	24.2	100.0	100.0
Textiles	89.8	59.1	90.9	97.9	52.2	85.2	100.0	100.0
Wood and pulp	82.8	100.0	—	—	100.0	100.0	—	—
Chemical products	77.1	50.5	92.8	74.4	74.6	87.4	100.0	100.0
Iron and steel	86.6	27.9	100.0	—	81.9	100.0	—	—
Nonmetallic products	97.8	65.4	100.0	100.0	54.7	87.8	81.1	100.0
General machinery	98.7	91.8	98.9	100.0	59.1	61.6	100.0	97.1
Electric machinery	98.3	75.8	51.7	81.5	27.7	29.8	67.1	56.6
Electronics machinery	95.5	80.8	80.3	84.8	44.3	72.6	100.0	94.9
Transport machinery	99.5	29.8	99.7	72.9	46.4	83.4	100.0	95.9
Precision instruments	99.5	93.7	92.3	99.4	50.9	89.2	79.0	100.0
Coal and petroleum products	100.0	99.4	—	100.0	—	78.9	100.0	—
Other manufacturing	98.4	78.2	96.1	74.1	29.4	77.9	98.6	100.0

Note: The figures indicate the share of intra-firm transactions in total transactions.
Source: METI, Kaigai Jigyo Katsuodo Kihon Chosa, No. 34, [Comprehensive Survey of Overseas Affiliates of Japanese Firms], 2004.

FDI regimes. In addition, a favourable macroeconomic environment, reflected in relatively stable price levels, a predictable and stable business environment and supporting institutions for private sector activity, and a relatively well-developed infrastructure together with an abundant supply of well-educated, low-wage labour contributed to the expansion of exports and FDI inflows.

Externally, the substantial realignment of exchange rates, particularly the yen–dollar exchange rate in the mid-1980s, was crucial. The appreciation of the currencies of the NIEs against the US dollar in the late 1980s promoted FDI outflows from the NIEs to other East Asian countries. In addition, remarkable technical progress in information technology facilitated trade and FDI by reducing the cost of communications. Finally, increased competition among MNCs, which resulted partly from liberalisation and deregulation in various sectors in many countries, promoted their global activities, thereby expanding trade and FDI. The remainder of this Section examines the liberalisation in trade and FDI policies in East Asia that contributed to their rapid expansion.

7.4.1. *Unilateral liberalisation*

In the 1980s and 1990s, East Asian economies embarked on unilateral liberalisation of trade and FDI policies and deregulation in domestic economic activities as part of more comprehensive structural reform policies. Such policy changes were induced partly by their commitments to the World Bank and the IMF for obtaining economic assistance and largely by the realisation by the East Asian economies that these changes would promote economic growth. Liberalisation of trade and FDI regimes led to the expansion of exports and inward FDI because they shifted the incentives from import-substituting production to export production and increased the attractiveness of these economies to foreign MNCs.

East Asian economies unilaterally liberalised their import regimes by lowering high tariff rates and non-tariff barriers from the early 1980s to the early 2000s (Table 7.16). The notable exceptions were Hong Kong and Singapore, which had longstanding virtually free-trade regimes.

Table 7.16. Trade liberalisation in selected East Asian economies.

		All products			Primary products		Manufactured products		
		Binding coverage	Unweighted averages	Import-weighted averages	Unweighted averages	Import-weighted averages	Unweighted averages	Import-weighted averages	Ad valorem equivalent of non-tariff barriers
China	1992		40.4	32.1	36.1	14.1	40.6	35.6	
	2004	100	9.8	6.0	10.0	5.6	9.7	6.0	1.5
Indonesia	1989		19.2	13.0	18.2	5.9	19.2	15.1	
	2003	96.6	6.4	5.2	8.0	3.1	6.1	5.8	0.5
Japan	1988		4.2	3.6	8.3	4.4	3.5	2.7	
	2004	99.6	2.9	2.4	5.3	3.9	2.4	1.6	1.6
Korea	1988		18.6	14.0	19.3	8.3	18.6	17.0	
	2002	94.4	15.5	9.5	20.9	19.0	7.8	5.0	0.0
Malaysia	1988		14.5	9.7	10.9	4.6	14.9	10.8	
	2003	83.7	7.3	4.2	4.5	2.1	7.8	4.6	1.7
Philippines	1988		28.3	22.4	29.9	18.5	27.9	23.4	
	2003	66.8	4.5	2.6	5.7	5.0	4.2	2.0	0.4
Singapore	1989		0.4	1.1	0.2	2.5	0.4	0.6	
	2003	69.8	0.0	0.0	0.0	0.0	0.0	0.0	0.5
Thailand	1989		38.5	33.0	30.0	24.3	39.0	35.0	
	2003	75.0	14.0	8.3	16.4	4.4	13.5	9.3	0.3
Vietnam	1994		14.8	20.6	20.9	46.7	13.9	13.1	
	2004		13.7	13.7	18.1	16.7	12.9	12.5	

Source: World Bank, World Development Indicators (2005).

Among the nine East Asian economies shown in the table, Japan and Singapore are the only two countries with average tariff rates lower than 10 percent while China, Thailand and the Philippines had particularly high tariff rates. From the mid-1990s, all the economies pursued liberalisation policies. By the early 2000s, China and the Philippines had reduced their tariff rates dramatically to an average tariff rate of less than 10 percent. Other economies also liberalised, but the magnitude of their cuts was less dramatic. Nevertheless, some economies still maintain relatively high tariff rates and the average rates for Korea and Thailand were around 15 percent in the early 2000s. The primary sector remained relatively more protected than the manufacturing sector and the average tariff rates for primary products are higher in all the economies in the table except for Malaysia and Singapore.

In addition to trade liberalisation through reduction in tariff rates and non-tariff barriers, several other policies adopted by East Asian economies promoted exports. One is the duty drawback system that returns to the producers tariffs paid on imported parts and components used for the production of exports. This system has virtually the same effect as free trade for the producers of exported products. Another is export-processing zones (EPZs) or free-trade zones (FTZs), wherein exporters or producers of export products can take advantage of free trade on imported inputs. Many EPZs offer incentives to foreign producers such as income tax holidays to attract export-oriented FDI. Many East Asian countries established EPZs and FTZs in the 1980s and 1990s after seeing the success in Taiwan and Korea in the 1960s and 1970s. It should also be noted that trade liberalisation promoted inflows of FDI with an export motive.

Although it is difficult to quantify the restrictiveness of an FDI regime, in the mid-1980s many East Asian economies began to liberalise their policies towards FDI inflows.[15] This liberalisation continued, because the East Asian economies realised that FDI inflows promote

[15] Japan PECC (2002) examined the impediments to FDI in APEC economies and found that many East Asian economies reduced the number and the level of impediments by liberalising FDI policies.

economic growth. Restrictions on FDI take various forms, including restrictions on market access, most-favoured-nation treatment and national treatment. Many East Asian economies reduced restrictions on market access by reducing the number of sectors and industries on the negative list and by relaxing the limits on foreign equity ownership. To attract foreign investors, Indonesia, Korea, Malaysia, the Philippines, and Thailand adopted substantial FDI liberalisation measures. Furthermore, recognising the important contribution that FDI may make towards economic growth, a number of economies introduced incentives such as tax breaks to attract FDI. Indeed, there has been keen competition in the region to attract FDI by reducing barriers and providing incentives.

7.4.2. *Liberalisation under the regional framework*

Liberalisation of trade and FDI also progressed in regional contexts in the 1990s. ASEAN members initiated the ASEAN Free Trade Area (AFTA) process in 1992 to make ASEAN a competitive region for exports and for attracting FDI. The 1992 agreement provided for the liberalisation of tariff and non-tariff measures under the Common Effective Preferential Tariffs scheme. The target year for achieving tariff and non-tariff liberalisation was originally set for 2008, but was later moved forward to 2002. The AFTA has been in effect among the original five ASEAN members — Indonesia, Malaysia, Singapore, Thailand and the Philippines — since January 2002 when the tariff rates were reduced to 0–5 percent, though the exclusion list is long and individual country circumstances vary. Furthermore, Vietnam was to comply with the same tariff standards by 2003, Laos and Myanmar by 2005, and Cambodia by 2007. By 2010, ASEAN is expected to be free from tariffs with the exception of Cambodia, Laos, Myanmar and Vietnam, which have later deadlines. FDI liberalisation in the ASEAN has been under way since the creation of the ASEAN Investment Area in 1998, which provides coordinated investment cooperation and facilitation programs, market access and national treatment of all industries. However, some ASEAN members continue to maintain sizeable sensitive and exclusionary lists from FDI liberalisation.

Another regional framework that promotes trade and FDI liberalisation in East Asia is the Asia–Pacific Economic Cooperation (APEC) forum. This trans-regional forum, which was established to promote economic growth in the region, includes not only East Asian economies but also economies in North and South America and Oceania. One important characteristic of APEC is its inclusion of China and Taiwan as members. Indeed, APEC was the only international economic forum in which both China and Taiwan pursued trade and FDI liberalisation before they became members of the World Trade Organization (WTO) in 2001 (China) and 2002 (Taiwan).[16] Following the Bogor Declaration in 1994 calling for full liberalisation of trade and FDI by 2010 for developed-economy members and by 2020 for developing-economy members, APEC members agreed to prepare and implement individual action plans specifying near- and medium-term liberalisation measures. Peer pressure has played a crucial role in the implementation of liberalisation schemes. All APEC members have made significant progress towards freer trade and FDI regimes and also helped both China and Taiwan to join the WTO.

7.4.3. *Liberalisation under the multilateral framework*

Turning to the multilateral level, the Uruguay Round of multilateral trade negotiations under the GATT started in 1986 and ended in 1994. Although it lasted eight years, twice as long as was targeted, the Uruguay Round made substantial progress towards liberalising trade and FDI. The achievements include a reduction in tariff rates; framework agreements on trade in services, on intellectual property rights and on trade-related investment measures; a timetable for phasing out all quantitative restrictions on trade, including those on textiles under the Multi-Fiber Arrangement; the first steps towards bringing agriculture more firmly under a multilateral discipline; a stronger dispute settlement mechanism; and the establishment of the WTO. Although

[16] They are also members of the Asian Development Bank.

it is difficult to estimate the impact of these achievements individually, there is no doubt that the GATT/WTO has promoted trade and FDI liberalisation in East Asia.

As we observed above, China reduced its tariff rates dramatically, largely in order to join the WTO. It committed to liberalising trade further after joining the WTO.

New multilateral negotiations did not begin until six years after the establishment of the WTO in 1995, mainly because of the differences in views between developed and developing members. The Doha Development Agenda (DDA), the first round under the WTO, started in 2001 but it has not entered real negotiation yet because of the differences in opinions on the contents of DDA not only between developed and developing members but also within the respective groups.

7.4.4. *Bilateral and regional frameworks: The recent surge in FTAs in East Asia*

East Asia was not active in the formation of regional trade agreements (RTAs), which include FTAs and customs unions, until recently (Table 7.17).[17] Indeed, AFTA was the only major FTA until Japan and Singapore enacted the Japan–Singapore FTA (formally named a New Age Japan–Singapore Economic Partnership Agreement, JSEPA) in 2002.[18] However, the situation has now changed dramatically and many economies in East Asia have formed FTAs with countries both inside and outside the region.

---

[17] In the GATT/WTO, RTAs, which violate one of its basic principles of non-discrimination, are permitted under GATT Article XXIV with several conditions. These include liberalisation of substantially all the trade of the members, not increasing trade barriers on non-members, and completing the RTA process within 10 years. For developing members, more lenient conditions are applied under the enabling clause. An FTA is considered to be a shallow form of regional integration because it only removes tariff and non-tariff barriers among the members, while a customs union is a deeper integration as it adopts common external tariffs on non-members, in addition to the removal of tariff and non-tariff barriers on trade among the members.

[18] AFTA was discussed in an earlier section. For discussions on FTAs in East Asia, see, for example, Aggarwal and Urata (2006), Urata (2005b) and Pangestu and Gooptu (2004).

Table 7.17. Major FTAs involving East Asian economies (as of December 2008).

In effect		In negotiation	
Bangkok Treaty (1976)	Korea–Singapore (2006)	ASEAN–Australia/NZ	Korea–India
AFTA (1992)	Japan–Malaysia (2006)	ASEAN–India	Korea–Mexico
Singapore–NZ (2001)	Korea–EFTA (2006)	ASEAN–EU	Korea–EU
Japan–Singapore (2002)	Korea–ASEAN (2006)	China–Australia	Malaysia–Australia
Singapore–Australia (2003)	Singapore–Panama (2006)	China–NZ	Malaysia–NZ
Singapore–EFTA (2003)	TPP* (2006)	China–GCC	Malaysia–Pakistan
Singapore–US (2004)	Japan–Chile (2007)	China–Pakistan	Malaysia–US
Korea–Chile (2004)	Japan–Thailand (2007)	China–SACUFTA	Singapore–Canada
China–Hong Kong (2004)	China–Pakistan (2007)	China–Singapore	Singapore–Mexico
China–Macao (2004)	Malaysia–Pakistan (2008)	Japan–Korea	Singapore–Egypt
Singapore–Jordan (2004)	Japan–Philippines (2008)	Japan–GCC	Singapore–Qatar
Japan–Mexico (2005)	Japan–ASEAN (2008)	Japan–Vietnam	Singapore–Peru
China–ASEAN (2005)	Japan–Indonesia (2008)	Japan–India	Thailand–EFTA
Thailand–Australia (2005)	Japan–Brunei (2008)	Japan–Australia	Thailand–Australia
Thailand–NZ (2005)		Japan–Switzerland	Thailand–India**
Singapore–India (2005)		Korea–US**	Thailand–US
China–Chile (2006)		Korea–Canada	

Notes: *refers to the Trans-Pacific Strategic Economic Partnership Agreement whose members include Brunei, Singapore, New Zealand and Chile.
**indicates that the treaty has been signed and is awaiting ratification by the legislative bodies.
Source: WTO website and respective government sources.

Besides AFTA, ASEAN as a group and its members individually have become active in FTA discussions with other countries. One of the FTAs involving ASEAN that has received much attention is that with China. ASEAN and China enacted an FTA in the goods trade in July 2005 and are currently negotiating an FTA in the services trade. ASEAN also enacted FTAs with Korea in 2006 and Japan in 2008. It is currently negotiating FTAs with Australia–New Zealand and India among others. Several ASEAN members have become active in establishing bilateral FTAs. Singapore has enacted many FTAs with countries such as New Zealand, Japan, Australia, the USA, the EFTA and India and begun negotiations with other countries. Thailand has also been active in establishing FTAs; it has implemented FTAs with Australia and Japan and is currently under negotiations with the USA and others. Malaysia enacted an FTA with Japan and has begun negotiations with several economies, including the US. Both the Philippines and Indonesia enacted separate FTAs with Japan.

Compared to ASEAN countries in Southeast Asia, the economies in Northeast Asia, including China, Japan, Korea and Taiwan, were not active in FTAs until recently. However, China, Japan and Korea have now become very active. China has implemented FTAs with ASEAN, Hong Kong, Macau, Chile and Pakistan, and is negotiating FTAs with more than 10 other countries. Japan enacted eight FTAs with Singapore, Mexico, ASEAN and others and is currently in negotiations with Australia, Vietnam and others. Korea implemented FTAs with Chile, Singapore and ASEAN, and concluded an agreement with the US. It is currently negotiating FTAs with several countries, including the EU.

The idea of an FTA covering East Asian countries has emerged. At the Leaders' Summit of ASEAN+3 (China, Japan and Korea) in 1998 the leaders decided to set up the East Asia Vision Group to prepare a long-term vision for economic cooperation. The group has presented recommendations including the establishment of an East Asia FTA. Currently, the Expert Group, which was set up at the recommendation of ASEAN+3 Economic Ministers, is studying the possibility of an East Asian FTA comprising ASEAN+3.

Japan proposed the CEPEA (Comprehensive Economic Partnership in East Asia), which is an Economic Partnership Agreement including an FTA covering ASEAN+3+3 (India, Australia and New Zealand) or ASEAN+6, at the ASEAN+6 Economic Ministers' meeting in 2006. Members of ASEAN+6 also belong to the East Asian Summit, which was held for the first time in 2005. It has been argued that behind the CEPEA idea lies Japan's strategy of taking a leadership role in setting up regional institutions in East Asia, as China took the initiative in the EAFTA discussions. A specialist group is currently examining the feasibility of the CEPEA.

It should be noted that the US proposed an FTAAP, or Free Trade Area of the Asia–Pacific covering 21 APEC member economies, at the APEC Leaders' Meeting in 2006. At the Leaders' Meeting in 2007, the leaders agreed to examine the prospects of FTAAP. Behind the US proposal of an FTAAP is its concern that it would be excluded from East Asia, which would result in a decline in its economic activities in the region. It should be noted that the differences in the members between ASEAN+6 and APEC give rise to important implications of the groupings. Taiwan and Russia, important economic players, are included in an FTAAP, while India, a member of ASEAN+6, is excluded.

Various reasons account for the recent surge of FTAs in East Asia. First, the rapid expansion of FTAs in other regions has alerted the East Asian economies to the importance of establishing FTAs to maintain and expand their export opportunities. Indeed, the number of FTAs reported to the GATT/WTO by its members expanded sharply from the early 1990s and accelerated in the mid-1990s when the WTO was established. Second, a stalemate in the negotiations under the DDA turned the attention of WTO members with an interest in trade liberalisation to FTAs. Third, the Asian financial crisis in 1997–98 underscored the need for regional cooperation among the East Asian economies in FTAs in order to avoid another crisis. Fourth, rivalry among East Asian economies over gaining a leadership role in the region has activated their FTA strategies.

One notable characteristic of FTAs in East Asia is their comprehensiveness in coverage and thus some are referred to as an Economic

Partnership Agreement (e.g., JSEPA) or Closer Economic Partnership Arrangement (e.g., the China–Hong Kong CEPA), among others. These new types of FTAs typically include facilitation of foreign trade, liberalisation and facilitation of FDI and economic and technical cooperation in addition to trade liberalisation, which is included in traditional FTAs. It may be worth noting that the basic philosophy of these new types of FTAs is similar to that of APEC, whose three pillars are (1) liberalisation, (2) facilitation of foreign trade and foreign investment and (3) economic and technical cooperation.

Many FTAs in East Asia are new and therefore their impacts have not fully materialised. However, some evidence on the impacts of FTAs in the form of trade expansion has been reported. For example, bilateral trade between China and Thailand increased notably after the enactment of an early harvest program under the China–ASEAN FTA.

Although FTAs may bring benefits in the form of trade expansion to FTA members, several possible negative impacts have been pointed out by researchers, business people, policy makers and others.[19] First, some FTAs established in East Asia are of low quality in that a substantial number of commodities and/or important commodities are excluded from trade liberalisation. Critics argue that because of their low quality, such FTAs will not generate the expected trade expansion effect, but will only create distortions in the market. Second, the proliferation of FTAs with different rules of origin is likely to give rise to the spaghetti bowl effect, which would reduce trade volume by creating impediments to trade. Third, an increased interest in FTAs is likely to have a negative impact on WTO negotiations by diverting interest and negotiating resources away from the WTO.

7.5. Concluding Remarks

This paper began by observing the rapid expansion of foreign trade and foreign direct investment in East Asia, which played an important role in achieving successful economic growth in the region.

---

[19] See, for example, Lincoln (2004) for these views.

The subsequent analysis revealed some of the dramatic changes in the trade patterns of East Asian economies. First, intra-regional trade expanded faster than extra-regional trade, resulting in an increase in intra-regional dependency. Second, the composition of trade shifted from non-manufacturing to manufacturing, especially to machinery products. Among machinery products, electronics (office and telecommunications equipment) and electrical products increased their importance. Third, intra-industry trade expanded faster than inter-industry trade. Within intra-industry trade, a dominant portion is in the form of vertical intra-industry trade, although horizontal intra-industry is also increasing. Fourth, trade in parts accounts for a large part of total trade (trade in parts and finished products) and the share is increasing. This pattern reflects the increasing extent of the division of labour within East Asia as the region has become a factory for the world. Fifth, all the changes in trade patterns have resulted from the involvement of MNCs in FDI and foreign trade — MNCs took advantage of business opportunities arising from freer trade and the FDI environment that resulted from the trade and FDI liberalisation policies adopted by East Asian economies. Thus, these notable features of trade in East Asia were generated by market forces. Focusing on increasing intra-regional trade, observers have described such development as market-driven regionalisation.

However, market-driven regionalisation seems to be giving way to institution-driven regionalisation, as an increasingly large number of regional preferential agreements in the form of FTAs have been established in East Asia, similarly to the situation in other parts of the world. One important reason behind the proliferation of FTAs is a stalmate in the multilateral trade negotiations under the World Trade Organization. The current round of trade negotiations under the name of Doha Development Agenda (DDA) started in 2001 but practically no progress has been made in the area of trade liberalization because of the differences in opinions among 150-plus members. Under such circumstances, countries interested in trade liberalization establish FTAs with a like-minded country or countries. An interesting and important question is whether FTAs would lead to further promotion of the trends and patterns realised so far and thus achieve economic growth.

The impacts of FTA on trade among FTA members so far appear positive, being consistent with the outcome projected by the simulation analysis using economic models. Indeed, many studies, including Scollay and Gilbert (2001), of the possible impacts of FTAs using computable general equilibrium models indicate positive impacts on the trade and economic growth of members. One would predict further development of the recent patterns of foreign trade in East Asia as FTAs lead to a larger and freer trading environment.

However, concerns have been raised about possible negative impacts of FTAs for both FTA members and non-FTA members. To begin with negative impacts on FTA members, the proliferation of FTAs with different rules of origin complicates the trading system to result in a decline in trade. Furthermore, governments suffer financially as they lose tariff revenue. As for non-FTA members, it is clear that they suffer from reduced export opportunities as they are discriminated against by FTA members.

Recognising that global trade liberalisation is optimum in terms of the economic welfare for all the economies in the world, policy makers and researchers have to devise a scenario and policy to move from regional trade agreements such as FTAs to global trade liberalisation. In this regard, it is important to ensure that existing and future FTAs are consistent with GATT/WTO rules, although these rules themselves have to be improved so as to successfully turn FTAs into global free trade.

References

Aggarwal, VK and S Urata (eds.) (2006). *Bilateral Trade Agreements: Origins, Evolution, and Implications.* New York: Routledge.

Fukao, K, H Ishido and K Ito (2003). Vertical intra-industry trade and foreign direct investment in East Asia. *RIETI Discussion Paper* Series 03-E-01. Tokyo: Research Institute of Economy, Trade and Industry.

Japan PECC (Pacific Economic Cooperation Conference) (2002). An Assessment of Impediments to Foreign Direct Investment in APEC Member Economies. Tokyo: PECC.

Kawai, M and S Urata (1998). Are trade and direct investment substitutes or complements? An empirical analysis of Japanese manufacturing industries. In *Economic*

Development and Cooperation in the Pacific Basin: Trade, Investment and Environmental Issues, H Lee and D Roland-Holst (eds.), pp. 251–293. Cambridge, UK: Cambridge University Press.

Kawai, M and S Urata (2004). Trade and foreign direct investment in East Asia. In *Exchange Rate Regimes and East Asia*, G de Brouwer and M Kawai (eds.), pp. 15–102. London: RoutledgeCurzon.

Lincoln, EJ (2004). *East Asian Economic Regionalism*. Washington, DC: The Brookings Institution.

Ng, F and A Yeats (2003). Major trade trends in East Asia: What are their implications for regional cooperation and growth? *Policy Research Working Paper* 3084. Washington, DC: World Bank.

Pangestu, M and S Gooptu (2004). New regionalism: Options for China and East Asia. In *East Asia Integrates*, H Kharas and K Krumm (eds.), pp. 79–99. Washington, DC: World Bank.

Petri, PA (1993). The East Asian trading bloc: An analytical history. In *Regionalism and Rivalry: Japan and the United States in Pacific Asia*, JA Frankel and M Kahler (eds.), pp. 21–48. Chicago: Chicago University Press.

Scollay, R and JP Gilbert (2001). *New Regional Trading Arrangements in the Asia Pacific?* Washington DC: Institute for International Economics.

Urata, S (2001). Emergence of an FDI-trade nexus and economic growth in East Asia. In *Rethinking the East Asian Miracle*, J Stiglitz and S Yusuf (eds.), pp. 409–459. Washington, DC: World Bank and New York: Oxford University Press.

Urata, S (2005a). East Asia's multi-layered development process: The trade-FDI nexus. In *Policy Coherence Towards East Asia: Development Challenges for OECD Countries*, K Fukasaku, M Kawai, MG Plummer and A Trzeciak-Duval (eds.), pp. 347–410. Paris: OECD.

Urata, S (2005b). Free trade agreements: A catalyst for Japan's economic revitalization. In *Reviving Japan's Economy*, T Ito, H Patrick and DE Weinstein (eds.), pp. 377–410. Boston: MIT Press.

Urata, S (2007). The Changing Patterns of International Trade in East Asia. In *A New East Asia: Toward a Regional Community*, K Mori and K Hirano (eds.), pp. 100–155. Singapore: NUS Press.

Yeats, A (1998). What can be expected from African regional trade arrangements, *Policy Research Working Paper*, No. 2004. Washington, DC: World Bank.

Chapter 8

The Integration of the Electronics Sector in ASEAN

David Parsons and Hussain G. Rammal

The electronics sector is one of ASEAN's priority sectors and is set to become a single market and production base across its 10 member countries. To achieve this, ASEAN governments have established a roadmap for the integration of electronics that includes the elimination of tariffs and non-tariff measures as well as a wide range of other measures to facilitate integration. This chapter investigates the measures affecting this integration process, especially non-tariff measures, and other supply-chain impediments.

The findings of the study are based on trade data sourced from the ASEAN database (ASEAN Secretariat, 2006) and the UN Comtrade (2006) database, and interviews and consultations with individual firms and industry associations operating in ASEAN. An initial questionnaire was created for the interviews that focused on non-tariff measures. The industry feedback on the questionnaire indicated that a wider set of interests was of concern because non-tariff measures were not as prevalent as in some other sectors, and because issues relating to the environment for production as well as trade were deciding factors in the path towards integration. It was also noted that using a single formal questionnaire seeking determinate responses would not be successful in capturing the scope and richness of the concerns of industry. To help address this overall challenge, a strong emphasis was placed on consulting with industry associations as well as firms.

The chapter is divided into five sections. The first section provides an overview of the electronics sector and the importance of efficiency in the supply chain. The second section describes the electronics sector in ASEAN followed by details of the challenges to integration in Section 8.3. The fourth section details the issues that could influence the future integration of the electronics sector in the ASEAN region. The chapter concludes by providing key recommendations to assist ASEAN in addressing the industry's concerns.

8.1. The Electronics Sector

The electronics sector is considered more complex than other sectors, including manufacturing. At the heart of the electronics sector is the production of hundreds of components that make up a very diverse set of intermediate and final products for a wide variety of uses, from simple consumer goods to highly sophisticated equipment. These products are usually grouped into eight main sets (Reed Electronics Research, 2005):

1. Electronic data processing (EDP) (computers and peripherals and associated parts and accessories),
2. Office equipment,
3. Control and instrumentation,
4. Medical and industrial equipment,
5. Radio communications and radar,
6. Telecommunications,
7. Consumer products,
8. Components.

The integration, production and assembly process in the electronics sector is complex and highly specialised (Berry, Towill and Wadsley, 1994). A final product can take 200 or more components made by separate producers in several different countries. The whole procurement and production chain requires a highly efficient process of Systems Integration. The task of Systems Integration is to lay out the requirements and objectives of the production chain, to determine the work breakdown specifications, to bring the components together and then to farm out the work in specific packages. When the production process is underway, Systems Integration is required to track and guide the whole process, including procurement of components, sub-assembly and assembly, until the final product is achieved. This whole process points to the need for seamless flows of communication and component parts across the network that, as noted, could include several different countries.

The electronics sector worldwide has been considered a leader in the development and management of the supply chains for more than a decade. Competition within the sector continues to force greater efficiency onto all producers in all aspects of the production chain, resulting in greater reliance on time, price and efficient information flows than within most other goods sectors. The cost margins of component suppliers in the supply chain are continually squeezed by the major players as they are forced to compete on final products in the market. An elaborate bidding process among potential component manufacturers led by the major players means that higher-cost producers are quickly eliminated from the market if they cannot perform to specifications and price requirements. While factory-level costs are important, government-imposed costs can be a significant problem.

The electronics sector is subject to rapid levels of technological change and innovation. Application and diffusion of digital technology and chip technology are having the most significant influence on these changes. Innovation in design and functions of products is also occurring more rapidly at the consumer end of the market, and with communication and industry-related products. The rapid shift in demand from VCR technology to DVD technology, the emerging shift to plasma and LCD televisions, and monitors from CRT-based televisions and screens are examples of rapid technological change and innovation. However, these changes are just as pervasive in components and final products. The competition for market share in products such as computers and mobile phones is intense and is translated into the production and launching of new products every six months. This increases the pressure on component producers to adapt quickly to the changes demanded by new technology by adjusting management and labour. Price pressures add a further dimension to the challenge.

8.2. The Electronics Sector: ASEAN

The four main product groups consisting of components, EDP, communications and radio, and consumer products make up 94 percent of production in ASEAN's electronics sector. In 2005, the share of intra-ASEAN trade in these product groups stood at about 18 percent of exports and 20 percent of imports. As shown in Table 8.1, these shares are slightly lower than intra-ASEAN shares in the region's total trade, which were about 21 percent of exports and 23 percent of imports. The intra-ASEAN trade shares have marginally reduced since 2002 although exports have nearly doubled in value and imports have increased more than three and a half times in value in the period 2002–2005.

The ASEAN trade figures show that among the nine ASEAN priority sectors[1] in 2005 (ASEAN Secretariat, 2001), only automobiles

Table 8.1. ASEAN trade shares at a glance.

	Share of intra-ASEAN trade in total trade	Share of intra-ASEAN trade in total electronics trade	Share of electronics in total ASEAN trade	Share of electronics in intra-ASEAN trade	Increase in ASEAN electronics trade 2002–2005
Exports	21%	18%	46%	39%	Nearly 2 times
Imports	23%	20%	43%	37%	Nearly 3.5 times

Sources: ASEAN Secretariat (2006) and UN Comtrade (2006).

[1]The nine priority sectors are agro-based products, fisheries, health care products, rubber-based products, wood-based products, textiles and garments, electronics, information and communication technology, and automotive.

had a higher share of intra-ASEAN exports than electronics. But in intra-ASEAN imports, electronics ranks fourth after agro-based products, fisheries, and wood-based products. However, it is important to note that the electronics sector is much larger than the other sectors, with the four electronics product groups accounting for nearly 40 percent of total intra-ASEAN trade. The impact on integration is therefore substantial.

ASEAN trade in electronics is led by Singapore and Malaysia, which account for nearly three-quarters of total ASEAN exports and imports. Only 6 of the 10 ASEAN countries engage in significant trade in electronics (see Fig. 8.1). Vietnam has the smallest trade share of the group of electronics producers but its production and trade has been increasing relatively rapidly in the last two years. Singapore's high trade share includes its role as a key port for electronics exports and imports for other ASEAN countries, especially its nearer neighbours, as well as its role as a producer of high-value electronics products.

Overall, ASEAN's electronics sector is dominated by its trade and investment with large international players in Asia, the European Union (EU) and the United States of America (USA). In 2005, five major partners, Japan, Korea, China, the EU and the USA,

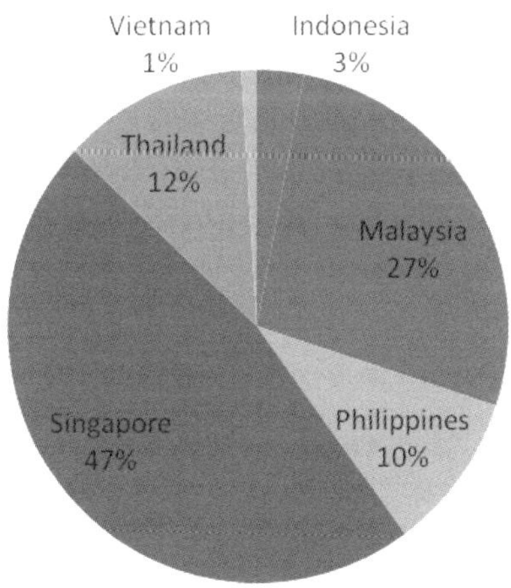

Fig. 8.1. ASEAN trade shares in electronics by country (2005).
Sources: Ozaki (2006) and UN Comtrade (2006).

accounted for 44 percent of ASEAN electronics exports and 45 percent of its imports. Taiwan is also a major partner but comparable trade data are not available. The USA and the EU are larger markets for electronics exports from ASEAN but relatively larger shares of imports come from within the Asian region. Of these countries, China is just ahead of Japan as the largest source of electronics imports for ASEAN. These trends reflect the investments and supply chains of large multinational companies that drive the electronics sector in ASEAN and are key determinants of the integration of electronics in ASEAN.

The review of country trade flows for the individual products show that trade in components and EDP products are the most important for all countries, even the smaller producers. The scale of these two subsectors and the role of small component suppliers mean that they provide considerable opportunity for greater integration within ASEAN. However, the level of integration is likely to be determined by the large international companies that direct the supply and production chains. For consumer and communications products, the most important trading relationships are outside the region with the large markets of the USA and the EU. Within the region, Singapore is an important trading centre for these products, but is less so for the Philippines and Thailand. With income levels rising, ASEAN itself is likely to grow as a market for these products; however, differences in consumer tastes in each ASEAN country means that companies do not necessarily see the region as a single market for many consumer electrical products.

A review of the non-tariff measures shows variation across the ASEAN countries in the electronics sector. These are detailed below:

8.2.1. *NTMs in electronics in perspective*

The non-tariff measures (NTMs) in the electronics sector in ASEAN are generally less prevalent than in some other sectors. For the components sector, which comprises nearly half of trade and production, trade-distorting NTMs are rare. A majority of the more prohibitive

NTMs, used across all countries, are imposed for non-economic purposes. These include the use of prohibition and licensing by governments to:

- control equipment and products that can be used, for example, in counterfeiting and mass duplication of DVDs, CDs and video for piracy or for pornography;
- inspect tapes, discs and videos;
- restrict and control specialised radio and telephone equipment for security and a range of machines for gambling and amusement.

However, for some products, particularly consumer products, NTMs are used to impede or block the flow of imports to protect domestic industry. As would be expected, these products are generally included on the negative list of the country that applies the NTMs and are therefore scheduled to be eliminated by 2010 as part of the second stage of liberalisation of the electronics sector. Technical measures are widely used to control safety standards but in some cases these may also be used to impede imports.

8.2.2. *Para-tariffs, price control measures and finance measures*

In the areas of para-tariffs, price control measures and finance measures, the electronics sector is free of NTMs. However, in Indonesia and the Philippines a domestic value-added tax is applied to all exports. In Indonesia, companies must apply to have this tax reimbursed after the product has been exported. The business sector claims the reimbursement process can be long and cumbersome and can require informal payments. Businesses therefore complain that significant amounts of funds can be tied up in this process, disadvantaging the export sector.

8.2.3. *Automatic import licensing*

Among the ASEAN nations, Indonesia is the heaviest user of automatic licensing. Licensing is applied to a wide range of electronics and electrical items and components. According to the Indonesian Government, automatic licensing is used to ensure greater consumer protection and to differentiate between legally imported and smuggled goods. There are proposals to label legally imported products. The Indonesian Government announced that in early 2007 it would adopt electronic licensing to facilitate the process. Brunei and Singapore also apply automatic licensing to some specific communications equipment, electrical products and replication equipment to monitor these imports.

8.2.4. *Quantity control measures*

The quantity control measures are applied through non-automatic licensing and import prohibition and quotas. In most cases non-automatic licensing and import prohibition are used for non-economic purposes to control sensitive items related to security, piracy, illegal and undesirable activities, unlicensed radio or communications transmission and health and medical equipment. Thailand prohibits the import of refrigerators using chlorofluorocarbons (CFCs) and Vietnam prohibits the import of used refrigerators and other used electrical items. Indonesia uses both non-automatic import licensing and quotas to control the imports of a range of computer machinery, electrical appliances and refrigerators. It also uses enterprise-specific restrictions by giving selective approval to importers for computers and machinery. It is claimed that these measures are to monitor consumer protection and to prevent smuggling and other illegal trading, but there is the risk that they may lead to increased smuggling.

8.2.5. *Monopolistic and technical measures*

Monopolistic measures appear to be applied in three countries. Indonesia applies a single channel for certain heavy-duty equipment, electronic equipment and household electronic appliances for sole importers. The Philippines applies this to shipments bound for the Philippines Government and, in addition, requires that any imports made under government loans and credit should be loaded on Philippines-flagged vessels. Finally, Vietnam uses a single channel for imports of machinery and paper used for money, vouchers and certificates.

Singapore lists the largest number of technical measures of any ASEAN country. They are applied to a wide range of consumer items to ensure that these products meet Singapore's safety standards and receive a Safety Mark from the Productivity and Safety Board. Laos lists the second largest number, but it appears to use technical measures for security, health and safety reasons where other countries use different instruments for this, as outlined above. This contrasting approach to technical measures between the most developed and least developed ASEAN countries illustrates the scope for interpretation and intervention on standards. For instance, Brunei lists no technical measures, but interviews in Brunei revealed complaints about consumer protection and adherence to stated manufacturers' standards on many imported electrical items. Indonesia is concerned about an unbalanced approach on standards and testing. Because of government policy and smuggling, this means that many imports are not tested or do not require specific standards, while producers for the domestic and export market are required to meet specific standards.

8.2.6. *Other non-tariff measures and current and emerging trends*

The review and surveys did not reveal other systematic NTMs not included in the ASEAN database that affect the electronics sector. There are cases of NTMs that are not specifically directed towards electronics that nonetheless impede efficiency in the supply chain. For example, the seamless road transport across the Malaysian–Thai border is impeded by a regulation designed to protect transport operators. This process requires that the goods be unloaded at the border from the truck registered in one country and reloaded onto another truck registered on the other side of the border. This naturally creates delays that fall heavily on electronics producers, and is an example of where the intention is to prevent integration. There are likely to be more regulations that are not specifically directed towards electronics but have an impact on intra-ASEAN trade, including the electronics trade. Overall, traditional NTMs are not used as a major form of impediment in ASEAN except in specific countries and for some goods.

8.3. Challenges to Integration

To understand the challenges to integration of the electronics sector in ASEAN, interviews and consultations were conducted with a range of electronics firms and industry associations from eight ASEAN countries. Laos and Myanmar were not included in the interview process because they have no significant electronics sector and trade remains very small. The challenge in consultations was to take into account the great diversity in the electronics sector in ASEAN. This diversity arises from:

- the differences in the nature of the sub-sectors,
- the interests of importers and exporters,
- the interests of ASEAN companies versus foreign multinationals and smaller component suppliers that do not trade, and
- the differences in the production and trade profiles of different countries.

Consultations with the electronics industry revealed two broad levels of issues that are of concern to companies and affect the integration process in the electronics sector in ASEAN. The first level relates principally to impediments in the supply chain that raise the cost of existing intra-ASEAN trade in electronics. These costs may be significant, but eliminating them may or may not lead to significantly deeper integration among existing electronics companies in ASEAN. The second level of issues relate to what could broadly be called competitiveness and capacity. These issues include factors such as the investment climate, infrastructure, the costs of production and the quality of available labour and other inputs, and influence whether electronics companies locate more of their production within ASEAN.

The relative costs in the supply chain also form part of this larger calculation about competitiveness. It is evident that addressing the bigger set of policy issues in combination with impediments in the supply chain will have the greatest impact on integration. In the case of the electronics sector in ASEAN, the industry nominates specific and high priority concerns from each of these two levels for policy action. They do not necessarily separate supply chain issues from competitiveness issues but they do tend to think of two tracks: one that the government should address urgently and another that should already be underway but will take longer to address. It should be noted that smuggling and the less-pervasive problem of hijacking are of great concern to the industry because they undermine formal supply chains and the orderly development of industrial development for regional integration. Smuggling is symptomatic of significant price differences and inadequate policing of borders.

Typically, both domestic and international firms give the highest priority to factors that affect the bottom line on current profitability. Companies believe that these are issues that governments should address in the short term. The efficiency of the supply chain is the focus of these concerns, particularly inefficiency and uncertainty created by poor administration, processing and policing in areas that are the responsibility of government, such as licensing, customs and standards. For the industry, informal payments, which are endemic in these systems, typify the administrative approach taken by many government agencies. A second set of concerns nominated by firms for action in the shorter term that also affects the efficiency of the supply chain and forms a subset of the competitiveness challenge results from a lack of government policy and action rather than intervention and includes issues such as poor domestic transportation systems and associated transport infrastructure.

All electronics firms and industry associations interviewed for this study expressed concerns in relation to the factors affecting competitiveness and capacity. Most identified economy-wide as well as industry-specific issues. At the economy-wide level were uncertainty in policy regimes and lack of transparency while law and order, the credibility and consistency of the rule of law and the overall level of corruption were listed as specific issues that affected the investment and business climate. Firms also looked at the pace of economic growth and level of incomes. This was not just to assess the strength and prospects for domestic demand but was also used by some firms as an overall indicator of the bigger "dynamics" of an economy and of a government's approach to reform and economic management.

8.4. The Future for the Integration of the Electronics Sector

The electronics industry has been active in apprising the ASEAN governments of their concerns at both country and regional levels. These priorities have guided ASEAN in developing its "Roadmap for Integration of the Electronics Sector" and specific initiatives such as the "ASEAN Mutual Recognition Agreement on Electronics and Electrical Equipment". The roadmap includes initiatives to address nearly all of these issues and has a broad timetable for implementation.

The electronics industry in general supports the initiatives taken by ASEAN. However, firms and electronics industry associations are concerned about the gap between what is planned and the actual implementation of policies, and about delays as well as the process of reform. The roadmap involves many different ministries and departments that will need to work together to establish this environment. There is concern that this is not being done in a coordinated way. This has led to a credibility gap in most ASEAN countries and doubts about the ability and resolve of individual governments to press ahead with effective changes according to agreed timetables. As of April 2007, only two governments had fulfilled their commitments under the "Common Effective Preferential Tariff" (CEPT) to eliminate tariffs on electronics products in the coverage list by 1 January 2007. Most governments were in the process of doing this, but some did not yet have an approved list of products to be included. Slow implementation generally has a direct impact on the profitability of current trade and constrains the process of integration. However, it has a potentially more damaging influence on how electronics firms shape their longer-term integration plans as they examine ASEAN's relative attractiveness and competitiveness as a location for new production or production growth. Some firms, particularly international and regional firms presently operating in several Asian countries, indicated that ASEAN was less attractive as a place to invest for future production because, among other things, governments were not moving fast enough on improving competitiveness.

Firms and electronics associations have identified several key priority concerns comprising a mix of supply chain impediments, areas in which capacities are insufficient for expansion and areas where competitiveness remains weak. Firms tend to identify those factors that impact on current levels of profitability as the most urgent to be addressed by the government, and they have understandably focused much of their efforts on seeking improvements in these areas. Customs remains a high priority issue in many ASEAN countries, along with informal payments. Of other non-tariff measures, a few raised standards and testing as an issue of concern. However, addressing these urgent factors alone will not be enough to tip the balance towards deeper integration. Over the medium to longer term, other seemingly less urgent issues are likely to be more important factors because of their contribution to improving competitiveness and capacity.

Addressing these urgent factors as well as issues that have a strong influence on decisions about where to locate growth in production and trade will be more effective in deepening ASEAN integration in electronics. This is in line with ASEAN's formally agreed approach, as shown in the roadmap. Realistically, in each economy the full range of improvements should be running concurrently as a mix of policy reforms with different timetables. With considerable diversity in cost structures and different levels of development, ASEAN countries have the potential to keep production within their region by preparing lower- and middle-level producing countries to take up the production of goods that can no longer be competitively manufactured by a higher-cost neighbour. For the electronics sector, facing strong competition for new investment from outside ASEAN and with the continuing need to climb the value-added ladder to remain competitive, it is becoming increasingly urgent as well as important to focus on the implementation of the wide-ranging and coordinated reform agenda.

The constituency for reform among firms tends to be less pressing for issues that might not have an impact on current balance sheets. As a consequence, individual governments in ASEAN may not give sufficient attention to mapping out and implementing plans outlined in the roadmap that are specifically needed by the electronics sector. It is unclear whether there is a monitoring process and, if so, whether this includes the views of the business community, and whether such a process would be effective in improving implementation. Some industry associations and the leadership of the ASEAN Electronics Forum consider that business groups could do more to catalyse cooperation and integration among themselves through practical measures. Some such initiatives are included in the roadmap. Industry associations and chamber representatives revealed that cooperation between associations at the working level has not been easy to foster and does not occur in all ASEAN countries on a systematic and ongoing basis.

The ASEAN Electronics Forum now has a register of all electronics companies operating in the ASEAN region. This is an important tool for increased cooperation and business matching but it will require a strong commitment from the industry itself to seek out and take up opportunities and to drive a process of specialisation. Part of the challenge of cooperation arises from the varying levels of value placed on ASEAN integration by the electronics sector in each country and questions about who or what is the driver for integration. Many in the sector are focused on working with their large international partners, while others are sceptical about the benefits that ASEAN integration can bring. In Indonesia, for example, which has the largest market for electronics products in ASEAN, the domestic industry is concerned about losing domestic market share to other ASEAN countries and gaining very little in return.

However, there is generally a clear understanding within the industry of the opportunities that are offered by integration and the importance of using integration to enable ASEAN to compete more effectively with China, already a large producer, and India, as it emerges as a producer. Some larger firms that are operating from Singapore indicated that China had benefits over ASEAN because of scale and because all suppliers, large and small, could be located within close proximity, thereby reducing the costs in the supply chain. These firms also stated that they would prefer to locate future production in India because they believed India could also offer the economies of scale and clustering advantages. Their criticism of ASEAN included a lack of coherence in regulations and administration and corruption.

The business sector has been making representations to the governments in ASEAN for many years about poor customs procedures and associated informal payments. Over this same period, major advances have been made in international customs cooperation through international and regional organisations, in the technology available for electronic processing and in the systems and their linkages. Some countries within ASEAN and many outside the region have been at the forefront of these developments and have implemented highly efficient and user-friendly customs procedures. Yet customs procedures still remain a major concern to the electronics sector in many ASEAN countries. Part of this may be the result of constraints in capacity and knowledge and a lack of funds in adopting new technology and better practices.

While some ASEAN countries are well underway with electronic processing and the adoption of the National Single Window for one-stop paperless trading, paper can be still be an overwhelming part of the export process. In Indonesia, a company can be obliged to prepare and submit 40,000 to 60,000 pages a month to fulfil customs requirements. If the processing is not carried out correctly, they can be subject to an audit, which may result in large informal payments of, at a minimum, the equivalent of about $10,000. Companies are required to pay the salaries and overtime of customs officials, whose so-called "wet signatures" are needed to approve the appropriate documentation to enable shipments to leave the factory. International companies in many ASEAN countries have difficulties in making these informal payments because of laws in the home-office country prohibiting such payments.

In the case of Thailand, where the development of the National Single Window is well under way, the industry reported that customs procedures were now improving with electronic processing. While it was cumbersome in the first stage of the process, the administrative burdens were subsequently much less. It was also reported that in Thailand informal payments had been reduced but official fees had increased markedly. However, the industry generally believed they were better off. In the case of Cambodia, which is on a slower track, electronic processing is being adopted alongside paper processing but the electronic processing can take longer. Businesses reported that ongoing training was needed for exporters and importers and customs officials, with more published information on procedures. Informal payments were up to five times higher than official fees because of low government wages.

The electronics industry is highly supportive of the development of National Single Windows in the ASEAN-6. However, there are concerns about ASEAN's ability to build an effective ASEAN Single Window because of different systems and problems in implementation. While the less-developed ASEAN-4 have until 2012 to implement National Single Windows, some in the industry expressed concern that the different timelines would deepen the gap between the ASEAN-6 and the less-developed countries and it was therefore in their interests to move as rapidly as possible with this initiative. The elimination of informal payments remains a high priority in the development of the ASEAN Single Window. Industry also believed that National Single Windows must be accompanied by faster clearance times.

The setting, testing and certification of standards are critical to international and regional integration in the electronics sector. International agreement already introduced on many standards used in the electronics industry has enabled the industry to become one of the most internationalised sectors. ASEAN has established a formal framework and procedures for an ASEAN Mutual Recognition Agreement (MRA) on Electronics and Electrical Equipment. This includes agreement on the definition of particular standards and provisions for approval of the testing authorities and certification. The MRA now includes 58 electrical appliances standards, 71 electrical safety standards and 10 electromagnetic component standards; however ASEAN countries are in varying stages of signing on to these standards. The MRA allows for goods that have been tested and certified in one country to pass freely to the other countries that are signatories of the MRA.

The issue of standards remains of concern in some countries because of several factors, including the fall-out from smuggling, credible testing and that many products are not included in formal MRAs.

With regard to smuggling, smuggled products are by definition not tested and approved. Smuggling, which is widespread in ASEAN, brings many cheap and sub-standard products into the ASEAN market, undercutting products that do comply with standards and creating safety and consumer protection concerns. Testing can be a costly and time-consuming process. Buyers in some markets can often stipulate the testing authority that should be used, although this more often occurs for buyers outside the region. For example, buyers of some Indonesian electrical products nominate a testing laboratory in Singapore. While this generally works smoothly, it can create additional burdens.

Smuggling of electronics goods occurs on a large scale in ASEAN. Most ASEAN countries have some level of smuggling in electronics products but, by its very nature, it is difficult to quantify in every economy. In Indonesia, the industry estimates that about 40 percent of electronics goods entering the country are smuggled. In Thailand, the industry complains of porous land borders through which large quantities of cheap consumer products enter the country. Smuggling is facilitated by a comprehensive network of international and domestic traders and by government officials who receive incentives to turn a blind eye to the large shipments that enter through mainstream ports as well as secondary channels. The rapidly increasing production of relatively low-cost consumer products in China has created a wave of smuggling into ASEAN from the north. Some of these products may be moved through smaller operations, but large quantities are also officially exported from China and some other ASEAN countries and transhipped through smuggling operations. For example, industry representatives cite the case where nine million electric fans were imported into Singapore from China while in the same period one-third of that number was officially imported into Indonesia. Smuggling is driven by two main factors:

1. Significant differences between domestic prices and international prices on electronics goods, which tip the balance between risk and return towards smuggling.
2. A lack of standards or policing of standards in a country, which enables products that do not meet adequate safety or consumer standards to be sold domestically.

Within a number of ASEAN countries, domestic prices are higher than international prices through a combination of import duties and domestic taxes. To cut these differences within ASEAN, the ASEAN-6 agreed that from 1 January 2007 the Common Effective Preferential Tariff (CEPT) rate on about 85 percent of electronics products would be reduced to zero. As of April 2007, only Malaysia and Singapore have implemented this agreement, although all countries are working on implementation. In relation to China, the source of many smuggled electronics goods, the ASEAN–China Free Trade Agreement stipulated that the import duty was scheduled to be reduced to 8 percent in 2007.

The next section provides key recommendations for the electronics sector in the ASEAN region.

8.5. Recommendations

In summary, the ASEAN governments are aware of the industry concerns and are addressing them through the development of the Roadmap for the Integration of the Electronics Sector and the ASEAN Mutual Recognition Agreement on Electronics and Electrical Goods. The review of the regulations in ASEAN reveals that the electronics sector is relatively free from burdensome NTMs. However, the industry consultations and feedback process identified a number of impediments to the integration of the electronics sector in ASEAN and the attractiveness of the region as an investment destination. These impediments include poor customs procedures and associated informal payments made by organisations; reliance on paper rather than electronic processing of business activities; and the setting and testing of standards, smuggling of goods, and price differences.

These issues have a direct impact on the supply chain and value-adding activities of the electronics sector. Since the sector is highly sensitive to price and time issues, these impediments risk the long-term profitability of companies operating in the ASEAN region. To ensure that foreign producers do not move their production to countries such as China and India, the governments of the ASEAN countries need to respond quickly to address these industry concerns and sustain the sector's growth potential. Some recommendations to address these impediments deal with customs procedures and addressing management and labour skills in the electronics sector.

ASEAN should continue to place the highest priority on the development of an ASEAN Single Window for Customs Administration through implementation of world-class National Single Windows. The National Single Windows should not only result in efficient paperless procedures but also have a real impact on the predictability and certainty of handling times and produce clear and formal-only payments systems. To ensure that the standard of custom procedures is uniform, ASEAN should develop capacity-building measures to fast-track National Single Windows in the less-developed ASEAN countries before the end date of 2012.

In the electronics producing countries, governments should allocate more resources to technical education institutions for certified training at the school and college level and for workers and managers already employed in the electronics sector. The latter is especially important in meeting the needs of smaller producers to continually update their skill levels. As part of the allocation, relevant authorities should step up the training of trainers and the upgrading of machinery used for teaching, including through cooperation programs with ASEAN partners. These steps could specifically include instructions on production and supply chain management so that managers are better able to meet chain requirements. Finally, in those countries leading the electronics sector, market incentives for research and development and innovation should be fostered, with a focus on providing services for regional production and supply management.

References

ASEAN Secretariat (2001). An investigation into the measures affecting the integration of ASEAN Priority Sectors (Phase 2): Review of regional trade and available tariff rate data. Jakarta, Indonesia: ASEAN Secretariat.

ASEAN Secretariat (2006). *ASEAN Statistical Yearbook*. Jakarta, Indonesia: ASEAN Secretariat.

Berry, D, DR Towill and N Wadsley (1994). Supply chain management in the electronics products industry. *International Journal of Physical Distributions & Logistics Management*, 24(10), 20–32.

Ozaki, H (2006). World Electronics Profile, ASEAN, and Direction Towards Integration. 7th Asian Electronics Forum. Manila, Philippines, June.

Reed Electronics Research (2005). *Yearbook of World Electronics Data.* UK: RER Publications.

UN Comtrade (2006). United Nations Commodity Trade Statistics Database. Available at http://comtrade.un.org/.

Chapter 9

Regional Value Chains and Asian Regionalism*

Richard Pomfret

One of the unifying features of Bijit Bora's work was his longstanding interest in multinational corporations and in regionalism, reflected in, for example, Bora and Findlay (1996), Gilbert, Scollay and Bora (2001) and Bora (2002). Geographically, his focus after moving to Australia in 1991 was on East Asia and the Pacific. Much of this was on APEC, and Bijit would have found my treatment of APEC disappointing, but his analysis of the internationalisation of China's economy (Bora and Chen, 1997) foreshadows a central theme of this paper.

A striking feature of international economic relations in Asia in the half century after 1945 was the absence of significant policy-driven regional integration. Since the late 1990s, however, the gap has been

*My published collaboration with Bijit was limited to a chapter on Australia's trade policies towards manufacturing (Bora and Pomfret, 1995), whose practical counterpart was the shared use of a Ford Capri — a symbol of misguided subsidies to the car industry. We co-taught international economics courses in the joint Adelaide–Flinders Honours Program in the 1990s, as well as sharing many discussions in Adelaide's cafes.

filled by a plethora of bilateral and plurilateral agreements. This paper argues that the extent and nature of regional agreements has been driven by the emergence of regional value chains, which were initiated by Japanese multinationals in the late 1980s but increasingly involve arms-length transactions. Since the mid-1990s, regional value chains have been centred on China as well as being driven by Japan, and one symptom has been a heightened struggle for regional leadership.

Because the successful export-led growth in East Asia was by the 1990s generally associated with low applied tariffs and absence of import quotas, the content of regional agreements has not focused on tariffs or quantitative restrictions to trade. Far more important have been measures to reduce trade costs. Such trade facilitation measures have succeeded insofar as trade costs fell faster for the participating East Asian countries (ASEAN+3) than for other countries.

Before the mid-1990s, trade was primarily between individual Asian countries and countries outside the region. Section 9.1 documents the shift towards intra-Asian trade associated with the emergence of regional value chains. The second section connects this phenomenon to the rise of Asian regionalism in the decade after 1997 and analyses the content of trade agreements in the region. A major difficulty in assessing trade facilitation measures is determining which are cosmetic and which have a significant impact on trade costs. Section 9.3 reports results from a dataset that provides quantitative evidence on the reduction in trade costs associated with East Asian countries' international trade. The final section draws some conclusions.

9.1. Patterns of Development and the Emergence of Regional Value Chains in East Asia

Economic development in East Asia in the second half of the 20th century was characterised by waves of economies experiencing rapid export-led growth. Japan was the first, and to a remarkable extent dominated the regional economic scene by the mid-1980s.[1] Hong Kong,

[1] According to the World Bank's World Development Indicators, Japan's GNP at current prices in 1987 was $2470 billion. India's GNP was $273 billion. The next largest

Taiwan, South Korea and Singapore followed a similar path in the 1960s and 1970s, succeeded by China after the reforms of 1978–79, Malaysia, Thailand and Indonesia from the early 1980s and Vietnam after the *doi moi* reforms of 1986–89. As each successor specialised in labour-intensive manufactures, previously successful exporters became uncompetitive in such goods and moved up the quality ladder to goods and services requiring more human and physical capital. The outward-oriented development path was reflected in the concentration of economic activity around a handful of port cities (Pomfret, 1994); in Thailand in the 1990s, for example, over half of the GDP was produced in Greater Bangkok, home to only an eighth of the country's population.

The outward-oriented growth of East Asian economies in the second half of the 20th century was based on multilateralism. Japan in the 1950s and 1960s, the new industrialised economies of the 1960s and 1970s (Hong Kong, Taiwan, South Korea and Singapore) and China in the 1980s and 1990s all benefited from the openness of the multilateral trading system, even before they were GATT/WTO members and although they suffered from some special trade barriers. A corollary to this was that they avoided preferential trading arrangements that might appear to discriminate against their major trading partners in North America or Western Europe. The only significant regional organisation in East Asia was the Association of Southeast Asian Nations (ASEAN), established in 1967, and its economic impact was tiny before the 1990s.

Producing goods for markets beyond Asia always faced protectionist threats, from the textiles and clothing agreements initiated in the 1950s and culminating in the Multifibre Arrangement to restrictive "voluntary" export restraint agreements such as that imposed by the USA on Japanese car exports in 1981. The biggest challenge to Japan's export-led growth came, however, when the large depreciation of the yen against the US dollar in the first half of the 1980s was followed by an even sharper appreciation of the yen in 1985–87 that threatened the

---

East Asian economies' GNP in billion US dollars were China 268, Australia 224, South Korea 140, Indonesia 76, Thailand 51, and Hong Kong 50. Taiwan is not included in the source. No other East Asian economy had a 1987 GNP over $40 billion.

competitiveness of Japanese manufactures. Japanese firms responded by investing heavily in Southeast Asia, off-shoring labour-intensive production processes to remain internationally competitive. The main markets for final goods were still outside Asia, but the subsidiaries began to supply the growing local markets, e.g., car sales in the booming Thai economy were dominated by Japanese models assembled in Thailand.

A similar trend towards integrated production chains began to emerge as some of the most dynamic Asian cities spread their economic activities to neighbouring regions. The pattern was clearest around Hong Kong and Singapore. As wages increased in Hong Kong and Singapore and land costs constrained their ability to absorb migrants as cities in the larger new industrialised economies continued to do, firms began to shift labour-intensive activities outside these territories. This involved cross-border outsourcing or the creation of subregional economic zones as they were known at the time (Pomfret, 1996).

Hong Kong's influence was largely restricted to China and in particular to the Pearl River Delta region of the neighbouring Guangdong Province. When Hong Kong's dollar-pegged currency appreciated sharply in 1983–85, producers of labour-intensive manufactures found that they were no longer competitive. In large numbers, Hong Kong firms moved the most labour-intensive of their production activities to China, where the post-1978 reforms had increased agricultural productivity, freeing literate low-wage labour for the manufacturing sector. Both sides benefited from the match between Chinese labour, perhaps using second-hand equipment such as sewing machines from no-longer-competitive Hong Kong factories, and Hong Kong entrepreneurs with expertise in manufacturing and exporting goods to the exacting standards of Western purchasers.

Slightly later Singapore experienced a similar loss of competitiveness in labour-intensive activities where its firms had substantial management and marketing expertise. The solution was to move such activities to the neighbouring parts of Malaysia and Indonesia. This subregional zone became known as Sijori after the initial letters of Singapore, Johor state in Malaysia, and Riau province in Indonesia. A key to such subregional integration was the reduced costs of moving people and goods across the national borders.

During the 1990s intra-regional trade and investment in East Asia began to increase rapidly.[2] By 1996 intra-regional trade accounted for 50 percent of the East Asian countries' total trade, compared to about a third at the start of the 1980s. The share of intra-regional trade in total exports dipped after the Asian Crisis, but climbed back to 52 percent in 2004, when the import share was 57 percent (Munakata, 2006, p. 47).[3] Trade intensity indices also show increasing trade within the East Asia region during the 1990s (Sohn, 2002; Ng and Yeats, 2003).

Intra-regional trade was in part a reflection of rising Asian incomes and demand. In particular, the later industrialisers found a growing market in Japan. Such demand-driven trade should have resulted in simple bilateral patterns of inter-industry trade. However, in the 1990s intra-industry trade (IIT) was increasing faster than inter-industry trade, especially for China. Xing (2007) calculates IIT (measured at the three-digit SITC level) to have accounted for 6 percent of China's bilateral trade with Japan in 1980, 18 percent in 1992 and 34 percent in 2004 and finds that Japanese foreign direct investment performed a significant role in enhancing IIT. Zhang, van Witteloostuijn and Zhou (2005) have comparable estimates of IIT.

Regional value chains, along the lines of Sijori or the Pearl River Delta, became more common and complex during the 1990s and regional networks became denser, with China playing an increasingly central role (Gaulier, Lemoine and Ünal-Kesenci, 2006; Athukorala, 2007). The increased IIT reflected production fragmentation as different stages of production were carried out in different locations. Kimura, Takahashi and Hayakawa (2007), Haddad (2007) and Gruenwald and Hori (2008) provide evidence that intra-industry trade in Asia is the vertical IIT associated with fragmentation of production rather than the horizontal IIT due to product differentiation observed

[2]The increased regionalisation of the East Asian economy is documented in Frankel and Kahler (1993), Hatch and Yamamura (1996), Aggarwal and Morrison (1998, pp. 65–86), Lincoln (2004, pp. 42–113), Munakata (2006, pp. 37–61), and Rajan (2006).

[3]These are higher than equivalent measures for NAFTA and similar to those for the EU in the mid-1980s.

in Europe. Ando and Kimura (2005) calculate very high shares of machinery (HS84-92) in East Asian countries' trade in 1996 and 2000, and conclude that this structure is especially suited to production fragmentation.

The pattern of emerging regional value chains is documented in greater detail in the "Emerging Asian Regionalism" project of the Asian Development Bank (ADB, 2008). The rapid growth of regional value chains created pressures for trade facilitation because fragmentation of the production process is only profitable if the cost of moving components across borders is low in terms of both money and time (Pomfret and Sourdin, 2009). This had already been a feature of Sijori, where by the early 1990s formalities for goods and people moving between Johor or Riau and Singapore had been substantially streamlined. For the wider East Asian region the pressure for trade facilitation could be addressed unilaterally (e.g., by reducing the paperwork associated with importing, exporting or travel), bilaterally (e.g., in coordinating opening times for border crossing points) or plurilaterally (e.g., by setting common standards for border procedures). Pressure for regional coordination became entwined with political pressures for Asian regionalism after the 1997–98 Asian Crisis.

9.2. Regionalism in East Asia

In sharp contrast to developments in Europe, Latin America and the Caribbean, Africa and North America, the Asian economic landscape in the second half of the 20th century was, apart from ASEAN, characterised by the absence of regional trading arrangements (RTAs). Japan, South Korea and Taiwan were the only major economies in the world not involved in preferential trading arrangements, beyond the Generalised System of Preferences for developing countries (Pomfret, 2001). This situation began to change after the 1997–98 Asian Crisis, when Asian countries felt let down by global multilateral institutions such as the International Monetary Fund and Japan began to put the case for Asian regional institutions, especially in the monetary field. After the turn of the century, the focus shifted to RTAs, in the context of the growth of regional value chains described in the previous section.

The Association of Southeast Asian Nations (ASEAN) was formed in 1967, but for a quarter of a century made little progress in regional trade liberalisation. Even after the announcement of the ASEAN Free Trade Area (AFTA) in 1992, progress in cutting intra-ASEAN tariffs was slow, with lengthy exclusion lists. Empirical studies of the impact of tariff preferences within ASEAN report generally small magnitudes.[4]

There were, however, steps towards reducing trade costs, with ASEAN members adopting common documentation and moving towards a single window (i.e., one stop at the border for immigration, customs, quarantine and so forth) and single border crossings (rather than separate stops for exit and entry). Already in the early 1990s, the emergence of sub-regional economic zones, especially Sijori, reflected areas of ASEAN where trade costs were being reduced to support economic integration and regional value chains. This process was extended and consolidated with the expansion from 6 to 10 members during the second half of the 1990s and accelerated progress towards AFTA.[5] Reflecting the accelerated pace of regional integration, an initiative to establish an ASEAN Economic Community was launched at the 2003 ASEAN summit in Bali, and at the February 2007 summit the target date for creation of a single ASEAN market was brought forward

[4]Manchin and Pelkmans-Balaoing (2008) survey the literature, and point out that preference margins were reduced by MFN tariff cuts. Singapore and Brunei have such low MFN tariffs that preferential treatment is trivial, and for the other four original ASEAN members the preference margins on over four-fifths of intra-ASEAN trade were less than 5 percent in 2001–03.

[5]AFTA was formally completed in 2002, when internal tariffs had been reduced to 5 percent or less, but the real issue is the number of excluded sensitive items. The pace of establishing AFTA noticeably accelerated in the late 1990s as unprocessed agricultural products were phased in and manufactured and processed agricultural products were transferred to inclusion lists. The climax was Malaysia's removal in 2005 of assembled and knocked-down automobiles from its exclusion list, signalling that even its most high profile import-competing industry would be opened up to free trade within ASEAN. By 2006 all temporary exclusions had been brought on to the inclusion lists of the original six ASEAN members and the unprocessed agricultural products still considered "sensitive" (less than 150 tariff lines) will be included by 2010, leaving only a General Exceptions List of 377 tariff lines, representing less than 1 percent of all tariff lines and mainly connected to the protection of national security, public morals and articles of historical significance (Bchir and Fouquin, 2006).

to 2015. The ASEAN Economic Community project is an attempt to unify and extend the ASEAN Free Trade Area, the ASEAN Investment Area and the ASEAN Framework Agreement on Services, and is clearly aimed at facilitating trade. Although trade facilitation measures within ASEAN are agreed at a regional level or among a subset of members, most trade facilitation is non-discriminatory; improved documentation, port logistics and so forth reduce costs of trade with all partners.

In 1989 Malaysia proposed a more extensive East Asian RTA to include China, Japan and South Korea as well as the ASEAN countries. This was opposed by the USA, and, with Japan's support, the Australian proposal of Asia–Pacific Economic Cooperation (APEC) was adopted in 1989 as an alternative, non-discriminatory forum for promoting trade liberalisation.[6] APEC initially focused on reducing traditional trade barriers. At the November 1994 Bogor summit APEC leaders adopted the goal of trade liberalisation by APEC's developed country members by 2010 and by the developing economies by 2020. In the mid-1990s APEC addressed sectoral issues, and in 1996 the USA pushed the Early Voluntary Sectoral Liberalization (EVSL) Initiative for APEC liberalisation in 15 sectors, but by 1998 the EVSL had collapsed acrimoniously.[7]

After the 1997–98 Asian Crisis there was an upsurge of interest in Asian regionalism, initially in the monetary sphere. Japan canvassed the idea of an Asian Monetary Fund, but this was gradually watered down, and the process culminated in the 2000 Chiang Mai Initiative that created formal swap arrangements among the central banks of the 10 ASEAN countries plus China, Japan and Korea (the ASEAN+3 group). Despite some advocacy of a uniquely Asian sequence of regional

---

[6] APEC now includes Australia, Brunei, Canada, Chile, China, Hong Kong, Indonesia, Japan, South Korea, Malaysia, Mexico, New Zealand, Papua New Guinea, Peru, the Philippines, Russia, Singapore, Taiwan, Thailand, the USA and Vietnam.

[7] Japan in particular was unhappy that the USA considered EVSL provisions as binding for developed countries. APEC was also discredited by its failure to address the 1997–98 Asian Crisis. Although APEC summits continue to provide a venue for leaders from the USA, China, Japan, Russia and other members to meet in a fairly informal setting, the economic impact of APEC has become negligible.

arrangements, the money-first approach made little progress after 2000 (Pomfret, 2005). In the 21st century, East Asian regional agreements have primarily concerned trade.

The spread of trade agreements in Asia has been documented by Kawai and Wignaraja (2007) and ADB (2008). Menon (2007) reports that by October 2006 the number of bilateral agreements signed between individual ASEAN members and other Asian countries and between Asian countries and other countries had reached 176, of which 50 had been implemented. Including South Asia and Australasia as well as the East Asian countries, Tumbarello (2007) counts 32 such agreements coming into force between 2001 and June 2007. However, it is difficult to generalise about the agreements' scope, and many lack much serious content (Pomfret, 2007a,b).[8] The agreements are not primarily about tariff barriers, but more often about reducing at-the-border and behind-the-border trade costs.

ASEAN was pivotal. At the same time as ASEAN was deepening its own regional integration through trade facilitation, it looked for new institutional arrangements with its northeast Asian trading partners. In 2000 ASEAN was considering a proposal for integration among ASEAN+3, but foot-dragging by Japan and Korea (Munakata, 2006, pp. 117–118) led to ASEAN and China moving swiftly in 2001 towards negotiating a trade agreement. In November 2002 ASEAN and China signed the framework agreement on Comprehensive Economic Cooperation that foreshadowed the establishment of an ASEAN–China Free Trade Area within 10 years. In June 2003 China and Thailand signed an early harvest agreement to eliminate tariffs on 108 edible vegetables and 80 edible fruits and nuts from 1 October 2003, and early

[8]Some of the agreements are paper agreements only, and those that have come into force are often driven by a small number of specific issues. The Japan–Thailand agreement, for example, excluded areas with significant trade barriers such as rice; its principal results were to reduce the tariff on components imported by the mainly Japanese-owned carmakers in Thailand and to ease restrictions on temporary migration of Thai chefs into Japan. Some recent agreements have been driven by areas not covered by other bilateral agreements, and would previously not have merited the name RTA (such as bilateral tax agreements in the past). Some cross-regional agreements involve trade flows that are, and always will be, tiny, such as Korea–EFTA and Thailand–Bahrain.

harvest measures involving other ASEAN members were introduced on 1 January 2004. In November 2004 the formal Agreement on Trade in Goods between ASEAN and China was signed; it envisaged the establishment of a free trade area with China by 2010 for six ASEAN members and by 2015 for the four newest ASEAN members. In addition, the framework agreement foresaw more comprehensive liberalisation, with agriculture, human resource development, information and communication technology, investment, and development of the Mekong River Basin identified as priority areas (Sen, 2004, p. 76) and collaboration on illegal immigration, drug smuggling, counterterrorism and other security concerns also on the agenda (Kwei, 2006, p. 121). The accelerated pace and broad scope of China–ASEAN negotiations reflected the growth of regional value chains involving China and Southeast Asian nations and the corresponding need to reduce trade costs.

At the eighth ASEAN+3 summit in 2004, it was agreed to convene a regular East Asia Summit. In the early preparatory stages China had proposed holding the first summit in Beijing, but Chinese policymakers quickly recognised that Chinese over-presence might stimulate concerns within the region about a Chinese threat. Hence, China was happy to let ASEAN play the leadership role, and the First East Asia Summit met on 14 December 2005 in Kuala Lumpur. It was preceded by arguments about whom to invite, with China favouring a guest list limited to ASEAN+3.[9] Japan argued successfully for Australia,

[9] In 2004 and early 2005 the USA lobbied Japan not to cooperate with proposals for an East Asia Summit, because the summit was designed to enhance the influence of China, while others suspected that the goal was to exclude the USA (Munakata, 2006, p. 15). In general, however, the USA showed less concern about East Asian regionalism in the early 2000s than it had in the 1990s. This reflected other priorities, especially the war on terrorism after September 2001, but also the Bush administration appeared to have few principled opponents of discriminatory trade arrangements whether signed by the USA or by other countries. Fostering ASEAN integration had become US policy (US Department of State, 2002), influenced by the increased involvement of US transnational corporations in Asian production networks. Within APEC, the USA shunned a 2003 Thai initiative to revive the Bogor Goals and a 2004 proposal for a Free Trade Area of the Asia–Pacific that was supported by Australia, New Zealand and Singapore (Barfield, 2007).

India and New Zealand to be included, so that the East Asia Summit configuration is sometimes referred to as ASEAN+6. At the summit China argued for Russia's inclusion, but no agreement was reached and the second East Asia Summit held in Cebu in January 2007 had the same participants as the first.[10] There was also no clarification of the relative roles of the East Asia summits and the ASEAN+3 summits in the evolving regional architecture.

One consequence of the East Asia Summit was to highlight the competition for regional leadership.[11] Even though China gave way to Japan on the invitation list, the summit was a Chinese initiative and Japan felt a need to respond. The Japanese proposal of a Comprehensive Economic Partnership in East Asia among the 16 East Asia Summit participants was controversial, especially because it seems even more than the EAEC to be an RTA that excludes the USA.[12] At the third East Asia Summit in Singapore in November 2007 it was decided that a report by the about-to-be-established Economic Research Institute for ASEAN and East Asia on the Comprehensive Economic Partnership in East Asia would be received at the fourth summit in Chiang Mai in March 2009.[13]

[10]Russia participated in the first EAS as an observer at the invitation of 2005 host Malaysia and its request to become a future member seems to be supported by China and India, but no formal progress has been made. Timor-Leste is seeking ASEAN membership and became a member of the ASEAN Regional Forum in July 2005; presumably any new member of ASEAN would also join the EAS.

[11]China's increased economic clout relative to Japan is illustrated by their respective gross national incomes at market prices; in 2000 Japan's GNI was US$4,393 billion and China's US$1,169 billion, but by 2007 the gap had narrowed to US$4,813 and US$3,120 billion (from the Key Development Data and Statistics section of www.worldbank.org [17 November 2008]).

[12]Tumbarello (2007) takes a guardedly more positive view of a pan-Asian FTA among the 16 East Asia Summit countries, arguing that such consolidation might help to unravel the current "noodle bowl" of overlapping trade agreements. Proposals for a Free Trade Area of the Asia Pacific among APEC members, which have been voiced in the Pacific Economic Cooperation Council (PECC), seem even more unlikely to be adopted.

[13]The Economic Research Institute for ASEAN and East Asia was formally established in June 2008. Until its own administration is established, the ERIA will be located with the ASEAN Secretariat in Jakarta.

Amid all this activity there has been little progress towards establishing effective new RTAs in East Asia. The various forums reflect great power competition, with Japan using the broader East Asia Summit membership to counterbalance China's success with a more functional approach towards relations with ASEAN and in various bilateral agreements.[14] There has, however, been considerable activity aimed at reducing trade costs in East Asia.

9.3. Reducing Trade Costs in East Asia

Trade facilitation efforts have centred on ASEAN since the early 1990s, and have subsequently included China and to a lesser extent Japan and Korea. This has coincided with increased regionalisation of East Asian trade and the growing importance of regional value chains, which have driven unilateral, bilateral and regional moves to reduce trade costs. In other parts of the world, regional agreements and trade facilitation measures were at a low ebb between the early 1990s and the start of the 21st century.[15] In the wider Asia–Pacific context, APEC shifted its attention to trade facilitation in 2001, when APEC members agreed to reduce trade costs by 5 percent over five years; in 2006 a target of a further 5 percent cut over the next quinquennium was adopted. Countries announced lists of trade-facilitating measures, but despite the quantitative goal there is no benchmark against which to gauge whether the announced measures actually reduced trade costs by 5 percent. At a global level, trade facilitation was brought into

---

[14]India is a latecomer to the competition. As well as participating in the East Asia summits, India promotes the Asia–Pacific Trade Agreement (APTA), a preferential trading arrangement open to all members of the UN Economic and Social Commission for Asia and the Pacific (ESCAP). APTA's current members are Bangladesh, China, India, South Korea and Sri Lanka. So far APTA has had little impact on regional trade flows.

[15]There had, of course, been important trade facilitation measures before the early 1990s, e.g., in the EU the Single Market program was completed in 1992. A global lull in RTA formation followed the completion of the EU92 program, the signing of the North American Free Trade Agreement in 1993 and the completion of the Uruguay Round of multilateral trade negotiations in 1994.

the Doha Development Round of multilateral trade negotiations in 2005.[16]

To what extent have these agreements and statements of intent actually reduced trade costs in East Asia? Pomfret and Sourdin (2009) address this question using detailed trade data of a third country, Australia. The gap between the free on board (fob) value of goods leaving an exporting country and the cost, insurance and freight (cif) value of those same goods on arrival at the importing country provides a measure of trade costs (Hummels, 2007; Pomfret and Sourdin, 2008).[17] The cif/fob gap has fallen continuously for Australian imports over the period 1990–2007, but there are large variations from one trading partner to another in the level of trade costs and in the rate of change. Some of the variation results from geographic factors (such as distance or being landlocked) or to the commodity composition of a country's exports (bulkier or more time-sensitive exports are likely to involve higher trade costs), but variations in trade costs also reflect institutions and policies.

Table 9.1 reports the average *ad valorem* trade costs (cif–fob/fob) on Australian imports from 1990 to 2007. For the 10 ASEAN countries trade costs declined from 10.3 percent in 1990 to 3.9 percent in 2007, which is a much more pronounced drop than in the global average. The unweighted ASEAN average is, however, heavily influenced by some outlier observations, especially for Laos.[18] A more robust indicator of Southeast Asian countries' trade costs is the average for the five original ASEAN members (Indonesia, Malaysia, Philippines, Singapore and Thailand), which fell by over 50 percent between 1990 and 2007. A

[16]At the December 2005 Hong Kong WTO Ministerial meetings, an agreement was reached on the need to move towards text-based negotiations on trade facilitation proposals that could be classified in terms of GATT Articles X (transparency), VIII (fees and formalities) and V (goods in transit).

[17]By focusing only on dollar values of trade costs, we do not directly address the role of time, which some authors (Hummels, 2001; Evans and Harrigan, 2005) identify as more important than financial costs, at least for some goods.

[18]The extreme case of *ad valorem* trade costs for Laos being over 43 percent in 1993 explains the local peak in the ASEAN average, despite the five original ASEAN members having slightly lower trade costs in 1993 than in 1992.

Table 9.1. Average trade costs, Australian imports, 1990–2007.

Year	All imports	Air	Sea	ASEAN-5	ASEAN	ASEAN+3	Asian APEC	ASEAN/Total
1990	0.080	0.066	0.085	0.097	0.103	0.098	0.089	1.29
1991	0.076	0.057	0.082	0.090	0.085	0.084	0.077	1.12
1992	0.075	0.062	0.079	0.080	0.078	0.077	0.071	1.04
1993	0.073	0.061	0.076	0.078	0.103	0.096	0.086	1.41
1994	0.070	0.058	0.074	0.069	0.083	0.080	0.074	1.19
1995	0.067	0.055	0.071	0.062	0.075	0.073	0.068	1.12
1996	0.066	0.053	0.070	0.061	0.077	0.075	0.070	1.17
1997	0.066	0.054	0.070	0.057	0.063	0.063	0.060	0.95
1998	0.064	0.047	0.071	0.056	0.063	0.063	0.060	0.99
1999	0.056	0.041	0.062	0.050	0.060	0.060	0.057	1.07
2000	0.057	0.040	0.063	0.055	0.064	0.063	0.058	1.12
2001	0.057	0.040	0.063	0.053	0.070	0.066	0.061	1.22
2002	0.051	0.038	0.054	0.044	0.046	0.046	0.043	0.90
2003	0.051	0.037	0.056	0.048	0.053	0.053	0.049	1.04
2004	0.055	0.040	0.061	0.057	0.071	0.068	0.062	1.29
2005	0.055	0.039	0.060	0.059	0.052	0.053	0.050	0.95
2006	0.051	0.037	0.055	0.051	0.043	0.045	0.043	0.84
2007	0.049	0.036	0.053	0.046	0.039	0.042	0.041	0.79

Note: The means in the first three columns are import-weighted (*ad valorem* trade costs = $\Sigma cif/\Sigma fob - 1$) and hence biased downwards because goods or trading partners with higher trade costs will be under-represented. The ASEAN averages are unweighted means for the original 5 members, the 10 current members, and the current members plus China, Japan and South Korea. Asian APEC includes ASEAN+3, Hong Kong, Taiwan and Papua New Guinea. The final column is the ASEAN average divided by the world average.

similar picture applies to the Asian APEC members.[19] By any aggregate measure, East Asian trade costs fell faster than the global average over this period, with most of the relative improvement occurring between 1993 and 2002.

Figure 9.1 shows the *ad valorem* trade costs of individual ASEAN countries' exports to Australia from 1990 to 2007. The original five ASEAN members experienced a substantial decline in trade costs during the 1990s with convergence towards the lowest-cost country, Singapore, while in the 2000s there is no clear trend. For Laos and, to a lesser extent, Brunei and Cambodia, the values are volatile, reflecting the small number of trade items. Trade costs of the other two newer members, Myanmar and Vietnam, fell significantly after they joined ASEAN in the late 1990s. For seven of the ASEAN countries, average trade costs converged from above to a range of 4–5.5 percent in 2007, with Brunei, Cambodia and Laos below this level.

The variations in East Asian countries' trade costs for 2007 are small. Indeed, all ASEAN+3 countries have trade costs below the median value for all countries in 2007. China has the highest trade costs (6.3%), followed by Indonesia (5.5%), reinforcing the fact that trade costs depend on factors other than distance or the size of bilateral trade. The lowest trade costs among the ASEAN+3 in 2007 were for Laos (1.6%) and Cambodia (2.5%), suggesting that commodity-specific factors are important.

If we control for country and commodity characteristics and scale, we can draw conclusions about the reduction in trade costs that may be explained by policy or administrative reforms rather than by changes in the commodity-composition of trade. Table 9.2 shows the baseline regressions for Australian imports from all countries, reported in greater detail in Pomfret and Sourdin (2008). Distance and bulkiness are associated with higher trade costs, while scale (measured by total

[19]The Asian APEC column in Table 9.1 includes ASEAN+3, Hong Kong, Papua New Guinea and Taiwan. New Zealand is omitted because the Closer Economic Relations Agreement involves deeper integration with Australia. Russia, whose *ad valorem* trade costs are higher than any of the countries covered and are volatile, is omitted because it is unclear how actively Russia has embraced the APEC trade facilitation targets.

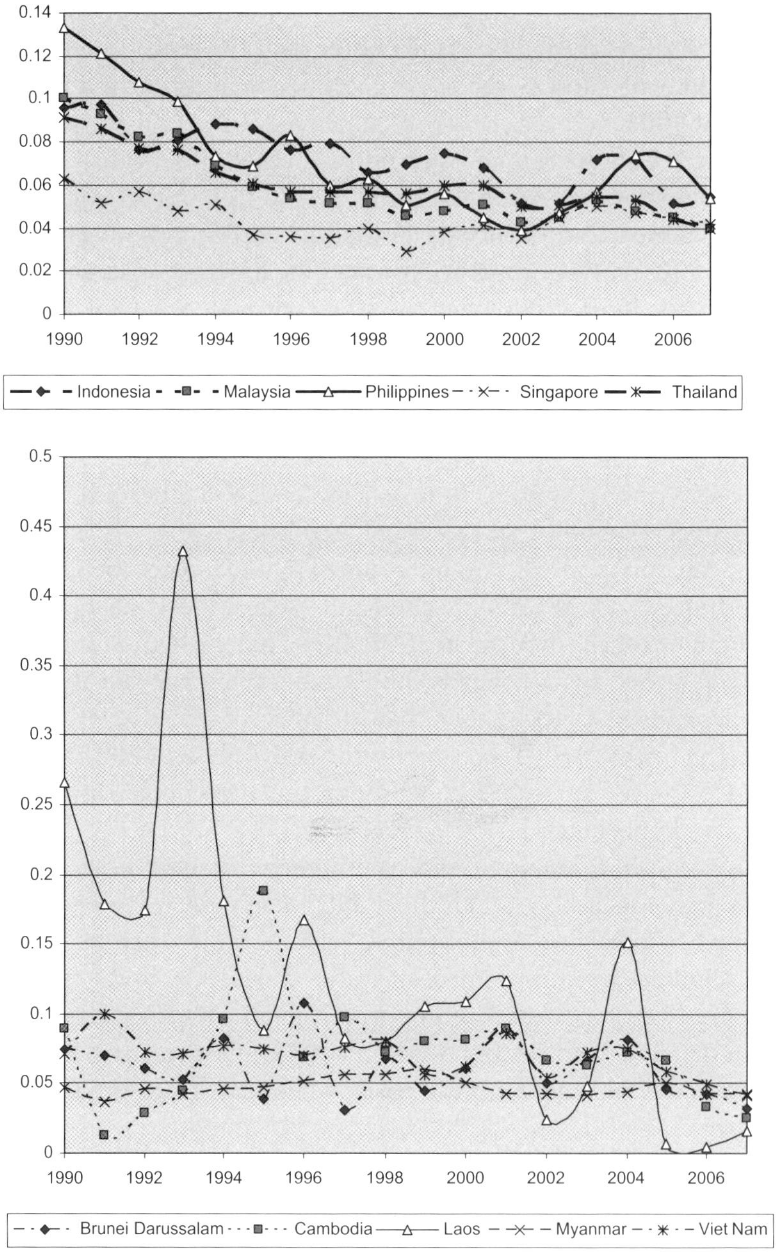

Fig. 9.1. Average trade costs, ASEAN member countries, 1990–2007.
Source: Pomfret and Sourdin (2009).

Table 9.2. Baseline regressions, 2006: Dependent variable log((cif–fob)/fob)*ik*.

	Full sample	Air only	Sea only
Log distance	0.297 (0.0126)	0.182 (0.0258)	0.349 (0.0136)
Landlocked	−0.174 (0.0272)	−0.269 (0.0566)	−0.199 (0.0292)
Log value/weight	−0.310 (0.00359)	−0.250 (0.006)	−0.381 (0.00465)
Log total imports	−0.0238 (0.00304)	−0.0189 (0.0075)	−0.379 (0.00457)
TI corruption index	−0.0167 (0.00260)	−0.0586 (0.0060)	0.00339 (0.00264)
Sea	−1.467 (0.0150)		
Constant	−2.978 (0.142)	−2.835 (0.289)	−4.723 (0.152)
Number of observations	18,682	5,716	12,966
F	F(6, 18675) = 1992.89	F(5, 5710) = 389.64	F(5, 12960) = 1592.34
R-squared	0.390	0.254	0.381
Root MSE	0.800	0.996	0.681

Note: Standard errors are in parentheses.
Source: Pomfret and Sourdin (2009).

bilateral imports) is associated with lower trade costs. These variables are statistically significant for both sea and air transport, with a stronger impact on costs of seaborne trade. Institutional quality, measured by the Transparency International Corruption Perception Index, is also statistically significant; less corrupt countries (with a higher TI index value) have lower trade costs, but this relationship is stronger for airborne than for seaborne trade. An important point from these baseline results is that trade costs depend not only on variables such as geography, bulk and scale, but also on institutions.

Table 9.3 reports results of country-fixed-effects regression for the entire panel for 1990–2007. Country fixed effects incorporate distance, landlockedness and institutional factors, so the estimating equation includes as explanatory variables the value/weight ratio of each commodity and the total exports of each country to Australia, as well as year fixed effects and an interaction term between ASEAN countries and year.[20] The negative and statistically significant time dummies in

[20]The usable dataset of 525,469 observations is smaller than the total dataset because consistent weight data were not available for all commodities. The interaction term is between all 10 current ASEAN members and year. Running the regressions with ASEAN-5 interaction terms made little difference, probably because there are relatively few commodities exported by the five non-founding members.

Table 9.3. Regressions with ASEAN–year interaction terms, 1990–2007: Dependent variable log((cif–fob)/fob)*ik*.

	(1)	(2) Sea	(3) Air		(1)	(2) Sea	(3) Air
Log(value/weight)	−0.291***	−0.345***	−0.248***	Constant	−1.206	2.475	−8.989***
	(0.001)	(0.002)	(0.002)		(0.025)	(0.025)	(0.785)
Log(imports)	−0.040***	−0.046***	−0.042***	Sea	−1.408***		
	(0.001)	(0.001)	(0.001)		(0.004)		
1991	−0.032***	−0.026**	−0.042**	ASEAN10*1991	0.031	0.027	0.036
	(0.008)	(0.009)	(0.016)		(0.026)	(0.026)	(0.062)
1992	−0.054***	−0.048***	−0.055***	ASEAN10*1992	0.022	0.021	0.033
	(0.008)	(0.009)	(0.016)		(0.025)	(0.025)	(0.063)
1993	−0.081***	−0.061***	−0.102***	ASEAN10*1993	0.050*	0.017	0.140*
	(0.008)	(0.009)	(0.016)		(0.025)	(0.025)	(0.062)
1994	−0.125***	−0.110***	−0.142***	ASEAN10*1994	−0.004	−0.033	0.062
	(0.008)	(0.009)	(0.016)		(0.026)	(0.027)	(0.062)
1995	−0.144***	−0.151***	−0.133***	ASEAN10*1995	−0.009	−0.046	0.092
	(0.008)	(0.009)	(0.016)		(0.025)	(0.025)	(0.060)
1996	−0.188***	−0.196***	−0.182***	ASEAN10*1996	−0.018	−0.053*	0.103
	(0.009)	(0.009)	(0.017)		(0.025)	(0.025)	(0.063)
1997	−0.133***	−0.158***	−0.101***	ASEAN10*1997	−0.055*	−0.121***	0.127*
	(0.008)	(0.009)	(0.016)		(0.025)	(0.024)	(0.061)
1998	−0.127***	−0.158***	−0.083***	ASEAN10*1998	−0.028	−0.037	0.034
	(0.008)	(0.009)	(0.016)		(0.025)	(0.024)	(0.062)

(*Continued*)

Table 9.3. *(Continued)*

	(1)	(2) Sea	(3) Air		(1)	(2) Sea	(3) Air
1999	−0.352***	−0.278***	−0.481***	ASEAN10*1999	−0.045*	−0.075**	−0.033
	(0.008)	(0.009)	(0.015)		(0.023)	(0.023)	(0.056)
2000	−0.327***	−0.258***	−0.444***	ASEAN10*2000	0.038	0.019	0.035
	(0.008)	(0.008)	(0.015)		(0.023)	(0.023)	(0.056)
2001	−0.284***	−0.215***	−0.393***	ASEAN10*2001	−0.032	−0.046*	−0.051
	(0.008)	(0.008)	(0.015)		(0.023)	(0.023)	(0.057)
2002	−0.345***	−0.310***	−0.402***	ASEAN10*2002	−0.116***	−0.155***	−0.029
	(0.008)	(0.003)	(0.015)		(0.023)	(0.023)	(0.056)
2003	−0.383***	−0.371***	−0.409***	ASEAN10*2003	−0.053*	−0.076***	0.016
	(0.008)	(0.003)	(0.015)		(0.023)	(0.023)	(0.057)
2004	−0.354***	−0.321***	−0.414***	ASEAN10*2004	0.090***	0.085***	0.071
	(0.008)	(0.008)	(0.015)		(0.022)	(0.023)	(0.055)
2005	−0.333***	−0.273***	−0.430***	ASEAN10*2005	0.065**	0.054*	0.038
	(0.008)	(0.008)	(0.015)		(0.022)	(0.023)	(0.056)
2006	−0.349***	−0.300***	−0.437***	ASEAN10*2006	−0.046*	−0.074**	0.026
	(0.008)	(0.008)	(0.015)		(0.023)	(0.023)	(0.059)
2007	−0.407***	−0.386***	−0.441***	ASEAN10*2007	0.006	−0.008	0.092
	(0.008)	(0.008)	(0.015)		(0.023)	(0.023)	(0.058)
R-squared	0.389	0.350	0.239				
N	525,469	332,512	192,957				

*$p < 0.05$, **$p < 0.01$, ***$p < 0.001$

Note: Fixed effects; robust standard errors in parentheses.
Source: Pomfret and Sourdin (2009).

Table 9.3 indicate the declining trade costs associated with exports to Australia over 1990–2007. Controlling for country fixed effects, commodity characteristics and scale, *ad valorem* trade costs fell relative to 1990 and the magnitude of the decline was larger in 1999–2007 than in 1990–98. The rate of decline was generally faster for goods sent by air than for goods shipped by sea (columns 2 and 3), although this was not true for 1995–98. The aggregate pattern and especially the accelerated rate of decline are primarily driven by the falling costs of air freight after 1999.

The ASEAN-year interaction term in Table 9.3 indicates that in 1991 and 1992 *ad valorem* trade costs fell by less for Southeast Asian countries than for the rest of the world, although the coefficients are not statistically significant. Over the decade 1994–2003, however, trade costs associated with ASEAN exports to Australia fell more rapidly than those for the rest of the world. The differences are small for 1994–96 and only statistically significant (at the 5 percent level) for four years (1997, 1999, 2002 and 2003), but the signs are consistently negative and the coefficients are fairly large for 1997–2003. The picture for 2004–07 is less clear; these are years of substantially lower trade costs for all countries and the ASEAN countries are sometimes ahead of the rest of the world in trade facilitation (2006), sometimes behind (2004–05) and sometimes on par (2007).[21]

9.4. Conclusion

The pattern of Asian trade began a dramatic shift in the late 1980s towards more intra-regional trade, and this shift has accelerated since the mid-1990s. The driving force has been intra-industry trade, reflecting the development of regional value chains. The policy counterpart has been concerted attempts to reduce the costs of crossing

[21] Breaking the sample down by mode of transport suggests that ASEAN-specific trade facilitation has reduced trade costs on maritime trade with third countries more than it has reduced costs associated with airborne trade. This may reflect the specific trade facilitation measures introduced by ASEAN countries over the last dozen years, which may have a maritime bias.

borders. This has been most pronounced in the trade facilitation measures introduced among the original five ASEAN members, but applies to some extent to all ASEAN+3 countries.

Trade facilitation measures have not been empty statements. The impact of the Southeast Asian countries' concerted attempts to reduce trade costs during the 1990s and 2000s is evident in the reduced *ad valorem* trade costs on ASEAN members' exports to Australia, which fell from more than 10 percent in 1990 to less than 4 percent in 2007, compared to the drop from 8 percent to 5 percent in the *ad valorem* trade costs on all countries' exports to Australia. For the five original ASEAN members the decline was concentrated in the decade before 2002 when AFTA was being established, and for the two large new member countries it occurred after joining ASEAN in the late 1990s. This suggests that the importance of AFTA lies in the environment for trade facilitation, as well as in the preferential tariff reductions stressed in the literature, but often found to be limited in their impact.

The evidence on ASEAN trade costs falling faster than the trade costs of other countries is less clear for 2004–07. This may be because the opportunities for reducing trade costs run into diminishing returns; the evidence is of convergence to the regional leader, which is easier than improving regional best practice. It may also be that other countries have begun to pay greater attention to trade facilitation, reflected in the inclusion of trade facilitation in the Doha Development Round of multilateral trade negotiations after the December 2005 WTO Ministerial meetings in Hong Kong.

The plethora of trade agreements being negotiated by East Asian countries since the turn of the 21st century suggest that interest in reducing trade costs has become even stronger in the region. The spread of RTAs and the falling trade costs had a common origin, the emergence of regional value chains, which put pressure on governments to reduce trade costs both by unilateral measures and by bilateral and plurilateral agreements. Whether a result of trade agreements or not, the trade facilitation measures introduced by ASEAN countries after the mid-1990s are visible in the reduced costs of trade with a third country.

References

ADB (2008). Emerging Asian Regionalism: A Partnership for Shared Prosperity. Manila: Asian Development Bank.

Aggarwal, V and C Morrison (eds.) (1998). *Asia–Pacific Crossroads: Regime Creation and the Future of APEC*. New York: St. Martin's Press.

Ando, M and F Kimura (2005). The formation of international production and distribution networks in East Asia. In *International Trade in East Asia*, T Ito and A Rose (eds.), pp. 177–213. Chicago: University of Chicago Press.

Athukorala, P (2007). China's rise and East Asian export performance: Is the crowding-out fear warranted? *APEC Economies Newsletter*, 11(9), available at http://www.crawford.anu.edu.au/publish/forward_to.php?r=/pdf/newsl/APEC11_9.pdf.

Barfield, C (2007). US trade policy: The emergence of regional and bilateral alternatives to multilateralism. Background paper for the Forum on Competing Regionalism, summarised in *Intereconomics*, 42(5), 236–259.

Bora, B (2002). The international distribution of international production. In *Research Issues and Foreign Direct Investment*, B Bora (ed.), pp. 46–61. London: Routledge.

Bora, B and C Chen (1997). The Internationalisation of China. In *China the Emerging Giant*. Canberra: East Asian Analytical Unit, Australian Department of Foreign Affairs and International Trade.

Bora, B and C Findlay (1996). *Regional Integration and the Asia Pacific*. Melbourne: Oxford University Press.

Bora, B and R Pomfret (1995). Policies affecting manufacturing. In *Australia's Trade Policies*, R Pomfret (ed.), pp. 91–111. Melbourne: Oxford University Press.

Evans, C and J Harrigan (2005). Distance, time and specialization: Lean retailing in general equilibrium. *American Economic Review*, 95(1), 292–313.

Frankel, J and M Kahler (1993). *Regionalism and Rivalry: Japan and the United States in Pacific Asia*. Chicago: University of Chicago Press.

Gaulier, G, F Lemoine and D Ünal-Kesenci (2006). China's emergence and the reorganisation of trade flows in Asia. *CEPII Working Paper No.2006-05*, Centre d'Etudes Prospectives et d'Informations Internationales, Paris. Revised version published in 2007, *China Economic Review*, 18, 209–243.

Gilbert, J, R Scollay and B Bora (2001). Assessing regional trading arrangements in the Asia Pacific. *Policy Issues in International Trade and Commodities Study Series No. 15*. Geneva: UNCTAD.

Gruenwald, P and M Hori (2008). Intraregional trade key to Asia's export boom, *IMF Survey*, March, 45 — summary of Chapter 4 of International Monetary Fund, *Asia and Pacific Regional Outlook*, October 2007.

Haddad, M (2007). Trade integration in East Asia: The role of China and production networks. World Bank Policy Research Working Paper 4160, January.

Hatch, W and K Yamamura (1996). *Asia in Japan's Embrace: Building a Regional Production Alliance*. Cambridge UK: Cambridge University Press.

Bchir, MH and M Fouquin (2006). Economic integration in Asia: Bilateral free trade agreements versus Asian single market. Paris: *CEPII Working Papers* No. 2006–15, October.

Hummels, D (2001). Time as a trade barrier. http://www.mgmt.purdue.edu/faculty/hummelsd/research/time3b.pdf [21 December 2008].

Hummels, D (2007). Transportation costs and international trade in the second era of globalization. *Journal of Economic Perspectives*, 21(3), 131–154.

Kawai, M and G Wignaraja (2007). ASEAN+3 or ASEAN+6: Which way forward? *ADB Institute Discussion Paper* No. 77, September.

Kimura, F, Y Takahashi and K Hayakawa (2007). Fragmentation and parts and components trade: Comparison between East Asia and Europe. *North American Journal of Economics and Finance*, 18(1), 23–40.

Kwei, E (2006). Chinese trade bilateralism: Politics still in command. In *Bilateral Trade Agreements in the Asia-Pacific: Origins, Evolution, and Implications*, V Aggarwal and S Urata (eds.), pp. 117–139. London: Routledge.

Lincoln, E (2004). *East Asian Economic Regionalism*. Washington DC: Brookings Institution Press.

Manchin, M and A Pelkmans-Balaoing (2008). Clothes without an emperor: Analysis of the preferential tariffs in ASEAN. *Journal of Asian Economics*, 19, 213–223.

Menon, J (2007). Bilateral trade agreements. *Asian–Pacific Economic Literature*, 21(2), 29–47.

Munakata, N (2006). *Transforming East Asia: The Evolution of Regional Economic Integration*. Tokyo: Research Institute of Economy, Trade and Industry and Washington DC: Brookings Institution Press.

Ng, F and A Yeats (2003). Major trade trends in East Asia: What are their implications for regional cooperation and growth? *World Bank Policy Research Working Paper* 3084, June.

Pomfret, R (1994). The localisation of economic growth in East Asia. *Australian Economic Review*, 107, 20–28.

Pomfret, R (1996). Sub-regional economic zones. In *Regional Integration and the Asia Pacific*, B Bora and C Findlay (eds.), pp. 207–222. Melbourne: Oxford University Press.

Pomfret, R (2001). *The Economics of Regional Trading Arrangements*. Oxford: Oxford University Press.

Pomfret, R (2005). Sequencing trade and monetary integration: Issues and application to Asia. *Journal of Asian Economics*, 16(1), 105–124.

Pomfret, R (2007a). Is regionalism an increasing feature of the world economy? *The World Economy*, 30(6), 923–947.

Pomfret, R (2007b). Asian regionalism: Threat to the WTO-based trading system or paper tiger? Posted on VoxEU http://voxeu.org/index.php?q=nod/309, 22 June 2007.

Pomfret, R and P Sourdin (2008). Why do trade costs vary? *University of Adelaide School of Economics Working Paper* 2008–08.

Pomfret, R and P Sourdin (2009). Have Asian trade agreements reduced trade costs? *Journal of Asian Economics*, 20, 255–268.

Rajan, R (ed.) (2006). Asian regionalism: A symposium. *North American Journal of Economics and Finance*, 17, 231–302.

Sen, R (2004). *Free Trade Agreements in Southeast Asia*. Singapore: Institute of Southeast Asian Studies.

Sohn, BH (2002). Regionalization of trade and investment in East Asia and prospects for further regional integration. *Journal of the Asia Pacific Economy*, 7(2), 160–181.
Tumbarello, P (2007). Are regional trade agreements in Asia stumbling or building blocks? Some implications for the Mekong-3 countries. *IMF Working Paper* 07/53.
US Department of State (2002). ASEAN Cooperation Plan, *Fact Sheet*, 4 December.
Xing, Y (2007). Foreign direct investment and China's bilateral intra-industry trade with Japan and the US. *BOFIT Discussion Papers* 1/2007. Helsinki: Bank of Finland Institute for Economies in Transition.
Zhang, J, A van Witteloostuijn and C Zhou (2005). Chinese bilateral intra-industry trade: A panel data study for 50 countries in the 1992–2001 period. *Review of World Economics* (*Weltwirtschaftliches Archiv*), 141(3), 510–540.

Chapter 10

Recent Developments in the Literature on Foreign Direct Investment and Labour Markets

Noel Gaston

"Levi Strauss, Ohio Art, and Radio Flyer are examples of the many American companies — from small manufacturers to giants like Boeing and Microsoft — that are outsourcing jobs overseas, to countries where labor and other costs are lower than in the U.S. Since 2001, the U.S. has lost nearly 3 million factory jobs.

But it's no longer only manufacturing jobs that are moving (or being created) overseas. Technology has made it easier for many types of jobs to be located almost anywhere. As a result, thousands of software development and call-center jobs, for example, have moved abroad. [...]

China, which manufactures 80 percent of the toys sold in the United States, has 8,000 toy makers competing fiercely for business by getting their production costs as low as possible. Kin Ki Industrial, which makes Etch A Sketch in China, stays competitive, its workers say, by paying them 24 cents an hour in Shenzhen, where the legal minimum wage is 33 cents. When the Etch A Sketch line shut down in Ohio, wages for the unionized workforce had reached $9 an hour."[1]

"A senior politician sparked the current debate on capitalism in Germany by comparing foreign investors to a plague of locusts ... SPD party secretary Franz Müntefering unleashed a stream of rhetoric likening foreign investors to a swarm of insects.

'Some financial investors spare no thought for the people whose jobs they destroy,' he told the mass-circulation tabloid *Bild*. 'They remain anonymous, have no face, fall like a plague of locusts over our companies, devour everything, then fly on to the next one.'"[2]

In recent times, foreign direct investment (FDI) has grown far more rapidly than international trade.[3] According to UNCTAD (2007), between 1982 and 2006 the outward stock of FDI grew nearly 19-fold. In a similar fashion, sales of foreign affiliates grew by more than eight times. Over the same period, exports of goods and services grew by a factor of "only" five. Clearly, there has been a massive shift in the location of global production activities.

This chapter deals with the impact of these production shifts on labour markets. The usual motivation for research on FDI or multinational firms and labour market effects is straightforward. For developed countries, a prominent concern is the relocation of domestic productive activities to lower labour cost locations offshore. The opening quotation is from an article written during the 2004 US presidential campaign. The suggestion, of course, is that the three million lost factory jobs in the United States were lost because of outsourcing

[1]Made in the USA?, *New York Times Upfront*, *Joseph Kahn* and *Ralph Blumenthal*, 26 February 2000. Available at http://findarticles.com/p/articles/mi_m0BUE/is_13_136/ai_n17206945.

[2]The Year of the Locust, *Deutsche Welle*, Deanne Corbett, 20 May 2005. Available at http://www.dw-world.de/dw/article/0,1564,1589069,00.html.

[3]UNCTAD (2004, p. 32) defines FDI as "investment involving a long-term relationship and lasting interest in and control by a resident entity in one economy in an enterprise resident in another economy. In FDI, the investor exerts significant influence on the management of the enterprise resident in another economy."

and moving production overseas. The "delocalisation" of production is often linked with the popular view that growing trade and immigration, particularly from low-wage countries, have adverse labour market consequences for domestic unskilled workers. Indeed, less-developed countries (LDCs) have attracted a markedly greater share of FDI inflows in the past two decades (UNCTAD, 2007).

Bhagwati (1999) notes the ironic "about-face" in policy-making circles concerning the impact of globalisation in the last 20 or so years of the 20th century. Post-World War II concerns about neo-colonialism and the dependency of LDCs on developed countries raised questions for the poorer countries about the desirability of increased integration and trade. This view has been supplanted, almost completely, by developing country enthusiasm for trade and inwards foreign investment. Reservations are now expressed by many developed countries, which worry about the consequences for their domestic workers if integration via trade, migration or investment in LDCs continues unabated. Fears about domestic firms "sending jobs overseas", whether to other developed countries or to LDCs, are an extension of the more traditional concerns about "hollowing out" the manufacturing industry and the loss of "key" manufacturing activities and "good jobs" overseas.

For host countries, even apart from issues to do with national sovereignty or cultural identity, the concerns are no less controversial. The second opening quotation was written during the last federal election in Germany and points to the perceived "footloose" nature of capital in a global economy, viz. the plague of locusts. In some countries, the union movement has drawn attention to the mobility of capital and the possibility that foreign investors seem less willing to invest in worker training and human capital than are domestic capitalists who "live in the community".[4] Another concern relates to the "race-to-the-bottom" in social policies for countries competing for new investment projects. Added to the list of concerns is whether multinationals, owing

---

[4]According to UNCTAD (2006, p. 5), private equity and hedge funds are a rapidly growing source of FDI. Obviously, these funds have a shorter time horizon than more traditional sources of FDI.

to their relatively greater demand for skilled workers, have contributed to the growing earnings inequality.

As for a direct labour market linkage with FDI, note that if a feature of multinational behaviour is the exploitation of wage differentials across countries, then this behaviour could have effects that are observationally equivalent to shifts caused by skill-biased technological change. For the majority of economists, rapid technological advancement is the most obvious explanation for the increased earnings inequality experienced by both advanced countries and LDCs during the 1980s and 1990s. An intra-industry shift in labour demand towards relatively more skilled and/or more highly educated workers would increase the skilled wage premium across all industries. Associated with this feature is the concern, for both source and host economies, that FDI may aggravate earnings inequality.

The lay view is that outward FDI or capital outflows may exert downward pressure on the wages of domestic production workers. Implicit in this view is the characterisation of multinational corporations as being predominantly vertical in nature.[5] That is, "slicing up of the value added chain" involves relocating unskilled labour-intensive parts of the production process to unskilled labour-abundant countries, commonly referred to as off-shoring. Hummels *et al.* (2001)

[5]FDI and multinational activity are traditionally distinguished by the motives for firms to locate some part of their production overseas. The activities of vertical multinationals and the international fragmentation of the production process are often motivated by cost considerations arising from cross-country differences in technologies or factor prices. In contrast, horizontal multinationals are firms that replicate most or all of the production process in several different locations. The motives are often potential savings of transport and trading costs and the possibility of gaining a strategic edge over overseas competitors in an oligopolistic industry. Of course, things are never this simple; the distinction between vertical and horizontal FDI has become increasingly blurred. For example, a firm might manufacture goods in a foreign subsidiary and then sell the output primarily in neither the home market nor the foreign market; this is referred to as "export-platform FDI". Hanson *et al.* (2001) and Yeaple (2003) describe a complex array of roles played by the foreign affiliates of multinationals. They can be any or all of export platforms, links in the value-added chain and wholesale distributors in foreign markets. Hanson *et al.* (2001) conclude that the distinction between horizontal and vertical FDI does not fully capture what multinationals do.

show that vertical specialisation, measured as the share of imported intermediates in exports, increased by 28 percent between 1970 and 1990 in 13 OECD countries, and that this increase accounted for 30 percent of total export growth for these countries. As discussed below, the growth of off-shoring and FDI constitute a plausible explanation for the increases in the relative demand for skilled labour observed in both host and source countries.

In the next section, the most recent theoretical developments that can explain some or several aspects of the impact of FDI on labour markets are briefly reviewed. The primary focus is on partial equilibrium models that seek to explain the activities of multinational corporations. In Section 10.2, the recent empirical work on FDI and labour market outcomes is evaluated in the light of the theoretical developments. Section 10.3 concludes.

10.1. Recent Theoretical Developments in Understanding the Effects of FDI

There are essentially two broad types of models that investigate the relationship between FDI and labour markets: general equilibrium and partial equilibrium models. A general equilibrium framework is particularly useful when dealing with questions about the relationship between trade and FDI.[6] A partial equilibrium or micro-analytic approach is more valuable for understanding what it is that multinational firms "do", how they are structured, how they operate, their impact on competitive conditions in particular industries or markets, and so on. The latter approach is best suited for understanding how multinational corporations not only directly affect wage and employment determination at the microeconomic level, but also for studying the impact on industrial relations, the "stance" taken by labour and capital in collective bargains and the pressure on labour market institutions to adjust. Thus, in the discussion below, the direct and

[6]The less recent literature and general equilibrium or trade models are reviewed in greater detail by Gaston and Nelson (2002).

indirect labour market impacts of FDI and multinational behaviour are distinguished.[7]

10.1.1. *The "new" trade and industrial organisation models*

At least since the publication of Hymer's (1960) dissertation, it has been clear that the arbitrage model of international factor mobility lacks something essential. Specifically, to the extent that doing business in another country entails a variety of costs not borne by local firms, multinational firms were thought to possess some form of competitive advantage to permit them to function profitably in foreign markets. Where early developments, including Hymer's own work, emphasised essentially monopolistic elements, more recent work has stressed oligopolistic and monopolistically competitive elements. International business researchers began to develop models of the international firm built on internalisation considerations, viz. why production in different locations is performed by one firm rather than contracted out to separate local firms.[8]

In recent years it has become increasingly clear that globalisation of production extends far beyond FDI (see Hummels *et al.*, 2001). This has resulted in theoretical and empirical work on what is variously referred to as outsourcing, off-shoring, production fragmentation, production sharing and slicing up the value chain, among others.[9]

---

[7] The effects of globalisation may operate on the labour market indirectly by transforming the structures that support one set of equilibria and induce change in those equilibria. Gaston and Nelson (2004) refer to these as the indirect effects of globalisation.

[8] Notably, Dunning's (1981) "eclectic theory" involves three major determinants of FDI decisions: location, ownership and internalisation.

[9] The commonly made distinction between outsourcing and off-shoring is that the former involves a domestic firm importing intermediate goods from foreign unaffiliated firms, while the latter is when the firm imports intermediate goods from one of its overseas affiliates; see EEAG (2007), for example. Bhagwati *et al.* (2004) are highly critical of the way in which the expression "outsourcing" is used. They argue that outsourcing is not the off-shore purchases of manufactured components or FDI by firms; outsourcing is more properly defined as the off-shore trade in arm's length services.

The effect of production fragmentation is to transform the aggregate production structure. This transformation will generally have labour market effects.

In a large body of work, Helpman and various co-authors have explored the various ways in which international production is organised.[10] In the most directly relevant work on the labour market effects of FDI, Antràs *et al.* (2006) show how multinational activity can be viewed as the outcome of a matching process of agents with different skill types. Globalisation and economic integration permit greater opportunities for forming more productive "value-added teams" of workers by altering the feasible matches between agents of different skill types.

In a one-sector, two-country model it is assumed that the North has a distribution of skills with a relatively high mean, while the South has a distribution of skills with a lower mean. Highly skilled agents in the North have a comparative advantage in knowledge-intensive (or managerial) tasks and can work with either unskilled domestic production workers or more skilled production workers in the South. There is also heterogeneity within each class of managers and production workers. Relatively better managers are able to increase the productivity of all the workers in their team; while the more able are production workers, the larger the team that can be formed. Hence, complementarity between manager and worker abilities determines which agents work for which teams and the size of teams. Comparative advantage drives occupational choices of economic agents, and the distribution of skills determines the types of teams that can be formed as well as the distribution of wages.

The two key features of the model are the degree of "skill overlap" (i.e., similarity in the distribution of skills in the North and the South) and the cost of communicating knowledge within teams (which determines the extent to which managers can utilise their knowledge in larger teams). It is shown that globalisation leads to the formation

[10] Grossman and Helpman (2002, 2003, 2004, 2005), Helpman *et al.* (2004), Antràs and Helpman (2004) and Grossman *et al.* (2005, 2006).

of teams in which Northern managers supervise teams of Southern workers. Hence, the South becomes a net exporter of manufactured goods, while the North is a net exporter of "knowledge services".

As discussed in Section 10.2, another advantage of this modelling approach that matches empirical facts is that, on average, Southern workers employed in multinational firms receive higher wages than Southern workers employed in domestic firms. In a consistent fashion, globalisation leads to an increase in wage inequality for workers with equivalent skills in the South. These changes result from improved worker–manager matches and the higher productivity of these workers and the fact that more Southern agents become workers (i.e., rather than inefficient Southern managers). As for wage inequality in the North, on the one hand, the fact that the better agents become managers, and not workers, lowers wage inequality. This is a compositional effect, i.e., globalisation increases the proportion of managers in the North and decreases the proportion in the South. However, there is also a competition effect whereby globalisation increases the relative supply of low-skilled workers in the North and high-skilled workers in the South. In addition, an integrated world places a premium on the efforts and time of more highly skilled managers; in turn, this magnifies the difference in the value added of more-skilled and less-skilled workers. Hence, if highly skilled managers are scarce, then globalisation increases Northern wage inequality.[11]

10.1.2. *Labour models with location perspectives*

An empirically tractable methodology to study the impact of foreign-owned firms on labour market outcomes eschews the question of why multinational corporations exist. This approach provides a transparent bridge between theory and empirical work. For example, the study of wages and patterns can be extended by examining questions such

[11] Kremer and Maskin's (2003) matching model provides a similar punch line. Yeaple (2005) also highlights the importance of worker heterogeneity for understanding the differential impact that globalisation may have on different workers.

as: "What does foreign ownership do?" and " Do multinational firms respond to labour cost differentials?"

Feenstra and Hanson's (1997) model of product differentiation identifies some of the likely determinants of location decisions. Gaston and Nelson (2002) provide a model that focuses on the impact of labour market policies on firm location. Models of this type provide testable predictions about skilled and unskilled labour demand and also have ready application to the effects of economic integration, capital market imperfections and international labour standards. An impetus behind the development of models such as these is that they generate predictions of growing earnings inequality in both the North and the South.[12]

A common theme of these models is how firms locate themselves in response to the policy choices adopted by different national policy-makers. Thus, among the main issues highlighted is the way in which policies interact with the "footloose" nature of capital in a global economy and how this affects the demand for less-skilled labour in both the source and host countries.

The central ideas can be easily captured by considering a model of production fragmentation. An implication of a Heckscher–Ohlin model with multiple cones of diversification is that different regions with different skill endowments have different relative wages. In equilibrium, regions abundant in skilled labour offer relatively lower wages for skilled workers. For present purposes, it is sufficient to simply recall that, for a variety of reasons, factor price equalisation does not hold. In fact, an obvious explanation for the existence of multinational operations is the fact that factor prices are not equalised across countries. If the modern world is viewed as an integrated economy, the logic extends from regions within countries to different countries within an

[12]As Feenstra (2007, p. 5) argues: "I think that we can reconcile the wage changes with international trade, but not with the Heckscher–Ohlin model or other traditional theories of international trade. Instead, we need to adopt a new paradigm, which emphasizes how tasks or activities can be sent across borders, as with outsourcing. In this new paradigm, it is fairly easy to predict that more skilled workers will gain in all countries due to increased outsourcing."

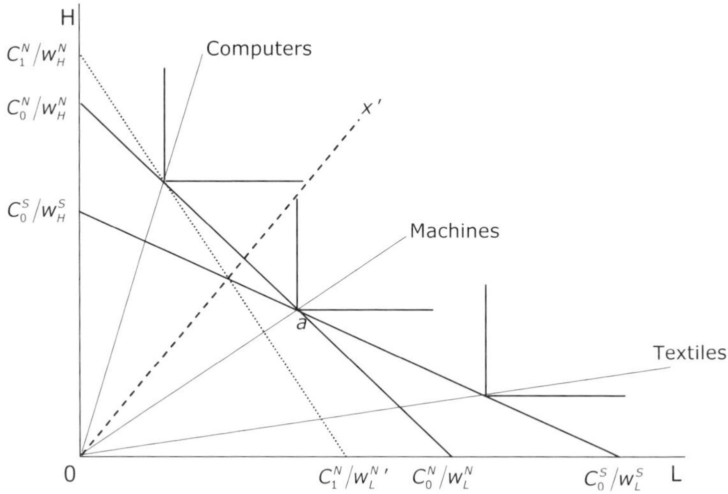

Fig. 10.1. Firm location and labour costs.

integrated global market. It follows immediately that countries exhibit systematic differences in production structure. It also follows that the type of industry varies with the relative wages and that firms adjust production across and within regions and countries in response to relative wage differences.

When regions are abundant with skilled labour, they are attractive to skilled labour-intensive industries. Consider Fig. 10.1, which is adapted from Bernard *et al.* (2005). There is a continuum of industries ranked by their skilled labour intensities, even though the unit-value Leontief isoquants for just three of these industries are shown. Three goods are produced: skilled labour-intensive computers, unskilled labour-intensive textiles and intermediate skill-intensity machinery. Compared to the South, the North is relatively skilled labour-abundant (H) and the relative wage of skilled workers is lower. Obviously, the North–South production structure also differs. The North produces goods C and M, while the South specialises in M and T. Note in particular that a firm (or industry) producing machines is indifferent to locating in the North or the South, i.e., the cost of production is the same in both countries at point a. Once the possibility of locationally indifferent industries or firms is admitted, the potential influence of different policy settings in one of the countries will affect the location of firms and industries.

10.1.2.1. *Higher labour standards and "runaway plants"*

First, consider a more stringent legally binding standard imposed in the North. The policy-maker's instrument is effectively a per capita tax on workers (which consequently disproportionately affects the cost of hiring unskilled workers) or it could be something that directly affects relative wages, such as minimum wages. An important assumption is that the cost of a higher "standard" or "tax" is not simply shifted backwards onto workers in the form of lower wages.[13] Accordingly, assume that the higher standard unambiguously increases operating costs for firms located in the North, i.e., $W_L^{N'} > W_L^N$ and $C_1^N > C_0^N$. Profits for industries, firms and plants in the North will fall. Moreover, firms producing machines in the North will find it worthwhile to move to the South (alternatively, they go out of business). Note that:

1. In Fig. 10.1, all producers using technologies with $H/L < x'$ will produce in the South. This extreme result is partly a consequence of the Leontief (no factor substitution) assumption. With the relatively easy factor substitution of H for L, fewer firms relocate. Overall, what causes delocation is a *substantial* policy shock. Note also that location decisions are related to both source and destination country labour market policies. Hence, an issue that needs to be addressed by empirical studies looking for race-to-the-bottom effects is that they have to identify a *natural experiment* involving a sufficiently large policy shock. In the absence of large shocks, shifting production off-shore is unlikely to occur and is difficult to empirically identify. At a point in time, the location of firms is not only determined by

[13]That is, higher labour standards may have little impact on the cost of production for firms, and therefore not lead to delocalisation (see Ehrenberg, 1994). However, there is a cost in the form of lower take-home pay for the workers benefitting from the more stringent regulations.

policy-maker preferences, but just as critically by differences in firm technologies;
2. The "movers" could be plants rather than entire firms, of course, and hence this example provides one explanation for off-shoring. The movers may use more unskilled labour than they did when they were located in the North, although they use less than their domestic counterparts. *Ipso facto*, movers will probably not relocate to the most unskilled labour-intensive industries or the industries with the very lowest labour standards. Delocation by Northern firms increases the relative demand for skilled labour in the South. The firms that relocate are those that are most vulnerable to increased stringency of the already higher Northern standards and are those that are relatively more reliant on unskilled labour. Overall, the relative demand for skilled labour increases in the North as well as the South. Consequently, the Northern firms that relocate to the South are likely to have higher average compensation and wages than incumbent Southern firms;
3. For all firms, except the marginally indifferent firm, movers' profits fall, but so too do the profits of Northern non-movers. In the long run, with production technologies that allow some factor substitution, non-movers will substitute away from using the relatively more expensive unskilled labour. On the other hand, community welfare may be increased by the higher standard.

10.1.2.2. *Race-to-the-bottom*

Competition for FDI, even among developed countries, can be intense and has provoked fears among some commentators that social standards will decline. The manifestation of such competition could be strategic reductions in "social" wages and labour standards in the North.

4. In Fig. 10.1, the marginal Southern firm (i.e., at point *a*) now migrates to the North, as the marginal cost of employing unskilled labour falls. Note that the "mover" will still be reliant on relatively

less-skilled labour than incumbent Northern firms. With factor substitution possible, the movers will use less unskilled labour than they did when located in the South, but they still use more unskilled labour than their domestic counterparts. The profits of all firms rise, the movers as well as the incumbent Northern firms. In both the North and the South, there will be a compositional change and structural shift towards greater demand for less-skilled workers. A consequence is that a "race-to-the-bottom" should contribute to *reduced* wage dispersion. Thus, the twin concerns about the "race-to-the-bottom" in social standards and expenditures and increasing wage inequality are mutually incompatible.

10.1.2.3. *Harmonisation of labour standards*

Now consider international labour standards that are imposed internationally.[14] The outcome of such standards is to increase the cost of unskilled labour in the South. In the extreme, this may induce relocation of firms to the North, with the analysis akin to that in the previous sub-section. Further notable points are:

5. For all bar the marginally indifferent firm, the profitability of all firms producing in the South falls. Policy harmonisation reflects the concerns expressed in LDCs that labour standards are a "backdoor" form of protection that deny the LDCs of what it is they do most efficiently.
6. As to the effect on inequality, the impact on the North is for it to fall, as the demand for unskilled labour increases there. In the South there are two conflicting effects. The movers have relatively high skilled-labour demand (relative to other Southern producers), thus their moving lowers demand for skilled labour. However, the firms remaining in the South now use relatively more skilled labour. The

[14] An example would be the widespread adoption of the core labour standards as embodied in the ILO's Declaration on Fundamental Principles and Rights at Work; see Martin and Maskus (2001).

impact on the dispersion of the income distribution in the South is therefore indeterminate.

There are also other factors to be considered. For example, Grossman and Rossi-Hansberg (2006) note that the off-shoring of production may improve the real wages of *all* workers because there are improvements in labour productivity due to a more effective division of labour.[15]

To summarise, the most obvious point is that if firms locate from the North to the South, there is likely to be an increase in the demand for skilled labour in both countries. Consequently, the income distribution becomes less equal in both countries. Overall, while there is a possibility that firms moving from the North start using relatively more unskilled labour, the combination of effects is more likely to bias the demand for labour away from unskilled labour. Integration, as the public fears, may therefore exacerbate income inequality between skilled and unskilled labour.

10.1.3. *Bargaining models*

Bargaining models provide some insight into why firms choose FDI over licensing activities or arm's length contracting. For instance, investing overseas, which may entail substantial investment in plant and equipment, provides a credible threat to use overseas workers in lieu of domestic ones; licensing in all likelihood will not. In the language of bargaining models, such investments may shift the threat point in bargaining games with unions in favour of the employers. In addition, strategic considerations involving unions in developed countries

[15]On the other hand, Blinder (2006) argues that, because of the international fragmentation of production, the traditional boundary between being a skilled or an unskilled worker is being increasingly eroded. Even highly skilled workers face competition from workers in LDCs where wages are much lower; see also Feenstra (2007). The idea is that a characteristic feature of globalisation is the unbundling of tasks. What tasks are profitable for firms to off-shore may have little to do with the skill content of those tasks. For example, the increased outsourcing of services can involve either skilled tasks (e.g., software programming) or non-skilled tasks (e.g., operators at call centres); see EEAG (2007).

are consistent with two-way FDI within the same industry, which is a prominent feature of modern FDI.

There are two basic issues that bargaining models, which examine how the existence of production facilities overseas affect the domestic wage and employment bargains struck between global firms and organised workers, must address. One is whether a global firm can credibly move production facilities to alternative locations if it does not receive bargaining concessions from the union (or unions). The second is whether any union can potentially "hold up" a vertically-integrated firm or whether workers will be pressured to reduce wages by dint of the increased competition from workers at foreign affiliates and the threat of producing some parts of the value-added chain overseas. In the latter case, it may seem obvious that unions can be played off against one another, but this depends crucially on whether the workers in separate unions (or "bargaining units") are complements or substitutes for one another.

The ability to move production overseas shifts the domestic collective bargaining outcome in favour of the firm. That is, when it bargains with a domestic union, the firm can threaten to close the domestic plant and switch production to the foreign country. During any dispute, the domestic firm supplies the market from abroad. The threat point of the firm is therefore its reservation profit when its production facilities are moved off-shore. Presumably, if foreign and domestic workers are equally productive and the foreign wage is less than the domestic wage (e.g., owing to the absence of unions in the foreign country), there are some additional fixed costs of moving overseas or taxes on overseas production, otherwise production would never occur at home. In addition to the *threat point effect*, Zhao (1998) also identifies a *collusion effect* whereby firms in different countries can collude to weaken the union's bargaining power. Since intra-industry FDI lowers the union wage, Zhao concludes that workers dislike both outward *and* inward FDI.

Ulph (1989) shows that multinational firms make capital investments in production facilities overseas in order to make credible the threat to use other workers. That is, this tilts the bargaining outcome in their favour. However, he also notes that these investments have two offsetting effects on workers. Although unions may get a smaller slice, a larger pie may more than compensate. Gaston (2002a,b) argues that the union movement's compliance with the decentralisation of collective bargaining in Australia is an optimal response by unions to the growing global nature of the firms that employ their members. He further shows that union leaders prefer a more wage-oriented bargaining posture when negotiating with multinational firms. Accordingly, this rationalises the empirically small effects of locating production overseas on domestic wages that are observed.

The punch line for most of the bargaining models is fairly straightforward. Multinational corporations and their overseas investments pose a threat to unionised workers because multinationals can use, or threaten to use, lower cost, non-unionised workers overseas. Compared to the bargaining power of domestic firms, the bargaining power of multinational firms is greater. The liberalisation of FDI amplifies and makes credible off-shoring threats and serves to moderate, and perhaps even lower, the wages of unionised workers in multinational corporations.

10.2. The Recent Evidence on the Labour Market Effects of FDI

In his survey of the literature, Hanson (2001) concludes that FDI is sensitive to both host-country tax policies and factors such as the education level of the labour force. Overall market size and the size of the local industrial base are also important and point to the relevance of agglomeration economies.

Possibly the most obvious point to make is that most FDI is directed to industrialised countries. Over the last few decades "the Triad" (the United States, Japan and the European Union) have never accounted for less than 60 percent of inward FDI flows. In 2005 it accounted for 70.3 percent of all inward flows (UNCTAD, 2006). Furthermore, the top 10 exporters of direct investment capital accounted for more than 90 percent of the world total in the period 1989–1993; while the top 10 recipients accounted for more than 75 percent of reported inflows. Six of the top 10 capital exporters were also among the top 10 recipients. In addition, the capital exporter group has been extremely stable over time. However, also notable is that LDCs have become increasingly important sources of FDI. Much of this FDI is directed to other LDCs.[16]

Together, these facts suggest that the substitution of low-wage labour in LDCs for domestic unskilled labour in developed countries is not the most important factor behind FDI growth.[17] Moreover, while foreign ownership has characteristically been heavily concentrated in manufacturing, since the early 1990s it has been directed increasingly towards tertiary industries, such as finance and real estate. The latter trend tends to reinforce the developed country–developed country nature of patterns of FDI.

As for the direct impact on developed country labour markets, Lawrence (1996) argues that the evidence for a large globalisation effect, via either increased trade or capital flows, is largely absent. In particular, from a trade-theoretic viewpoint it should be expected that, if using unskilled workers in LDCs is empirically important, the skilled wage premium should rise in developed countries and fall in the LDCs. Associated with this should be falls in the proportion of skilled workers employed in developed countries. This has simply not happened. Lawrence, like a number of other trade economists, has opted for the skill-biased technological change explanation for the increased wage inequality experienced in a number of countries — both developed and developing — since the early 1980s. However, recall that rising skilled wage premiums in the developed countries and LDCs are consistent with the predictions of the partial equilibrium models described in Section 10.1.

---

[16]UNCTAD (2006, p. 6) argue that this development reflects the stronger ownership advantages of LDC firms, which is in turn related to the economic success of their home economies. In addition, the share of manufacturing FDI as a proportion of total FDI has been declining quite sharply. The respective shares of FDI in services and primary commodities have grown rapidly (UNCTAD, 2006, p. 6). The massive record investment by both Japan and China in Australia's natural gas and coal industries is an obvious manifestation of the latter.

[17]The recent surge of FDI into China may warrant some moderation of this view in the future.

10.2.1. *Location decisions*

Gaston and Nelson (2002) conclude that the evidence indicates two strong empirical realities: (i) FDI is mainly horizontal and (ii) relative labour costs matter, but not directly.

As to the first point, evidence for the United States indicates that FDI is concentrated in industries in which US direct investment abroad is highest. That is, FDI is industry-specific. This argues against the vertical slicing up view of FDI and multinationals. That is, FDI is generally horizontal, designed with explicit competition-affecting or strategic considerations in mind.[18] In other words, reciprocal horizontal investments are occurring in countries with roughly similar factor costs.

Second, and related to the above, is the fact that FDI is largely directed towards high wage and high skill-intensity industries. Cooke (1997) paints a more complete picture by showing that the FDI decisions of US firms are negatively related to the presence of high levels of union penetration, centralised collective bargaining structures, unfavourable industrial relations environments and governmental restrictions on layoffs. Of course, these findings support the view that global firms are attracted by favourable expected unit labour cost differences.

Overall, caution is best exercised in jumping to the conclusion that the exploitation of labour cost differentials is a minor consideration for FDI. Cross-country studies of the determinants FDI find mixed evidence that labour costs matter. In particular, confirmatory or negative findings are sensitive to regression specification. For example, in a parsimonious regression specification Farrell *et al.* (2001) show that Japanese FDI responds significantly to labour cost differentials. However, when country fixed effects are allowed for, the effect becomes insignificant. One interpretation of such a finding is that FDI is attracted to relatively lower labour costs; but that such

---

[18]However, Yeaple (2003) finds stronger evidence of vertical FDI. Specifically, he finds evidence that US outward FDI flows towards skilled labour-scarce countries in the least skilled labour-intensive industries.

cost advantages are highly correlated with country effects, such as low rates of unionisation of a potential host country's labour force or "favourable" industrial relations laws.[19]

10.2.2. *Outsourcing,, off-shoring and fragmentation*

Feenstra (1998) provides a clear exposition of the relationship between product market integration and production process disintegration or off-shoring. He argues that analyses which focus on final goods imports severely understate the "true" impact of globalisation because the intermediate goods imports by multinational corporations are ignored. That is, it is inappropriate to "assess the proximate cause of the decline in employment and wages of unskilled workers by attributing all within-industry shifts in labor demand to technology, and allowing trade to operate only via between-industry shifts" (p. 41).

He argues that measuring the importance of trade by the traditional openness measure (i.e., total trade to GDP ratio) diminishes the importance of outsourcing. He shows that merchandise trade as a share of merchandise value-added is significantly higher and growing faster than the traditional openness measure. On the one hand, researchers who claim the irrelevance of trade for large wealthy countries are, by using traditional measures of trade openness, providing lower bound estimates of the "true" effect of greater openness. On the other hand, the disintegration of production is inextricably linked to trade openness. It is not only final goods, but also intermediate goods that flow across national borders with greater frequency. In fact, many countries rely heavily on imported intermediate inputs to produce finished goods. This is occurring even in the most advanced economies. Feenstra (1998, p. 37) reports statistics which indicate that US firms are increasingly importing goods at more advanced stages of processing,

[19]Egger and Egger (2003) show that relocation of production facilities to Eastern Europe has been low-wage seeking and motivated by falling trade barriers. Further, this overseas production has been associated with increases in the relative employment of skilled workers. Overall, the high rate of unionisation led to large changes in relative employment and not in relative wages.

i.e., these firms have been substituting away from goods produced by domestic suppliers.

Feenstra also argues that off-shoring and outsourcing have an *observationally equivalent* impact on employment and wages *vis-à-vis* skill-biased technological change. As discussed in Section 10.1.2, if advanced countries procure intermediate inputs from lower labour cost, unskilled labour-abundant countries, then this lowers relative demand for domestic unskilled labour. As a corollary, he questions the usual distinction that is made between "trade" versus "technology" explanations for lower relative demand for unskilled labour. In particular, off-shoring activity itself may relate intrinsically to improvements in information and communication technologies (ICT) and the speed with which product quality and design can be monitored. That is, technological improvements can spur such activity.

Using an estimation procedure to distinguish the effects of skill-biased technological change and outsourcing, Feenstra and Hanson (1999) find that outsourcing can explain up to 40 percent of the change in US relative wages for the 1980s. Similarly, Hijzen *et al.* (2005) find a strong negative impact of international outsourcing on labour demand for low-skilled labour in UK manufacturing industries between 1984 and 1995.

Geishecker and Görg (2008) investigate the link between international outsourcing and wages using data from the German Socio-Economic Panel Study for the period 1991–2000. Germany is an interesting case to analyse because of its economic integration with low-wage Eastern and Central European economies and the potential for outsourcing. In addition, even though increases in Germany's wage inequality have been negligible, its labour market is more highly regulated and unionised than those of Anglo-American countries. So it is interesting to see whether economic integration and outsourcing lead to union wage moderation in bargaining between firms and unions, as suggested in Section 10.1.3. In fact, the authors find evidence of large wage effects. Specifically, a one percentage point increase in outsourcing reduces the wage for workers in the lowest skill categories by up to 1.5 percent, while it increases wages for highly skilled workers by up to 2.6 percent.

In her study of the French manufacturing industry, Strauss-Kahn (2004) finds that outsourcing explains 10 to 15 percent of the decline in the share of unskilled workers in total employment between 1977 and 1985 and 25 percent of the decline between 1985 and 1993. Yan (2006) studies the impact of dramatic increases in expenditures on ICT and in purchases of foreign intermediate inputs on the demand for skilled workers in Canadian manufacturing industries over the period 1981–1996. He finds that both ICT and foreign outsourcing are important contributors to the demand for skilled workers.

10.2.3. *Direct effects*

Figlio and Blonigen (2000) show that FDI location decisions are affected by incentives awarded by local governments and that the government expenditure incurred in attracting foreign investment seems much higher than that for attracting domestic investment. However, they show that the addition of an average-sized new foreign (domestic) manufacturing firm is associated with a 2.3 percent (0.3 percent) increase in real wages for all workers. Budd *et al.* (2005) show that cross-border flows of capital, labour, goods and information affect profit-sharing between workers and firms. Foreign affiliate wages increase with higher parent profits per worker. Since multinationals tend to be more profitable, their result explains why their wages are, on average, higher than for domestic firms.[20]

It is reasonably clear that the wage premium paid by multinationals is primarily a result of their larger size. Moreover, Globerman *et al.* (1994) show that foreign affiliates are larger, more capital intensive and pay higher wages in Canada. Using data from the Australian Workplace Industrial Relations Survey, Wooden and Bora (1999) find that foreign ownership, the significance of export markets and location are

[20]In contrast, Fabbri *et al.* (2003) show that multinationals have more elastic labour demands than do domestic firms. While this finding is consistent with a view that globalisation matters little (for wages, at least), multinationals are more likely to shut down their plants than are domestically owned firms and the presence of multinational tends to lower the bargaining power of workers.

among the most important workplace-level influences on wages. Doms and Jensen (1998) find that higher wages and productivity are not just particular to foreign affiliates, but to any plant connected with a multinational, be it foreign- or US-owned. Further, Feenstra and Hanson (1996, 1997) show that the foreign affiliates of global firms are more likely to rely on imported intermediate inputs than are domestically owned firms. Overall, multinationals have different types of labour demand than do their domestic counterparts.

Why larger firms pay higher wages is one of the most long-standing, yet largely unresolved issues in labour economics. Specifically, how can larger firms stay competitive if their labour costs are higher? The size–wage premium is empirically and economically large. Not surprisingly, there has been a proliferation of theories and explanations (see Oi and Idson, 1999). Prominent among these, for present purposes, is that large firms have more productive employees and that the higher wages reflect rent-sharing with large organisations, which tend to be more profitable. In the former case, this reflects the fact that larger firms have more capital, tend to adopt new technologies faster and therefore demand more skilled workers. In the latter case, larger firms are likely to have greater market power and profits which, when faced with organised workers, plunge us into the economics of bilateral monopoly and bargaining models. A safe conclusion is that jobs at smaller domestic firms are different from jobs at large multinational firms.

It could be argued that the fact that the impact of multinational firms on the host country's wage structure is negligible, once size is controlled for, implies that there is no impact on wages attributable to multinational enterprises. However, this is faulty reasoning. The point is that the majority of multinationals are large firms with economies of scale, operating in imperfectly competitive product markets. Controlling for size therefore biases the wage impact of multinationals towards zero.

10.2.4. *Indirect labour market effects*

Of the three strands of economic globalisation — trade in goods and services, labour migration and flows of capital — it is the latter that is most likely to have associated with it both direct and indirect impacts on the labour market. Specifically, increased globalisation may initiate changes to the labour market institutions, such as collective bargaining practices, that have historically served to bolster the position of less-skilled workers in the economy. Lindbeck and Snower (1996) show that, in the age of the new global firm, which stresses multitasking activities by employees, centralised wage bargaining is inefficient. Efficiency dictates the switch to less-centralised forms of wage bargaining and a greater reliance on individual employment contracts.

Greater reliance on market-based contracts and movements away from centralised wage bargaining would by themselves increase the dispersion of labour market earnings. Some recent evidence consistent with this line of argument is presented by Haskel *et al.* (1997) who show that increasing labour market flexibility in the United Kingdom has resulted in labour input being more closely aligned to the business cycle. Blomström *et al.* (2000) conclude their study of the impact of inward FDI for Japan by noting the existence of various pressures for fundamental structural changes. Among these is the pressure for the Japanese labour market to become increasingly flexible.

In similar fashion, Slaughter (2001) shows the elasticity of labour demand for US production workers has increased as off-shoring has increased. The finding applies to other developed economies as well; based on data for 11 OECD countries and 20 industries, OECD (2007) report significantly larger elasticities of labour demand from 1980 to 2002. The latter finding applies to manufacturing rather than service sector industries and seems to be driven by increased off-shoring (once again, measured as the share of imported intermediate inputs in value added). Of course, higher wage elasticities weaken the bargaining position of workers and lower subsequent wage demands.

EEAG (2007) findings for the advanced European Union economies suggest that the adverse employment effects of globalisation (which include measures of imports from low-wage economies and outward FDI stock in low-wage economies) are eliminated once the differences in labour market institutions (such as the degree of unionisation and employment protection legislation) are controlled for. These findings suggest the importance of institutional and policy changes and their role in neutralising the direct effects of globalisation on the labour market.

10.2.5. *Evidence from developing countries*

As mentioned, one motivation behind the development of the models discussed in Section 10.1 is the simultaneous occurrence of higher demand for skilled labour and increasing wage inequality in both developed and developing countries.[21] As mentioned, workers employed by foreign affiliates of multinationals enjoy higher wages than those employed by domestic firms. For example, Aitken *et al.* (1996) find that foreign affiliates pay higher wages than do comparable domestic firms in Mexico and Venezuela. Harrison and Scorse (2005) utilise Indonesian manufacturing data and find that foreign affiliates paid up to 10 percent more to their unskilled workers and up to 35 percent more to their skilled workers compared to domestic firms.[22]

Lipsey and Sjöholm (2003) show that takeovers by foreign firms increase the wages of both white-collar and blue-collar workers in Indonesia. Plants taken over by domestic firms had smaller wage rises, although similarly high average wages. Thus, it is not the case that foreign firms take over high-wage plants; rather plants become high wage plants as a result of foreign takeovers. But, once again, foreign takeovers tended to be of the larger plants and domestic takeovers were of the smaller plants.

Evidence on whether the presence of foreign firms raises wages at domestic firms is mixed.[23] Aitken *et al.* (1996) find that FDI is associated with higher wages for foreign firms only, i.e., there is little evidence

[21] Evidence supporting this prediction is found by Anderton *et al.* (2002). Recent evidence on the relative wages for production and non-production workers painting the same picture is presented for the United States and Mexico by Feenstra (2007).

[22] On the other hand, Ramstetter (1999) finds no systematic link between the higher productivity of foreign affiliates and employees' wages for Hong Kong, Indonesia, Malaysia, Singapore and Taiwan.

[23] Fosfuri *et al.* (2001) argue that these spillovers could occur through the provision of training by foreign firms and subsequent worker mobility. Hanson's (2001) assessment of the productivity-enhancing benefits of foreign firms spilling over to domestic firm performance is rather grim. Based on case study evidence, Pack and Saggi (2006) are far more positive.

of wage spillovers for domestic firms. They conclude that FDI is not a vehicle for "catch-up" for LDCs. The higher wages are paid only in the foreign-owned firms and this effect, in turn, largely results from their larger size and capital intensity. Using data for Ghanaian manufacturing firms, Görg *et al.* (2002) find that workers who receive training in foreign firms experience more rapid wage growth than workers trained in domestic firms.

One explanation for the wage effect is that when domestic firms are taken over by foreign firms, average compensation rises and total employment falls, which suggests that low-paid and low-productivity employees are sloughed off, consistent with the findings of Lipsey and Sjöholm (2003). Driffield and Taylor (2000) show that any beneficial impact of inward FDI in terms of higher real wages may be offset by increases in wage inequality. This occurs because multinationals rely more heavily on skilled labour and induce copycat behaviour by domestic firms. Thus, two factors serve to increase income inequality: increased demand for skilled workers in an industry or region, and technology spillovers from foreign to domestic firms.[24] The latter feature aggravates wage inequality, because domestic firms start skill-upgrading.[25]

Thus, while the higher wage paid by multinationals is largely attributable to productivity differences, they also have quite different factor demands than do domestic firms in the same industry. Of course, this feature is also affected by economic geography considerations

---

[24]As usual, there are some contradictory findings. Blonigen and Slaughter (2001) show that Japanese "greenfield" investment lowered relative demand for skilled labour. The latter type of investment is less likely to replicate the same type of relative factor usage. Javorcik (2004) found evidence of positive productivity spillovers from foreign affiliates and their local upstream suppliers in Lithuania. She also found evidence of knowledge spillovers. Blalock (2001) has qualitatively similar findings for Indonesian manufacturing. On the other hand, Hanson (2001) summarises the evidence as failing to reveal anything systematic about technological and other externalities from FDI. In fact, some studies even find negative spillovers.

[25]Hanson (2001) argues that the recent evidence points to the presence of multinationals depressing the productivity of domestic plants (perhaps by driving them into less profitable market segments). If Hanson is correct, this would provide another reason why the presence of multinationals results in income inequality widening in LDCs.

and is a feature evident in the models of location described above. Finally, consistent with Figlio and Blonigen's (1999) results, Amiti and Cameron (2007) use data for Indonesian medium- and large-sized firms to show the importance of location — specifically, access to intermediate good suppliers and to large consumer markets — for manufacturing wages. Their results indicate that the Indonesian government's attempts to spread the benefits of industrialisation to islands outside of Java have been futile.

10.3. Some Final Observations

In terms of recent theoretical developments, the FDI literature has distanced itself from the standard trade model and models that emphasise differences between countries and the homogenising influence of capital arbitrage. In addition to the bargaining models, matching models as well as the "new" trade and firm-theoretic models are at the frontier. In part, their popularity for explaining modern multinational activities stems from their ability to generate implications consistent with the observed growth of earnings inequality in both developed and developing economies. A feature of these models is that the reduction in communication costs present opportunities for a better matching of skills and a more efficient global division of labour. The models of location suggest that earnings inequality rises in both the North and the South. These models emphasise the effect of compositional changes due to the firms that now produce in different locations and the effect that such changes have on the relative demand for skilled labour. An implication of some of the newest of the new trade models is even stronger; in a world with more mobile capital and globalised production, with the possible exception of "superstar" workers and managers, most workers are now more vulnerable, i.e., both skilled and unskilled workers.

In assessing the recent research on FDI, the most sensible conclusion that can be drawn is that the evidence, as well as the interpretation of the evidence, is mixed. At one extreme is the still influential stance taken by economists such as Bhagwati who argue that the international outsourcing of intermediate inputs is fundamentally "just" a trade phenomenon. In the long run, we will all most assuredly be better off. In terms of labour market effects, the ubiquitous skill-biased technological progress explanation for the increase in the relative demand for skilled labour still reigns supreme. At the other extreme are the globalisation sceptics who emphasise the short-run costs of international production fragmentation and the lower demand for unskilled workers at home, i.e., the workers who find themselves in greater competition with workers at lower labour-cost locations overseas.

The evidence supporting the relocation or off-shoring of production facilities to low-wage locations in LDCs as the drivers of changes in the distribution of earnings in the developed nations is highly suggestive. On the other hand, if we accept Feenstra's argument that it is inappropriate to attribute all *within*-industry shifts in labour demand to technological change, then the "direct" impact of FDI on domestic wage and employment outcomes for industrialised countries seems to range from moderate to significant. It also seems clear that multinational activity is associated with a greater use of more skilled workers in larger, more capital-intensive plants.

The evidence for the presence of foreign firms contributing to the growing earnings inequality in many LDCs is more clear-cut. In addition, the most recent evidence provided for developed countries other than the United States is quite stark and paints a rather bleak picture. In general, multinational firms are large, more capital-intensive, adopt new technologies faster and also demand more skilled workers. The multinational firms have different factor demands than do domestic firms in the same industry. The higher wages paid by multinationals are attributable to greater skill and productivity differences. However, they are also more "footloose" and mobile than local firms and have more elastic labour demands. If we add to these latter features the evidence that workers are relatively immobile, and the lack of evidence of wage spillovers to the employees of local native firms, it is unsurprising that the impact of FDI on unemployment, wages and earnings inequality may, in some cases, be considerable.

In terms of the indirect labour market effects, the behaviour of multinational corporations is influenced by the presence of government tax policies and inducements, the degree of unionisation and the industrial relations environment both at home and abroad. Moreover, the presence of multinational firms affects local producers. At a minimum, the degree of product market and labour market competition is altered. For some countries, labour market institutions have evolved in response to the rise of the modern multinational enterprise. For example, at the microeconomic level there have been different schemes for compensating workers as well as changes in collective bargaining practices. Specifically, there has been a move towards more enterprise-level bargaining. It would be surprising if such effects did not have labour market consequences. However, we should *not* expect to find dramatic negative effects on all workers, particularly those workers with substantial bargaining power. Skilled workers and well-organised union workers are likely to be better off in the new global environment. Multinational firms in developed countries are likely to be concentrated in oligopolistic, high-rent industries, viz. the industries in which organised workers can share in greater rents and have the most to gain. However, it is also clear that the least-skilled or non-unionised workers may be at greater risk in the new global environment. In turn, this may stimulate further institutional and structural changes as well as encourage policy-makers to respond by regulating and reforming rules for investment in their countries.

References

Aitken, B, A Harrison and RE Lipsey (1996). Wages and foreign ownership: A comparative study of Mexico, Venezuela, and the United States. *Journal of International Economics*, 40(3/4), 345–371.

Amiti, M and L Cameron (2007). Economic geography and wages. *Review of Economics and Statistics*, 89(1), 15–29.

Anderton, B and P Brenton (1999). Outsourcing and low-skilled workers in the UK. *Bulletin of Economic Research*, 51(4), 267–285.

Anderton, B, P Brenton and E Oscarsson (2002). What's trade got to do with it? Relative demand for skills within Swedish manufacturing. *Review of World Economics*, 138(4), 629–651.

Antràs, P, L Garicano and E Rossi-Hansberg (2006). Offshoring in a knowledge economy. *Quarterly Journal of Economics*, 121(1), 31–77.

Antràs, P and E Helpman (2004). Global sourcing. *Journal of Political Economy*, 112(3), 522–580.

Bernard, AB, S Redding and PK Schott (2005). Factor price equality and the economies of the United States. Centre for Economic Policy Research Discussion Paper No. 5111.

Bhagwati, J (1999). Globalization: Who gains, who loses? In *Globalization and Labor*, H Siebert (ed.), pp. 225–236. Tübingen, Germany: Mohr Siebeck.

Bhagwati, J, A Panagariya and TN Srinivasan (2004). The muddles over outsourcing. *Journal of Economic Perspectives*, 18(4), 93–114.

Blalock, G (2001). Technology from Foreign Direct Investment: Strategic Transfer through Supply Chains. Berkeley, CA: University of California.

Blinder, AS (2006). Offshoring: The next Industrial Revolution? *Foreign Affairs*, 85(2), 113–128.

Blomström, M, D Konan and RE Lipsey (2000). FDI in the restructuring of the Japanese economy. NBER Working Paper No. 7693. Cambridge, MA: National Bureau of Economic Research.

Blonigen, B and M Slaughter (2001). Foreign affiliate activity and US skill upgrading. *Review of Economics and Statistics*, 83(2), 362–376.

Budd, JW, J Konings and MJ Slaughter (2005). Wages and international rent sharing in multinational firms. *Review of Economics and Statistics*, 87(1), 73–84.

Cooke, WN (1997). The influence of industrial relations factors on US foreign direct investment abroad. *Industrial and Labor Relations Review*, 51(1), 3–17.

Doms, ME and JB Jensen (1998). Comparing wages, skills, and productivity between domestic and foreign owned firms in the United States. In *Geography vs. Ownership in Economic Accounting*, R Baldwin, R Lipsey and JD Richardson (eds.), pp. 235–258. Chicago: University of Chicago Press.

Driffield, N and K Taylor (2000). FDI and the labour market: A review of the evidence and policy implications. *Oxford Review of Economic Policy*, 16(3), 90–103.

Dunning, J (1981). *International Production and the Multinational Enterprise*. London: Allen and Unwin.

Egger, H and P Egger (2003). Outsourcing and skills-specific employment in a small economy: Austria after the fall of the Iron Curtain. *Oxford Economic Papers*, 55(4), 625–642.

Ehrenberg, RG (1994). *Labor Markets and Integrating National Economies*. Washington DC: The Brookings Institution.

European Economic Advisory Group (EEAG) (2007). *The EEAG Report of the European Economy*. Munich: CESifo.

Fabbri, F, JE Haskel and MJ Slaughter (2003). Does nationality of ownership matter for labor demands? *Journal of the European Economic Association*, 1(2/3), 698–707.

Farrell, R, N Gaston and J-E Sturm (2001). Determinants of Japan's foreign direct investment: A panel study, 1984–1995. *Centre for Japanese Economic Studies*.

Farrell, R, N Gaston and J-E Sturm (2004). Determinants of Japanese foreign direct investment: An industry and country panel study, 1984–1998. *Journal of the Japanese and International Economies*, 18(2), 161–182.

Feenstra, R (1998). Integration of trade and disintegration of production in the global economy. *Journal of Economic Perspectives*, 12(4), 21–50.

Feenstra, R (2007). *Globalization and Its Impact on Labor, Global Economy Lecture.* Vienna Institute for International Economic Studies.

Feenstra, R and G Hanson (1996). Globalization, outsourcing, and wage inequality. *American Economic Review*, 86(2), 240–245.

Feenstra, R and G Hanson (1997). Foreign direct investment and relative wages: Evidence from Mexico's maquiladoras. *Journal of International Economics*, 42(3/4), 371–393.

Feenstra, R and G Hanson (1999). The impact of outsourcing and high technology capital on wages: Estimates for the US, 1979–1990. *Quarterly Journal of Economics*, 114, 907–940.

Figlio, DN and BA Blonigen (2000). The effects of foreign direct investment on local communities. *Journal of Urban Economics*, 48(2), 338–363.

Fosfuri, A, M Mottac and T Røndee (2001). Foreign direct investment and spillovers through workers' mobility. *Journal of International Economics*, 53(1), 205–222.

Gaston, N (2002a). Foreign direct investment and enterprise bargaining: Cheshire cat unions revisited? In *Foreign Direct Investment: Research Issues*, B Bora (ed.), pp. 132–151. London: Routledge.

Gaston, N (2002b). The effects of globalisation on unions and the nature of collective bargaining. *Journal of Economic Integration*, 17(2), 377–396.

Gaston, N and D Nelson (2002). Integration, foreign direct investment and labour markets: Microeconomic perspectives. *The Manchester School*, 70(3), 420–459.

Gaston, N and D Nelson (2004). Structural change and the labour market effects of globalization. *Review of International Economics*, 12(5), 769–792.

Geishecker, I and H Görg (2008). Winners and losers: A micro-level analysis of international outsourcing and wages. *Canadian Journal of Economics*, 41(1), 243–270.

Globerman, S, J Ries and I Vertinsky (1994). The economic performance of foreign affiliates in Canada. *Canadian Journal of Economics*, 27(1), 143–156.

Görg, H, E Strobl and F Walsh (2002). Why do foreign firms pay more? The role of on-the-job training. Discussion Paper No. 590, IZA, Bonn.

Grossman, G and E Helpman (2002). Integration versus outsourcing in industry equilibrium. *Quarterly Journal of Economics*, 117(1), 85–120.

Grossman, G and E Helpman (2003). Outsourcing versus FDI in industry equilibrium. *Journal of the European Economics Association*, 1(2/3), 317–327.

Grossman, G and E Helpman (2004). Managerial incentives and the international organization of production. *Journal of International Economics*, 63(2), 237–262.

Grossman, G and E Helpman (2005). Outsourcing in a global economy. *Review of Economic Studies*, 72(1), 135–159.

Grossman, G, E Helpman and A Szeidl (2005). Complementarities between outsourcing and foreign sourcing. *American Economic Review*, 95(2), 19–24.

Grossman, G, E Helpman and A Szeidl (2006). Optimal integration strategies for the multinational firm. *Journal of International Economics*, 70(1), 216–238.

Grossman, G and E Rossi-Hansberg (2006). Trading tasks: A simple theory of offshoring. NBER Working Paper No. 12721. Cambridge, MA: National Bureau of Economic Research.

Hanson, G (2001). Scale economies and the geographic concentration of industry. *Journal of Economic Geography*, 1(3), 255–276.

Hanson, G, RJ Mataloni, Jr. and MJ Slaughter (2001). Expansion strategies of U.S. multinational firms. In *Brookings Trade Forum*, D Rodrik and S Collins (eds.), pp. 245–294. Washington DC: Brookings Institution.

Harrison, A and J Scorse (2005). Do foreign-owned firms pay more? Evidence from the Indonesian manufacturing sector 1990–99. Working Paper No. 98, International Labour Office, Geneva.

Haskel, J, B Kersley and C Martin (1997). Labour market flexibility and employment adjustment: Micro evidence from UK establishments. *Oxford Economic Papers*, 49(3), 362–379.

Helpman, E, MJ Melitz and SR Yeaple (2004). Export versus FDI with heterogeneous firms. *American Economic Review*, 94(1), 300–316.

Hijzen, A, H Görg and RC Hine (2005). International outsourcing and the skill structure of labour demand in the United Kingdom. *Economic Journal*, 115, 860–878.

Hummels, D, J Ishii and K-M Yi (2001). The nature and growth of vertical specialization in world trade. *Journal of International Economics*, 54(1), 75–96.

Hymer, S (1960). *The International Operations of National Firms: A Study of Direct Foreign Investment.* Cambridge, MA: MIT Press.

Javorcik, BS (2004). Does foreign direct investment increase the productivity of domestic firms? In search of spillovers through backward linkages. *American Economic Review*, 94(3), 605–627.

Kremer, M and E Maskin (2003). Globalization and inequality. Working Paper, Harvard University.

Lawrence, RZ (1996). *Single World, Divided Nations? International Trade and OECD Labor Markets.* Washington DC: Brookings Institution and OECD.

Lindbeck, A and DJ Snower (1996). Reorganization of firms and labor-market inequality. *American Economic Review*, 86(2), 315–321.

Lipsey, R and F Sjöholm (2001). Foreign direct investment and wages in Indonesian manufacturing. NBER Working Paper No. 8299. Cambridge, MA: National Bureau of Economic Research.

Lipsey, RE and F Sjöholm (2003). Foreign firms and Indonesian manufacturing wages: An analysis with panel data. NBER Working Paper No. 9417. Cambridge, MA: National Bureau of Economic Research.

Martin, W and KE Maskus (2001). Core labor standards and competitiveness: Implications for global trade policy. *Review of International Economics*, 9(2), 317–328.

Oi, WY and TL Idson (1999). Firm size and wages. In *Handbook of Labor Economics*, Vol. 3B, O Ashenfelter and D Card (eds.), pp. 2165–2214. Amsterdam: Elsevier Science.

Organisation for Economic Co-operation and Development (2007). *Employment Outlook.* Paris: OECD.

Pack, H and K Saggi (2006). Is there a case for industrial policy? A critical survey. *World Bank Research Observer*, 21(2), 267–297.

Ramstetter, E (1999). Comparisons of foreign multinationals and local firms in Asian manufacturing over time. *Asian Economic Journal*, 12(2), 163–203.

Slaughter, M (2001). International trade and labor-demand elasticities. *Journal of International Economics*, 54(1), 27–56.

Strauss-Kahn, V (2004). The role of globalization in the within-industry shift away from unskilled workers in France. In *Challenges to Globalization: Analyzing the Economics*, RE Baldwin and LA Winters (eds.), pp. 209–231. Chicago: University of Chicago Press.

Ulph, A (1989). The incentives to make commitments in wage bargains. *Review of Economic Studies*, 56(3), 449–466.

United Nations Conference on Trade and Development (UNCTAD) (2004, 2006, 2007). *World Investment Report*. New York and Geneva: United Nations.

Wooden, M and B Bora (1999). Workplace characteristics and their effects on wages: Australian evidence. *Australian Economic Papers*, 38(3), 276–289.

Yan, B (2006). Demand for skills in Canada: The role of foreign outsourcing and information communication technology. *Canadian Journal of Economics*, 39(1), 53–67.

Yeaple, SR (2003). The role of skill endowments in the structure of US outward foreign direct investment. *Review of Economics and Statistics*, 85(3), 726–734.

Yeaple, SR (2005), A simple model of firm heterogeneity, international trade, and wages. *Journal of International Economics*, 65(1), 1–20.

Zhao, L (1998). The impact of foreign direct investment on wages and employment. *Oxford Economic Papers*, 50(2), 284–301.

Chapter 11

Competition Policy in International Airline Markets: An Agenda and a Proposed Solution

*David K. Round**
and Christopher C. Findlay

11.1. Introduction

Few major airlines operate in a purely domestic environment. More so than most areas of business, airlines work on an international scale, with most flying at least to adjoining countries. However, while many international airlines pursue global strategies, their regulation is still largely national. Local regulators control firms in their jurisdiction in a vacuum, not usually taking into account the firms' operations and their economic spillovers (good or bad) elsewhere. In reality, it is

*Earlier versions of this paper were presented to the 17th International ECMT/OCED Symposium on Transport Economics and Policy "Benefiting from Globalisation: Transport Sector Contribution and Policy Challenges", Berlin, October 2006 and to the conference on Comparative Experience in Competition Policy Reform: Australia, Japan and East Asia, Australian National University, Canberra 22–23 September 2008. Thanks to Greg Cutbush and Henry Ergas for comments on the latter. Findlay's contribution to the revisions was supported in part by a grant from the Australian Research Council.

not possible for one economy to successfully regulate a multinational airline, as decisions will likely be made in favour of local welfare, which may not correspond with either the firm's private optimum or with the international socially optimal outcome. Just as sector-specific competition policies within a given country can lead to regulatory inconsistencies and potential for capture, uncompromising country-specific competition policies may stand in the way of achieving regional or global consensus and the benefits that can follow from harmonised approaches to making markets work competitively. This is especially true when dealing with sectors exhibiting strong network effects.

Mergers and alliances between airlines benefit all participants. Airlines can become more efficient and offer better price–product–service packages to passengers and those organisations seeking timely delivery of freight. However, airline mergers and alliances cannot be evaluated fully within a purely national framework. They must be evaluated in a global rather than in a local context.

We believe that an integrated international policy position on promoting competition in air transport markets is valuable. Piecemeal, uncoordinated developments in competition policy and enforcement in international airline markets will not lead to a global optimum and will result in conflicting outcomes as well as in static and dynamic inefficiencies.

In this chapter we present a brief consideration of the regulatory environment and of recent dynamic developments in the sector, especially with respect to mergers and alliances. History tells us that regional or international policy initiatives are never easy or conclusive. The Qantas and Air New Zealand's trans-Tasman experience between 2003 and 2005 is highlighted as a case study.

Discussion then follows on regulatory errors. While a global authority is less likely to make decisions that are globally welfare reducing, which can happen with separate national authorities, there are considerable challenges in the establishment and successful operation of such an agency and in the implementation of its decisions. Consideration of such an authority and the role it might play facilitates a discussion of the transitional paths that might be called for. We conclude with suggestions as to how, when and by whom an agenda for a truly international airline competition policy framework can be developed.

11.2. Mergers and Alliances in Airline Markets

The "three pillars of stagnation" is a phrase coined by Giovanni Bisignani, Director General of the International Air Transport Association, to describe the bilateral system of exchanging air transport traffic rights, national ownership rules, and the approaches taken by competition authorities. In his view these three factors limit change and profit prospects in international air transport markets.[1]

The regulation of international air transport services involves a complex web of over 3500 bilateral agreements that establish rules to identify the airlines that can be designated to fly on each route, determine the capacity that they can deploy, and limit the capacity that can be offered by airlines from third countries. Rights of designation usually depend on local ownership and control, which constrain the scope for mergers across international borders. The system imposes country-specific quotas in each country-to-country market pair, and competition on each route is limited to those suppliers designated by the relevant bilateral agreement.[2] As a result of these restrictive entry conditions, some carriers earn substantial profits on some routes, but this is far from a universal condition, and so it is claimed that regulation is not working and that reforms are urgently needed.

The regulatory system itself has also increased the airlines' costs. They have been forced to construct networks through a maze of bilateral agreements. These can in part be overcome through alliances and code sharing but this is likely to be a second-best solution.[3] Some routes are undoubtedly being served inefficiently because of limitations on market access associated with bilateral agreements.

In the last decade airline markets have witnessed a flurry of corporate restructuring and horizontal and vertical integration and diversification through internal or external growth and through consensual

---

[1] https://iata.org/pressroom/speeches/2003-03-22-01 (accessed 15 September 2008). Findlay and Round (2006) consider the challenges for air transport reforms that are posed by these three pillars.

[2] Descriptions of the system are provided by the Productivity Commission (1998) and WTO (2000 and 2001a).

[3] Cooperative arrangements between carriers are reviewed in WTO (2001b). Oum, Park and Zhang (2000) provide an analysis of alliances.

amalgamations and alliances. Some mergers have been approved by competition authorities, both within countries as well as in a regional setting, such as the Air France/KLM and Lufthansa/Swissair amalgamations. Alitalia merged with Air One at the end of 2008 and sold 25% of the company to Air France/KLM in early 2009. The Lufthansa/Swissair group was in mid-2009 seeking competition authority approval to take over Austrian Airlines. In the US, Northwest and Delta merged in October 2008. Other proposals have been blocked: Ryanair's bid for Aer Lingus was blocked in 2007 by EU competition authorities. Singapore tried but failed to take over China Eastern in January 2008 There are recent reports of a merger between China Eastern and Shanghai Airlines. Zhang and Round (2008) examine a burst of mergers in the Chinese market in 2002 following domestic deregulation.

Some alliances have not been approved consistently between jurisdictions, as in the attempt by Qantas and Air New Zealand to form a formal and comprehensive trans-Tasman alliance in 2003.[4] Other alliances, such as that between Qantas and British Airways on the so-called "kangaroo route" from Australia to England, have been approved (twice, the most recent approval occurring in 2004) on public benefit grounds. In this case their combined market share was a much lower 40 percent (compared with the approximately 80 percent combined market share of Qantas and Air New Zealand across the Tasman), and the two airlines faced real competitive constraints from Singapore Airlines and Emirates, among others, on the route.

There appears to be little doubt that such corporate activity has been privately beneficial. Executives have argued that the Air France–KLM merger had been a success because the separate brands had been retained (but customers could combine fares from both), and the two airlines had largely operated complementary networks.[5] It has also been

[4]More recently Virgin Blue has been presented as a merger partner for Air New Zealand, and in July 2009 entered into an alliance with Delta.

[5]Interview in *The Australian*, 29 April 2006, with Patrick Alexandre, executive vice-president of the international commercial division of Air France. The Air France–KLM amalgamation aimed for cost savings from many sources, including combining local

argued that the success showed that mergers were not just a matter of cutting routes, but could lead to real synergies. Thus, the model of the future could be one bottom line with two brands and two networks, but with inter-operable networks.

In the presence of restrictions on foreign ownership and the bilateral regulatory system that governs international airline operations, which together give limited access to country-pair traffic rights, cross-border amalgamations such as those that have occurred in Europe are unlikely to feature strongly in the medium term. Brand franchising may occur, and alliances are another way to gain some of the advantages of a merger. Code sharing can work too, in so far as brand presence is achieved on a route or, as in the operating alliance that had been proposed by Qantas and Air New Zealand, where the two airlines would each have been able to maintain a full network presence while eliminating some of the excess capacity (thereby gaining more efficient use of aircraft) that is a feature of the trans-Tasman market.[6]

Freedom to merge or form alliances gives airlines greater ability to respond to market forces, yet with these greater freedoms there are likely to be calls for attention to competition issues including, *inter alia*, entry conditions, mergers and the use of market power.

Bisignani, however, has argued that competition authorities are too cautious, referring to "dogmatic competition policies [that] also restrict our freedom". He observes that despite the existence of strong competitive forces in these markets, including LCCs and fifth freedom operators, decisions on mergers or alliances by single-country

---

and regional management teams, joint ticket counters, joint airport handling contracts, shared airport lounges, and renegotiated catering contracts.

[6]Their LCC subsidiaries appeared not to have been included in the code-sharing proposals, but would abide by some form of agreement that would eliminate fierce competition. If the proposal had been authorised by the Australian Competition and Consumer Commission, the airlines would have coordinated pricing and marketing initiatives as well, in the process eliminating the losses that had emerged in this sector due to excess capacity and heavy discounting by new entrants. It was estimated in April 2006 that there were 3120 vacant seats every day on trans-Tasman flights. See Qantas, Air NZ try to mop up spare Tasman seats, *Sydney Morning Herald*, Rod Myer, 21 April 2006.

regulators take much time and competition authorities everywhere are over-cautious with air transport. He asks:

> What other global business is more fragmented than air transport? Where are the multi-national players, the Daimler–Chrysler's or the Pharmacia–Upjohn's of air transport? Some industries requiring large investments are fiercely competitive even with just a few very large players. In spite of that, most airline alliance projects, or the few merger attempts face long delays ... We need the economies of scales [sic] that mergers or acquisitions can provide with the proper competition supervision ... the regulators must take up the challenge of change![7]

Some caution may however be warranted, not just because of the effects of mergers on concentration in air transport markets, but because the effects of all these types of conduct transcend national boundaries.

If regulation occurs through an uncoordinated network of national authorities, and mergers are denied, airlines will develop strategies to capture the gains from networking, including alliances with airlines based in other countries. That is, as noted earlier, they will respond to policy decisions and seek to re-engineer their operations and institutional environment in their own self-interest. From an overall social perspective, these responses and the initiating policies may well be second-best outcomes. Here, the gains from consolidation are not lost but are attenuated through a less socially optimal regulatory regime.

The alternative, providing for a regional or global airline merger authority, will produce the opposite set of outcomes, generating social efficiency gains but in all likelihood creating national concerns about competition effects and damage to national champions. It is unlikely that the long-run first-best option for an international regime for transport competition policy will be immediately achievable. History will work against that. But having adopted such a policy goal, we can consider various strategic paths for its implementation. The first steps

[7] https://iata.org/pressroom/speeches/2003-03-22-01 (accessed 15 September 2008).

may have to be small. It is important to get the culture for competition right before moving on. One step at a time is better than two steps forward and one step back. Evenett (2005, p. 17) stresses the value of such an approach in his discussion of recognising the implications of cross-border spillovers:

> Competition enforcement agencies may see advantages in coordinating and sequencing investigations, and even in specializing in certain types of investigations, much in the same way that certain national competition law enforcement agencies in the same jurisdiction cooperate with one another. Arguably the current discussions on international cooperation on competition law and enforcement are a long way from this type of outcome, but the goal [should be] not to show what is practicable immediately but where the logic of internalizing cross-border spillovers leads to in terms of international collective action.

We return to the sequencing of reform in later sections, but first illustrate the issues in uncoordinated action in a case study of decision making across the Tasman.

11.3. Intersection of Regional and Domestic Policies: A Trans-Tasman Case Study

Currently, with the exception of the EU, cross-border mergers between firms domiciled in different countries are independently assessed in their respective countries. Mergers are evaluated under each country's statutory provisions, which demand assessment in terms of national priorities and objectives. Even in geographically, commercially and culturally close countries such as Australia and New Zealand that over the past decade have signed several MOUs on the harmonisation of trans-Tasman business laws,[8] the statutory objectives of enhancing national

[8] See Round *et al.* (2005) for details on these MOUs. For example, a company with a substantial degree of power in a trans-Tasman market (one with a geographic dimension of either within Australia or New Zealand or both) must not take advantage of that power for one of three proscribed anti-competitive purposes in any market in

welfare are squarely national, not trans-Tasman. The competition authorities from the two countries meet frequently, undertake staff exchanges, use similar guidelines, and cooperate in investigations and coordinated enforcement where appropriate. Yet there are significant differences in analytical approaches, in attitudes to public consultation, in attempts to quantify anti-competitive detriments and public benefits, and in the welfare standards used to assess "public" benefits. In addition, differing appeal procedures and decision-making authorities mean that complete business law harmony is far from being achieved.[9]

The problems of multiple merger jurisdictions are strikingly demonstrated by the competition regimes of Australia and New Zealand. Both countries prohibit mergers that have the purpose, effect or likely effect of substantially lessening competition. Agreements, arrangements or understandings between competitors are similarly proscribed. A somewhat unique feature of the Trade Practices Act in Australia and the Commerce Act in New Zealand is that both types of conduct can be administratively authorised (rendered immune from prosecution) if the parties can demonstrate *ex-ante* that any anti-competitive detriments arising from the conduct will be outweighed by public benefits directly attributable to it. This process can be lengthy and cause significant commercial delays. If the parties are domiciled in separate countries, the authorisation process has to be undertaken in each one separately. Despite essentially the same law being applied to the same set of facts, different outcomes can result.

either Australia or New Zealand. A misuse of market power in any market in the two countries can be attacked by the competition agency of either country in its own court system.

[9]In a press release dated 23 July 2006, the Australian Competition and Consumer Commission and the New Zealand Commerce Commission announced an in-principle agreement to a protocol to enhance their cooperation in dealing with trans-Tasman mergers, including the sharing of information, assistance with merger reviews and the synchronisation of their timing, and the gathering of information on behalf of each other. See http://www.accc.gov.au/content/index.phtml/itemId/754797/fromItemId/142 (accessed 15 September 2008).

Nowhere has this been more starkly demonstrated than in the attempt that began in 2002 by Qantas and Air New Zealand to set up a trans-Tasman agreement whereby the two airlines would coordinate schedules and pricing for all flights within, originating from, and arriving into the two countries. Qantas also sought to acquire a 22 percent stake in the equity of Air New Zealand. The requirements of the bilateral air services agreements of both countries require that their airlines retained their separate identities. However, any cooperative agreement between the airlines required authorisation by the competition authorities of both countries, since such pricing cooperation was highly likely to have been assessed as having the effect of substantially reducing competition. Had a merger been possible, a different process would have been followed in which proceedings would have been less public and in which the competition authority would have had to demonstrate that the merger would substantially lessen competition, rather than the proponents having to argue for the authorisation by demonstrating that the public benefits arising from the alliance outweighed the anti-competitive detriments. The merger, therefore, had it been possible, might have led to a different regulatory result.

The proposals for authorisation were denied by the Australian Competition and Consumer Commission (ACCC) and by the Commerce Commission in New Zealand on largely structural grounds, based on a likely combined trans-Tasman market share of around 85–90 percent (Air New Zealand did not fly domestic routes in Australia, and appeared unlikely ever to do so, and Qantas operated only very limited services within New Zealand, and appeared to have no wish to expand these).[10] Qantas and Air New Zealand appealed both decisions to the relevant appeal bodies, the Australian Competition Tribunal in Australia[11] and the High Court in New Zealand. The appeal was

[10]It is the normal practice of the ACCC not to oppose mergers, even though they will result in a duopoly, if there is evidence of sustained and sustainable levels of import competition.

[11]David Round is a Member of the Australian Competition Tribunal, and was one of the three Members who sat on the appeal. Nothing that is said in this paper, in general or specifically in relation to this appeal, should be ascribed to the Tribunal, but rather should be read as his personal views.

denied in New Zealand, but was granted in Australia. The proposals were abandoned, however, at least temporarily, as they needed approval in both jurisdictions.

Why was it that the two regulators agreed, but the appeal authorities produced quite different decisions? The problem lay in the differing nature of the appeal procedures. In Australia, the appeal was to the Tribunal, a body consisting of a judge of the Federal Court of Australia as President, and two lay members appointed for their expertise in commercial matters, economics or the law. For appeals on agreements and equity acquisition issues, the process is a *de novo* one (rather than a review of the papers that were before the ACCC) in which a complete rehearing occurs, with updated evidence, new witnesses, and new arguments and submissions being heard. For New Zealand, the appeal was before the High Court of New Zealand, in which a judge sat with one lay member, with only limited admission of new evidence, the purpose of the appeal being to determine whether the Commerce Commission had made an error in its decision.

In a market that was highly dynamic, it came as no great surprise that the two appeal authorities handed down quite different decisions. In the intervening period between the regulators' decisions and the appeal hearings, the market for passenger flights between Australia and New Zealand had changed markedly. Significant new entry had occurred by Virgin Blue, an Australian carrier, and Emirates, a large international carrier that used its "dead" turnaround time in Australia to fly a return leg across the Tasman. Both airlines offered much lower fares (and, in the case of Emirates, true international class service) than had previously been charged by Qantas and Air New Zealand, resulting in a steep drop in market share for the two established carriers.

Using a behavioural rather than a structural approach (in contrast to the ACCC at first instance, which focused heavily on market shares), the Tribunal found that in the presence of such fierce competition, there could be little prospect of future anti-competitive detriment, as it would not be in the commercial interests of Qantas and Air New

Zealand to raise their prices or significantly restrict their schedules,[12] in the face of these low-priced entrants that appeared to be committed to the trans-Tasman market in the long term, and for whom there appeared to be no barriers to expansion.

In contrast, in New Zealand the High Court sought to find whether there was any error in the findings of the Commerce Commission, paying little regard to developments in the market, especially with respect to new entry. In authorisation matters, New Zealand has generally sought a greater level of quantification of anti-competitive detriments and public benefits than has been the case in Australia, and, while the Court did find some errors that worked to the airlines' advantage, they were not sufficient to lead to a reversal of the regulator's decision. A further appeal was open to the airlines, but they chose not to take this opportunity.[13]

Following their failure to have the arrangements approved, it appeared that each airline would go its own way, with Qantas in particular focusing on LCC operations in Asia. However, in April 2006 the two airlines submitted a new proposal to the ACCC for authorisation, in the form of a trans-Tasman code-sharing alliance that controlled capacity and prices. This application relied on the findings of the Tribunal, and effectively by-passed the Commerce Commission, as in New Zealand inter-country airline agreements (the new proposal contained no equity acquisition component) need only to get the approval of the Minister for Transport, who had supported the previous set of proposals as the relevant minister (but who of course had no control over the independent Commerce Commission). On the assumption that such approval

---

[12]Some readjustment of schedules had been proposed by the airlines to eliminate wasteful wingtip flying and to introduce aircraft of optimum capacity for each flight, rather than continue with the inefficient scheduling of parallel flights and large aircraft resulting in excess capacity.

[13]It is worth noting that New Zealand appeal authorities have always been reluctant to find against the Commerce Commission, on the grounds that it is a specialist regulatory body with the knowledge and ability to investigate and analyse commercial matters.

should now be a "shoe-in",[14] the two airlines presumably decided that they could apply to the ACCC for authorisation, confident that even if the application were to be rejected, in the face of what was by then a highly competitive trans-Tasman airline passenger (and freight) market, any appeal would likely still find favour with the Tribunal. However, early in November 2006, the ACCC issued a draft decision rejecting this new application, and the airlines announced shortly thereafter that they would not proceed with yet another appeal.

The moral of the trans-Tasman position is clear. For internationally traded goods or services such as country-to-country airline services, within-country assessments of commercial activities may differ significantly from country to country, with the potential to disrupt or deny globally or regionally efficient strategies from coming into operation. An unduly restrictive statute is likely to damage welfare, especially when dealing with industries where network effects are important, and where the firms subject to the vagaries of introspective regulation have the commercial opportunity to choose other locations in which to base their operations or to locate part of their commercial network.

11.4. Regulatory Errors and Multiple Competition Authorities

As illustrated in the previous section, when firms located in two different jurisdictions seek to merge or engage in an alliance, two independent regulators will assess the conduct. In markets that are as interconnected as airline markets, decisions on the competitive process by one country will almost certainly affect competition in airline markets in other countries. Findlay and Round (2003) observed that different decisions could emerge between countries on a merger, either for reasons of political economy, or because of differences in

[14]Warren Truss, the New Zealand Minister for Transport, was reported in *The Australian* on 15 June 2006 as saying that the proposed new agreement between Qantas and Air New Zealand would help both airlines bring about needed capacity rationalisation, helping them to survive in a very competitive market in which they had been losing market share.

regulatory capacity, maturity, methodology or investigatory procedures, or because of different attitudes towards the costs of decision errors. Regulators may also come to different conclusions because of differences in data provided to them (certainly this was the case in the Qantas–Air New Zealand alliance application). But most importantly for the purposes of this chapter, each regulator will examine the impact of a proposed merger or alliance on the welfare of its own country's population and the firms domiciled in that country (or the share of profits accruing to its nationals if the firm is partly foreign owned). If benefits or costs accrue to foreign nationals, they will not normally be considered.

In this scenario, for a proposal to go ahead it must be approved by both regulators. Under what circumstances could one regulator accept a merger application while the other rejects it? More to the point, could a proposed merger that reduces global welfare be accepted, or could one that improves global welfare be rejected due to its assessed impact in one country? Many academic papers have considered these kinds of issues. National authorities that concentrate on the effect of mergers on national welfare will usually overlook the possibility that such mergers could have an effect on producer surplus accruing to foreign firms, and could result in increased prices in international markets — external effects not within the country in question, but in other countries.[15]

Tay and Willmann (2005) model cross-border mergers as random events that yield asymmetric consequences in the two countries affected by them. They conclude that a first-best global competition policy can only be achieved through a global competition authority that can internalise cross-border externalities, and point out that such an authority would free poorer countries from the expense of setting up their own independent competition authority. Haufler and Nielsen (2005) use a Cournot model to show that under certain circumstances actions taken by national merger authorities towards national mergers will be

[15]There is a considerable literature now on these external effects. See, for example, Farrell and Shapiro (1990), Barros and Cabral (1994) and Head and Ries (1997).

too restrictive from the perspective of global efficiency. They argue that there is

> "an important asymmetry between national and cross-border mergers in markets where national players dominate. In these markets a national merger will indeed reduce the number of firms that actively supply the market, whereas an international merger will not ... [T]he conditions for an international merger to be in the interest of the participating firms are unambiguously stricter than in the case of a national merger, but when indeed proposed, international mergers will not be vetoed by neither [sic] national nor regional merger authorities" (p. 25).

Findlay and Round (2003) have assessed regulatory discordance in the context of two sources of conflict between regulators: differences in structures between the two economies and the resultant differing weights given by regulators to consumer and producer interests, and different approaches to the need to look forward in the assessments and how to handle the ensuing uncertainty that emerges in any assessment of dynamic market efficiency.

Differences in reactions by regulators to merger proposals can arise because of differences in the structures of their own economies. From a global perspective a merger proposal should be rejected if it reduces total welfare — that is, if the expected loss of consumer surplus exceeds the likely gain in producer surplus. But each regulator will make this assessment according to its own views on the appropriate measurement, and the relative distribution, of these surpluses. One country, for example, could account for a relatively high share of producer interests and a relatively low share of consumer interests and would discount the total cost to consumers and take into account a greater share of the impact of the proposal on producers. It is possible for such a country to approve a proposal that does not enhance global welfare as its large share of a relatively small gain to producers exceeds the cost to its consumers; when this happens, the other country (in a two-country world) will reject the same proposal. If approval by both regulators is required, the merger would not go ahead, avoiding the risk that global welfare will be reduced. Additionally, a merger that increases global welfare could be rejected by one country if its loss in consumer welfare is relatively large compared to its share of producer gains.

Clearly, it is possible that one country could be worse off when a merger that reduces global welfare is rejected, but it is unlikely that a scheme could be set up to compensate that country. In contrast, if a country seeks to stop a merger that enhances global welfare, compensation may be feasible, although it would need to be checked that this country is not "gaming" the situation. Establishing such a scheme would be costly, however, and the assessment of the appropriate compensation would not be easy, especially in view of the possible long-term incentive effects.

All regulatory decisions are subject to the possibility of error. Type 1 error occurs when a merger that will be welfare enhancing is rejected, while Type 2 error results from the approval of a socially undesirable merger. In the latter case, it may be hard to undo the damage, as once the eggs have been scrambled it is rarely possible to revert to the original position. However, if a Type 1 error is made, the proposal can always be resubmitted, with no lasting social (or private) damage. Type 1 and Type 2 errors are inversely related; any regulatory scheme to reduce the probability of one occurring automatically increases the chance of the other taking place. Avoiding the risk of accepting a merger that will reduce welfare means that there will occur a greater rejection rate of all mergers, good as well as bad. The trade-offs can be reflected in the threshold that is applied in the statute. For example, the higher the threshold for rejecting a merger (an easier regime), the greater the implied risk of making a Type 2 error. Findlay and Round (2003) note that in open economies with few entry barriers, Type 2 errors may correct themselves over time, as any excessive profits made as a result of the increased market power will encourage entry into the market. While Type 1 errors may only entail short-run social costs, they will involve irretrievable losses to both consumers and the firms involved. To guard against this situation becoming a long-run problem, firms must be able to re-apply, or to appeal to an independent review body for a speedy rehearing of the case.

In airline markets, where entry possibilities are often closed off by other regulations, the consequences of making a Type 2 error could be damaging, and so regulators should investigate merger proposals in great detail, and may be more likely to reject mergers that increase competition. Depending on national goals and stages of development, and on the relative short-run and long-run costs of these errors (and the costs of reducing them), different countries may evaluate the consequences of the two different errors in different ways. Such inter-country differences create major problems for cooperation on competition policy issues.

When two countries assess a merger independently and when agreement by both is required before a merger can proceed, the country that is more concerned about a Type 2 error (and therefore more likely to reject an application) is likely to prevail and determine the final outcome. Such a country is likely to be at a later stage of development, or to have a stronger antipathy towards big business, to have a longer established culture of competition, or to regard entry barriers as being relatively high.

If regulators follow different ideological approaches to assessing the competitive process, further opportunities arise for different decisions. For example, one regulator might favour a structural approach and the other a dynamic approach that focuses on strategic behaviour by firms.[16] This situation might arise, for instance, between a relatively new regulator and an experienced one. A regulator following a strategic behaviour approach may approve more mergers than one following a structuralist approach. The gap could be expected to diminish over time, including through higher levels of transparency in decision making. Consultation, cooperation and capacity building clearly will also help produce a more coordinated regulatory vision.

The message here is unequivocal — independent decision making may not lead to the "right" answer on mergers and alliances,

---

[16]As was the case in the evaluation of the Qantas–Air New Zealand alliance in Australia, where the ACCC took largely a structural approach, and the Australian Competition Tribunal on appeal favoured an analytical method based on the examination of strategic behaviour in the relevant markets.

globally speaking and assuming that the goal will always be to maximise total welfare. We have just noted ways in which the gaps between the positions of domestic regulators might close over time. Another response to this problem is to create a supranational authority to deal with these issues. The feasibility of this response is examined in the next section, and that discussion also provides insights into ways in which regulatory capacity within countries might be developed.

11.5. Steps towards a Multilateral Competition Policy for Airline Markets

The idea of an international competition policy and a global "super-regulator" for competition and consumer protection issues is not new.[17] However, a move towards a single authority is still far from being a reality, if for no reason other than that we do not know the objective functions of the respective national authorities.[18] The gains

[17] For an interesting early assessment of the need for competition policies for an integrated world economy, and a proposal for international competition policy instruments that would seek to promote competition while at the same time have a low impact on national sovereignty, see Scherer (1994). It is interesting to note Scherer's final sentence in his book: "It is important to emphasize that extraterritorial application of domestic antitrust law must be a solution of last resort so as to place a priority on promoting cohesive and converging competition policies in an increasingly international market."

[18] Many issues need to be agreed on before such an authority could be successfully established. For example, should it be bureaucratic, administrative or judicial? Should it operate under a current international body or start afresh? What will be the national composition of the authority? Will membership be legal, other professions, or business people, and in what proportions? Will membership rotate, and if so, how often? How will the chair of the authority be selected, and what tenure will this person have? To what superior authority or institution will the group report? What will be the nature (legal or administrative) of the review/appeal stage of the process, and on what grounds will appeals be heard? Should its procedures be inquisitorial or adversarial? Agreement is also needed on whether the objective should be efficiency in airline markets — allocative, productive and dynamic — or whether equity issues should be given much weight. As Western countries with a long experience of competition policy have not in the past necessarily agreed on these objectives (Europe, for example, has tended to favour the latter while the US has generally emphasised the former), it is unlikely that ready multinational agreement will occur on these goals.

from setting up such a body would in all likelihood not be distributed evenly, and would be likely to fall especially to countries that do not already enjoy extraterritorial powers. In the absence of a mechanism for compensation or side payments, such a body will be difficult to establish with any sort of universal support. Nevertheless, the benefits from embracing a competitive culture are likely to be so high that the winners could in theory compensate the losers (an equity argument rather than an efficiency one), and there would still be a credit balance at the end of the process. In practice, of course, such processes do not happen, as there is no mechanism that can easily be used to bring about this redistribution.

Countries should, of course, be free to choose the competition policy they think is locally optimal, but they must be conscious of any spillovers to other countries from their decisions. At the very least there should be some consistency in national laws on the worst anti-competitive practices, but different economies at different stages of economic development will always face different problems with respect to competition policy.

Our interest here has been the treatment of competition issues in international airline markets. There is an argument that multi-purpose regulators are generally preferable to single-sector regulators as they present less opportunity for regulatory capture, and promise greater consistency in assessment of all types of conduct and all kinds of markets. From a cross-border perspective, a trade-off also exists between having a single regulator, perhaps lacking detailed knowledge of each relevant economy, and the more specific expertise of single-country regulators. From this, one might conclude therefore that a transnational, single-market authority dealing with airlines is subject to major organisational as well as operational difficulties — treating issues in an inconsistent way with other antitrust authorities, being subject to capture. Yet it does offer the prospect of proper consideration of all the network-wide effects of airline behaviour, and of internal consistency in evaluating airline behaviour.

Our suggestion is that, first, a commitment to the principle that spillovers between jurisdictions are important should be sought. It will be much harder to reach an agreement on the detail of how to respond.[19] Such cooperation, albeit limited, would be an improvement on the current situation of uncoordinated and unsystematic attempts to control mergers, especially cross-border amalgamations. Agreement would be needed on many issues — the type, focus, detail and coverage of the laws, as well as the degree of proscription and prescription; the nature of enforcement; and the penalties that could be incurred for breaches of the statute. As Round (2005, p. 239) has said in relation to the need for East Asian countries to develop a harmonised approach to competition law and policy:

> The pursuit of a cooperative regional policy and enforcement stance requires the flexibility to handle economy-specific problems, and should promote a convergence to a broadly agreed set of goals, standards, prohibitions and methods that will provide a transparent regulatory framework and incentives for businesses and consumers to get the most out of market processes, thus enhancing private and social welfare. A harmonised approach would involve each economy taking account of what is happening in its neighbouring economies, and through consensus following a common path on as many issues as possible, including policy development, legislation, administration, education, enforcement, penalties and review. The keywords should be communication and convergence ...

---

[19] If broad agreement on the joint treatment of airline competition issues could be established by a small number of countries, this could induce other governments to pursue similar policies, if only because domestic firms not used to competitive pressures may find it much harder to compete in regional markets where competition policies have been effective and where buyers are better informed and more demanding that their requirements be met by firms, whether domestic or foreign. Plurilateral agreements are already used in air transport markets, for example in Europe and among groups of APEC members. A plurilateral agreement could emerge from negotiations on air transport market access between Europe and the US (see Open skies hits turbulence, *Australian Financial Review*, 14 February 2004, where it is suggested that sticking points are the American position on 49% foreign ownership cap for US airlines, and limits on foreign carriers' access to domestic routes). However, plurilateral structures do not necessarily lead to global free trade, either because their architecture makes intersection difficult or because they create new interests that preclude further extensions to their membership (see Andriamananjara, 2002, 2003).

There is some guidance from other multilateral activities. Much debate has occurred in recent years over the need to develop a viable multilateral competition policy to be administered through the WTO, and also to develop best practice guidelines for competition policy and enforcement through agencies such as the OECD and the International Competition Network. Europe has shown the way in promoting international competitiveness.[20] It is now up to other regional groups to follow this lead, and for international bodies such as the WTO to encourage the development of an international merger policy regime for the airline sector that promotes efficiency and competition.

Piecemeal competition-related provisions have been included in many WTO Agreements, including, for example, in various GATT (General Agreement on Tariffs and Trade) Articles mainly related to anti-dumping provisions and state-owned enterprises; in GATS (General Agreement on Trade in Services) provisions with respect to monopoly and anti-competitive behaviour, as well as domestic regulation; and in the TRIPs (Trade Related Aspects of Intellectual Property Rights) provisions against conduct that unreasonably restrains trade or adversely affects the transfer of technology. Trade Policy Reviews frequently deal with issues related to competition as well. ICAO (the International Civil Aviation Organisation) has drafted a model clause on competition safeguards that lists examples of conduct that may be anti-competitive in air transport markets. This clause also provides for consultations and for a dispute resolution mechanism with respect to those behaviours.[21] The clause could be combined with other material

---

[20]Neelie Kroes (2006), the European Commissioner for Competition Policy, has observed that cross-border mergers, especially in sectors where large national incumbents have been present, tend to be more favourable in terms of competitive outcomes than amalgamations between national players in the same sectors. As Kroes points out, the single market rules of the EU, and Article 21 of the EC Merger Regulation, forbid national governments from using unjustified steps to prevent the consummation of cross-border mergers that have a European dimension (and hence the approval given to the Air France–KLM merger).

[21]See http://www.icao.int/icao/en/atb/atconf5/docs/ATConf5_conclusions_en.pdf (accessed 15 September 2008).

into a GATS Reference Paper on Air Transport Services, which could include the principles to be applied to domestic regulation as well as detail on desirable levels of international cooperation.

Competition law and enforcement philosophies and practices within economies will always reflect the local underlying political, economic and legal culture and history of the country. Views will differ on reasons, content, objectives, processes, instruments and timetable.[22] Immediate or full agreement cannot be expected. But a timetable and a commitment to a process of convergence on principles and methods, a harmonising yet flexible process of developing a shared multinational approach, is essential to promote efficient airline markets. With such cooperation, experience and capacity can be shared and the complete intersecting picture and all of its implications can be assessed. Such integration could begin simply with information exchanges and then expand into the more complex process of shared commitments, building policies and infrastructure (including an appeals mechanism), and educating the industry on its new regulatory environment. These gains, however, will not be free of adjustment problems, nor will they be symmetrical in their occurrence. But transition problems should not be used as an excuse for a lengthy delay in getting the system rolling.[23]

11.6. Summary and Conclusions

Pressure is mounting for airlines to become more efficient globally and proposals for mergers and alliances are increasing. Different countries will face proposals that will simultaneously affect the competitive process in markets that lie within or overlap their jurisdictions,

---

[22]Or, in other words, the economist's Magnificent Seven list of questions: what, who, where, how, how much, for whom, and when.

[23]The Closer Economic Relations Trade Agreement between Australia and New Zealand has shown that harmonisation is possible in the enforcement of competition laws, especially in the context of predatory behaviour. A company with a substantial degree of power within Australia or New Zealand, or both, must not take advantage of that power for one of three proscribed anticompetitive purposes. A misuse of market power in any market in the two countries can be attacked by the competition agency of either economy. See Round *et al.* (2005) for further details of this Agreement.

as well as in markets over which they have no regulatory mandate. When competition regulators act independently and where agreement is required before a merger can go ahead, a country that seeks to reduce the likelihood of approving a socially damaging merger is more likely to reject merger applications. The deliberations and priors of that country on the trade-off between the two types of regulatory error therefore become dominant. However, while independent assessment may lead to the rejection of mergers or alliances that will enhance global welfare, the cost of that risk may be less than that of building a more complex set of institutions to avoid the problem.

If producer interests have a powerful influence over regulatory agencies (a likely situation in the early stages of the development of any new competition policy), there will be a higher probability that mergers which lower global welfare will be approved, although this outcome will be less likely if the countries and their regulators are at different stages of developing a culture for competition. It is also less likely when regulators are independent of any political influence.

Different countries will display differing attitudes to regulatory decision-making errors and their consequences. A relatively less-developed country might approve mergers that will damage the competitive process on a wider scale, on the grounds that the costs of this error will be short lived (although this is not necessarily the case) and that lowering the risk of making such an error would involve considerable regulatory effort (this is undoubtedly true, but carries with it a much greater and more geographically dispersed long-run social benefit). In contrast, a merger could be rejected under one regime even though on a more global evaluation the transaction could be welfare enhancing.

Developed countries should be heavily involved in programs of capacity building to share their experience on methodologies, errors and outcomes with countries and institutions at earlier stages of development. The goal must be to deepen and shorten the learning period, and to bring together policy procedures and methodology, so that when cooperation or assessment of the same or similar factual situations is required, any differences of opinion will be minimised. Then we can be more confident that socially good airline mergers and alliances will be approved, and socially damaging ones will be rejected.[24] And, as appealing as this goal might be, it is still likely to be a second-best one: The first-best would see methods to capture the spillovers between domestic regulatory practice. A single international authority to consider the numerous competition issues that arise in international airline markets is one solution, although its implementation involves a considerable set of challenges.

Thinking about the operation of a supranational authority provides some guidance for a work program on these issues. Certainly a focus on national welfare is a critical first step, and transparency in national decision making about competition policy is a valuable contributor to that. It is also desirable that one country, or group of countries, takes the lead in promoting common policy directions, statutory coverage and language, and also in encouraging regulatory capacity building and cooperation towards a harmonised approach to common issues. However, as Round (2002) has noted, the reality and speed of convergence of competition policies, removing differences in approach, ideology and method, depend on the development of a joint culture for competition and an appreciation of its contribution to efficiency and social welfare. History shows that convergence to common competition policies and enforcement procedures, let alone jurisprudence and precedent, rarely emerges quickly, as different countries' stakeholders respond to, and are driven by, different incentives, endowments, aspirations, and micro- and macro-economic environments. Despite these

[24]The horizontal and vertical alliances and mergers in the airline sector to date (whether voluntary or defensive) have been designed to protect the market positions of the participants. It may now be difficult, if not impossible, to unwind these at any geographical level. The situation is not unlike that of regulating a market faced with what is known as creeping acquisitions. Here, no single acquisition that adds incrementally to market share can be assessed as substantially lessening competition, but a point is reached when the acquirer clearly has amassed significant market power and it is too late to rely on structural remedies — and behavioural remedies are much harder to implement and enforce. This point-of-no-return must be carefully anticipated. Use of trigger mechanisms may help to manage the problem, as can carefully developed merger guidelines that are revised through experience and changing market circumstances.

differences, regulatory authorities will have to interact if they are to come up with sensible answers.[25]

The way to start is to find a champion or two committed to the goal. Research into perceived problems could be undertaken, and detailed assessments could be made of what controls might be desirable, and whether current existing methods and precedents from single countries can be adopted, or whether a new regulatory method is called for. The question should not be whether a converged treatment of airline market competition will happen, but rather when it will occur, how it will occur, based on what model(s), with what efficiency and distributive goals, in what legislative manifestation, and with what agreed enforcement priorities and methods. What is now called for is the establishment of understandings on principles, sequencing, capacity building, methods, enforcement, remedies and review.

References

Andriamananjara, S (2002). On the size and number of regional integration arrangements: A political economy model. *Journal of International Trade and Economic Development*, 11(3), 279–295.

Andriamananjara, S (2003). On the relationship between preferential trade agreements and the multilateral trading system. Remarks prepared for the PECC Trade Forum Meetings at the Institute for International Economics, Washington, DC. Available from http://www.iadb.org/intal/foros/LAandriamananjara_paper.pdf [15 February 2004].

Barros, PP and L Cabral (1994). Merger policies in open economies. *European Economic Review*, 38, 1041–1055.

Evenett, SJ (2003). The cross border mergers and acquisitions wave of the late 1990s. NBER Working Paper Series, Working Paper 9655, Cambridge, National Bureau of Economic Research.

Evenett, SJ (2005). What can we really learn from the competition provisions of regional trade agreements? Unpublished paper, 23 August 2005.

Farrell, J and C Shapiro (1990). Horizontal mergers: An equilibrium analysis. *American Economic Review*, 80(1), 107–126.

[25]The recently proposed merger consideration protocol between the Australian and New Zealand competition authorities (outlined in footnote 9 above) may, in time, provide a useful model for consideration by other, wider groups of countries.

Findlay, C and D Round (2003). Issues in international competition policy coordination. In *Regulation and Market Access*, A Sidorenko and C Findlay (eds.), pp. 157–173. Canberra: Asia Pacific Press.

Findlay, C and DK Round (2006). The "three pillars of stagnation": Challenges for air transport reform. *World Trade Review*, 5(2), 251–270.

Haufler, A and SB Nielsen (2005). Merger policy to promote 'global players'? A simple model. CESifo Working Paper No. 1523, Munich: CESifo.

Head, K and J Ries (1997). International mergers and welfare under decentralized competition policy. *Canadian Journal of Economics*, 30(4b), 1104–1123.

Kroes, N (2006). Challenges to the integration of the European market: Protectionism and effective competition policy. Burrell Lecture, June 12, 2006, Institution of Electrical Engineers, London.

Oum, TH, J-H Park and A Zhang (2000). *Globalization of Strategic Alliances: The Case of the Airline Industry*. Oxford: Elsevier Pergamon.

Productivity Commission (1998). *International Air Services*. Report No. 2, Canberra: Productivity Commission.

Round, DK (2002). Market power in East Asian economies: Its origins, effects and treatments. *Review of Industrial Organisation*, 21(2), 107–112.

Round, DK (2005). Regional cooperation in competition policy. In *Competition Policy in East Asia*, EM Medalla (ed.), pp. 231–256. Oxford: Routledge.

Round, DK, J Tustin and KA Round (2005). Australasian competition law: History, harmonisation, issues and lessons (unpublished paper, available from the first author at david.round@unisa.edu.au).

Scherer, FM (1994). *Competition Policies for an Integrated World Economy*. Washington: The Brookings Institution.

Tay, A and G Willmann (2005). Why (no) global competition policy is a tough choice. *Quarterly Review of Economics and Finance*, 45, 312–324.

Word Trade Organization (WTO) (2000). Developments in the air transport sector since the conclusion of the Uruguay Round, Part 3: Background note by the Secretariat. World Trade Organization, S/C/W.163/Add.2, 10 November 2000.

World Trade Organization (WTO) (2001a). Developments in the air transport sector since the conclusion of the Uruguay Round, Part 4: Background note by the Secretariat. World Trade Organization, S/C/W.163/Add.3, 13 August.

World Trade Organization (WTO) (2001b). Developments in the air transport sector since the conclusion of the Uruguay Round, Part 5: Background note by the Secretariat. World Trade Organization, S/C/W.163/Add.4, 15 August.

Zhang, Y and DK Round (2008). China's airline deregulation since 1997 and the driving forces behind the 2002 airline consolidations. *Journal of Air Transport Management*, 14(3), 130–142.

Index